Human Sacrifice, Militarism, and Rulership

Teotihuacan was one of the earliest and more populous pre-Columbian cities, and the Feathered Serpent was its vital monument, erected *circa* AD 200. This work explores the religious meanings and political implications of the pyramid with meticulous and thorough analyses of substantially new excavation data. Challenging the traditional view of the city as a legendary, sacred, or anonymously governed center, the book provides significant new insights into the Teotihuacan polity and society. It provides interpretations of the pyramid's location, architecture, sculptures, iconography, mass sacrificial graves, and rich symbolic offerings, and concludes that the pyramid commemorated the accession of rulers who were inscribed to govern with military force on behalf of the gods. This archaeological examination of the monument shows it to be the physical manifestation of state ideologies such as the symbolism of human sacrifice, militarism, and individual-centered divine authority, ideologies that were later diffused among other Mesoamerican urban centers.

SABURO SUGIYAMA is a Professor in the Graduate School of International Cultural Studies, Aichi Prefectural University, Japan and a part-time member of the research faculty at the Arizona State University. He has contributed to a number of edited works on Mesoamerican archaeology including *Mesoamerican Archaeology: Theory and Practice* (2003).

NEW STUDIES IN ARCHAEOLOGY

Series editors

Wendy Ashmore, *University of California, Riverside*
Clive Gamble, *University of Southampton*
John O'Shea, *University of Michigan*
Colin Renfrew, *University of Cambridge*

Archaeology has made enormous advances recently, both in the volume of discoveries and in its character as an intellectual discipline: new techniques have helped to further the range and rigour of inquiry, and have encouraged inter-disciplinary communication.

The aim of this series is to make available to a wider audience the results of these developments. The coverage is worldwide and extends from the earliest hunting and gathering societies to historical archaeology.

For a list of titles in the series please see the end of the book.

SABURO SUGIYAMA

Human Sacrifice, Militarism, and Rulership

Materialization of State Ideology at the Feathered Serpent Pyramid, Teotihuacan

CAMBRIDGE
UNIVERSITY PRESS

PUBLISHED BY THE PRESS SYNDICATE OF THE UNIVERSITY OF CAMBRIDGE
The Pitt Building, Trumpington Street, Cambridge, United Kingdom

CAMBRIDGE UNIVERSITY PRESS
The Edinburgh Building, Cambridge CB2 2RU, UK
40 West 20th Street, New York NY 10011-4211, USA
10 Stamford Road, Oakleigh, VIC 3166, Australia
Ruiz de Alarcón 13, 28014 Madrid, Spain
Dock House, The Waterfront, Cape Town 8001, South Africa

http://www.cambridge.org

First published 2005

Printed in the United Kingdom at the University Press, Cambridge

Typeface Plantin 10/13 pt.   *System* LATEX 2ε   [TB]

A catalogue record for this book is available from the British Library

Library of Congress Cataloging in Publication Data

Sugiyama, Saburo.
   Human sacrifice, militarism, and rulership: materialization of state ideology at the
Feathered Serpent Pyramid, Teotihuacan / by Saburo Sugiyama.
      p. cm. – (New studies in archaeology)
   Revision of the author's thesis (Ph.D.)–Arizona State University, 1995.
   Includes bibliographical references and index.
   ISBN 0 521 78056 X (alk. paper)
      1. Teotihuacán Site (San Juan Teotihuacán, Mexico)   2. Quetzalcoatl (Aztec deity)
   3. Indians of Mexico–Mexico–San Juan Teotihuacán–Politics and government.   4. Indians of
   Mexico–Mexico–San Juan Teotihuacán–Rites and ceremonies.   5. Indians of
   Mexico–Mexico–San Juan Teotihuacán–Antiquities.   6. Human sacrifice–Mexico–San
   Juan Teotihuacán.   7. Excavations (Archaeology)–Mexico–San Juan Teotihuacán.   8. Human
   remains (Archaeology)–Mexico–San Juan Teotihuacán.   9. San Juan Teotihuacán
   (Mexico)–Antiquities.   I. Title.   II. Series.

F1219.1.T27S84 2005
972'.52 – dc22
                                                                            2004056819

ISBN 0 521 78056 X

To Kumiko, Yosei, Masano, and Nawa
in memory of Masako and Jusaku Sugiyama

CONTENTS

FIGURES

TABLES

ACKNOWLEDGMENTS

This study is a result of my long-term research into the Feathered Serpent Pyramid (FSP) and the Ciudadela (Citadel). A major portion of the study was first published as my dissertation at Arizona State University (ASU) in Tempe, Arizona in 1995. *Human Sacrifice, Militarism, and Rulership: Materialization of State Ideology at the Feathered Serpent Pyramid, Teotihuacan* is a revised version of the dissertation, into which I have integrated new data and whose analyses and interpretations I have further refined.

The ideas expressed here developed through projects supported by several institutions and grants. My first fieldwork at the FSP was carried out as part of the Proyecto Arqueológico Teotihuacán 1980–82, directed by Rubén Cabrera Castro of the Instituto Nacional de Antropología e História (INAH) in Mexico. Further excavations for the same project during the 1983–84 seasons gave me an opportunity to focus on the sacrificial burial complex. I sincerely express my deep gratitude to Rubén Cabrera for his continuous support.

As a result of the early work, a new, joint project of INAH and ASU (formerly Brandeis University before the author's move to ASU) was formed: Proyecto Templo de Quetzalcoatl (PTQ88–89), or Project Feathered Serpent Pyramid in English. Cabrera and George Cowgill served as codirectors; I was their principal assistant. Funding was granted by the National Geographic Society, National Endowment for the Humanities, Arizona State University Foundation, and other sources; the Consejo de Arqueología of INAH in Mexico authorized the project. I received independent aid from the National Science Foundation's (NSF) Dissertation Research Program for the analysis of the data described in this publication. Much of the interpretation and writing of the text were carried out at Dumbarton Oaks, where I was a Resident Junior Fellow in 1993–94. Further funding for analyses and publications from the National Endowment for the Humanities and NSF, for which I was coprincipal investigator with Cowgill, also contributed to the present study.

During the length of the study, I was encouraged and assisted by many people. I am most grateful to George Cowgill, my teacher, mentor, and friend, who made invaluable contributions, including raising most of the funding that made the study possible. Without his support and trust in my decisions in field and laboratory work, the study would not have been realized. It is hard to express my indebtedness to René Millon, with whom I first discussed the joint project around 1986 and from whom I have received strong, continuous support since then. I sincerely

appreciate his contribution and patient discussions with me on the results of excavations and on Teotihuacan archaeology in general. I still remember that his visit
with George from the United States during the difficult field season of 1989 was a
great incentive and encouragement to me. I am fortunate that several other scholars
patiently provided criticism and advice on earlier versions. I am particularly thankful
to Emily Umberger, Barbara Stark, and Christopher Carr for their lengthy, careful,
and straightforward comments. Conversations with many other colleagues in various
fields, like Elizabeth Boone, Javier Urcid, Debra Nagao, Chris Beekman, Frances
Hayashida, Andy Darling, John Carlson, Sue Scott, Mike Spence, John Pohl, Bill
Perry, and Ben Nelson, were especially beneficial. This book would not have been
published without the strong support of Wendy Ashmore and David Freidel with
their critical suggestions and critiques. Although the book benefited from the comments of all my colleagues, misinterpretations and errors remain the sole responsi-
bility of the author.

I am also thankful to members of the Proyecto Templo de Quetzalcoatl 1988–
89: Carlos Serrano, Emily McClung de Tapia, Oralia Cabrera, Alejandro Sarabia,
Martha Pimienta, Alfonso Gallardo, Lillian Thomas, Don Booth, Clara Paz, and
many others who worked in the field and/or provided me information of different
kinds. Don Pedro Baños and Don Zeferino Ortega assisted substantially in the excavation of PTQ88–89. I am deeply thankful to all of them, including the local
workers who worked with me on the hard task of tunneling during the 1988–89
seasons.

At ASU, Elizabeth Dinsmore helped me by digitizing graphic data for the com-
puter. Drawings by Kumiko Sugiyama, Verónica Moreno, and Nawa Sugiyama are
included in the volume; Jamie Borowicz deserves special credit for his excellent ink
drawings of the victims' bodies. I am also very thankful to Debra Nagao, Mary
Glowacki, Jan Barstad, and Claudia Garcia-Des Lauriers for editing work on earlier versions, and to William Phillips, who handled editing of the final version with
professional care. I received assistance from Kumiko and Yuko Koga in preparing
figures for this version; sacrifice of Kumiko in the private sector also deserves much
credit. Many thanks to everyone.

I finally should mention that, as a consequence of the research described here, a
new excavation project was carried out at the Moon Pyramid from 1998 to 2004
by Rubén Cabrera, my codirector of the INAH in Mexico, and me. The continuing
research was motivated by what the FSP project did and did not resolve. However,
as the fieldwork is still underway, I have only added general data here very briefly
with a few references to preliminary reports. Ongoing analytical studies with substantially new and unique data would strikingly shift our view of major monuments
in Teotihuacan, affecting the interpretations presented here. In fact, new insights
provided by the recent excavations formed a part of my "excuse" for the extended
delay in publishing this, for which I owe profound thanks to the editors of Cambridge
University Press, Jessica Kuper and Simon Whitmore. I am very grateful for their
unusual patience, warmth, and continuing support. At any rate, I believe that the results of the studies discussed in this book formulate a body of substantial information

that we should return to, in order to integrate it into more comprehensive comparative studies of Teotihuacan monuments for the coming years. I have simply tried to present here what René Millon (1992: 401) says will be of lasting importance to students of Teotihuacan archaeology, a richly illustrated analytic study. (See also complementary information at http://archaeology.asu.edu/teo.)

1

Introduction: cognition of state symbols and polity

Motivations and ends

When the Spanish hurried by a ruin near Otumba during their war against the Aztecs in 1521, they apparently did not recognize the huge mounds they passed as historical monuments. Even after the Conquest, they could not learn the history of the ruins from the Aztecs, who had fundamentally mythological visions of the site. The Aztecs called the place Teotihuacan (in the Nahuatl language "place where gods lived") eight centuries after the city's fall, but its original name, the language spoken by its inhabitants, and the ethnic groups who created the city were unknown to them and are not understood today. The archaeological recovery of Teotihuacan history began only in the twentieth century.

To understand this early society, many surveys, excavations, and studies of materials have been carried out since the beginning of the twentieth century with different motivations, approaches, and techniques. Since Manuel Gamio (1922) undertook the first scientific, interdisciplinary approach in 1917–22, several explorations have successfully revealed specific cultural traits and have situated Teotihuacan prehistory within the Mesoamerican chronological framework (Table 1). The Teotihuacan Mapping Project (called hereafter TMP) directed by René Millon (R. Millon 1973; Millon et al. 1973), and the Settlement Survey Project in the Basin of Mexico directed by William Sanders (Sanders et al. 1979), largely contributed to our current view of the city (Fig. 1). Independent explorations in the city's residential compounds also provided substantial information about social life and about people of different categories and levels.

According to these studies, the sacred center seems to have originated sometime during the first century before Christ (Patlachique phase: 150–1 BC);[1] however, this is based mainly on surface collections of ceramics, and excavation data on this incipient period are still too sketchy to reconstruct the dawn of the new center. During the next stage (Tzacualli phase: AD 1–150), Teotihuacan quickly became the largest and most populous metropolis in the New World. By AD 150 the urban area had expanded to approximately 20 km² and contained some 60,000 to 80,000 inhabitants, according to Millon (1981: 221). Construction of major monuments was apparently concluded by AD 250 and many apartment compounds were also built during this period (Miccaotli and Early Tlamimilolpa phases: AD 150–300). Unmistakable influences of Teotihuacan began to be felt during the fourth century throughout most parts of Mesoamerica (Late Tlamimilolpa phases: AD 300–400). During its prosperous period (Xolalpan and Metepec phases: AD 400–650), Teotihuacan was the

Table 1 *Chronology of Teotihuacan and other relevant sites*

(Approx.)	Mesoamerica in general	Basin of Mexico	Teotihuacan Valley	Oaxaca Valley
1500	LATE	AZTEC IV	TEACALCO	
1400	POSTCLASSIC	AZTEC III	CHIMALPA	LATE MONTE ALBAN V
1300	-------------			-------------
1200		AZTEC II/I	ZOCANGO	EARLY MONTE ALBAN V
1100	EARLY		ATLATONGO	
1000	POSTCLASSIC	MAZAPAN	MAZAPAN	-------------
900	-------------			
800	(EPI-CLASSIC)	COYOTLATELCO	XOMETLA	MONTE ALBAN IV
700	LATE CLASSIC	-------------	OXTOTIPAC	-------------
600		METEPEC	METEPEC	MONTE ALBAN IIIb
500	MIDDLE CLASSIC	XOLALPAN	XOLALPAN	
400	EARLY CLASSIC			MONTE ALBAN IIIa
300	-------------	TLAMIMILOLPA	TLAMIMILOLPA	
200	TERMINAL	MICCAOTLI	MICCAOTLI	
100	FORMATIVE	TZACUALLI	TZACUALLI	
0		CUICUILCO	PATLACHIQUE	MONTE ALBAN II
100	-------------		-------------	
200				MONTE ALBAN Ic
300	LATE	TICOMAN III	LATE CUANALAN	
400	FORMATIVE	TICOMAN II	MID. CUANALAN	MONTE ALBAN Ia
500	-------------	TICOMAN I	EARLY CUANALAN	-------------
600	MIDDLE			ROSARIA PHASE
700	FORMATIVE	ZACATENCO	CHICONAUHTLA	GUADALUPE PHASE
800				

Source: Adapted from Millon 1981: fig. 7–7; Mastache and Cobean 1989: table 1; Cowgill 1996: table 1.

sixth largest city in the world, with an estimated population of 125,000 (Millon 1993: 33). In this latter period, until its sudden collapse, the city seems to have functioned as a well-developed urban center apparently with a multiethnic population (Cowgill 1996: 329; R. Millon 1988a).

Accumulated information delineates historical trajectories and cultural traits, mostly of the affluent periods following the incipient stage. One of Teotihuacan City layout's most evident and distinctive features was a highly organized political structure that can be called, in an evolutionary view, a preindustrial state system. In addition to its immense population, a highly planned city layout with vast monumental structures and some 2,000 residential apartment compounds suggest that several kinds of institutional organizations administered the urban life. In particular, standardized architectural traits, rigid space control, and a systematic water management program seem to indicate formal constraints imposed by the state. Orderly channelization of drainage and large-scale canalization of the San Juan River were integrated into the grid system that persisted under the control of the government throughout the city's history.

In residential compounds life would have been complex in terms of social differentiation, labor divisions, economic transactions, and other routine activities. Recent osteological and mortuary analyses indicate that those living in an apartment compound (usually housing 60 to 100 residents) had patrilineal links, with significant social stratification within the compound (Sempowski and Spence 1994; Storey 1992).

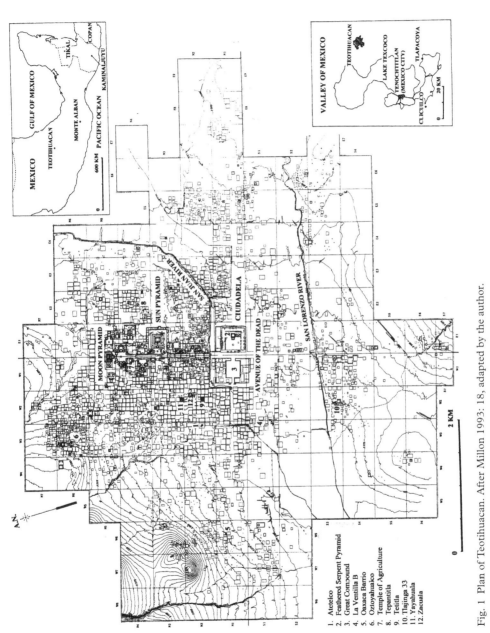

Fig. 1 Plan of Teotihuacan. After Millon 1993: 18, adapted by the author.

Mortuary remains seem to indicate that social differentiation was also conspicuous among apartment compounds. Economic activities, such as specialized manufacturing and redistribution of practical and prestige items, were carried out primarily in apartment compounds, as amply demonstrated by analytical studies (Manzanilla 1993; Múnera 1985; Spence 1987; Turner 1992; Widmer 1987). As Millon (1992: 382) has suggested, marketplace institutions also would have existed at Teotihuacan, beginning at least in the second century AD. For these urban activities, the state would have functioned administratively, legislatively, and judicially in return for labor and agricultural, craft, and other products as state revenue (Millon 1992: 377). Data from enclaves discovered at the Merchant's Barrio (Rattray 1990) and Tlailotlacan (Spence 1992) suggest certain constraints imposed on foreigners or immigrants by the state. In addition, widespread distribution of Teotihuacan products and symbols in contemporaneous Mesoamerican societies substantially demonstrates that a state system with interregional dominance was functioning centrally in this multiethnic metropolis.

Although social complexity has been thus indicated by various kinds of materials, the political form of the early state has not been well understood. Little is known about the founding of the new center, largely because of little archaeological record from the early period. However, I believe that the uncertainties are also due to an insufficient cognition of the different qualities of available data and the scarcity of holistic interpretation. This book, dealing as it does with the symbolism of an early monument, is explicitly directed to the issue of an emerging state polity at Teotihuacan.

From a macroscopic view, it can readily be recognized that the data do not represent the different sectors of Teotihuacan society evenly, despite the quantity of research during the last century. Data about people of the highest social status are still scarce in every period of the city's history. We have not even identified residences of the ruling group that could have been distinguished in material culture from the others. Royal families are absent from burial data, despite the fact that more than 800 single or multiple graves with more than 1,400 skeletons have been discovered to date in Teotihuacan (Rodríguez 1992). Although a population of low, intermediate, and higher status is evident in the city, people of the *highest* social status have still not been identified in the data from residential areas.

Interpretations of political structure thus seem to be influenced significantly by the lack of palace and royal graves in the archaeological record. The fact that specific paramount individuals have not been identified in works of art also restrains researchers from explicitly discussing rulers or ruler-centered political structures. The "uniqueness" of Teotihuacan in material culture has been stressed mostly as a reflection of the special political form of the Teotihuacan state (e.g., Pasztory 1992), and also has led some to propose a collective polity for Teotihuacan (Blanton et al. 1996). The invisibility of Teotihuacan rulers contrasts greatly with other Mesoamerican societies such as Olmec, Maya, and Aztec, in which ruling individuals were conspicuous or at least visible in mortuary practices, works of art, and written records.

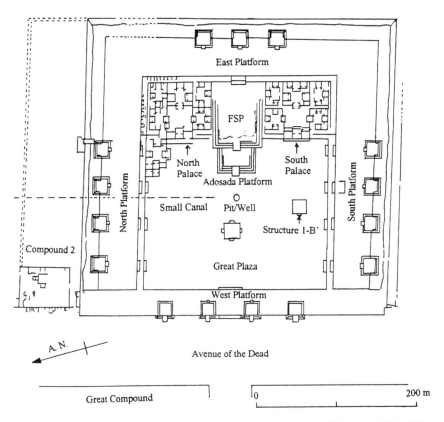

Fig. 2 Plan of the Ciudadela. Drawing: Kumiko Sugiyama, from Berrin and Pasztory 1993: 1020.

New discoveries, analytical studies, and holistic interpretations, described in this volume, suggest that this interpretative framework needs modification. A different kind of data set is the focus of this book. While excavations in residential areas provide continuous information about subsistence, technology, trade, and social life in Teotihuacan, excavations of monumental constructions reveal other aspects of the state. The monuments, apparently representing ideational realms of the ruling group in a symbolic manner, were excavated mainly by Mexican archaeologists of national institutions, currently called the Instituto Nacional de Antropología e Historia (INAH), as the nation's interest in its cultural heritage and history has been raised in certain social and political contexts since the beginning of the last century.

Leopoldo Batres (1906) first excavated the Sun Pyramid, one of Teotihuacan's major monuments, in the early 1900s (Fig. 1). In 1917, Manuel Gamio (1922) extensively explored the Ciudadela (Citadel) complex, including parts of the Feathered Serpent Pyramid (FSP) (Fig. 2). In 1962–64, an INAH macroproject directed by Ignacio Bernal (1963) excavated and consolidated the Moon Pyramid complex and a major portion of the temple-residence complexes along the Avenue of the Dead (Acosta 1964). Two decades later, another INAH presidential project,

Fig. 3 Principal facade of the FSP. Photo: author.

the Proyecto Arqueológico Teotihuacán 1980–82 (PAT80–82), directed by Rubén Cabrera (Cabrera, Rodríguez, and Morelos 1982a, 1982b, 1991), mainly excavated the southern section of the city's core, including most structures in the Ciudadela that Gamio did not excavate. In the early 1990s, Eduardo Matos (1995) of the INAH coordinated excavations of the Sun Pyramid complex, uncovering the base of the northern and eastern parts of the pyramid and the large platforms surrounding the pyramid.[2]

Significant amounts of information have been provided by these national projects, which have contributed to our understanding of the monuments of Teotihuacan. However, the question of how these monuments were specifically involved in state affairs remains poorly understood. These major pyramids and other monumental programs should be intensively and systematically explored further in an appropriate methodological and interpretative framework. In this book, I discuss one of the major monuments, the Feathered Serpent Pyramid located in the Ciudadela, in order to explore the nature of early government of the Teotihuacan state. This monument was the third largest pyramid and, perhaps, the one reflecting the highest energy expenditure in Teotihuacan, as indicated by its extraordinary sculptural facades (Fig. 3). The pyramid's physical features establish that the monumental construction was totally directed by the state administration.

As a consequence of long-term explorations at the pyramid, accumulated data, although they are not exhaustive, deserve a thorough examination, with a focus on state affairs. The structure provides much higher quality and quantity of data than any other monument excavated earlier at Teotihuacan. The FSP was one of the excavation fronts of the PAT80–82, in which I have been involved since 1980 (Cabrera and

Sugiyama 1982). As a complementary operation to PAT80–82, burials associated with the FSP were searched for, and a part of the burial complex was found on the south side of the pyramid in 1983–84 (Sugiyama 1989a, 1991a). Subsequently, a joint project called the Proyecto Templo de Quetzalcoatl 1988–89 (PTQ88–89) was formed with members of two institutions with which I was associated at the time; we explored this monument more intensively and extensively (Cabrera, Sugiyama, and Cowgill 1991).

These new discoveries comprise three construction levels, a large-scale grave complex of apparently sacrificed people, material symbols, and a systematic termination program including the looting of multiple burials.[3] The rest of an earlier construction prior to the Feathered Serpent Pyramid was uncovered with a corresponding sacrificial burial. The second level, corresponding to the Ciudadela and the Feathered Serpent Pyramid, which has been dated to the early third century, was one of the most monumental construction programs in the city. The Adosada platform was the third construction level at this location. It covered the front facade of the main Feathered Serpent Pyramid sometime in the fourth century (Sugiyama 1998c). One of the most significant discoveries was the more than 137 individuals that were found with abundant symbolic offerings of exceptional quality in and around the pyramid. The distribution pattern of the graves clearly indicates a materialization of the Teotihuacan worldview; significant numbers in Mesoamerican cosmology and calendric systems were evidently used in organizing the burials. Although we intentionally left some graves unexcavated, we believe that more than 200 individuals were buried during the construction of the pyramid.

In this volume, I mainly discuss the FSP in terms of its symbols and their sociopolitical implications in the broader context of the city and beyond. My goal is to explore the nature of an early state and the process of urbanization of a nonindustrialized city in the New World, given the current immature state of our understanding of the Teotihuacan polity.

A holistic approach is chosen for this purpose. I explore the symbolism of the location, monumental architecture, sculptures, burial complex, and offerings discovered at the FSP. An underlying notion is that the various symbolic acts associated with the pyramid would have been manipulated meaningfully by the state administration. One of the main propositions is that, as in other Mesoamerican states (López 1994; Marcus 1992a; Schele and Miller 1986; Umberger 1987a), rulership of the Teotihuacan state also may have been encoded metaphorically and systematically in architectural features, graves, and offerings found at the monument. Knowledge of ritual meanings expressed in each material assemblage may lead us to a better understanding of a cohesive symbolization program by the state.

Much of the book is devoted to the interpretation of ritual and cosmological connotation of materials, explored with descriptive and analytical tools. The fundamental objectives of this process are, specifically, to search for coherent significance and to discuss sociopolitical implications. Finally, I discuss the FSP as a state symbol and relate it to the early polity in Teotihuacan and beyond, arguing patterns of Mesoamerican state politics and preindustrialized urbanization processes.

Structure and brief summaries

This book is structured in the following way to arrive at the goals mentioned above. In the second half of this chapter, I discuss current theoretical and methodological issues dealing with symbols in archaeology, touch upon the degree to which we can deal with ritual behavior, and explore the question of how we can decode ritual behavior from archaeological materials. I especially stress the feasibility of relating rulership to religion in the Teotihuacan state. I believe that the materials recovered from the FSP over the last two decades are detailed, precise, and specific enough to allow us to consider the ideological and cosmological issues involved.

In Chapter 2, I provide brief background information of two quite different types: sources of data discussed in this book and some Mesoamerican ideational features. The chapter presents the framework for the discussion of analyses and interpretations in the following chapters. I first summarize the history of exploration and excavation at the FSP to provide a setting for the studies, referring to the discoveries of different kinds of materials during the last eighty years. Descriptive detail in published and unpublished reports varies significantly from one discovery to another. Numerous objects found earlier are no longer accessible; therefore, data from excavations after 1980 are the main sources for analysis, and the previous information has been re-interpreted retrospectively from newly discovered, comprehensive data. Particularly, the materials obtained by PTQ88–89 form the core of the data studied.

In the second half of Chapter 2, I briefly introduce Mesoamerican mythology and other ideational factors that we may recognize through analyses of archaeological materials in Teotihuacan. I stress cosmological structures, indigenous concepts of time, space, deities, and cosmogonical myths, that probably were shared by Mesoamerican societies since the Preclassic periods.

The next five chapters are intended as a bridge between the data and ideational realms, both summarized in Chapter 2. In Chapter 3, I begin an analytical interpretation of possible meanings attached to the location of the Ciudadela in which the FSP stands as the principal pyramid. The locational data are examined in terms of a worldview materialized in the city layout, which I have proposed elsewhere had existed since an early stage of the city's formation (Sugiyama 1993). My study of the measurement unit used in Teotihuacan (TMU) is a basic tool for this assessment, together with information about the topography, orientation, and architecture of the city. This study suggests that the Ciudadela, with the FSP, was located topographically and conceptually at the lowest point on the Avenue of the Dead and may have been constructed for ritual displays related to the mythological Underworld.

Study of the architecture and iconography of the FSP comprises Chapter 4, a discussion of the cosmogonic aspects of the building. Interpreted in the contexts of Teotihuacan iconography are the architectural style and sculptured facades, as well as burned clay fragments (which may have been walls of the temple once situated atop the FSP) found in the construction fill of the Adosada, a stepped platform later built over the front of the FSP.

The sculptural facades of the FSP seem to have commemorated a myth of the creation of time (López et al. 1991). More concretely, the facades can be read as the following: the Feathered Serpent brings time from the watery Underworld to the present world; it bears a calendar sign on its body in the form of a headdress that represents the Primordial Crocodile, a Teotihuacan antecedent to the Aztec creature, Cipactli. As my survey of later representations of the Feathered Serpent elsewhere in the city suggests, the Feathered Serpent at the FSP seems to have borne symbols of warfare, human sacrifice, and most explicitly rulership.

The core of this volume, found in Chapters 5 through 7, is a discussion of the massive burial complex found at the FSP. In total, 132 complete skeletons plus fragmentary remains have been found with rich offerings around and in the FSP; the majority of the interments chronologically correspond to the stages of construction of the pyramid. Many were found with their wrists crossed behind their backs as if they had been tied. Many of the people buried were identified as soldiers because of the types of offerings associated with them (Cabrera, Sugiyama, and Cowgill 1991; Sugiyama 1988b, 1989a). Based on the excavation contexts, the remains have been interpreted intuitively as those of human sacrifice with militaristic implication, although there is no direct evidence of cause of death from the bones (R. Millon 1988b: 109).

In this book, I endeavor to interpret the data from the burial complex more specifically, systematically, and comprehensively. Chapter 5 deals with burial patterns at the FSP. The grave complex may have been, rather than the result of a single event, a complicated ritual process that involved many burials. I consider several alternative explanations inductively in the context of the excavation, and present interpretations of each grave based on stratigraphy, association with architecture, and differences in treatment of the dead among the graves.

After a diachronic review, I examine hypothetical propositions that the graves were highly patterned to express the state's ideological concerns, and that social hierarchy among burials existed in a metaphoric religious manner. Mortuary features – locations and morphologies of the graves, number of individuals buried in each grave, positions, orientations, and forms of bodies, ages, sex, and other physical traits of the burials – are used to plot the spatial distribution of bodies in a search for patterns. The studies indicate that the burials found at different spots in and around the FSP manifested a foundation program integrated into the monument.

A royal burial or burials might have been included in the graves discovered at the FSP, in addition to the dedicatory burials. Unfortunately, the "candidates" for royal burial, two graves found near the center of the pyramid and a large pit in front of the staircase, were heavily looted in ancient times (Sugiyama 1998c). Although we cannot know for certain whether the body of a ruler was included in the graves at the FSP, the issue is discussed in the light of circumstantial field data and the burial patterns. Preliminary conclusions are that almost all graves found at the FSP, including the central grave, were essentially sacrificial and dedicated to the erection of the monument, and that one or two elite burials might have been integrated into the monument sometime after the construction was completed. They suggest that rulership was not only symbolically involved in the monument, but also that ruling individuals may have been physically integrated into the grave complex. These hypothetical interpretations, however, remain, for the present, unverified.

Chapter 6 consists of analyses of burial offerings, organized by type of material. Many formal analyses of the obsidian, greenstone and other stone materials, shell, pottery, and organic materials have been completed, and a few are still underway. Detailed descriptive information will be published in Spanish and in English in the near future. In addition, an extensive World Wide Web page publication is already available on the internet as a complementary report (see Chapter 1, note 3). Therefore, after a brief description, I discuss these materials mainly in terms of their symbolic significance.

Offerings are first classified on the basis of morphology and quantitative data. I then analyze locational data using a GIS program (MapInfo Corporation 1992–94) in reference to the classifications and visually display distributional patterns of the offerings, interrelation among burials, and hierarchical groups of graves. After possible emic classifications are suggested with locational data, ritual meanings are discussed in the light of Teotihuacan iconography.

In Chapter 7, before overall conclusions are stated, results from the mortuary studies are evaluated in the comparative context of the city and beyond. Sacrificial burials and elite graves in other parts of the city and Teotihuacan-related sites are briefly reviewed. This includes hypothetical propositions about the graves associated with major monuments in Teotihuacan. I first review other sacrificial burials in Teotihuacan, in order to compare them with the instances at the FSP. Mortuary forms of sacrifice in residential areas contrast considerably with the cases at the FSP. Second, elite burials associated with monuments at Teotihuacan and Teotihuacan-related sites are reviewed in general. Particularly, burials discovered by Kidder, Jennings, and Shook (1946) at Mounds A and B in Kaminaljuyú are useful to distinguish possible elite graves from sacrificial ones at the FSP.

In Chapter 8, I synthesize the information. Several implications can be deduced through different approaches: the cosmological nature of the materials recovered from this central monument of the city; the cohesiveness of meanings in various kinds of materials in terms of a citywide program, which in effect materializes a Teotihuacan worldview. I end the book with a discussion of sociopolitical implications of these ritual behaviors in Teotihuacan and beyond and argue that the huge amount of material at the FSP can best be interpreted as official symbols manipulated by ruling groups to create a New Era brought by the Feathered Serpent. The two important sociopolitical institutions – militarism and human sacrifice – seem to have been woven metaphorically into this "net" of cosmogonic meanings. These institutions were most likely connected with individualistic rulership, which was proclaimed to be given by the Feathered Serpent at the monument. State symbols thus established at the FSP in Teotihuacan about AD 200 seem to have diffused as a social power, in time and space, to other Mesoamerican societies.

Theories and strategies
For some years, many archaeologists focused their research on the material side of early human society, such as human ecology, subsistence, economic systems, and technologies. In recent years, there has been a growing tendency to investigate

the mental side, or what may be referred to as ideation. This widening of research interest in archaeology seems to reflect shifting theories in anthropology and the social sciences in general. Particularly, a simplistic polarity between materialist versus mentalist is no longer tenable (Ortner 1984). Instead of looking for outside factors governing human behavior, many sociocultural anthropologists are focusing more closely on individual practice, praxis, experience, or decision-making processes. A central focus of these action-based approaches is the dynamic *inter*relationship between agent and ecology, structure, system, or Bourdieu's concept of "habitus" (Bourdieu 1978). Particularly, rituals are considered by symbolic anthropologists as one of the primary matrices for the reproduction of consciousness (Geertz 1973: 55–86).

As I deal with archaeological materials used for ritual purposes, my interpretations are grounded in the symbolic anthropologists' perspective that rituals are central social institutions that structure, and are reproduced or transformed by, participants' actions (Eliade 1959; Geertz 1973: 87–125). In archaeology, the idea has been applied to explanations of complex preindustrial societies (Renfrew and Zubrow 1994). For example, the religious forces found in sacred landscapes, which I discuss with regard to Teotihuacan, have been pointed out as crucial factors in the establishment of political legitimacy in early complex societies (Bender 1993; Demarest and Conrad 1992). In the case of complex Mesoamerican societies, especially Postclassic societies for which abundant ethnohistorical and ethnographic records are available, religion was an essential institution integrated into, and therefore constrained by, social, political, and economic organizations (e.g., Broda 1978; Carrasco 1978; López 1973; Matos 1987; Umberger 1987b). Religion and worldview are extensively explained by some Mesoamerican archaeologists as a prime variable in social change, including the process toward state complexity (Coe 1981; Marcus and Flannery 1996).

The rise of the Teotihuacan state has been discussed from different points of view, including ecology (Sanders 1981), subsistence (McClung de Tapia 1987; Nichols 1987), economics (Charlton 1978; Spence 1981), and politico-religious perspectives (Cowgill 1992a; Millon 1981; Manzanilla 1992). While archaeologists develop evolutionary views of the urbanization process, studies of religion in Teotihuacan had been largely in the charge of historians and art historians who reconstructed ritual meanings using Postclassic written references. Iconographers focus on state religion and worldview through works of art from a more synchronic point of view without touching on their political functions and relevant social histories. Before the 1970s, the sacredness of the city's architecture, and its impersonal, anonymous, abstract, or mythological imageries, often dominated iconographic interpretations and veiled our perception of sociopolitical organizations which works of art may have reflected.

After the 1970s, the Teotihuacan politics symbolized in the religious materials increasingly has been emphasized from archaeological perspectives. The role of sacred places, like the cave under the Sun Pyramid, and the religious authority expressed by particular symbols, have been integrated into explanations of politics by archaeologists (R. Millon 1973, 1981; C. Millon 1973). It was René Millon (1988b: 112) who first argued that charismatic despotic rulership in religious quality was fundamental to the founding of the city. Manzanilla (1992) stressed that the Teotihuacan trade network was organized and controlled by hierarchies conceived in overwhelmingly religious terms. Integrating discoveries at the FSP in the 1980s, R. Millon (1988b: 112) and Cowgill (1992a) intuitively suggested that the construction of the FSP, occurring at an early stage of the city's history, was a glorification of personal power. Following these interpretative frameworks, I provide an analytical view from the FSP about the relationship of religion with state polity and synthesize studies of material symbols into an archaeological and anthropological explanation.

In this book, I stress the social nature of symbols as cultural products; I follow Geertz's (1973: 3–30) definition of symbols as vehicles of meanings, integrated echoes, and worldview of a society. Unlike icons and indexes that are understandable cross-culturally, symbols have an arbitrary relationship of culturally constituted contiguity between expression and object, like signifier and signified in any language. Symbols are therefore products of conventional linkage relevant exclusively among members of a social or cultural unit. Rather than being locked inside people's minds, symbols function by determining social actions and thus embody culture in a fundamental way (Geertz 1973: 3–30; Schneider 1976). Victor Turner defines symbols as "what might be called *operators* in the social process, things that, when put together in a certain arrangement in a certain context (especially ritual), produce essentially *social* transformations" (Ortner 1984: 131; italics in original text). In this study, I discuss the symbolism of a monument in terms of a public operating system, which arbitrarily and conventionally links ritual meanings with their sociopolitical functions.

A fundamental question is how we can approach the public operation system involved in material symbols in political contexts. In order to understand public symbols, Geertz (1984) emphasizes the study of culture from the actor's point of view. He argues that culture is a product of acting social entities trying to make sense of the world in which they find themselves, and that, if we are to make sense of a culture, we must situate ourselves in the position from which it was constructed. In dealing with highly symbolic materials, I try to approach an emic point of view using various kinds of strategies, in order to understand native meanings conveyed by symbols at the FSP, and by extension, to recognize the native way in which the symbols of the state functioned in the public political sphere. In archaeology, when dealing with cultural remains, approaches may be indirect, and it is necessary to specify methodologies and strategic tools.

I use analogies among materials that can be found within particular social boundaries (namely Teotihuacan and directly Teotihuacan-related sites), and I consider similarities in possible historical contexts reconstructed by archaeology. To approach an emic point of view, objects are first categorized in etic terms based on morphological differences; then these categories are tested in their contexts, mainly using their spatial patterns. The mental structures or cognitive systems of the ancient Teotihuacanos may be elucidated partially through these processes. Study of the city layout may be a simple instance, as described in detail in Chapter 3; through analysis of the city's layout using our metric system, I try to approach the native measurement unit system and then observe, from an emic point of view, how possible religious, cosmological meanings were involved in space management. The studies of iconography, burials, and offerings associated with the FSP were also carried out with the intention of approaching native categories from morphological classifications. Finally, results of these analyses are contextualized, as these materials of different kinds were once associated. It is hoped that this procedure strengthens the interpretation of meanings and functions of the FSP symbolism as a social operating system.

Before I move on to specific strategies and further theoretical discussion, I must clarify the procedure of examining my underlying proposition. It is proposed that the monument studied is comprised of several components; rituals and other ideological factors embodied in its erection may be better comprehended as various programs or facets of the same symbolization process. Location would have been important to the pyramid's meaning. Architectural, sculptural, and mortuary programs were apparently involved in the foundation ceremony of the FSP. In particular, a mass mortuary program seems to have taken place with special significance for the erection of the pyramid. However, the cohesiveness or consistency among meanings was not taken for granted during the analyses. Graves and offerings are studied and interpreted, independently from one another, in their own configurations; later, the results are integrated into the concluding explanation. In this way, principles of symbolic organization or structure of the assemblage may be examined through what remains, even though the details of a past culture are lost forever (Leone 1982: 743).

City layout

Except for archaeoastronomers' studies of the city's orientation, spatial analysis and interpretation of the Teotihuacan city layout have previously been carried out mainly in search of functions rather than ritual meanings of specific locations and structures (R. Millon 1973, 1981; Cowgill 1983). Strong attention to the chronology of each building may have kept archaeologists from discussing interrelated meanings among city structures. Even though available data are fragmentary, it is still somewhat surprising that possibly correlated meanings among the three major monuments in Teotihuacan – the Sun Pyramid, the Moon Pyramid, and the Ciudadela – have not been systematically and extensively studied. In Chapter 3, I explore the city layout using the Teotihuacan Measurement Unit (hereafter called TMU) as a strategic tool, as I mentioned above. Although the objective had been specified since the beginning of the study, the process was fundamentally inductive and resulted in a preliminary indication of unexpectedly highly patterned city layout with built-in cosmological meanings. The result seems to make sense in light of other kinds of information from Teotihuacan as discussed in the last chapter.

Iconography

During the last century, Teotihuacan iconography was intensively studied by scholars of various disciplines from different points of view.[4] In general, the studies relied strongly on Postclassic written records to interpret religious meanings in Teotihuacan imagery. Historical and contextual interpretations, keenly integrating politics and sociocultural transformation of the society studied, began in the 1970s fundamentally with Clara Millon (1973) and increased in the 1980s. Janet Berlo (1984), following earlier scholars who stressed cultural continuity, elucidated through analyses of artwork the nature of the relationship between Teotihuacan and one of its provinces in Guatemala. James Langley (1986), who carried out the first systematic, computer-aided approach to iconography, likewise stressed the importance of ritual sacrifice in Teotihuacan imageries. Among major outcomes of his work is the identification of Teotihuacan notational calendrical signs, which may have been related to actual rituals and historical individuals. René Millon (1988b), Clara Millon (1988b, 1988c), and Pasztory (1988) interpreted newly disclosed murals through careful comparative analyses, confirming that a main theme of Teotihuacan murals, and presumably real life, was in fact human sacrificial rituals.

Following these recent methodologically developed studies, I interpret meanings of iconographic representations of the FSP in reference to archaeological data. My iconographic study is grounded in social contexts within a chronological framework (AD 200 to 600). Analogous instances from later Teotihuacan periods are compared morphologically in search of general meanings attached to each iconographic component. Extracted general meanings are then combined for reconstruction of symbolic messages that were socially created in particular historical contexts. Conventional relationships between symbols and conveyed meanings are searched, to understand the underlying social significance of the symbols. During this process, it becomes clear that symbols used at the FSP are related to a cosmological program in which the importance of warfare, sacrifice, and authority are stressed: the last as the bearer of time brought by a mythical entity. Social implications of these meanings are discussed in the final chapter, in which historical, social, and political contexts are considered archaeologically.

Mortuary program

Graves associated with monuments should be considered as a socially produced symbolic program. However, features involved in burials should not be proposed simply as direct reflections of social factors of the individuals interred. Literature of mortuary analysis during the last quarter-century provides underlying theories.

An earlier premise was that mortuary practices were reflections of beliefs about death and the afterlife and therefore unstable and arbitrary with regard to social factors (Kroeber 1927). In contrast, processual archaeologists of the 1970s, especially Binford (1971), proposed that mortuary forms and social dimensions of the dead can be correlated (Braun 1981; Chapman et al. 1981; Tainter 1978). A large number of studies with middle-range theoretical propositions and statistical devices was applied to burial data to reconstruct social features. Recently, a large number of burials from Teotihuacan have also been studied with statistical analyses, as previously mentioned (Rodríguez 1992; Sempowski and Spence 1994). However, Binford's proposition has been criticized by postprocessual archaeologists (Hodder 1986; Parker Pearson 1982), who cite the complexity of symbolic behaviors, in which mortuary practices sometimes mask social relations. Carr (1995) demonstrates, through a cross-cultural survey of mortuary practices, that philosophical-religious beliefs should be considered beyond social determinants for holistic and multidisciplinary approaches.

The mortuary program at the FSP seems to have been extensive, systematic, highly ritualistic, and apparently related to state religion, as indicated by the monumentality of the building with which the burials were associated. In addition, since the persons interred were possibly sacrificial victims, the mortuary form was unlikely to be correlated in any simple way with their social positions. Social dimensions reflected in the mortuary practices may have been metaphorical and meaningful on their own terms. Moreover, as Turner (1977) pointed out, complicated sacrificial rituals may have to be considered as processes rather than events. Archaeological data from the FSP clearly indicate that the burials were part of a foundation ceremony performed during the process of erection of the monument. Because of this complexity, I review, among various explanatory theories, three models of human sacrifice that I believe are relevant to defining the specific meanings and functions of the cases at the FSP.

Human sacrifice
In some instances of official sacrificial rituals in ranked societies around the world, sacrifices were dedicated to or served dead rulers. In other cases, the sacrifices could have been, by themselves, manifestations of kingship (Valeri 1985). The "retainers-for-king" theory is appropriate in many burials in ancient states, such as the royal tombs at Ur (Woolley 1954), the Shang dynasty (Chang 1980), or the Moche royal tombs of Sipán (Alva and Donnan 1993). Examples of the same sacrificial burial type are widely observed in Mesoamerican societies. Different mortuary treatments between a king's burial and those of sacrificial victims are usually conspicuous in tombs at major pyramids (Ruz 1968). In the case of Aztec kings, their tombs have not been identified because cremation was probably involved (Umberger, personal communication, 1992). Nevertheless, sacrifice of retainers seems to have been common, as described by Sahagún (1952: 43). In Teotihuacan, no examples of retainer sacrifice have been identified to date. However, the concept may be relevant if royal burials can be identified at the FSP or other monuments.

The "contract with the gods" theory seems to explain mythological beliefs underlying Mesoamerican sacrificial rituals in general. An Aztec version of this theory was interpreted thus by Pasztory (1983: 58):

> The gods themselves were not immortal, and remained within this cycle
> of death and rebirth. The processes of living and dying were frequently
> reduced to the metaphor of eating. When humans were eating maize
> they were actually eating the flesh of the maize god Centeotl; this had to
> be restored to the god in the form of human sacrifices – the blood into
> which the maize had been transformed. The dead, whether people or

gods, were eaten by the earth, imagined as a great monster. One of the most powerful images of Aztec art is the open jaw of the earth monster ready to devour its victims.

A general conception of the divine contract seems to have existed in the minds of Teotihuacanos, as many representations of deities carrying out human sacrificial rituals suggest. Numerous temples and public spaces in Teotihuacan, including the FSP, may have been used for rituals grounded in beliefs of divine contract. Since the burials at the FSP were unusually associated with sculptural imagery of deities, as later explained, faith in a divine contract could have been an underlying concept.

Another possible explanation of the mass human sacrifice at the FSP is the "foundation" theory, which interprets sacrifice of victims as a dedication to the monument. Human sacrifices were often carried out to spiritualize monuments and/or to attach specific ritual, cosmological, or calendrical meanings to them. Examples can be found over long periods of time and space around the world (Davies 1984). Human sacrifice dedicated to specific monuments was also common in Mesoamerica. In Teotihuacan, possible foundation sacrifices have been excavated at other monuments as described in Chapter 7, although data are still scarce.

Within the Mesoamerican cultural sphere, mortuary forms of human sacrifices varied largely (Boone 1984). In fact, several specific meanings and functions seem to have been attached to the burial complex at the FSP, as in the case of the Templo Mayor, Tenochtitlán, which Matos (1984) and López (1994) persuasively demonstrate within a different religious and sociopolitical context. The explanatory theories mentioned above were not mutually exclusive; it may have been an event involving meaning of a contract with certain gods, a dedication to supernatural forces, and spiritualization of the monument. As discussed later, had one of the burials contained a ruler, the overall mortuary program should also be considered a possible retainer complex serving the deified dead ruler (the case was not confirmed because of earlier looting) (Nagao 1985: 38–39). Following these explanatory frameworks, my goal is to arrive from the data at a more specific and precise interpretation of the ritual meanings and political functions involved, useful for holistic perspectives on social changes in ancient states (Demarest 1984). Theories of human sacrifice indicate that this peculiar mortuary form requires special treatment for analysis and interpretation.

In summary, it appears that while formal mortuary analysis has tended to focus on the relations between the dead and the grave contents, interpretation of mass human sacrifice needs to take into account the primary role of the sacrificers who were responsible for the mortuary practices (Hubert and Mauss 1964). By no means can the relations of the dead (sacrificed) and the grave contents be supposed to have been direct. In other words, we may be dealing with the symbolic behavior of the sacrificers, rather than that of the sacrificed. This is why the final chapter discusses the burials in relation to other ritual actions that took place at Teotihuacan. I search for cohesive acts of those responsible for the diverse programs to explain their primary involvement in politics.

In my research, this proposition became clearer as analyses of the offerings progressed. The burials discovered at the FSP were not just individuals who were sacrificed and simply buried at the pyramid: the production of the offerings seems to have been systematically planned, and they were placed in specifically assigned graves according to overall ritual meanings, in order to express certain ideational concerns of the sacrificers. My studies reveal that the burials were explicit manifestations of ritual warfare and the significance of human sacrifice. This symbolic action can better be understood in terms of a political proclamation by the state. I believe that the burial complex was, like the location, architecture, and iconography of the pyramid, part of a larger program of materializing a consistent belief system manipulated by the ruling group.

The Ciudadela was constructed with the largest plaza for ritual display at a critical location of the city; the FSP with its colossal sculptures was intentionally highly monumental to be worshiped by numerous people; mass-sacrificial rituals taking place at the erection of the FSP must have been impressively commemorative. I believe that this series of constructive works and funerary actions comprised integrative functions of religion, cosmology, and politics. The symbolism and rituals registered in such pivotal context at the FSP must have been public and well understood by the sustaining populace for political arguments of the relevance to be convincing.

In this chapter, I have described motivations, ends, theoretical background, and strategies in the search for ideological factors involved at the FSP. Discussions on methodology continue in each chapter. In Chapter 2, before the description of studies and interpretations, I specify the sources used and Mesoamerican ideational factors that can be inferred from the archaeological data, in order to give readers directions on which the analyses will focus.

2

Background: data and ideation

In the first half of Chapter 2, I describe the history of excavations and interpretations of the Feathered Serpent Pyramid (FSP) to demonstrate the different qualities of data analyzed. I evaluate the research contexts, since contextual details are often crucial for the reconstruction of ritual behavior in time and space. An action is sometimes imprinted between layers and can be restored through careful interpretation of its archaeological context. In the second half, I review Mesoamerican cosmology, to provide a background for what ritual meanings we might expect to find at the Ciudadela and the FSP. The following chapters are efforts to build a bridge between the data and ideational realms outlined here.

Excavations at the Feathered Serpent Pyramid

The pyramid was separately excavated by several archaeologists at different times. Graves found in and around the pyramid were reported as independent graves unrelated to each other. Since 1985, however, I have believed that almost all these graves were part of a sacrificial burial complex associated with the building of the pyramid (Sugiyama 1986 and 1989a). My hypothesis of a cohesive relationship among the burials is analyzed with new, more detailed data in Chapters 5 and 6. In this section, excavation contexts are discussed and in some cases reinterpreted. The cohesiveness of the architecture, graves, and caches found around the FSP, and related stratigraphy, is also discussed.[1]

Discoveries before 1980

The Ciudadela is a huge enclosure located geographically at the center of the city of Teotihuacan and measuring about 400 m on a side (about 160,000 m^2); the interior space is surrounded by four large platforms surmounted by pyramids (Fig. 2). The main plaza had a capacity of 100,000 persons without much crowding (Cowgill 1983: 322); and one can easily suppose that the main function of this huge, enclosed space was for ritual performance. The FSP was the central structure of the complex (Fig. 3). Two apartment compounds adjacent to the pyramid were apparently for residences and/or administrative offices of elites (Compounds 1D: N1E1 and 1E: N1E1: Millon et al. 1973; hereafter they are called North Palace and South Palace respectively).

The FSP, measuring 65 m on a side (about 4,225 m^2), was once completely covered with stone blocks. The walls were of tablero-talud form, an architectural feature characteristic of Teotihuacan combining a rectangular portion (tablero) set on top of a trapezoid form (talud). Huge sculptural heads jutting from the tablero portions evidently represented mythical entities in the forms of Feathered Serpents and headdresses, as later discussed in great detail. The Adosada platform was later attached to the FSP, covering a major portion of the pyramid's principal facade (Figs. 4 and 5).

In 1917 Ignacio Marquina, a member of Manuel Gamio's national project (1922 [1979]), began to excavate the Ciudadela complex extensively for the first time. The excavation area included large platforms, parts of palaces, and the FSP (later called the Temple of Quetzalcoatl). The monumental architecture and sculptural decoration of the main facade (discussed in Chapter 4) have been exposed since that time. The early excavation process was described by Marquina (1922) and Reygadas (1930) with useful maps and photos, but the details of the excavation, such as data on the west (principal) and south facades of the FSP and the palaces, do not appear in any of these reports.

Together with the impressive carved stone facade of the pyramid, burials and precious artifacts made of greenstone, obsidian, shell, and ceramics were found during the 1917 excavation. At the beginning of the exploration, three burials of fragmented bones without apparent anatomical relationships were discovered on the top of the mound, and the discoverer interpreted them as bones exhumed from other graves. I became suspicious of this interpretation in 1984; they also could have been remains of primary burials, as later discussed (Sugiyama 1989a: 103).

In 1925 Pedro Dosal (1925a, 1925b) unexpectedly discovered four graves, one at each of the four corners of the FSP (Fig. 5), each containing a human skeleton and associated offerings. Dosal reports that these individuals were found under floors within pits made in a rock-like volcanic ash subsoil. Although the report lacks precise stratigraphic data, the general excavation context accords with burials found on the south side of the pyramid. The locations, so directly associated with the pyramid, suggest that these graves were related to the construction of the FSP. Associated offerings include 14 obsidian projectile points and 400 or more pieces of shell worked into the form of perforated rectangular plaques simulating human teeth (Siliceo 1925), identical to those found in graves in the 1980s. This striking similarity supports the idea that they were part of the same burial complex. Before the excavations of the 1980s, burial contexts led some researchers to surmise that the people buried at the corners of the structure were sacrificial victims (Armillas 1950: 44; Dosal 1925a: 218; Millon 1981: 213; Sempowski 1983).

In 1939, under orders from Alfonso Caso, José R. Pérez (1939) dug pits and tunnels at different places near the FSP. Many offerings were found in front of the staircase of the FSP, others under the staircase of the Adosada, and were interpreted simply as offerings associated with the two buildings respectively. I was also skeptical of this interpretation because of inconsistencies in the excavation reports: both sets of offerings seemed to correspond to the construction phase of the FSP (Sugiyama 1989a, 1991a). Two brief reports on these excavations are available, the first written fifteen days after the conclusion of fieldwork by Pérez (1939), who headed the excavation; this unpublished report provides much more detailed field contexts and

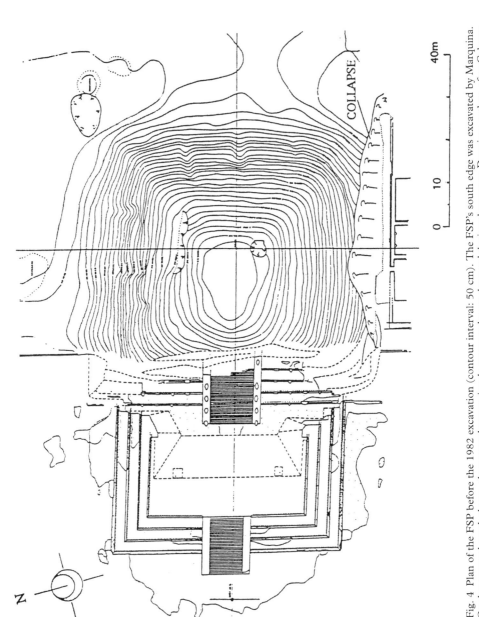

Fig. 4 Plan of the FSP before the 1982 excavation (contour interval: 50 cm). The FSP's south edge was excavated by Marquina. On the east and north slopes, three trenches previously excavated were detected during the survey. Drawing: author, after Cabrera and Sugiyama 1982: 175.

COLLAPSE

N

0   10   40m

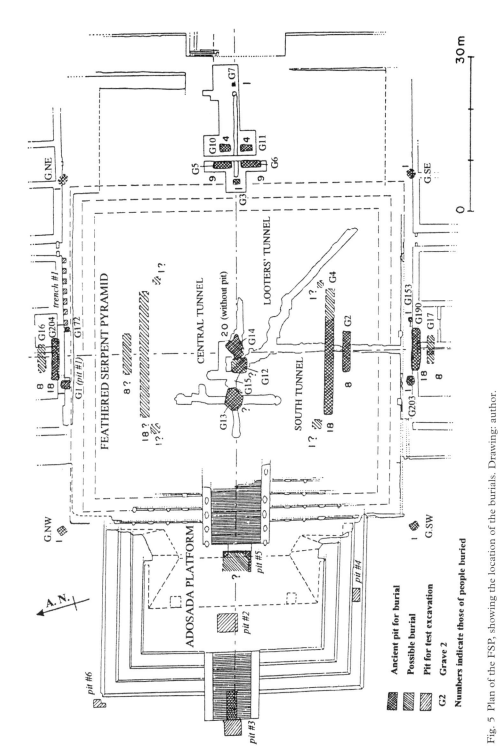

Fig. 5 Plan of the FSP, showing the location of the burials. Drawing: author.

concrete description of discoveries than the brief account published eight years later by Daniel Rubín de la Borbolla (1947). Pérez's report led me to consider the finds part of a massive sacrificial burial complex. This idea was confirmed in 1988, when a test pit was excavated during PTQ88-89 (pit 3, Fig. 5), and it was possible to verify that both of the rich caches described by Borbolla were earlier than the construction of the Adosada and perhaps pertained to the FSP.

Apart from the stratigraphic question of the caches, I wondered if Pérez had found a grave pit in front of the staircase of the FSP. Sempowski (1983) also suspected that bones found at the FSP staircase originally belonged to two probable burials. Although he did not clearly mention it, some of Pérez's words, like "a vertical cut (in the subsoil)" and "a depth of 1.72 m" suggested that he found offerings in or around a grave pit in front of the FSP (Sugiyama 1989a: 99–100). To clarify the uncertainty in his report, another test pit was dug in front of the FSP stairway (pit 5, Fig. 5). The results are described in Chapter 5. Although Pérez's excavation report caused some confusion, his were the primary data that, along with the discoveries made on the south side in 1982, triggered my thoughts about a large-scale dedicatory complex at the FSP, an idea that finally resulted in even more extensive explorations.

Discoveries between 1980 and 1987

The Ciudadela complex was not extensively excavated again until the 1980s. In the 1960s, the TMP directed by René Millon dug a stratigraphic trench in the Ciudadela's East Platform and two test pits near the FSP, which yielded stratigraphic information related to the palaces (Millon 1992). The TMP also produced, for the first time, an accurate map of the city that included the Ciudadela, at a scale of 1:2,000 (Millon et al. 1973).

An INAH project, the Proyecto Arqueológico Teotihuacan (PAT80–82) (Cabrera, Rodríquez, and Morelos 1982a, 1982b, 1991) was formed in 1980–82 as a major presidential program for Mexico. The project, directed by Rubén Cabrera, consisted of about 600 people working on excavation and conservation mainly on the southern part of the Avenue of the Dead. This area was chosen as complementary to an earlier presidential project, which in 1962–64 uncovered the northern half of the city's central part along the avenue (Bernal 1963; Acosta 1964). The Ciudadela complex was one of the main excavation areas of PAT80–82.[2]

The project was designed to remove all post-Teotihuacan layers from this huge square precinct in order to expose Teotihuacan's monuments. Virtually all the buildings in the Ciudadela, except for a small area east of the FSP, were excavated and consolidated for public display, including the North and South Palaces (Jarquín and Martínez 1982).

As a member of PAT80–82, in 1982 I was assigned to explore the south facade of the FSP (Cabrera and Sugiyama 1982). Although no previous excavation records remained, our excavation confirmed that a major area of this section had been excavated once before, probably by Marquina (1922), and that the east–west corridor along the south edge of the pyramid was re-covered later by natural silting. So the excavation's first stage was the removal of new fill in most of the area. After the

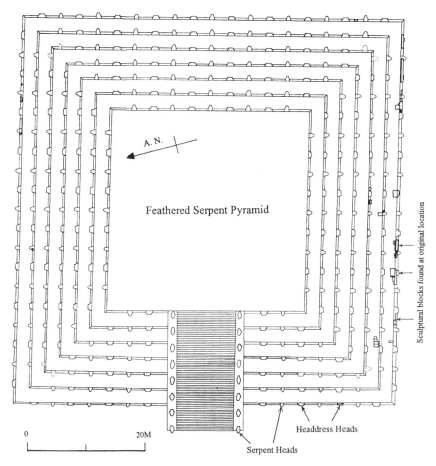

Fig. 6 Plan of the FSP reconstructed by the author in 1982, based on blocks and sculptural heads found in situ (bold lines). Sculptural blocks including large heads once covered four sides of the pyramid completely. After Cabrera and Sugiyama 1982: 179.

uppermost Teotihuacan construction level was exposed, the second stage was to dig trenches and test pits into the pyramid's facade and corridor floors, to understand the pyramid's stratigraphic relationship to the South Palace. In one of these test pits, a single burial (Grave 153), one male with thousands of small shell beads around his thorax, was discovered by accident. The stratigraphy indicated that the grave was sealed by floors during construction of the FSP. This discovery motivated the search for more burials.

The grave was not on the north–south centerline of the reconstructed pyramid (Fig. 6), as one might expect. This anomaly led me to open another pit exactly on the pyramid's north–south centerline, since I realized that graves and caches previously discovered also follow a symmetrical pattern at the pyramid (Dosal 1925a; Marquina 1922; Pérez 1939).[3] Subsequently, the edges of a long east–west pit, excavated from the subsoil level, were found exactly on the centerline under the masonry north wall of the South Palace. During the PAT80–82's 1983–84 field season, eighteen people buried with offerings were uncovered (Grave 190, Fig. 5). Stratigraphic data indicate that a long pit for a multiple burial was made at the time of the construction of the FSP, exactly across the north–south centerline of the FSP.

After the excavation's completion, another individual burial (Grave 203), corresponding to Grave 153 with respect to the north–south centerline and containing a significantly different type of offering, was uncovered west of Grave 190. The stratigraphic data recovered from the south side, and the spatial distribution pattern of the graves, strongly indicated that the FSP still contained undiscovered graves on the north and east sides, as well as in the interior of the pyramid.

In 1986, a multiple burial (later recorded as Grave 204) was unearthed in a practice excavation by students of physical anthropology of the Escuela Nacional de Antropología e Historia (ENAH) at the place I had proposed as another grave site in 1985 (Sugiyama 1988b). The burial contexts and associated materials were similar to those of Grave 190 on the south side. Because of the lack of data, this monograph does not discuss the two graves (Graves 172 and 204) excavated on the north side by Martínez and Jarquín. Only general information published in a Mexican popular journal (Mercado 1987) was considered.

Discoveries by the PTQ 1988–89
With this background, a new, international project was formed in 1987, called Proyecto Templo de Quetzalcoatl 1988–89 (PTQ88–89) and coordinated by Cabrera, Cowgill, Carlos Serrano, and myself. The excavation area was separated into three fronts. Front A, coordinated by Cabrera and Rodolfo Cid, was an extensive excavation on the east side of the FSP, the only area untouched by previous excavations in the Ciudadela. Under about 4 m of debris from the collapse of the pyramid were three Teotihuacan concrete floors, all considerably damaged. Seven pits in subsoil were uncovered under these floors, sited apart from several smaller pits; six of the pits were considered primary graves forming parts of the sacrificial burial complex (Graves 3, 5, 6, 7, 10, and 11).

The Front A excavation area was completely filled in with earth at the end of the PTQ88–89 exploration. A new INAH project, formed by Cabrera, Rubio Chacón, and others in 1993–94, finally removed all post-Teotihuacan layers on the east side of the FSP. The entire Ciudadela is now free from all post-Teotihuacan natural and cultural accumulations.

Front B, supervised by George Cowgill and others, is a series of pit excavations on the north and west sides of the FSP and in and near the Adosada platform, carried out during the 1988 season. Grave 1 was found on the north side of the pyramid in pit 1, mirroring Grave 203 (Fig. 5). The stratigraphy, grave pattern, and offerings indicated a similarity with Grave 203, although there were also significant differences.

To date the Adosada, pit 2 was excavated atop the structure. The excavation was carried down more than 5 m, in mostly loose, rocky fill, until it reached undisturbed deposits. The most striking discovery, among a myriad of other materials in this pit, was many fragments of intricately modeled, fired-clay walls (described in detail in Chapter 4). The stratigraphy indicates that the fragments were from a razed structure, probably the temple atop the FSP; they may have formed part of a frieze adorning the structure's facade.

Pit 3 reopened the 1939 excavation and tunnel at the foot of the Adosada staircase, to verify the stratigraphy according to my proposal that the offerings found by Pérez under the Adosada corresponded to the FSP rather than to the Adosada. The excavation could not confirm this, but it provided more information to support my hypothesis. Additional offerings, similar to those reported by Rubín de la Borbolla (1947), were found near Pérez's excavation. That excavation indicated that the sacrificial burial and cache complex at the FSP may have extended to the west beyond a grave pit in front of the staircase of the FSP. The discovery hints at even more graves and caches within a certain distance from the pyramid, on the east–west and north–south centerlines.

Pit 4 was dug in apparently in situ deposits sealed by a small section of Teotihuacan concrete floor atop the lowest body of the stepped Adosada platform. The pit was dug to obtain additional materials with which to date the structure. Ceramics recovered from the pit indicate a significant shift between the FSP and the Adosada;[4] a section of talud from a possible substructure was also found, suggesting that the Adosada itself replaced an earlier structure.

We also reopened the 1939 excavation at the foot of the staircase of the FSP (pit 5) to examine several earlier questions (Sugiyama 1989a: 99–100) (details are discussed in Chapter 5). We found a large pit that had been looted before the Adosada platform was constructed.

Pit 6 was opened in the Great Plaza of the Ciudadela, at the northwest corner of the Adosada, to check if another grave was present, since the FSP had graves at its four corners. The result was negative and confirmed that the Adosada marked a significant change, at a time when the FSP was partially covered by the Adosada and when several sacrificial burial complexes were looted.[5]

In 1988, a series of test pits called Trench 1 were dug between Grave 172 and the northeast corner of the FSP to search for more graves near the pyramid's facades. The search for burials around the FSP using test pits originally focused on the structure's south side; the pattern found there was confirmed later on the north side, since the excavations of Trench 1 did not detect any graves. Based on the symmetry principle indicated by burials discovered at the FSP to date, it is unlikely that more graves will be found around the pyramid, at least near the facades, although additional parts of the burial/cache complex might still exist outside the pyramid, especially on the east–west centerline.

Front C refers to a tunnel excavation I coordinated in 1988 and 1989, to investigate the possibility of additional interments under the FSP, to verify the existence of earlier structures, to acquire information on construction materials and techniques, and to obtain data that could help date the structure more precisely (Sugiyama forthcoming). The initial excavation consisted of horizontal tunneling into the base of the platform, starting at the south facade's centerpoint at the level of the subsoil upon which the pyramid's foundations rested. The tunneling operation proceeded northward from that point along the structure's north–south central line (Fig. 7) and revealed that the pyramid fill was homogeneous throughout. Numerous unfaced, roughly made rock walls set in mud mortar ran somewhat irregularly north–south and east–west, intersecting to form cells. Two walled burial chambers were encountered during the excavation: the first (Grave 2), located 10 m inside the pyramid, contained eight individuals with offerings; the second (Grave 4), found 13.5 m north of the tunnel entrance, contained eighteen individuals with substantially richer offerings.

Beyond these two burial chambers, our tunnel continued north toward the center of the pyramid. At 24 m, it intersected an ancient tunnel, the existence of which was not suggested by either the topography of the pyramid mound or any ethnohistorical, archaeological documents (Fig. 7). The entrance to this old tunnel was completely sealed and apparently had been so for centuries (Sugiyama 1998c, 1998d); it was a large, irregular, hollow passage left by the removal of a large volume of stones and mud by looters. Its discovery forced us to make radical changes in our original excavation strategy, but it also provided an unexpected opportunity: to study the pyramid's construction and burial complex more intensively, besides presenting new questions about the tunnel itself. We surveyed it and excavated a series of test pits along its entire route to obtain stratigraphic data and any materials that the looters might have left behind. Our understanding of the architecture and the grave pattern that I describe later was greatly enhanced by this exploration.

The looters' tunnel originated at the southeast corner of the pyramid and probably had been left open for a long time. It runs diagonally toward the center but misses the exact center by 2 m. West of the central north–south axis, it passes over a large grave pit containing Grave 12 (which the looters disturbed) and proceeds west, where a still larger, looted grave pit (Grave 13) was encountered (Fig. 8). At this point, three branches of the tunnel go north, south, and west from Grave 13, and another short branch extends north from the area around Grave 12. Small portions of two Teotihuacan-type floors were seen in the wall of the looters' tunnel near the western edge of the Grave 12 pit. Beneath these traces of earlier structures, we found the burial of a single individual, registered as Grave 15 (Fig. 9). The condition of the bones suggested heart sacrificial ritual (described later).

The stratigraphy of the area in and around Grave 13 indicates that this grave was seriously looted before the looters' tunnel was later extended. Test pits in the southern extension revealed more remains of pre-FSP substructures consisting of small areas of typical Teotihuacan concrete, earth floors, and plastered walls. Only a few sherds were recovered on which to base a temporal assignment.

Given the failure of the looters' tunnel to pass through the exact center of the pyramid's base, we took advantage of its proximity to explore the center, and we initiated a new tunnel excavation starting at the east wall of the tunnel about 3 m north of Grave 12. At the exact center of the pyramid base, a twenty-people multiple burial (Grave 14) was unearthed, with exceptionally rich offerings (Figs. 10 and 11). Our exploration ended with the excavation of an extension tunnel farther east of Grave 14 that confirmed that there was no grave corresponding to Grave 13 with respect to the pyramid's north–south central line.

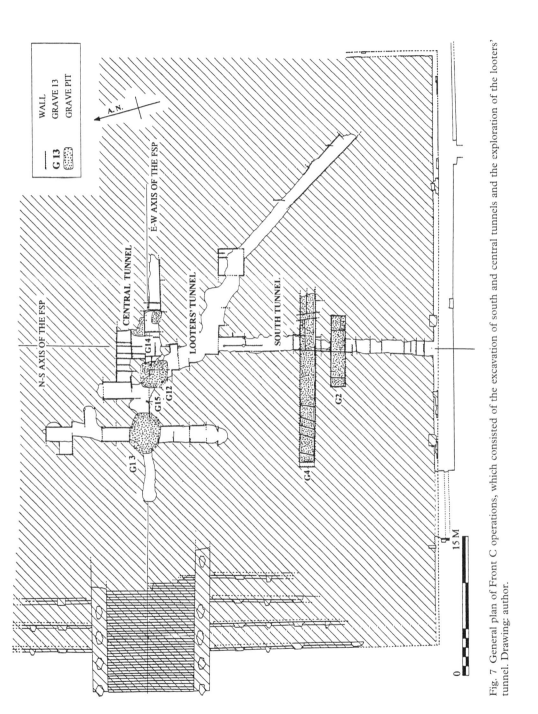

Fig. 7 General plan of Front C operations, which consisted of the excavation of south and central tunnels and the exploration of the looters' tunnel. Drawing: author.

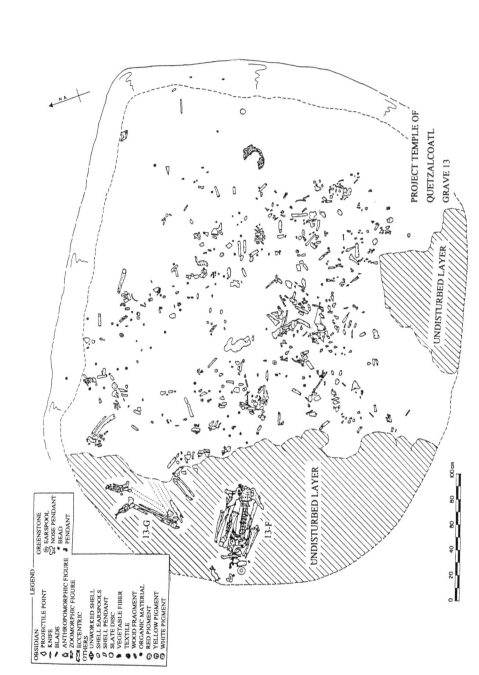

Fig. 8 General plan of Grave 13. Most bones and offerings were disturbed by looters. In an untouched layer, one complete skeleton (13-G) and parts of extremities of another individual (13-F) were discovered in anatomical relationship. Drawing: author.

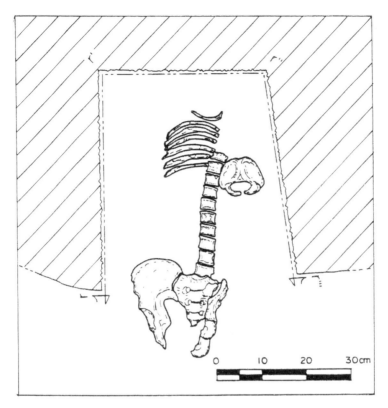

Fig. 9 Plan of Grave 15. Drawing: Kumiko Sugiyama.

After the conclusion of PTQ88–89's fieldwork, Mexican archaeologists reinvestigated the FSP. In 1993–94, Rubio and others excavated the east side, removing all post-Teotihuacan layers to display the uppermost Teotihuacan floor. The excavation included exploration of the entrance to the looters' tunnel near the southeast corner of the pyramid. Rubio also excavated test pits north of Grave 5 and south of Grave 6 to seek other graves on the east side of the FSP. The search revealed that there were no more graves that corresponded to Graves 153 and 203 found on the south side, or to Graves 1 and 172 on the north side.

Rubio and students of physical anthropology from the Escuela Nacional de Antropología also excavated two more graves already detected by PTQ88–89 as a part of the FSP's sacrificial burial complex: one north of Grave 204, underneath the North Palace (1D: N1E1), and another south of Grave 190, underneath the South Palace (1E: N1E1), called Graves 16 and 17 respectively (Fig. 5). They confirmed that eight people were included in each grave, with artifacts similar to those found in Graves 10 and 11.

The several projects described above explored the burial complex before and after our project; availability of data and recording systems varied significantly, so that this study cannot discuss all of them. In any case, I believe my information, mainly from PTQ88–89, is comprehensive enough to discuss grave patterns and offerings.

Fig. 10 Plan of Grave 14, showing a large amount of offerings distributed in certain patterns, reconstructed with 73 field drawings, many photos, and notes. Drawing: author.

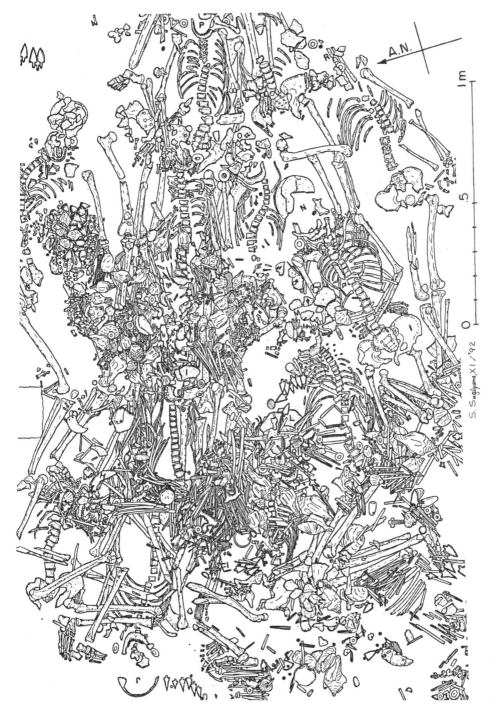

Fig. 11 Central section of Grave 14. Drawing: author.

An implication of this complicated exploration history is that, during the series of excavations in the 1980s, the graves were not accidentally discovered by random excavations but were sought through pit excavation using symmetry principles suggested by graves discovered earlier and by architectural features. Because of preservation issues at the monument, extensive excavation into later-period structures to search for early burials was impossible, so that additional graves might still remain, undetected, at subsoil level. It is also possible that there are more graves within the pyramid, above the subsoil but below the top of the FSP. The principle of symmetry was repeatedly hypothesized and tested at other spots of the pyramid, and proved in some cases, rejected in others. Certainly, results indicate that all known graves related stratigraphically to the FSP were evidently distributed in a symmetrical relationship with respect to the pyramid's centerlines. This feature is considered as a distribution principle for further interpretations of burials and offerings.

Mesoamerican cosmology

It is well known that there were elaborate calendar systems throughout Mesoamerica, probably from early stages of cultural formation. Ethnohistorical and epigraphic information indicates that various time-reckoning systems functioned simultaneously, relating each to the other, and that the passage of time was explicitly marked by rituals. Calendar systems seem to have derived from cycles of astronomical bodies, and time seems to have been conceived of as cyclical, although a lineal concept of time also seems to have been developed by certain societies, particularly by the Maya (Sharer 1994: 559–75). It was a fundamental feature in Mesoamerica that the calendar systems clocked decisive political, military, and social events with regard to astronomical cycles.

The 365-day solar calendar system, divided into eighteen months of twenty days plus five days, was used as a principal time scale. Since many natural phenomena and related human activities depend on sun cycle and annual environmental changes, rituals related to seasonal events, like those connected with agriculture, were carried out according to this solar calendar (Sahagún 1981: bk. 2). Another important calendar was the 260-day ritual calendar. Called the Tonalpohualli by the Aztecs and the Tzolkin by the Maya, this cycle is composed of twenty day signs, combined with a prefix number from 1 to 13; specific days were designated by a number and name and reappeared every 260 days. Although its origin is not yet well understood, it is well known that the ritual calendar was long used primarily for divination. These two calendars were combined to make a larger cycle, called the Sacred Round. This cycle is completed in fifty-two years of the 365-day solar calendar, or seventy-three "years" in the 260-day cycle ($365 \times 52 = 260 \times 73$). The cycle is well documented in Maya and Postclassic Central Mexico, since it was often used in combination with others to record dates of historical events.

In addition to the 365-day and 260-day calendar systems, the Maya wanted each cycle to relate to "the beginning of time" and so elaborated the Long-Count system. A day was named with units of twenty days, 360 (20×18) days, 7,200 ($20 \times 18 \times 20$) days, and 144,000 ($20 \times 18 \times 20 \times 20$) days; these were used in combination with the Tzolkin and other cycles of celestial objects to create periods of diverse lengths with astrological or cosmological significance. For the Maya, an 819-day ($7 \times 9 \times 13$) cycle also seems to have existed, although its origin and functions are not understood (Macleod 1989; Schele and Freidel 1990: 78; Thompson 1960: 212–17).

Besides these calendars, the 29.5-day lunar cycle and the 584-day Venus cycle appear to have played important roles in Mesoamerica at least since Late Preclassic time (Freidel and Schele 1988a; Justeson and Kaufman 1993). The lunar cycle was widely recorded via its gradual waxing and waning stages, while the Venus cycle was recognized as having four periods: visible as morning star (236 days), invisible at superior conjunction (90 days), visible as evening star (250 days), and invisible at inferior conjunction (8 days). Recent studies of correlation between war-related dates inscribed on Maya monuments and Venus cycles at the same time (Nahm 1994; Aveni and Hotaling 1994) reveal that the Classic Maya seems to have carried out war campaigns, victory celebrations, and other war-related events according to the stages of the Venus cycle rather than by the solar calendar (see also Carlson 1991). Venus's movement seems to have been viewed as relating to the solar calendar and the Sacred Round in some Mesoamerican societies, as indicated by a larger cycle of 104 years in the 365-day solar calendar, 146 cycles in the 260-day ritual calendar, or 65 cycles in the Venus calendar, intermeshing the 3 cycles ($365 \times 104 = 260 \times 146 = 584 \times 65 = 37{,}960$ days).

In addition, movements of other planets, comets, or eclipses were observed and may have been integrated into time-reckoning systems. Particular attention was evidently paid to eclipse cycles. As suggested by Aveni (1980: 182) and Nahm (personal communication 1994), the lunar eclipse cycle seems to have been related to the 260-day ritual calendar, because three times the lunar node passage interval (173.31 days) fits neatly into two rotations of the 260-day cycle ($3 \times 173.31 = 519.93$ or about 520; $2 \times 260 = 520$). Although ritual and astrological meanings attached to each calendar system may have varied considerably, the structure of the cycles seems to have persisted as the principal scales by which Mesoamericans conceived time's expanse, including mythical time, into the future and the past.

Two basic scales, horizontal and vertical, delineated the dimension of space but were metaphorically combined in indigenous perspectives. For example, the Aztecs conceived of the world as a multilayered vertical universe (Caso 1971: 336–37; Nicholson 1971: 406–8): the upper world was divided into thirteen layers in which celestial objects and deities were believed to reside, while the Underworld was divided into nine layers – hazard stations that dead souls had to pass successfully before reaching eternal rest (Fig. 12). Multiple layers in the heavens, earth, and Underworld were represented by gods, supernatural forces, celestial bodies, birds, mountains, water, rivers, obsidian knives, etc. Thus, supernatural and natural objects were arranged hierarchically in the vertical dimension.

Horizontal dimensions were also conceived in mythological and cosmological terms. These were divided into four quarters plus a center, with ritual meanings, colors, gods, birds, and trees in each division (Nicholson 1971: 403–4). Native interpretations about concrete objects and specific concepts vary considerably from

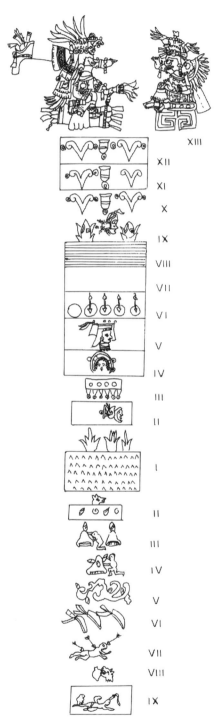

Fig. 12 Underworld and upper world depicted in *Codex Vaticanus* A. Space is layered with nine Underworld and thirteen upper world levels. Sun (IV), Moon (II), and Venus (V) each occupy one layer separately. Drawing: Kumiko Sugiyama, from Aveni 1980: 16.

region to region; as happens in many societies (see the Chinese instances mentioned in Chapter 3), in Mesoamerica ritual meanings of cardinal directions were often attached to objects or concepts related to the vertical dimension. The primacy of the east–west dimension seems to have been associated with the path of the sun, the moon, and other celestial objects as they passed along that axis; in fact, sixteenth-century maps of Mesoamerican cities and regions often placed east at the top (Ashmore 1991: 200; Roys 1933: 132; Thompson 1934). Moreover, the fact that principal pyramids at many religious centers (including Tenochtitlán and Teotihuacan in the Valley of Mexico) face toward the west suggests the primacy of the east–west axis and its association with objects in the sky.

The north–south axis also had various meanings and differed significantly from region to region. For the Aztecs, north represented Mictlan, land of the dead, Region of the Underworld, and south represented the Region of Thorns (Nicholson 1971: 403–4; Sahagún 1977: bk. 7: 21). In contrast, in some Mixtec codices (*Códice Borgia* 1963: 52; *Codex Cospi* 1968: 13; *Codex Fejérváry Mayer* 1971: 34) death and Mictlantecuhtli, Lord of the Underworld, were related to south, while in the Maya universe, north signified the direction of the ancestral dead, and south meant the right hand of the sun (Schele and Miller 1986: 42). Ashmore (1989, 1991) stresses the importance of the strongly marked north–south axis in the spatial organization of Classic Maya religious centers: in her interpretation, north stands for the celestial, supernatural sphere and south for the Underworld. In Schele and Miller's (1986: 276–77) discussion of the Mayan worldview, including the relation between the Underworld and the Heavens, the Maya identified the north sky as the place the ancestral dead finally arrive to assist and guide descendants after their journey into the Underworld, where the soul of the deceased faces a series of trials and competitions with the Lords of Death.

Natural and cultural phenomena seem to have been interpreted meaningfully and metaphorically within this three-dimensional cosmological structure. For example, water was conceived cosmologically as a fundamental element. According to the *Popol Vuh* (1985: 72), the Quiché Maya book about the creation of the world, only sky and water existed before the creation of earth. A crocodile-like creature, called Cipactli in the Aztec language of Nahuatl, was created from the water, and the earth was made later from this creature; thus time and worlds began with a primordial monster (Garibay 1965: 25). In the real world, water appeared as clouds or rain in the sky and as lakes, rivers, springs, and seas on earth, and oceans were regarded as the boundary of the world in the horizontal dimension. Underground water, often represented as the water in caves and springs, was believed to be connected with oceans and finally with the watery Underworld. We know from iconographic and epigraphic studies that the Classic Maya also thought of the Underworld as a watery world, or at least they believed that it was reached by a passage through or under water (Schele and Miller 1986: 267).

One of the most characteristic features of Mesoamerican belief systems was that time and space were intimately fused (Coe 1981: 161; Kubler 1962; León-Portilla 1963: 55–56).[6] The four directions and the vertical expanse were related to days,

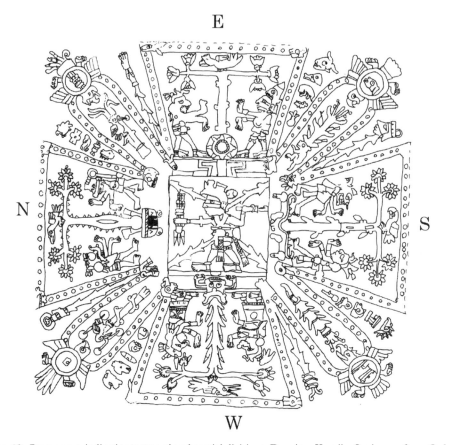

Fig. 13 Cosmogram indicating temporal and spatial divisions. Drawing: Kumiko Sugiyama, from *Codex Fejérváry Mayer*, 1971: 1.

months, years, and "centuries" in Mesoamerica (Fig. 13, *Codex Fejérváry Mayer* 1971: 1). In other words, space seems to have had a strong connection with cyclical movements or morphological transformations of natural objects. In indigenous concepts of the "universe," time and space were interdependent.

Dualism was another feature of Mesoamerican culture that complicated native perceptions of natural phenomena. Sun–moon, day–night, sunrise–sunset, hot–cold, sky–earth, man–woman, birth–death, youth–age, fire–water, etc., were interpreted dualistically as two phenomena opposed or linked to each other.

Many natural objects or phenomena were interpreted in relation to the complex of deities or supernatural forces dwelling in the Heavens or Underworld. Mesoamerican deities are complex and varied. At the time of the Spanish conquest, ceremonial centers in the Mexican Highlands were crowded with many individualized deities believed to control the various spheres of the universe. Most deities were conceived anthropomorphically, although zoomorphic representations were also abundant from Preclassic periods. Nicholson (1971) divides deities in pre-Hispanic Central Mexico into three major categories: celestial creativity, rain/agricultural fertility, and war/sacrifice. Some deities inherited from earlier cultures were believed to dwell in the celestial sphere, and/or were related to astronomical objects or phenomena.

These native interpretations of time, space, natural objects, phenomena, and deities seem to have been deeply rooted in the creation myth of the gods and mankind. Aztec accounts describe a contract with the gods at the time of the creation of the "universe," the Sun, the Moon, the earth, and mankind (*Codex Chimalpopoca* 1992: 142–52; Sahagún 1953: 4–9, 1950). According to the Mesoamerican worldview, man and the world came into being through the auto-sacrifice of the gods, and man must feed the gods by human sacrifice to sustain the universe. One of the principles that made Mesoamerican culture distinctive is the long-perpetuated primary myth of origin and beliefs associated with human sacrifice, which were most likely integrated into political structure since an early formation period of the Mesoamerican culture (Coe 1981; Welsh 1988b). My study deals with a version of this myth as one of the fundamental factors that may have structured Teotihuacan society and its material symbols.

Mesoamerican cosmological principles, including those mentioned above, seem to have endured long beyond ecological, societal, and temporal frames. As happened in the Olmec, Maya, Zapotec, or Aztec societies, ruling groups in Teotihuacan also may have metaphorically combined worldviews and cosmic events with specific historical circumstances and social events, and would have left a record of their political intentions and purposes in material symbols. In the following chapters, I look for underlying principles of Teotihuacan cosmology, involved in the city layout, monumental architecture, iconography, and burials.

3

The Ciudadela and the city layout

I have suggested that major public architectural complexes in Teotihuacan probably had specific ritual meanings and functions within city-wide contexts. If a master plan for the city layout existed, meanings attached to the FSP would have been an integral part of the sacred geography expressed by the whole city. I believe that finding such a master plan and the contents of the sacred geography will help us understand the symbolism of the FSP.

In fact, instances exist around the world in which an ancient city's monuments and public buildings functioned as meaningful parts of the sacred city. Such structures were used mostly as ritual spaces or administrative offices, legitimizing sacred authority and the political power of the state. For example, celestial archetypes, symbolic centripetality, and other kinds of cosmo-magical principles were a fundamental part of ancient Chinese city planning (Wheatley 1971). Monuments and important official buildings of governors and their associates – the interpreters of Heaven's messages – were arranged spatially according to cosmologically codified significance. Ethnohistorical records document that the Cuzco quadripartition also rendered the capital a microcosm of the empire, as well as a metaphor for the Inca universe. Spatial dual division of Cuzco reflected patterns of social, economic, political, and religious organization, particularly in association with specific lineages (or *ayllus*) that extended into spatial organization of provinces (Zuidema 1983). Kolata and Sangines (1992) archaeologically demonstrate that the city of Tiwanaku, political capital of a preliterate state, was conceived as the central point of the universe, located in the sacred Lake Titicaca, holy locus for many indigenous myths of creation. Tiwanaku seems to have represented a cosmogram that framed the natural and social order symbolically and coherently in the spatial arrangement of public architecture, sculpture, and an immense artificial moat.

Spatial analyses and interpretations of Teotihuacan architecture have been made in search of function rather than ritual meaning. This is because of a strong interest in the social hierarchies involved in each building's different functions. Major monuments in different architectural styles were assumed to have been associated with distinct social units. Different layout and distinctive architectural styles were also interpreted as indicators of chronological difference, so that the sequence of monuments could be explained in terms of changing sociopolitical functions or factions (Millon 1992; Cowgill 1983, 1992a) rather than in terms of different ritual meanings that may or may not imply sociopolitical shifts.

What follows is a very brief overview of a diachronic analysis of the city's space management, based by Millon on precise maps of the entire city and surface collections studied by the Teotihuacan Mapping Project (TMP) during the last three decades (Cowgill 1974, 1987, 1992b; Cowgill et al. 1984; Drewitt 1967; R. Millon 1967, 1973, 1974, 1976, 1981, 1992; Millon et al. 1973; see also Chapter 1, note 1 and Table 1).

The sacred center seems to have originated during the Patlachique phase, and the center's population is estimated at between 20,000 and 40,000 by the end of this phase (Cowgill 1974: 381–83; Millon 1981: 221). Oztoyahualco, in the northwestern section of the Teotihuacan Valley (Fig. 1), may have been occupied during this early period, according to preliminary studies of the TMP's surface collection (Cowgill 1992a: 91–102; R. Millon 1973: 38–39). Sometime after the early "Old City" was founded, the city's core shifted southeast. Based on Teotihuacan ceramic chronology, the Sun Pyramid was built during the Tzacualli phase. The existence of a subterranean cave seems to Heyden (1975, 1981) and Millon (1981) to have determined the location of the pyramid, which sits above it. The innermost stage of the Moon Pyramid also seems to have been built during this early period or earlier. Millon and others believe that the East and West Avenues existed at least by the second century AD as important routes intersecting the Avenue of the Dead near the Ciudadela (R. Millon 1973: 42, 52, 1974: 354). The Ciudadela and the uppermost part of the Sun Pyramid appear to have been constructed during the Miccaotli phase (AD 150–200) (R. Millon 1973: 54–55). Both the FSP and the Sun Pyramid underwent modification, including construction of the Adosada platforms, at least once during the Tlamimilolpa (AD 200–400) and Xolalpan (AD 400–550) phases, respectively (R. Millon 1973: 57, fig. 17a). It is also believed that the political center shifted from the northern Sun and Moon Pyramids to the southern complex by the Miccaotli or Early Tlamimilolpa phase and that the Ciudadela, as its geographically central location suggests, became the religious and political center of the whole city and remained so until the city's collapse. The city apparently entered its most stable period after about AD 350, and remained stable until the Metepec phase (AD 550–650) (Cowgill 1983, 1996; R. Millon 1973: 60–61): during this period, there is no evidence of marked change within the city, and Teotihuacan influences abroad are conspicuous in many sites throughout Mesoamerica, especially in the Maya area.

This view of Millon and his associates is based on ceramic chronology. On the basis of reconstruction of principal monuments, the function of other architectural complexes, such as political administrative headquarters, residential areas, space for economic activities, various kinds of workshops, sectors of foreign ethnic groups, and merchant barrios, have been interpreted spatially using data from surface collections and excavations (e.g., Barbour 1976; Kolb 1987; Rattray 2001; Spence 1992; Turner 1992). In this chapter, I present a version of the city layout that connects ideology to major monuments.

According to ceramic chronology, the time interval between the earliest monument (the Sun Pyramid and possibly others: Tzacualli) and the latest (FSP: transition from

Miccaotli to Early Tlamimilolpa, AD 200–250) was about 50 to 250 years.[1] This relatively short time span (still to be confirmed by further excavations, as well as C14 and other dating techniques) has led me to propose that the Teotihuacanos intended to manifest interrelated ritual meanings among the major monuments, including the Sun and Moon Pyramids, and the Ciudadela. It is possible that there was a master plan or plans that included spatial integration and meaningful coherence among the major monuments. If so, the FSP was probably integrated into the city's global symbolic manifestation, since it was clearly the Ciudadela's principal pyramid.

In this chapter, I summarize the study of the Teotihuacan measurement unit that led me to propose strong cohesiveness among the major monuments. I then discuss possible principles of city layout and major monuments, in order to "relocate" the Ciudadela within the sacred geography of the city (Sugiyama 1993).

Search for the Teotihuacan Measurement Unit (TMU)

Unusual uniformity in architectural style, orientations, and symmetrical and proportional spatial distributions of buildings in Teotihuacan suggest that the city was planned by means of a standardized measurement unit or units. Investigators have been searching for the measurement unit since the nineteenth century, but no consensus was reached hitherto because of the complexities of architectural units and modifications that covered or destroyed original layouts. Another obstacle to systematic studies is the fact that no one knows which parts of the structure the Teotihuacanos measured or how they did it. For example, complicated features of residential compounds, often from several different construction stages but exposed today as a single unit, make determination of original measurements difficult or impossible. Nor is there any reason to believe that the entire city was laid out with a single measurement unit: several units may have been used in different locations, and they may have changed through time.

In the nineteenth century, Almaráz (1865) suggested that a measurement unit of about 80 cm was used in Teotihuacan while Drewitt (1969, 1987) and Drucker (1971, 1974, 1977a) hypothesized 80.5 cm from maps of much higher quality and quantity. Séjourné (1966a: 212–13) independently proposed 60 m, while at one time Drewitt proposed 57 m (Drewitt 1967), and later 322 m (Drewitt 1987) as a large unit. Outside Teotihuacan, O'Brien and Christiansen (1986) hypothesized that 147 cm was used in Maya Puuc-style archaeological sites. Although the proposals of these measurement units appear reasonable from the limited data used for the studies, the question of how to verify any proposed unit has remained unresolved.

The present research was based on previous studies and began with the idea that the earliest structure of each monument probably reflects the original plan more explicitly than later construction. Measurement units used here are from construction during early phases of the city. Measurements used repeatedly at various locations were accorded special attention.

One of the few monumental buildings in Teotihuacan whose exact dimensions are known is the FSP. During my mapping survey of the monument, I noticed that the width of a balustrade (1.66 m) is roughly twice the measurement unit proposed by Almaráz, Drewitt, and Drucker, and that 1.66 m is also almost half the distance (3.29 m on the average) between the head sculptures jutting regularly from the west facades, and one-eighth the width of the staircase (13.06 m). The side-dimension of the square pyramid's lowest platform (about 65 m) is nearly forty times the same distance (1.66 m × 40 = 66.4 m), although the difference between them (65 m − 66.4 m) is significantly large.

These data led me to propose 82.3 cm as a measurement unit used at Teotihuacan during the pyramid's construction phase: an average calculated with distances taken from the pyramid. Similar units, between 80 and 85 cm, were hypothesized and applied to many other construction maps made at a scale of 1:100 (Sugiyama 1982). I have tentatively concluded from this study that 83 cm was the standard measurement unit (1 TMU or Teotihuacan Measurement Unit) most applicable to Teotihuacan architecture, although the calculations must be refined to determine possible variations through time and space.[2]

Ethnohistorical records seem to support the 80–83 cm unit, although precise assessment of Mesoamerican measurement units cannot be made from ethnohistorical documents alone. Castillo (1972) studied measurement units used by Nahua speakers and pointed out that linear units were based on proportions of the human body: the units were expressed by the names of body parts. For example, *cemacolli* (one shoulder) and *cenyollotli* (one heart) indicate that the distance (80–90 cm) between shoulder or heart and the tip of the finger in extended arm position was a unit before the Conquest. Castillo also suggested units of approximately 80 cm (*octácatl*, meaning model or pattern), and 1.60 m or a little more (*cennequetzalli*, "straight position of man" or the height of a standing man – and twice 80 cm). Harvey (1988), citing Alva Ixtlilxochitl (1975 [2]: 92–93), argues that the Texcocan linear measure for land was equal to three Spanish varas or 2.5 m, which is approximately 3 TMU (0.83 × 3 = 2.49 m). These data accord well with ethnohistoric documents on measurement methods based on the length of human body parts used by the Maya (O'Brien and Christiansen 1986: 145–49).

A principal reason for proposing an 83 cm measurement unit for Teotihuacan is that the distances between major points in the city, multiplied by round numbers such as 1,000, 2,000, or 4,000, correspond to it.[3] Moreover, when applied to Teotihuacan construction, this unit seems to reveal that the dimensions of monumental structures and distances between them correspond to specific numbers important in Mesoamerican calendar systems and cosmology. Although some of the measurements mentioned below are approximate, the congruences between them, in a seemingly planned city, can hardly be accidental. In the following sections, I explore the possible cosmological significance of spatial arrangements based on the TMU study.

Principles of space management in the city

Using the TMU, I analyzed maps made by the TMP (Millon et al. 1973) and my own at a scale of 1:100 (Sugiyama 1982), searching for an "emic" view of the city layout.

I used locational data of temple-pyramids for the purpose, since sacred monuments may have been more essential than residential buildings for space management and may have been integral to the city's symbolism. Axes of monuments (which often did not change despite later modification) and edges of monuments at original floor level especially were used as measurement points for calculating dimensions.

Figure 14 shows the extent of the ancient city ca. AD 600, with the locations of prominent mounds more than 2 m high, which have been interpreted as independent temple platforms by members of the TMP. In general, a high density of residential units lies north of the channelized Río San Juan. Major prominent buildings are clearly concentrated in the northern section around the Avenue of the Dead; their pattern of distribution seems to indicate a concentration of religious and sociopolitical activities in that area. Only a few temple platforms lie south of the San Juan: the Ciudadela seems to be the only outstanding complex with high temples and platforms south of the river. The Great Compound (interpreted as a possible bureaucratic center and/or locus of the principal marketplace) (Millon 1981: 229) completely lacks mounds, according to current topography. Thus, I argued that, given its monumentality, the area north of Río San Juan along the Avenue of the Dead was the city's most significant zone. The Ciudadela and the Great Compound may have been the only outstanding architectural complexes in the southern section of the city.

This deliberate division into north and south sections also can be detected in measurements of the city's layout (Fig. 14). The distance between the north limit of the Moon Pyramid and the south edge of the Río San Juan (1,662 m) is approximately the same as the distance between the south edge of the Río San Juan and the north edge of the Río San Lorenzo on the Avenue of the Dead (1,654 m). The division is further supported by the fact that these distances correspond approximately to 2,000 TMU (1,660 m); this suggests that two major zones of equal dimensions were created to represent north and south sectors. Although this argument is still highly hypothetical due to imprecise information,[4] some distances converted to the TMU system (which I describe later) make the proposition worthy of serious consideration.

A portion of the Río San Juan, from the northeastern part of sector S1W3 to the southeastern part of the sector N2E2, was evidently modified (Fig. 14), replaced by a 2,500 meter-long channel, presently 15–40 m wide, that runs north–south to east–west, in accordance with standardized Teotihuacan architectural orientations (15.5 degrees east of north and 16.5 degrees south of east). The Río San Lorenzo also appears to have been modified by the Teotihuacanos, as indicated by its unnaturally straight course. Millon and Cowgill (1992, personal communication) believe that part of the Río San Lorenzo's course was modified, possibly with specific directional significance. If this is true, the data imply that the Río San Juan and the Río San Lorenzo were parts of the principal water-management program integrated into the general city layout. The two channels have not been dated; however, a suggested deliberate division into two equal sections raises the possibility that the channels, along with the Moon Pyramid, were principal factors at the city's founding.

The TMP proposed that the East and West Avenues were major streets. In my opinion, this proposal is still in question, since there is little evidence of temple

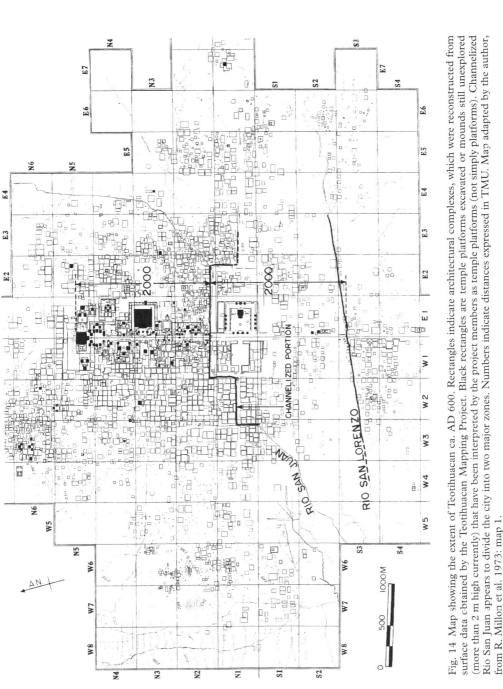

Fig. 14 Map showing the extent of Teotihuacan ca. AD 600. Rectangles indicate architectural complexes, which were reconstructed from surface data obtained by the Teotihuacan Mapping Project. Black rectangles are temple platforms excavated or mounds still unexplored (more than 2 m high currently) that have been interpreted by the project members as temple platforms (not simply platforms). Channelized Rio San Juan appears to divide the city into two major zones. Numbers indicate distances expressed in TMU. Map adapted by the author, from R. Millon et al. 1973: map 1.

platforms or long platforms delimiting the proposed streets in the current topography, and no excavation data to corroborate the presence of these avenues (although there are no data to reject it either). Instead, the east–west axis of the city may have been de-emphasized in favor of the north–south axis represented by the Avenue of the Dead.

The proposed continuation of the Avenue of the Dead to the south of the Ciudadela also remains to be verified by excavation. Only a few mounds (1 and 2 of S2E1, and 6 and 7 of S3W1 in Millon et al. 1973) might have limited the proposed southern portion of the avenue. Extensive excavation carried out on the Avenue of the Dead by the PAT80–82 uncovered evidence for two walls delimiting both sides of the street immediately south of the Ciudadela, but without clear evidence of construction farther southward (Cabrera et al. 1982a: 13; Romero 1982: 53). Given that the poor quality of these roughly made low walls is not comparable with the tablero-talud of the long, high platforms uncovered north of the Río San Juan, it can be argued that the data with which the East and West Avenues and the southern Avenue of the Dead were identified might have been remnants of small streets or low platforms, or remains of water-management programs. Thus, Millon and his project members once proposed a reconstruction of the city's plan as divided into four sections by two major avenues, with the Ciudadela at their cross-point, presuming analogy with the quadripartite layout of the Aztec capital, Tenochtitlan; this idea however is still to be tested fundamentally with excavation data. My own study, presented here, suggests an alternative.

The foregoing description indicates the centrality of the northern section, laid out along the city's north–south avenue with clear articulations at certain points. However, it is not clear what divided the space in the east–west direction. One possibility is suggested by three major architectural groups: the Sun Pyramid complex, the Ciudadela, and the Great Compound. The north–south axis of the Avenue of the Dead, which has been traced both in the field and on maps by the TMP, is a line that seems to be close to, if not exactly the same as, the main axis used by the original planners for the city's layout.

Two evidently planned lines lie parallel to this north–south axis (Fig. 15). The Sun Pyramid complex is clearly defined by the North, East, and South Platforms. The eastern limit of the complex (the east edge of the East Platform) was presumably measured from the city's axis when the Sun Pyramid was founded. This east–west measurement is almost identical to the distance between the axis and the eastern limit of the Ciudadela (431 m and 432 m respectively, according to the TMP's reconstruction maps). This apparent deliberateness is supported by the TMP study. The distance coincides with the measurement units multiplied by 520 TMU (0.83 m × 520 TMU = 431.6 m). The number is twice 260, the number of days in one Tonalpohualli sacred year. The 520-day interval was also related to eclipse cycles, since three times the lunar node passage interval (173.31 days) fit to a 520-day cycle (Chapter 2; see also Aveni 1980: 173–95). This coincidence cannot be accidental since the size of the Sun Pyramid itself measures half of this exactly (namely 260 TMU), as later mentioned. Therefore, the number seems to have represented a

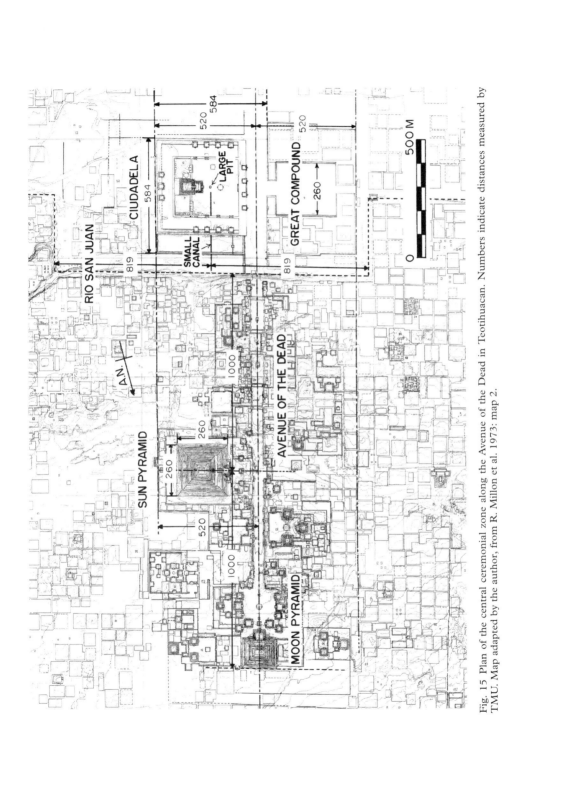

Fig. 15 Plan of the central ceremonial zone along the Avenue of the Dead in Teotihuacan. Numbers indicate distances measured by TMU. Map adapted by the author, from R. Millon et al. 1973: map 2.

larger cycle in which the ritual calendar and eclipse cycle were intermeshed. The study suggests that the Sun Pyramid complex and the Ciudadela were planned in close relation with each other, and that the line passing on their eastern limits forms another north–south axis of the city. This line, exactly parallel to that of the Avenue of the Dead, would have limited the central zone to the east.

The west edge of the Great Compound might have been the west limit of the central zone, located in a similar way. Although the distance from the axis of the Avenue of the Dead to the west edge of the Great Compound, in the reconstruction of the TMP, measures 425 m (512 TMU), originally this could still have been 520 TMU: the western limit of the compound's low platform has been disturbed and seriously damaged, leaving nothing for reliable reconstruction. It should also be noted that western limits of various architectural complexes in sectors N2W1, N3W1, and N4W1, reconstructed by the TMP, correspond generally to this proposed west edge line (Fig. 15).

In summary, it appears that the city was planned in a north–south rather than an east–west direction. If we put aside the East and West Avenues, no monumental construction exists to indicate a central east–west axis. Thus, I conclude that, instead of being divided into four quadrants, the city was constructed in two major zones, north and south, with high concentrations of monumental structures and residential compounds in its northern portion. The Ciudadela with the FSP at its central location seems to have stood as an exceptionally massive complex with specific ritual meanings in the south zone.

Monuments on the Avenue of the Dead
The principal north–south axis of the city was apparently created in combination with surrounding natural elements. Cerro Gordo in particular, with a cleft in its top, was evidently a principal natural reference selected for the city plan. This is indicated by the fact that the central north–south axis of the Avenue of the Dead points precisely to the cleft over the summit of the Moon Pyramid (Gamio 1922: vol. 1, 110; Linné 1934: 32–33; Tobriner 1972: 103). The Avenue of the Dead, whose axis may thus have been laid down from Cerro Gordo, begins at the Moon Pyramid and runs to the south. The architectural complexes between the Moon Pyramid and the Río San Juan were laid out symmetrically on either side of the avenue, suggesting that a strong relationship among architectural complexes was a principal condition governing the intraspatial arrangement of the city.

The Sun Pyramid was evidently erected as the city's main pyramid, because the east–west axis of the pyramid divides the most densely constructed zone – the city's northern section – into equal parts. The distance between the east–west centerline of the Sun Pyramid and the north limit of the Moon Pyramid measures 833 m, or 1,003.6 TMU (Fig. 15), and the distance between this axis and the current south edge of the Río San Juan is 829 m, or 998.8 TMU. Even considering possible errors in maps of the pyramids, the Avenue of the Dead, and the channel of the Río San Juan (presently 16 m wide), the almost-round TMU numbers suggest that the nearly equal distances on both sides of the axis of the Sun Pyramid were not accidental.[5]

Moreover, given their high visibility, the Moon Pyramid and the Río San Juan are most likely the limits of this central symbolic zone.

The Sun Pyramid has a square base. The completely excavated south side wall gives evidence at its base of two architectural stages, which are still visible. The older and smaller inner stage measures 216 m, while the exterior stage is 222.7 m. The earlier pyramid's dimensions appear to reflect the original plan as it fitted into the overall city plan: 216 m is half of the previously mentioned distance between the axis of the Avenue of the Dead and the east limit of the Sun Pyramid complex (431 m) and coincides with the proposed measurement unit multiplied by 260, the number of days in one Tonalpohualli sacred cycle ($260 \times 0.83 = 215.8$ m).[6] In summary, it seems that the Sun Pyramid was the principal temple-pyramid in Teotihuacan perhaps representing one of the most important ritual cycles. I believe this was why the pyramid was built to this particular size from the beginning.

Further south of the Sun Pyramid, apartment compounds with temple platforms are closely and proportionally aggregated along the Avenue of the Dead, which was divided into seven sections by six transverse platforms. The series of temple-apartment complexes ends with the channelized Río San Juan. Beyond the river to the south, the wider, flat floor of the avenue expanded between the Ciudadela and the Great Compound. As discussed previously, I question whether the Avenue of the Dead still continued to be served as the main avenue south of these two complexes.

The Ciudadela as an integral element of the city layout

The southern section of the city, limited by two channelized rivers, is at the lowest altitude on the city's central north–south axis. This altitudinal position may have been integrated into the city's sacred geography. Perhaps the Ciudadela was conceived as a representation of the watery Underworld (see Mesoamerican cosmology in Chapter 4). Abundant watery symbolism found in the Ciudadela supports this idea. It must have intentionally been built very near, if not on, the original course of the Río San Juan, in a swampy area. According to the TMU study, the channel might then have been brought into line with a distance 2,000 TMU from the Moon Pyramid.

Why the channelization of the Río San Juan took place in its specific form is unclear. While it may have served in functional roles – for drainage, transportation, and the city's water supply – data from the measurement unit study suggest that its role was also significantly symbolic. The portion of the straight channel running east–west and crossing the Avenue of the Dead perpendicularly would measure approximately 1,360 m, or nearly two times 819 TMU ($1360/0.83 = 1638.6 = 819 \times 2 + 0.6$ m), again the number of a calendric cycle known from Classic Maya inscriptions (see Chapter 2). This suggests that the channelization was associated with the calendar system, although measurement of the distance between the two corners of the river's straight portion was preliminary, measured as it was from the reconstruction plan.

For unknown reasons, the midpoint of the east–west portion of the channel does not correspond to the central axis of the Avenue of the Dead, as we might expect. However, the Teotihuacanos' knowledge of the midpoint can be reinforced by the fact that a large, deep, artificial round pit or well (5.67 m × 4.70 m in diameter and more than 5.5 m deep) was found in 1982 by Patricia Quintanilla (1982) in the great plaza of the Ciudadela directly to the south of the midpoint and exactly on the east–west centerline of the FSP (Fig. 15).

Quintanilla also found a small, north–south canal to the south of the midpoint. It started near the edge of the Río San Juan and passed beneath the Ciudadela's North Platform to the edge of the pit/well, as if the water was carried from the river through the canal to the pit/well (Rodríguez 1982: 56, 67, 68). Many shells were found in the canal near its southern end. That the canal and the North Platform formed an unitary construction at their intersection clearly indicates the contemporaneousness of the two features. This relationship of the Río San Juan, the small canal, and the pit/well with the Ciudadela indicates that a water-management plan was integrated into the Ciudadela's construction. Thus, the topography, location, and architecture of the Ciudadela suggest that the space was related to rituals with symbolism of water or the watery Underworld.

The TMU study suggests, besides cosmological meanings, that the Ciudadela was associated with calendar cycles, particularly the Venus calendar. As we have seen, the distance between the central north–south axis of the city and the eastern limit of the Ciudadela is 520 TMU. The distance between the eastern limits of the Great Compound and the Ciudadela (484 m, according to the TMP reconstruction maps) is approximately 584 TMU (584 × 0.83 = 484.72 m), the number of days in the Venus cycle. The distance between the south edge of the Ciudadela and the north side of the north wall that limits the extension space (Compound 2: N1E1 in Millon et al. 1973) north of the Ciudadela is 485–87.5 m, according to the reconstruction maps, which is approximately 584 TMU. Apparently, Compound 2 was built later than the North Platform of the Ciudadela; however, the 1980–82 INAH excavations demonstrated that the space was functionally part of the Ciudadela (Múnera 1985; Rodríguez 1982; Sugiyama 1998a). Therefore, the builders of Compound 2 might have known that the total size of the larger Ciudadela complex matched the cycle of Venus.

The dimensions of the Ciudadela itself might reflect days when Venus was visible. According to the reconstruction of the TMP, the distance between north and south limits of the Ciudadela (401–3 m) is 484.3 in TMU (402 m/0.83) and is approximately the number of days when Venus was visible as morning or evening star during a Venus cycle (236 + 250 = 486 days). Although this must be verified with precise data, my preliminary conclusion is that Venus cycles may have been encoded in the Ciudadela.

General discussion

Methodologically speaking, the cosmological and calendrical symbolism of the city's layout is still hypothetical, since it is based primarily on the study of the TMU, which was derived from a small number of accurate data and many that are imprecise. The TMU emerged as a possibility from earlier studies and some hints provided by major monuments. About 83 cm was then hypothesized and was applied to major

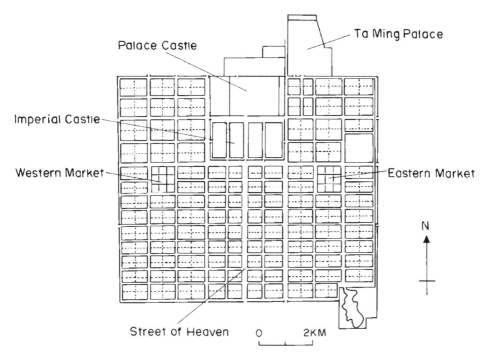

Fig. 16 Plan of the ancient Chinese capital of the Sui state, founded in AD 582; also called Ch'ang An of the T'ang dynasty in later periods. Drawing: Kumiko Sugiyama, from Kishi 1976: 106.

monuments for testing. Specific calendrical or cosmological numbers were thus disclosed through this process.

Although the TMU needs further, rigorous statistical testing with more accurate data (Freeman 1976), the preliminary study suggests cohesive meanings in the city's layout, into which the Ciudadela was probably integrated. Of course, it is necessary to research the details of each monument's substructures and chronologies further in order to detect the original city plan. As Millon has stated, using ceramic chronology, all of Teotihuacan's major monuments were probably erected sometime during the first two centuries AD and persisted throughout the city's life. Spatial relationships among the monuments suggest that they were not an aggregation of independently built monuments.

There are many instances of ancient sacred cities planned on a grand scale at their inception. For example, Daxing in China, an ancient capital of the Sui state founded in AD 582 (Ch'ang An of T'ang Dynasty in later periods), may provide relevant features for a comparison with Teotihuacan's layout (Fig. 16). Ethnohistorical records prove that highly proportioned, symmetrically planned cities often preserved the original city layout centuries after modification (Kishi 1976; Reiba 1976). The northern part of Daxing, called the "Palace Castle," was evidently planned as the residential complex of the ruler's family (the city's founder), and the "Imperial Castle," to the south, was the family's administrative offices. Both were located on the city's north–south axis, and the main avenue, the "Street of Heaven," was laid from the southern main gate of the Imperial Castle toward the south, on the same north–south axis. A residential zone for citizens extended on each side of the avenue; a grid system with one market center in each zone was laid out symmetrically. The northern section was conceived as the "right place" for elites, reflecting high status in the social hierarchy, while the south was designated for public and secular activities. Dedicated efforts of rulers for several generations were necessary for completion of the construction of the city. Later, new monuments, such as "Ta Ming Palace" northeast of the Palace Castle, were constructed and programs to modify earlier buildings often took place, partially covering or breaking the city's symmetry. However, the principal original factors remained highly visible along the city's axes, so that the master plan was discernible throughout the city's life. This sacred spatial pattern was continued in later Chinese and Japanese capitals, where the principal factors were essentially the same though reproduced in different sociopolitical contexts.

In Mesoamerican cities, complicated modification processes often covered large portions of their original foundation programs. Original layouts of major cities such as Tikal or Monte Albán, which functioned for many centuries, are difficult to comprehend, although the ideational factors behind site planning and spatial organization have been explored successfully (Ashmore 1991). The obscuring of plans may be indicated by the fact that no single major axis of these cities can be traced on the maps of later-period constructions. Teotihuacan seems to have been an exceptional case in which major monuments, the main avenue (the axis of the city), and large-scale channelization persisted as principles of spatial arrangement, from early periods until the end of the city, even though later modifications were abundant. This seems to indicate a strong cohesiveness among the major constructions and their lasting significance over the following centuries. The argument is also supported by the fact that virtually all structures in Teotihuacan maintained the same orientation, with coherent astronomical significance, throughout the city's life, much more rigorously than any other Mesoamerican city (Aveni 1980; Drucker 1977b; Malmstrom 1978; Dow 1967; Millon 1992: 387–88), making the hypothesis of a Teotihuacan master plan or master plans with enduring ideological principles worthy of exploration.

The following summarizes some hypothetical features of the erection of the Ciudadela within the context of the city plan.

1. The city's major monuments and grand channelization seem to have been principal parts of an original master plan, which apparently began by the second century AD and ended early in the third century. The Ciudadela and the Sun Pyramid complex seem to have been complementary to each other, although the construction of the latter may have begun earlier. This view contrasts with previous views, in which the Ciudadela was interpreted as a reflection of a new political order. Pasztory (1992) believes that the new architectural style of the Ciudadela, contrasting with the earlier Sun Pyramid, symbolized a political shift. Cowgill (1992a: 106) thinks "that the planners of the Sun Pyramid did not foresee the Ciudadela, and the Ciudadela probably represents new ideas about the symbolism of monumental architecture." I interpret the Ciudadela as representing meanings that complement those of the Sun

Pyramid; both seem to have been integrated parts of a single master plan, although the actual inauguration date of the Ciudadela may have been considerably later than that of the Sun Pyramid as suggested by ceramic chronology.

2. The city was apparently not equally divided into four sections with the Ciudadela/Great Compound as its center, as originally suggested by R. Millon (1973). The city plan more likely stressed two sections, northern and southern, divided by the Río San Juan. The importance of a heavenly east–west axis was clearly stressed by the major monuments facing west in Teotihuacan. However, the east–west axis might have been played down intentionally at the ground level in order to emphasize the north–south axis. The major ceremonial precincts were evidently planned along the north–south axis (Avenue of the Dead) to display cosmological significance through the spatial relations of the monuments.

3. The TMU study suggests that the city's layout was structured with four major constructions crossing the Avenue of the Dead: the Moon Pyramid (northern limit as reference point), the Sun Pyramid (central east–west axis, equating to the cave entrance under the Sun Pyramid), the channelization of the Río San Juan, and the Río San Lorenzo. This is suggested by distances between or combinations of these complexes that were nearly round numbers of TMU, such as 1,000 and 2,000.

4. The Avenue of the Dead may have been conceived as a hierarchical cosmos, possibly the passage from the Underworld to the Heavens in the horizontal dimension: cardinal direction may have been equated with vertical direction.[7] In Teotihuacan, north may have symbolized ascending direction, while south represented descending, perhaps toward the Underworld. It is well known from ethnohistorical records that, in Mesoamerica, terms indicating vertical (cosmological) dimensions were used to express religious political hierarchies. In Teotihuacan, the northern end of the Avenue of the Dead culminated in the Moon Pyramid complex. The higher elevation of the complex in the natural topography also may have been a favorable representation of the higher hierarchical position of this direction. Moreover, the exact setting of the Moon Pyramid against the silhouette of Cerro Gordo must have offered a view of the cosmological relationship of the pyramid with the mountain for people on the Avenue of the Dead. The notion is further supported by the fact that in the sky toward that direction, Polar North, around which celestial objects circle, was considered the center of the universe.

Archaeological data from the southern section also support the idea, which basically agrees with Coggins's (1980) and Ashmore's models (1989, 1991) about Classic Mayan cosmology reflected in city layout: that north represents the Heavens and south the Underworld. The notion introduced by Coggins (1980: 730–31), citing Brotherston (1975), strikingly matches the concept of the Teotihuacan city plan. Coggins argues that north and south signify "moments between" east and west (which seem to have been associated with astronomical objects) and between "above and below" in Yucatec Maya, a concept that may be traceable to the Late Preclassic period in different regions of Mesoamerica (Freidel and Schele 1988a).[8]

5. The northern section seems to have been the core of the city, indicated by a major concentration of public and residential buildings in the area. The Sun Pyramid

stands at the section's midpoint as the city's principal monument. The centrality of the pyramid is also suggested by the fact that its size apparently related to the pan-Mesoamerican calendar complex, particularly the 260-day ritual calendar.

6. The Ciudadela in the city's southern part seems to be an integral element with distinct cosmological meanings. The concept of a watery Underworld appears to have been attached to the southern location, suggested by the Ciudadela's low natural topography, its surrounding water management programs, including channelization, and other watery symbolic elements discovered there. The idea coincides with the Mesoamerican worldview, particularly Mixtec cosmology, where death and Lord of the Underworld were related to the south (Chapter 2).

7. One result of the TMU study is the possible "disclosure" of Mesoamerican cosmological meanings and a calendrical system materialized in the city's layout. As we have seen, time and space were intimately related in Mesoamerican life and myth. In Teotihuacan, time-reckoning systems, such as the 260-day ritual calendar, 365-day solar calendar, 584-day Venus year cycle, 520-day bundle related to the 173.3-day eclipse cycle, and perhaps the 819-day ritual calendar, seem to have been encoded into the city's expanse and monumental constructions in a very complicated way. The city's layout seems to have symbolized the equation of certain dimensions of space and time.

As a result of my preliminary study of the city's layout, it can be concluded that the city was conceived as the center of the cosmos. This notion can quite commonly be found in ancient cities around the world. This grand cosmogram may imply that a strong administration manipulated its materialization with a master plan on an unprecedented scale. If chronological data show that construction of the major monuments was completed within a few generations, it may mean that a strong rulership existed at an early period in Teotihuacan. The data suggest that the exceptional cosmogram invoked social power and was exploited for political ends at the state level. The Ciudadela and its principal monument, the Feathered Serpent Pyramid, may have played a central role in the overall scheme.

In the following chapter, I concentrate on the architecture and iconography of the Ciudadela and its main pyramid and focus on ritual meanings and deity representations manifested by those elements. They seem to have been consonant with the suggested cosmological and calendrical significance of the city layout and the Ciudadela that I have discussed here.

4

Architecture and sculpture

Monumental architecture and sculpture have been found at the FSP, and murals at related structures in the Ciudadela. The assumption underlying this chapter is that both architectural style and iconography at the FSP formed the final stages of a single construction program that began with the preparation of the burial complex and offerings discovered during excavation. One might logically expect to find some sort of coherent ritual meaning among architecture, iconographic representations on the sculptural facade, and the burial complex dedicated to that structure, all of which were related to the erection of the FSP and may also have been a part of a larger state program. Here, I discuss possible ritual messages encoded in the pictogram of the pyramid.

In the section on architecture, construction stages and other architectural features are discussed in terms of symbolic aspects; the second section deals with stone carvings on the facades of the FSP, which express the main visual messages of the pyramid; and the third section concerns burned clay fragments found on top of the Adosada, which were probably from walls of the temple atop the FSP and which were contemporaneous with and complementary to those of the facades. I end the chapter with some concluding remarks on the overall context of imagery at the FSP.

Architecture

That the FSP was the principal pyramid at the Ciudadela is suggested by its size and central location. We cannot precisely correlate it chronologically with the Ciudadela, due to lack of direct stratigraphic and architectural data; it could have been constructed either earlier or later than the Ciudadela, although ceramic analyses by Rattray (2001: 371; see also Millon 1992: figs. 6, 7) and Cowgill (1992a; Cabrera, Sugiyama, and Cowgill 1991: 88–89) indicate that both entities were built some-time during the Miccaotli–Early Tlamimilolpa phases. At present, ceramic analyses (Cowgill 1995, personal communication) suggest that at least the main bulk of the Ciudadela platform was built somewhat earlier than the FSP.

Evidence of earlier structures found in the FSP complicates the chronological assessment. Small portions of earlier construction were found in the pyramid around two looted pits (Graves 12 and 13); however, since we did not get any ceramic materials associated with these substructures, their chronology remains unknown. That they were found very near the center of the FSP suggests that they might have already been related to the Ciudadela. Early-phase ceramics (Patlachique and

Tzacualli phases) collected from the surface of the Ciudadela and in the 1988–89 excavations (Cowgill 1983: table 11.1; Cowgill and Cabrera 1991) suggest that the substructures were earlier than the construction of the Ciudadela itself. This conjecture will remain highly speculative until INAH project data are available.

Although the chronological relation of the FSP to earlier structures is not clear, it is evident that the spot was totally leveled to the subsoil about AD 200, and a new construction program began. The graves, construction of pyramid and temple, and facade sculptures belonged to this program. The FSP was the third largest pyramid in Teotihuacan, much smaller than the Sun Pyramid and the Moon Pyramid, yet the energy expenditure for its construction may have been as great. The PAT80–82 (Cabrera and Sugiyama 1982: 167) excavations confirmed that the facades on all four sides had been decorated with carved stones (Fig. 6), whose size varied greatly. The heavy stone heads must have involved an especially high energy expenditure in quarrying, transporting, manipulating, and carving at the site.

This type of pyramidal construction, covered with stone blocks and three-dimensional sculptured heads, can be found only at the FSP and the Adosada platform of the Sun Pyramid in Teotihuacan; they were distinct from other structures and contemporaneous with each other, according to the ceramic chronology (R. Millon 1973). They were also distinguished from other structures in Teotihuacan by being the two oldest instances of the city's characteristic tablero-talud profile, perhaps among the oldest in all of Mesoamerica.[1]

The tablero-talud form, one of Teotihuacan's most distinctive artistic features, was a combination of rectangle (tablero) and trapezoid (talud). A vertical, rectangular wall with moldings on its four sides rests on an inner-inclined trapezoid portion, the former always jutting out from the upper edge of the latter (Fig. 3). Similar forms appeared not only in architecture but also in pottery (supports of vases), in ornaments (nose pendants and possibly headdresses), and other types of visual representations. Because of the instability of the vertical elements, the form was evidently not in high demand in architecture for practical reasons.

Meaning seems to have determined shape. The tablero-talud form is reminiscent of the Teotihuacan year-sign, which is composed of an overlapping trapezoid and triangle, as pointed out by Heyden (1979). It is generally agreed that the trapezoid and triangle signs had calendrical functions in Postclassic cultures (Heyden 1979; Langley 1986: 148–53; von Winning 1979). A similar form often appears as a symbolic notational complex in headdresses and censer ornaments called the Manta compound[2] in Teotihuacan that also had a strong connotation of ritual calendrical meanings (Langley 1986: 153–67). Year signs often appear with other notational signs of the Mesoamerican almanac. If this is true for Teotihuacan, the distinctive architectural form, the tablero-talud, symbolized calendrical meanings, perhaps for the first time in early major monuments like the FSP and the Sun Pyramid's Adosada platform. This suggests that innovative calendrical significance may have been embedded in the monumental architecture itself at the time of their construction.

The FSP was exactly square, with sides about 65 m long, and it is currently 19.4 m high (Cabrera and Sugiyama 1982). Marquina (1951: 85) proposed that the pyramid had six stepped platforms with 366 sculptural heads, but this reconstruction is in error. I believe the pyramid had seven stepped platforms. If it had had six platforms, its original height would have been 17.4 m (2.9 m: height of a platform × 6), 2 m lower than the current height of the mound. Its top surface clearly shows the pyramid's nucleus (or original fill), indicating that it originally was higher. The reconstructed height of seven platforms, 20.3 m (2.9 m × 7), 0.9 m higher than the current mound, appears more correct. The pyramid's slopes and its western staircase also indicate that it consisted of seven stepped platforms. In Teotihuacan, staircases usually jutted out from a facade, and their inclinations were less steep than those of the facades, so that the uppermost step of the staircase joined the edge of the highest platform. The FSP apparently had the same form (Fig. 6). The current slope of the lower portion of the original staircase joins the slope of the stepped pyramid at the level of the seventh platform in the reconstructed plan.

The calendrical significance of the number of sculptural heads on the facades is complicated and still uncertain. As we have seen, Marquina's claim of some 366 heads at the FSP was not the case, as his reconstruction of the number of stepped platforms and the distance between heads is wrong. I preliminarily list here several possibilities for head numbers, from factual data.

At the FSP, the heads of Feathered Serpents (hereafter called serpent heads) alternate regularly with another type of head (hereafter called headdress heads for reasons set forth in the following section). It is likely that the same locational pattern of heads was repeated on the south side. In 1982, several heads were found in the fill, and a headdress head was found in its original place on the same side. Sculptural data from fallen blocks discovered on the north and east sides strengthen the idea that the same pattern was repeated all around the pyramid. I reconstructed the plan (Fig. 6) from field data taken on the pyramid's west, south, and north sides and tried to calculate the number of the heads at the FSP.

Difficulties stem from several unresolved questions. Data from the west facade indicate that a "corridor" on each stepped body of the pyramid consistently measures 2.60 m wide. This means that an upper platform measures 2.60 m less than the next lower platform at the corner, and the difference does not match the interval between the sculptural heads (3.29 m) jutting from the platforms. It also means that a higher platform did not necessarily always have two fewer heads than the next lower one. For example, the third platform, from the bottom to the top, may or may not have ended with serpent heads at the corners. There was space for serpent heads close to the corners, but whether heads were actually there would have depended on the representational context of the whole pyramid, which we only partly understand. More crucially, we have no data on the imagery at the corners; these parts have been heavily eroded, and the sculptural blocks near the corners did not yield any special iconographic data useful for the reconstruction.

For these and other reasons,[3] the total number of heads remains uncertain. Therefore, I list several possible ways to count them simply based on space availability. In my reconstruction plan (Fig. 6), the pyramid has a total of 361 sculptural heads: 175 serpent heads + 186 headdress heads (the same order is used for the following numbers in parentheses). There could have been 377 (191 + 186) heads, if the heads of the balustrades are included. These numbers do not include possible heads near the corners at the third platform; if these are added, the number of heads increases to 385 (199 + 186) with or 369 (183 + 186) without those of the balustrades. The numbers become even more complicated if we assume that Teotihuacan architects allowed equal intervals between heads on the four sides, including those that would have been covered by, or might not have been placed at, the staircase. (An analogous case is the Pyramid of Niches at El Tajín, which was adorned with 364 niches, including those covered by its staircase [Marquina 1951: vol. 1, 430].) The number of heads becomes 404 (200 + 204) with or 396 (200 + 196) without serpent heads at the corners of the third platform. None of these possibilities corresponds to calendrical numbers. Only the fact that the west – or principal – facade had eighteen headdress heads on each side of the stairway suggests calendrical meanings. The heads on the other sides do not indicate a clear association with meaningful numbers.

Although calendar relationships remain far from certain, the precise manipulation of sculptured blocks obviously indicates that the irregularity caused by the difference between the width of the stepped platforms and the interval between the sculptural heads was deliberate. Given Teotihuacan's high architectural standards (in which the FSP stands out in terms of monumentality, planning, and precision) some ritual meaning could have been encoded in the number of each type of head or the total number of heads. Additional heads on the upper portion of the pyramid, intentional irregularity of head locations at the corners, or heads integrated into the temple construction on top may have complemented the number of Feathered Serpent heads.

Sculpture of the facades

Previous iconographic studies were undertaken to understand the imagery of the pyramid's principal facade (Figs. 3 and 17a), with no convincing interpretation agreed upon by scholars. In particular, identification of the sculptured heads that alternate with the Feathered Serpent heads (previously called Tlaloc heads) has been controversial (Drucker 1974: 12–18).

The main motifs of both tableros and taludes were profiles of undulating Feathered Serpents with tail rattles. Tablero figures repeatedly appear with front-facing heads in high relief. Similar types of Feathered Serpent heads in high relief were also attached to the staircase balustrades. On the main (west) facade, all the Feathered Serpents' bodies, beginning with their heads, face toward the staircase. On the lateral facades (south and north), all the bodies probably faced west. Only compositional structure and directionality of the bodies on the back (east) side are unknown.

Feathered Serpent bodies on the tableros alternate with high-relief, front-facing heads of other entities. Identification of the entities' heads is still in doubt. Distinguished from the rest of the imagery by their greater three-dimensionality, they have led various scholars to interpret them, with the high-relief Feathered Serpent heads, as "dualistic" entities (Coe 1981: 168; Drucker 1974). However, Karl Taube (1992a)

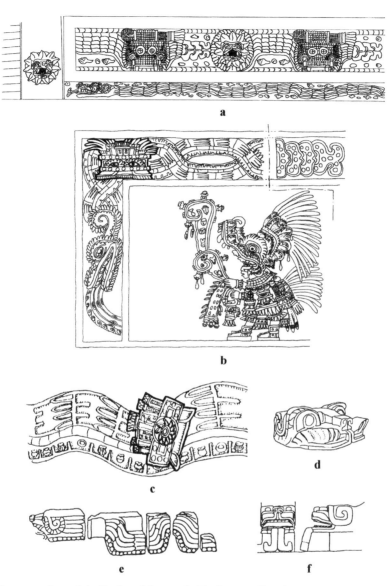

Fig. 17 Representations of the Feathered Serpent in Teotihuacan. Drawing: author. a Sculptures of the main facade at the FSP; b The mural of processional human figures at Tepantitla; the space was bordered by the Feathered Serpent wearing the headdresses. The human figure bears an elaborate costume and a headdress in the form of a coyote head topped with feathers and obsidian blades in a row (from Miller 1973: 100); c Mural of the Feathered Serpent with a headdress superimposed on its body, found in Zacuala Palace (from Miller 1973: 112–13, and Séjourné 1966a: fig. 9); d Sculpture of the Feathered Serpent, found in the Palace of Quetzalpapalotl (from the original); e Sculpture of the Feathered Serpent, found in the Palace of Quetzalpapalotl (from Acosta 1964: fig. 25); f Sculpture of the Feathered Serpent, found in the "West Plaza Compound" located on the west side of the Avenue of the Dead and to the north side of the San Juan River (from the original).

and I (Sugiyama 1989b, 1992) independently identified the heads as headdresses superimposed on the bodies of Feathered Serpents.[4]

Interpretation of the unidentified heads as headdresses is supported by a compositional pattern that governed Teotihuacan murals (Sugiyama 1992): headdresses superimposed on the bodies of Feathered Serpents were found in murals at Zacuala Palace and Tepantitla (Fig. 17b and 17c). In fact, elements overlapping the bodies of zoomorphic figures were a common feature of Teotihuacan iconography, and other iconographers now generally agree with the headdress interpretation (Millon 1992: 362; Carlson 1991; Coggins 1993: 144; James Langley 1991, personal communication). Therefore, my discussion here concerns the nature of Teotihuacan's Feathered Serpents and the identification of their headdress heads.

Other iconographic elements are motifs surrounding the bodies of the Feathered Serpents, which are immediately recognizable as various kinds of shells (see Chapter 6, on shell offerings).

Feathered Serpents

Only one realistic representation of a serpent is known in Teotihuacan iconography (Fig. 18a). All other figures with long, serpent-like bodies contain abstract features. The so-called Feathered Serpent was a creature composed of elements of both serpents and birds. Later, some representations of this creature became more complicated, acquiring elements of other entities, and in some cases the undulating bodies were combined in different ways with elements of other animals (Fig. 18b–d); in these scenes, Feathered Serpents may be undergoing a transformation into another creature. These combined or transforming creatures cause serious disagreements among iconographers trying to identify them.

Besides the realistic and the combined creatures, there are "conservative" serpent creatures which we conventionally call Feathered Serpents because of the apparent presence of feathers on their bodies (Fig. 17a–e). The identification of the principal figure at the FSP as a Feathered Serpent is unquestionable, since its components were diagnostic for Feathered Serpents known from ethnohistoric documents. During the Postclassic period in the Mexican Highlands, the figure was well known as Quetzalcoatl, god of the dawn, the wind, and the Morning Star (*Codex Chimalpopoca* 1992; Sahagún 1970: bk. 1: 9). However, the mythical nature of the figure in Teotihuacan needs to be considered in its own context (Kubler 1967).

The following discussion deals with structural analogies and correlation of elements of the figures I call the Teotihuacan Feathered Serpent group. Previously, I tentatively classified the mythical animals in Teotihuacan, including Feathered Serpents (Sugiyama 1988a). For this book, I add new data published since 1988, modifying and synthesizing my earlier classification, taking into account insights obtained from other recent studies (Carlson 1991; Carrasco 1982; Langley 1986; López 1973, 1990; López et al. 1992; C. Millon 1988a, 1988b; R. Millon 1988b, 1992; Pasztory 1988; Taube 1992a).

Feathered Serpents appear in Teotihuacan with considerable variety in form, structure, and context. In order to classify them, I defined the images from a diachronic

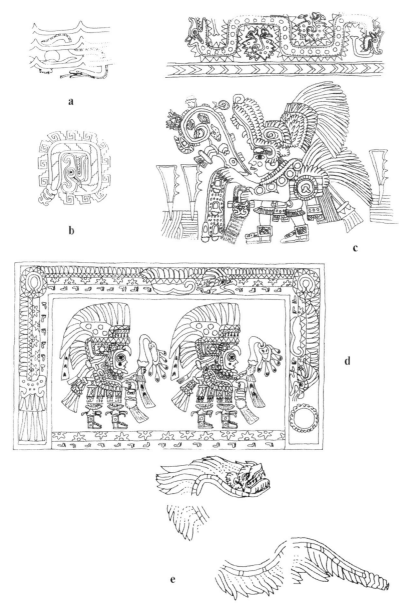

Fig. 18 Representations of serpent-like creatures in Teotihuacan. Drawing: author. a The most realistic serpent representation in a Teotihuacan mural (from Miller 1973: 73); b A mural found near the Sun Pyramid (from Miller 1973: 76); c A mural probably originating from Techinantitla, a large residential compound located 500 m east of the Moon Pyramid (from Miller 1973: 170); d Representations of two priests under the Feathered Serpent body carrying the bird symbols. The mural was uncovered in a residential complex near the northwest corner of the Sun Pyramid (from Séjourné 1966a: fig. 173; Kubler 1967: figs. 11, 12); e Feathered Serpent representation in the mural called "Mythological Animals," found near the Avenue of the Dead (from Fuente 1995: 100–101).

a

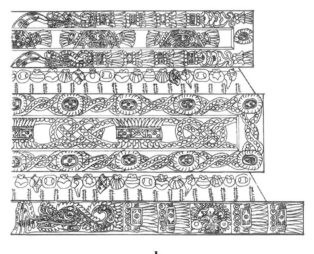

b

Fig. 19 Representations of the Feathered Serpent as a border motif in Teotihuacan. a Mural from Techinantitla, stored in the DeYoung Museum, San Francisco (drawing: author, from the original; after Berrin 1988: 138); b Mural on an altar excavated at Atetelco (drawing: Kumiko Sugiyama, from Miller 1973: 164).

point of view and took account of components at the FSP as diagnostic elements, because (as far as we know) the FSP serpent is one of the earliest representations in Teotihuacan and may have affected later representations (Millon 1992: 420–29; C. Millon 1972). In fact, it is a typical image of the entire body, and it contains most of the essential elements of the Feathered Serpent (Fig. 17a). The essential elements consist of serpent head, "bird eyes," curling snout, wide mouth with backward-curving fangs (without incisors or molars), bifurcated tongue, eyebrow with curled-up end, feathered body, and tail rattles. I believe that most of the images assembled in Figures 17, 18e, 19–21 are identifiable as Feathered Serpents, based on these elements. In the sections that follow, I summarize certain attributes of Feathered Serpents in order to point out some implications for the interpretation of the FSP.

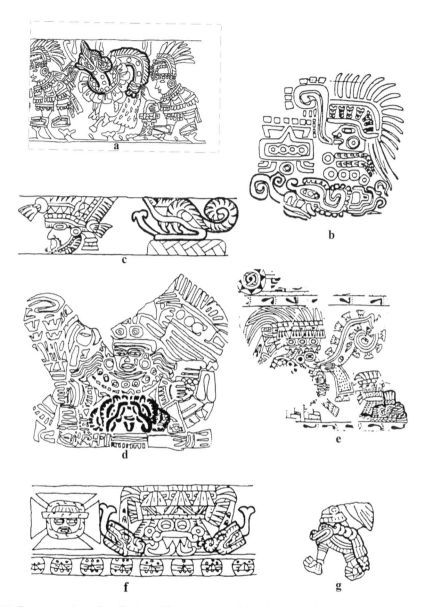

Fig. 20 Representations of the Feathered Serpent as an independent symbol. Drawing: author. a Ceramic bowl from Calpulalpan, excavated by Linné (1934) (from Séjourné 1966b: fig. 117); b Ceramic vessel found in Teotihuacan (from Séjourné 1966c: fig. 90); c Ceramic vessel found at Zacuala, Teotihuacan (from Séjourné 1970: fig. 83); d Ceramic bowl found in Teotihuacan; currently stored in INAH's local museum (from the original); e A mural at Techinantitla, Teotihuacan (from the original, after Berrin 1988: 118); f Ceramic vessel from Teotihuacan (from Caso 1967a: fig. 34b); g Ceramic plaque found in a workshop for censer production excavated to the north of the Ciudadela in 1982 (from the original).

Feathered Serpents characteristically appeared as sculptural figures attached to Teotihuacan staircase balustrades (Fig. 17d and f). Eventually, this became a Mesoamerican tradition and lasted well beyond the decline of Teotihuacan, as documented in Tula, Chichén Itzá, Tenochtitlán, and other ritual centers. The FSP serpents seem to have been among the oldest instances of this category in the city (Acosta 1964: fig. 20; Morelos 1993: 274). Feathered Serpents were also represented frequently in marginal parts of walls such as tablero moldings or talud borders (Figs. 17b and 19). This is especially true when a Feathered Serpent's whole body was depicted. Feathered-Serpent-like bodies combined with elements of other animals also appear in border areas (Fig. 18c and d). In this sense, the FSP (Fig. 17a) would have been an exception: here the Feathered Serpent is the single, central entity symbolized repeatedly in high relief on a very large scale at a major monument.[5]

Representing Feathered Serpents on architectural structures and on painted walls as a structural element in whole scenes may have been related to attributes of the Feathered Serpent (López 1990; 1989, personal communication). According to López's interpretation and that of Carrasco (1982), Feathered Serpents were related to time in a fundamental way; the creatures were believed to have brought time to this world and, by that act, to have defined space. López says they were often used as columns to keep space open so that other entities could live between or under them. This cosmogonical meaning may have underlain an emic view of Feathered Serpent representations on columns, balustrades, or moldings of pyramids or in border areas of murals that defined sacred space. This view seems to fit the interpretation of the headdress head carried by the Feathered Serpent on its body (which I describe later).

Feathered Serpent heads were often used as independent iconographic elements attached to anthropomorphic figures as if to identify the figures (Fig. 20), sometimes in the form of a headdress (Fig. 21a–d) or as an element attached to a headdress worn by certain types of anthropomorphic figures, including the Storm God (Fig. 21e–h). Feathered Serpent heads were frequently a main motif on ceramic vessels (Fig. 22a–h), often combined with other iconographic elements, such as heads represented in stamps (Fig. 22i) and ceramic plaques or "adornos" (Fig. 22j). This type of use was found mainly in portable items, where they were depicted in abbreviated or abstract forms.

Elements associated with Feathered Serpents make possible further arguments: one associated theme or dimension has been the Feathered Serpent's militaristic aspect. Various zoomorphic and anthropomorphic figures, including the coyote (C. Millon 1973, 1988b), the jaguar (Kubler 1972), and the bird (von Winning 1948), had military associations in Teotihuacan imagery; compared with the others, however, the Feathered Serpent was rarely represented with martial objects in Teotihuacan iconography. Contrasting with the scarcity of Feathered Serpents with military associations in Teotihuacan, Teotihuacan-style (feathered) serpents found abroad had a strong military association. In one Teotihuacan case, an individual wearing a Feathered Serpent headdress and a Feathered Serpent head at his waist is depicted with a shield and spear, establishing his military identity (Fig. 21b). Another example is a relief incised on a Teotihuacan vessel (Fig. 21d), in which a figure bearing a shield and spears wears a large Feathered Serpent headdress.

This scarcity of militaristic association at Teotihuacan agrees with the fact that the FSP's iconography did not have any overtly martial objects; however, the burial complex of sacrificed victims attired as soldiers clearly indicates the pyramid's strong

Fig. 21 Representations of the Feathered Serpent in the form of a headdress. Drawing: author. a, b Ceramic plaques from a workshop excavated to the north of the Ciudadela in 1982 (from the originals); c Ceramic vessel from Teotihuacan (from Séjourné 1966b: fig. 133); d Cylindrical tripod from Teotihuacan (from Séjourné 1964: fig. 8); e Cylindrical tripod from Escuintla, Guatemala. Three Feathered Serpent heads are indicated by arrows (from Berlo 1984: pl. 181; Sugiyama 1992: 214); f A mural found in the Palace of Jaguar near the Moon Pyramid (from Miller 1973: 57); g Ceramic fragment found in Teotihuacan (from the original stored in the INAH's local facility, after Sugiyama 1989b: 71); h Ceramic vessel from Teotihuacan (from Séjourné 1966b: 109).

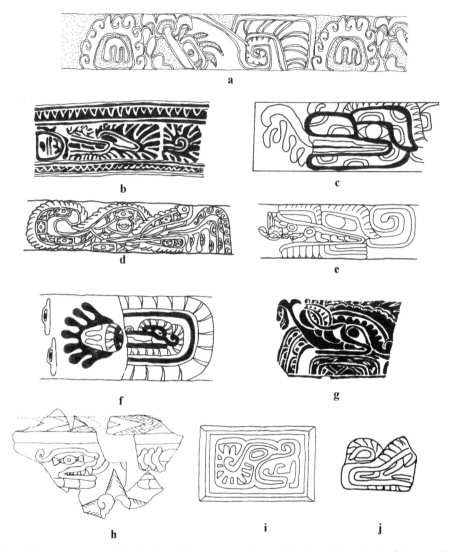

Fig. 22 Representations of the Feathered Serpent as main motif, often with symbols of heart and/or blood. a Ceramic vessel from Teotihuacan (drawing: author, from Séjourné 1966b: fig. 112); b Ceramic vessel from Teotihuacan (drawing: Kumiko Sugiyama, from von Winning 1987: vol. 1, 130–31); c Ceramic vessel from Zacuala, Teotihuacan (drawing: Kumiko Sugiyama, from Séjourné 1959: fig. 25); d A mural in Atetelco (drawing: Kumiko Sugiyama, from Séjourné 1966b: fig. 90); e Ceramic vessel from Teotihuacan (drawing: author, from Séjourné 1966b: fig. 195); f Painted vessel from Teotihuacan (drawing: Kumiko Sugiyama, from Séjourné 1959: fig. 132); g Ceramic fragment with a representation of the Feathered Serpent on a mat symbolizing authority (drawing: Kumiko Sugiyama, from von Winning 1987: vol. 1, 130); h Ceramic fragments found in the North Palace of the Ciudadela (drawing: author, from the original stored in the INAH's local facility); i Stamp from Teotihuacan (drawing: author, from Séjourné 1966c: fig. 140); j Ceramic plaque from a ceramic workshop discovered on the north side of the Ciudadela (drawing: author, from the original).

military association. In addition, Feathered Serpents were represented widely and intensively in the contexts of bloody rituals in the iconography of later periods. Like the Maya (who preferred to depict sacrificial rituals as victory celebrations instead of war scenes), the Teotihuacanos may have stressed the importance of warfare-related rituals in visual presentation more than the wars that often preceded them.

The association of the Feathered Serpent with sacrificial rituals is manifested abundantly and explicitly: on ceramic vessels, Feathered Serpent heads are often shown with a heart and/or drop sign, which likely represents blood (Fig. 22a, b, c, and f). On vessel fragments found in the North Palace of the Ciudadela (Fig. 22h), a serpent's head and a rattle tail with a trilobal sign representing a heart are incised with possible representations of knives below the chevron chain that Langley (1986: 62–67) interprets as martial symbolism. In later periods outside Teotihuacan, Feathered Serpents were also associated with ball games (Hellmuth 1975). In a Teotihuacan-type tripod found at Tiquisate, Guatemala, a figure, probably a ball game player, has a knife in his left hand, below which a human head is shown (Fig. 21e); three Feathered Serpent images are attached, one each to his headdress, his belt, and right knee; below them is an abstract, horizontal representation of an upper jaw.

Feathered Serpents also have been associated with water and fertility, with water flowing from their fangs and/or with watery representations surrounding them (Figs. 17b, 19, 22c, d, and g). In some cases, water symbols are not clearly distinguishable from blood symbols: water symbols used with shells (supposedly meaning water) appear frequently with hearts, most likely meaning blood, especially when painted red. In Figure 19a, water (painted blue) and possible blood (painted red) issue together from the fangs, making it probable that Teotihuacanos conceived of water and blood as metaphorically overlapping, similar to contemporaneous Maya, who related blood and water (Freidel 1985: 19).

Teotihuacan's Feathered Serpents also represented authority. In many cases (Fig. 20c–e), the serpent is shown resting on a mat, a symbol of authority and rulership well known throughout Mesoamerica (C. Millon 1988a: 119). It is important to note that the mat symbol in Teotihuacan appears almost exclusively with Feathered Serpent heads. In all cases I know of, the mat symbol appears only with Feathered Serpent heads, although Langley (1986: 273) cites a case in which, he says, the sign appears under a human being.

Another expression of authority is the association of Feathered Serpents with headdresses. The depiction of an independent headdress was so common in Teotihuacan that it suggests that headdresses were especially significant to the society (Langley 1986: 107–24). Clara Millon's studies (1973, 1988a) have made a persuasive case for the tassel headdress as a symbol of authority (which appears to be linked to the military), and as a symbol of Teotihuacan outside of the city. In the murals at Techinantitla, the Storm God carries a lightning bolt in his left hand and, in his right hand, a headdress similar to one he wears (Fig. 23a). The scene can be interpreted as the Storm God's delivery of the headdress, meaning accession to his office by the giving of regalia, the symbol of divine authority (Sugiyama 1992: 216–19). We do not know if this is a mythological depiction of the gift of divine authority or if it

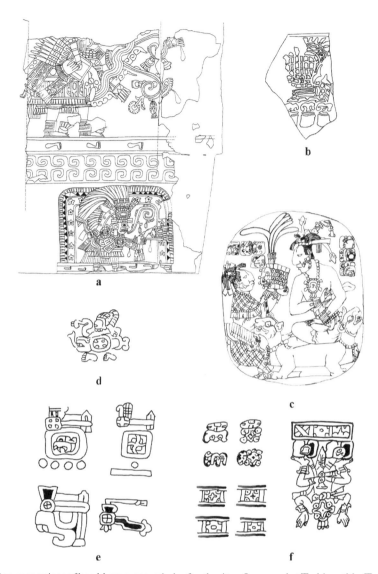

Fig. 23 Representations of headdresses as symbols of authority. a In a mural at Techinantitla, Teotihuacan, the Storm God (upper level) carries a headdress that seems to be a duplicate of the one worn by the Storm God in the lower level. This Storm God extends the same headdress toward someone, as if giving his own emblem or title of authority (drawing: author, from the original, after Berrin 1988: 102); b A headdress on a hand underlain by three shells: may represent accession in Teotihuacan (drawing: author, from von Winning 1987: vol. 1, 80–81); c Oval Palace Tablet in Palenque, Maya, ca. AD 652, shows accession scene of King Pacal. While Pacal is sitting on the double-headed jaguar throne, his mother, Lady Zac-Kuk, extends a drum-major headdress, the crown used by Palenque kings, toward her son (drawing: Kumiko Suigyama, from Schele and Miller 1986: 114); d Zapotec representation of a mythical serpent carrying a human head with a Teotihuacan-type headdress was sculptured on Stela 1 from Monte Albán, Oaxaca. A quincross-like sign is also on the body of the serpent (drawing: Kumiko Sugiyama, from Marcus 1983: 139); e Zapotec representations of year sign including an element similar to a quincross (drawing; Nawa Sugiyama, after López et al. 1991: 98); f Venus and quincross signs in Maya (drawing: Kumiko Sugiyama, from Seler 1963: vol. 1, 21, 191; Thompson 1972: 77). The quincross in the *Dresden Codex*: 58 also formed a celestial band element, from which Venus is descending.

implies divine sanction of an individual ruler or elite, since the entity to whom the headdress is being presented is intentionally omitted from the scene; however, the connection between the deity and the headdress is clear: the headdress apparently is an earthly manifestation of the authority of that deity.

This form of denoting accession is widespread in Mesoamerican iconography (Fig. 23b and c). As we have seen, the Feathered Serpent is often represented as a headdress, or it appears as an element attached to a headdress (Fig. 21), which probably carried the meaning of authority. The FSP is another example in which the Feathered Serpent is associated with authority, since it carries a headdress of a special type on its body. The next section focuses on the possible meaning of the headdress.

The Feathered Serpent also seems to have been related to Venus, perhaps as early as its first appearance in Teotihuacan iconography: among objects associated with it is the quincross sign that appears repeatedly on its body (Figs. 19b, 22d, and possibly 22c and 23d), a cross with a circle in the center that frequently appeared in pre-Columbian iconography; however, meanings attached to the cross at different times are not well defined. Hasso von Winning (1987: vol. 2, 11 and 66) thinks it represents water, especially fresh water. The Maya version of the same glyph, the Kan-cross (Glyph 281), was interpreted by Thompson (1962: 65–66) as a symbol for turquoise, "precious," and, by extension, water. Caso's interpretation of the Zapotec Glyph E (1967b: 145, fig. 2), equivalent to the quincross, as turquoise agrees with Thompson's. Pasztory (1976: 136–37) also agrees, adding a possible association with Tlaloc for Mexican Highland representations.

The quincross sign may have become more specific since early Teotihuacan times. Caso (1967b) further identified the glyph's function as that of a year bearer (Glyph E). Javier Urcid (2001: 113–23) distinguishes Glyph E from the quincross on head-dresses (Fig. 23e) because it lacks the central dot the quincross always carries; otherwise, the glyph is identical to an element used as a year sign in Zapotec headdresses. Seler (1963: 188–91) interprets the quincross as a representation of Venus, pointing out the relationship between it and the Maya hieroglyph for Venus (Fig. 23f). John Carlson (1991) further proposes that the glyph symbolized the five cycles of the Venus almanac which, combined with eight cycles of the 365-day vague year, represents a large cycle. Thus, although the specific meaning of the glyph is still uncertain, we can suggest an association between Venus and the Feathered Serpent, which often carries the quincross sign. If this association is valid, the Feathered Serpents of Teotihuacan also may have had symbolic associations with Venus.[6]

The relationship of the Feathered Serpent with Venus is further suggested by the discovery of a mural in the Great Plaza of the Ciudadela (Structure 1-B' in Fig. 2; Cabrera 1992: fig. 6). The function of the temple platform built independently in the plaza evidently had to do with ceremonies carried out in association with the FSP. Found in tableros, the mural consists of a row of double-cross signs, each with a central disk (Fig. 24a), reminiscent of the representations of Venus found in the *Codice Vindobonensis* (Fig. 24b). In Mixtec codices (Fig. 24c), a similar symbol is attached to the right waist of Tlahuizcalpantecuhtli, god of Venus. Analogous

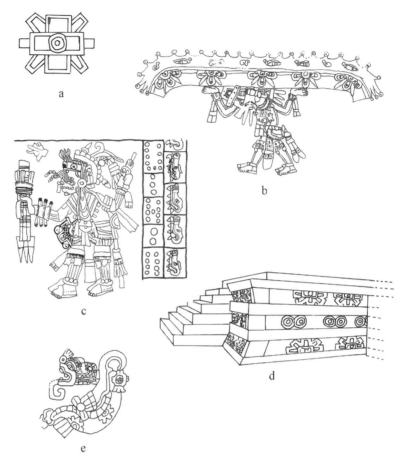

Fig. 24 Representations of Venus and symbols related to Venus in Mesoamerica. a Possible representation of Venus in a mural of a platform (1-B' in Fig. 2) excavated in the Ciudadela (drawing: Kumiko Sugiyama, from Cabrera 1992: 120); b Ehecatl Quetzalcoatl supporting a sky band, from which five star signs, possibly representing specifically five Venus (cycles), are suspended (drawing: Nawa Sugiyama, from *Códice Vindobonensis* 1992: 47); c Tlahuizcalpantecuhtli, a Venus deity, carrying a spear-thrower and spears, bordered with calendrical numbers and representations of Cipactli (drawing: Kumiko Sugiyama, from Seler 1963: vol. 2, fig. 118); d Teotihuacan-style structure in Tikal (drawing: Kumiko Sugiyama, from Pasztory 1978: 109); e Sacrificial knife overlapping with a serpent which carries possible Venus signs on its body; depicted on a stuccoed frieze of the palace in Acanceh, Yucatan (drawing: Kumiko Sugiyama, from Miller 1991: pl. 4).

symbols have been found at a Teotihuacan-style building in Tikal (Fig. 24d), and in Yaxha, a similar sign was represented on the body of a Teotihuacan-type serpent, overlapping a sacrificial knife (Fig. 24e). Although the Ciudadela mural has not been dated, it is logical to suppose that it was an integral element of the Ciudadela's symbolism for a certain period.

The headdress head on the Feathered Serpent's body
This head (Figs. 17a and 25a) has been puzzling since its discovery in 1918–22 and is something of a mystery even today, because its morphology is unique among

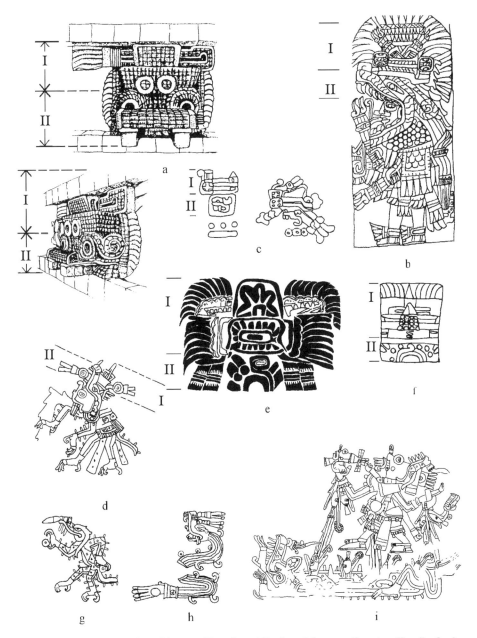

Fig. 25 Representations of headdresses, Cipactli, and Feathered Serpent. Drawing: Kumiko Sugiyama.
a Representation of Primordial Crocodile in the form of headdress at the FSP (from Caso and Bernal 1952:
fig. 184); b Priest wearing the headdress of the Feathered Serpent (II), which carries its own headdress (I).
Stone relief from Soyoltepec, southern Veracruz (from von Winning 1979: fig. 24a); c Zapotec headdress
(I) with year bearer M (II), according to Urcid. In Zapotec writing, headdress complexes with numbers
were used as date or name signs (from Urcid 2001: 122); d Cipactli in the Postclassic period, wearing
a headdress of year sign (I) (from *Códice Borgia* 1963: pl. 38); e Headdress (I) and "reptile eye" (II);
may have been an abstract form of the Primordial Crocodile with its title of authority. In the past, Beyer
(1969: 63), von Winning (1961), and others associated the glyph with the day Cipactli, while Caso (1962:
53) mentioned its relation to Ehecatl Quetzalcoatl (from von Winning 1987: vol. 2, 70–10a); f "Manta"
(mantle) compound as a combination of "reptile eye" (II) and "headdress" (I) including a year sign (from
von Winning 1987: vol. 2, 78–79); g Cipactli without a headdress in Postclassic period (from *Códice Borgia*
1963: pl. 51); h Feathered Serpent in Postclassic period (from *Códice Borgia* 1963: pl. 52); i Cipactli in
Postclassic period (from *Códice Borgia* 1963: pl. 27).

Teotihuacan mythological entities. It has been interpreted in the past as the head of various deities: Tlaloc (Gamio 1922: vol. 1, p. LXVI; Reygadas 1930: 166; Armillas 1945: 24–26; Drucker 1974); Youalcoatl, a form of Quetzalcoatl (Armillas 1945: 24); the Feathered Serpent (von Winning 1987: vol. 1, 151); Itzpapalotl, the obsidian butterfly (Linné 1934: 30); a terrestrial crocodilian tail-head (Coggins 1986); Cipactli, an alligator-like creature known from Aztec codices (Drucker 1974: 13); and Xiuhcoatl, or Fire Serpent (Caso and Bernal 1952: 113–16). Carlson (1991) has interpreted it as the Storm God, the name preferentially used among recent Teotihuacan iconographers to designate what was traditionally called Tlaloc, while Taube (1992a) recently interpreted it as the War Serpent.

At first, I interpreted the head as an abstract form of Feathered Serpent (Sugiyama 1988a, 1989b, 1992); subsequently I was influenced by Alfredo López's idea that it represents a predecessor of the Postclassic Cipactli (López et al. 1991). In order to avoid historical implications attached to the Nahuatl term *Cipactli*, I propose that the entity represents a Primordial Crocodile, which has a specific cosmogonic and calendrical significance. The concept of the Primordial Crocodile is close to that of Cipactli and may have been shared among many other Mesoamerican societies.

The Tlaloc, or Storm God, interpretation should be excluded on the basis of comparative studies with other Storm God representations in Teotihuacan. The headdress head has no Storm God elements except for two rings on the forehead, and these are not a diagnostic for the Storm God since they were used widely by other deities, mythical animals, and anthropomorphic figures. In addition, no evidence has been found that the Storm God ever appeared in the form of a headdress in Teotihuacan. Other interpretations are more difficult to prove or reject since they are views that project Postclassic deities into the past, and no clear evidence connects them.

A recent argument accepted widely in the United States (e.g., Weaver 1994: 87–88; Coe 1994: 98) is Karl Taube's 1992a proposition that the FSP represented the duality of the Feathered Serpent symbolizing fertility, and the War Serpent (headdress head) symbolizing warfare. As supporting examples, he used Mayan anthropomorphic representations of Teotihuacan-type headdresses, which carry serpents and other animal elements without feathers, and he stresses martial objects carried by these figures and the bead-like texture of the headdresses to argue for the origin of the Maya War Serpent at the FSP. However, there are significant spatial, temporal, and cultural gaps between the FSP and representations of Mayan War Serpents.[7] I do not believe the War Serpent (a phrase coined by Taube to designate an essentially Mayan entity with foreign elements) existed at Teotihuacan. At the FSP, the Feathered Serpent itself had strong military associations and was *the* divine entity to which the pyramid was dedicated. The headdress head put on its body probably represented specific attributes of the Feathered Serpent, rather than attributes of another, independent entity juxtaposed with the Feathered Serpent.

I have described why I believe that the "headdress head" was not itself a mythical entity but a real headdress (Sugiyama 1989b, 1992: 206–9). For further analysis, I divide the headdress into two parts: the head of a mythical animal in the lower half

(II of Fig. 25a) and the headdress on top of the head of this mythical animal (part of a double headdress) in the upper half (I of Fig. 25a). The two parts form the whole headdress complex carried by the Feathered Serpent. The idea is supported by a strong Mesoamerican tradition (Fig. 25b, c, and d): in Mesoamerican iconography, many animal heads used for headdresses often had their own, smaller headdresses. This tradition can be recognized as a structural feature in Teotihuacan imagery (Figs. 17b, 18d, 21c, and 25e). In the case of the FSP, there is no clear dividing line between the head and the small headdress, and a bead-like texture covers almost the entire surface of the headdress complex. However, I believe this division, into a mythical animal head and its own small headdress, is useful for further analysis. The lateral fringes of feathers seem to be attached to the whole headdress complex, and a nose pendant (discussed later in this section), another crucial emblem, is put together under the jaw (this element is evidently independent of the headdress complex).

The upper part (small headdress) consists of a small trapezoid above a larger trapezoid and a large knot with feathers on its upper and rear parts (Fig. 25a). Two rings are attached to the lower trapezoid section rather than to the mythical animal's forehead. This small headdress is typically Teotihuacan. James Langley, who has studied symbolic notation in Teotihuacan extensively and systematically, classified this form as the Feathered Headdress symbol; he points out that the elaborated headdresses occur as the contextual framework within which semiotic clusters are placed (Langley 1986: 114). I believe the headdress representations at the FSP also included such signs.

Langley also argues that the Feathered Headdress symbol is visually related to the so-called year-sign headdress (Langley 1986: 114, 293–94). The headdresses directly associated with the Feathered Serpent in different circumstances seem to be analogous in terms of compositional principles that may include cohesive meanings. Figure 26 shows a variety of headdresses carried by, or directly attached to, Teotihuacan Feathered Serpents. This grouping includes headdresses adorned with the year sign (Fig. 26e), the quincross (Fig. 26f), the blood drop sign (Fig. 26d), or tassels identified (in conjunction with headdress) as symbols of authority (Fig. 26c). The headdress worn by the Primordial Crocodile at the FSP, whose general form is similar to Figures 26a and b, might also carry an attribute of calendrical notation. The idea is supported by the bow sign at the upper level (Fig. 25a). The bow and knot sign, which appears in the Manta compound, had strong calendrical associations in Teotihuacan (Langley 1986: 153–67) as well as in some other Mesoamerican societies (Caso 1928: 27; Urcid 2001).

Following the lines laid down by Caso (1937, 1967b) in his search for calendrical symbolism, Langley (1986: 143) further argues that dots for numerical notation are sometimes integrated into the sign either as infixes or by inclusion inside a frame or cartouche. In the samples he cites (Fig. 27), dot signs appear in the glyph frames. In the cluster of headdresses associated with the Feathered Serpent (Fig. 26a–e), several rings, disks, or beads are attached on the inferior trapeze of the headdresses, which may have functioned as some kind of numerical notation. This raises a possibility that the two rings attached to the inferior trapeze of the headdress at the FSP also carried

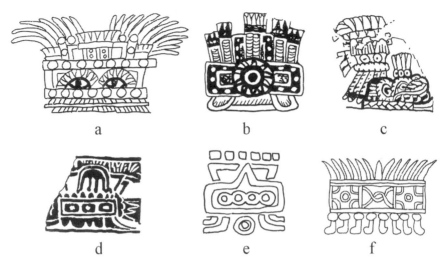

a   b   c

d   e   f

Fig. 26 Representations of headdresses associated with the Feathered Serpent, implying possible calendrical meanings and/or significance of authority (rulership) in Teotihuacan. Drawing: Kumiko Sugiyama. a Headdress on the body of the Feathered Serpent, depicted on a mural of Atetelco (see Fig. 17b; from Miller 1973: 112–13); b Headdress on the body of the Feathered Serpent, depicted on a mural of Zacuala Palace (see Fig. 17c; from Séjourné 1966a: fig. 9); c Tassel headdress attached to the Feathered Serpent in a mural looted from Techinantitla (see Fig. 20e; from the original, after Berrin 1988: 117); d Headdress juxtaposed with the Feathered Serpent on a tripod vessel (from von Winning 1987: vol. 1, 131–32); e Headdress associated with an anthropomorphic figure and the Feathered Serpent (see Fig. 20b; from Séjourné 1966c: fig. 90); f Headdress depicted on a mural of the alter dedicated to the Feathered Serpent in Atetelco (see Fig. 19b; from Miller 1973: 164).

Fig. 27 Possible dots signs in Teotihuacan, according to Langley. Drawing: Kumiko Sugiyama, from Langley 1986: 118 and 144.

numerical meaning; however, the two rings can be interpreted in different ways. The fact that many other entities carry only two rings in their foreheads reduces the probability of numerical meaning; instead, they may imply attributes of the Storm God, butterfly, or other entities who carry rings. Whether or not two rings had numerical meaning, the calendar-related function of the headdresses is strengthened by its combination with the lower portion that probably represented a mythological animal related to time division.

The identification of the lower part of the headdress complex (II of Fig. 25a) is more controversial. The components – "bird eyes," curling snout, upper jaw with incurved fangs, eyebrow with curled-up end – suggest that it represents the Feathered Serpent, as I identified previously (Sugiyama 1988a, 1989b, 1992); however, it is not covered with feathers but with a bead-like texture that often appears in helmet-style headdresses in Teotihuacan iconography and that may represent material used for headdresses.[8] Certain unknown symbolic meanings seem to have been involved in this texturing.

To me, a more convincing possibility is that this Primordial Crocodile represents a traditional symbolic deity of creation and divine authority involved in Mesoamerican cosmogonies; it is a predecessor of the Postclassic Mexican deity, Cipactli (López et al. 1991: 99), a successor of the Preclassic Olmec Dragon, or a contemporaneous Oaxacan reptile deity (Glyph V or M) and the Mayan celestial crocodilian monster, Yax Ain.

The Postclassic Primordial Crocodile, feminine and aquatic, is the original monster appearing widely as a crocodilian beast, occasionally as a sawfish or a snake, in pictorial and ethnohistoric records. In Postclassic imageries, the head of the Cipactli (a version of the Primordial Crocodile) is often indistinguishable from serpent representations when it lacks diagnostic body parts (Figs. 24a, 25d, g, h, and i). It is often covered with a bead-like texture and characteristically appears with only its upper jaw, which is the case at the FSP (see also the discussion of upper jaw pendants in Chapter 6). Cipactli was a sort of big fish or monster from which the earth was created, according to the *Historia de los mexicanos por sus pinturas* (Garibay 1965: 25–26). More importantly, it represented a calendar sign in the Postclassic period, appearing as the first day sign of the Tonalpohualli and as a sign of the beginning of larger cycles, carrying a strong, abstract sense of beginning. In addition, it seems to have been used as a calendar sign in combination with the Venus almanac (Fig. 24c) (e.g., *Códice Borgia*; discussed extensively by Seler 1963: 113–28).

The concept of a Primordial Crocodile apparently goes back at least to the Middle and Late Preclassic period in Mesoamerica. The so-called Olmec Dragon was perceived as a primordial monster floating on the surface of the waters of creation or dwelling in the sky, symbolizing both terrestrial and celestial aspects (Reilly 1996). It has the physical appearance of a crocodilian and shares with the Primordial Crocodile distinct features like scutes, the mosaic quality of the hide, the teeth, the snout, and eyes topped with flame or feather eyebrows. It was widely represented in monumental sculptures, stone artifacts, and ceramics found at ceremonial centers on the Gulf (e.g., La Venta) and Pacific coasts (e.g., Izapa; see Smith 1984) and in the Mexican Highlands (e.g., Chalcatzingo Tlapacoya). Reilly points out convincingly that the creature is frequently and explicitly associated with royal status particularly when the images appear in the context of royal burials or accession ceremonies.

Similar creatures representing cosmogonic significance also existed in Oaxaca, and the calendrical association of the primordial monster at Monte Albán seems

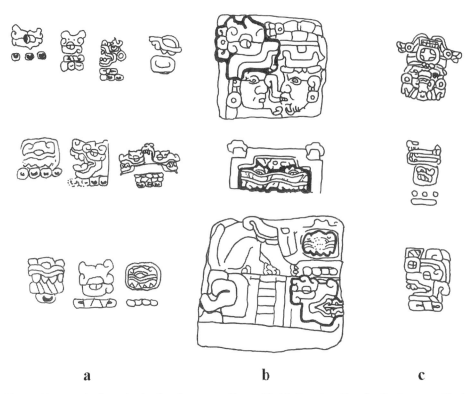

Fig. 28 Zapotec glyphs and calendar signs, according to Urcid. Drawing: Kumiko Sugiyama. a Glyph V (from Urcid 2001: 218); b Glyph V, as headdress or architectural motif (from Urcid 2001: 222); c Year Bearer M (from Urcid 2001: 191).

to be clearer and more explicit than at other sites. A version of an alligator-like creature at Monte Albán, classified visually by Urcid (2001) as Glyph V, was present by AD 200, approximately the time when the FSP was constructed (Fig. 28a). Some cases of Glyph V appear with numbers, as calendrical signs, in the form of headdresses, or in facade representations (Fig. 28b). Caso classified a larger group of representations of serpent-like creatures similar to the Primordial Crocodile as Cociyo (Glyph M in Urcid 2001), which often appears with a headdress as a year sign (Fig. 28c). Considering the strong relationship of this Oaxacan center with Teotihuacan (Marcus 1983), the above data seem to favor the interpretation of the Primordial Crocodile as a calendar symbol at Teotihuacan.

For the contemporaneous Lowland Maya, a version of the crocodilian creature would be Yax Ain, the celestial monster which, like the Feathered Serpent, identifies the royal association of the individuals who carry its symbol; Freidel et al. (1993: 59–122) think that Yax Ain was represented by the arching body of the Milky Way. A Tikal ruler, called Yax Ain I (First Crocodile), was explicitly portrayed with a mosaic helmet indicating cultural affiliation with Teotihuacan, particularly in Stela 31 (Martin and Grube 2000: 32–35). Yax Ain I was also portrayed in a ceramic found in his grave, bearing a headdress covered with mosaic hide and crocodile

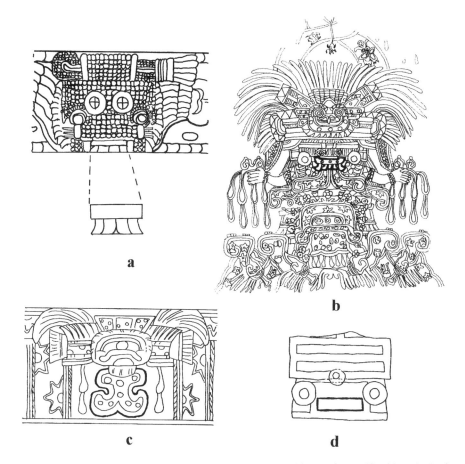

a

b

c

d

Fig. 29 Representations of headdress and nose pendant (bold) without a face. a Headdress in the form of Primordial Crocodile at the FSP with a type B nose pendant (drawing: author); b Anthropomorphic figure in "Tlalocan" mural at Tepantitla (drawing: Kumiko Sugiyama, from von Winning 1987: vol. 1, 138–39); c Headdress with type B nose pendant on pottery (drawing: Kumiko Sugiyama, from Séjourné 1966b: fig. 95); d Stone sculpture of headdress, nosebar, and earspools without face from the Palace of Jaguar (drawing: Kumiko Sugiyama, from Berrin and Pasztory 1993: 172).

features that identified or named him; the representation obviously carries some iconographic resemblance to the headdress head on the FSP. Unquestionable association, either political or biological, of Yax Ain I with Teotihuacan suggests that his version of the crocodilian creature, a symbol of rulership, originated in Teotihuacan. The Feathered Serpent may have been the supreme divine authority, which bore the title of Primordial Crocodile, as symbolized by the headdress head on the images at the FSP.

Below the Primordial Crocodile at the FSP is another element attached to the headdress complex. A nose pendant, composed of a rectangular plaque and four fang-like pendants, is clearly shown under the upper jaw (Fig. 29a) and evidently was not a part of the headdress complex. This type of nose pendant was associated both in and out of Teotihuacan with individuals often identified as deities or priests;

it seems to have symbolized authority and at the same time may have been an identification code for (a) particular individual(s) or social group, since it was combined
with the headdress complex composed of various possible calendar-related elements
(described above). Two similar nose pendants were found by PTQ88–89 inside the
FSP itself (see Chapter 6). The combination of headdress (often with the Feathered
Headdress symbol) and a nose pendant without a face was a pattern used instead
of realistic faces in the central section of entire scenes in Teotihuacan works of art,
as if these elements carried the most important emblems (Figs. 29b–d, 114). The
FSP may be one of the most monumental examples of this pattern in the city's early
period.

Temple sculpture

The upper part of the FSP was evidently completely destroyed, since Marquina's
1922 excavation and the recent excavation by the PAT80–82 (Cabrera and Sugiyama
1982) revealed only the nucleus of the pyramid at the apex of the current mound.
Only the square form of the pyramid suggests that it supported a single temple. No
data on the temple were available until the PTQ88–89 excavation unearthed some
remains.

The excavation (pit 2) was conducted at the top of the Adosada Platform and
uncovered within the fill many fragments of burned clay, with a variety of low-relief
motifs and varying in size from $43 \times 30 \times 20$ cm to tiny fragments. Their location
and stratigraphy indicate that they were derived from a nearby razed structure, and
their form suggests that they were parts of a frieze adorning a facade. Since there were
no nearby structures except for the temple, it is probable that the temple was razed
when the Adosada was built and the fragments used in the platform fill (Sugiyama
1998c). In other words, the frieze, which can be partially reconstructed from the
fragments, had been a part of the pyramid's decoration and should be integrated
into the whole visual message of the pyramid.

Despite their importance, the materials are too small a portion of the whole frieze
to give an understanding of its iconography. Moreover, many pieces came from inner
parts of the 20-cm-thick walls of the frieze, so that the pieces whose surface portion
contained iconographic information were very limited. Many fragments had only a
small, smooth, flat surface.

Along with these burned clay fragments, pieces of Teotihuacan concrete with
stucco and red painting were found in the Adosada fill, apparently parts of typical
Teotihuacan concrete walls and possibly those of the temple. A few burned clay
fragments with stucco and red paint, and several stones with a very thin burned clay
layer which was covered with stucco and red paint (perhaps parts of the juncture
between stone wall and clay frieze), were also unearthed.

The data suggest that the temple was a masonry building covered with stucco and
probably with red paint. No fragments painted with motifs were found in our test
pit (pit 2). The burned clay seems to have formed a large frieze or panel that may
have sat on the temple wall or roof. It is less likely that the temple walls were made of
rocks covered by burned clay decorations since we did not find any evidence of thick

Fig. 30 Burned clay fragments with representations of "feathers" in low relief, found in Adosada platform. Photo: author.

burned clay attached to the stones. Instead, some clay fragments had impressions of wood, suggesting that the frieze had been attached directly to a wooden wall, or to wooden pillars that functioned as an internal structure.

The motifs on the burned clay are large. Many fragments show only a portion of an iconographic element, and only a few have two or more elements, suggesting that the frieze may have been a large scene that could be observed at a distance. This seems logical, given the height of the FSP and the size of the Great Plaza, from which people presumably looked up to the principal temple.

Among the pieces providing some iconographic information, several elements have been recognized. A major portion of fragments with motifs is included here. Only smaller fragments without clear motifs, and others with unidentifiable lines, have been eliminated from this catalogue.

Feathers
Several large fragments clearly represented a cluster of feathers (Fig. 30), which usually measure 7–9 cm wide and taper gradually near their ends. They could have been part of a fringe adorning the main motif or part of a large headdress, but they could not have been part of the body of a Feathered Serpent.

Shells
A few fragments were unequivocally bivalve shells (Fig. 31) identical to those on the facades of the FSP. Other fragments also may have represented bivalves. The limited

Fig. 31 Burned clay fragments with representations of "shell" (two pieces at the top) and possible "plants" in low relief, found in Adosada platform. Photo: author.

samples do not seem to include representations of univalve shells, such as conches, that often appeared with bivalves. Shell sizes are similar to those on the facades of the FSP.

Scrolls

A series of scrolls with three parallel lines on their bases is pictured on a large fragment (Fig. 32), and many other smaller fragments seem to have the same scroll motif. The scroll is a typical liquid-related element that appears frequently in Teotihuacan iconography. I believe the combination of the scrolls with three sharply bent lines resembles a water complex (Shell Triplet in Langley 1986: 320) often associated with the Storm God (Figs. 33–35). This complex is usually composed of scrolls, three shells or "mountains," and a double bow with knots, also related to the Storm

Fig. 32 Burned clay fragment with representation of a "scroll" in low relief, found in the Adosada platform. Photo: author.

God (Figs. 33 and 34) and similar to the water symbol set being poured out from the "Tlaloc" jars in the Storm God representation at Tepantitla (Fig. 35a). In this case, the three "mountains" can be clearly identified as three shells (the shell sizes mentioned above would fit well as an element of a water complex). The main figure with which the motif is associated is again the Storm God. A similar motif can be

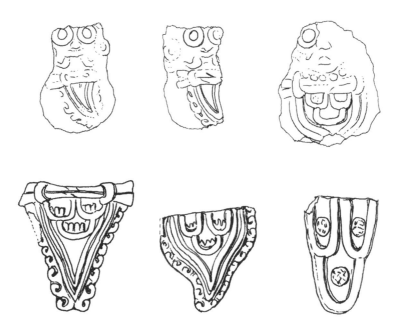

Fig. 33 Representations of watery scrolls associated with the Storm God at Teotihuacan. Triple "mountain" and Storm God complex on plaques found at a ceramic workshop north of the Ciudadela. Drawing: author, from Múnera and Sugiyama 1993.

Fig. 34 Triple "mountain" compound (left) and Storm God (right) on a Teotihuacan tripod vessel. Triple "mountain" compound includes double-knot elements with punctuation panels in upper portion. Drawing: Kumiko Sugiyama, from Caso 1967a: fig. 7b.

found in the profile of the Storm God in a talud border at Tepantitla (Fig. 35b), in which scrolls with parallel lines radiate from under the Storm God's face.

In these analogous examples, the meanings of objects with scrolls may vary case by case, but the similarity as a repeated pattern in Teotihuacan works of art is striking. If the fragments formed a part of these objects, the central image in the frieze of the temple at the FSP may have been the Storm God complex that Pasztory (1974) classified as Tlaloc A. Other elements described below also may have been integral

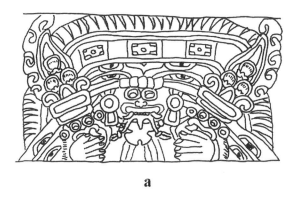

a

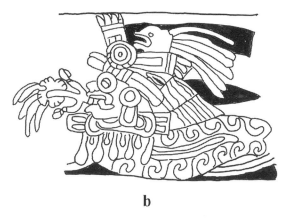

b

Fig. 35 Representations of watery scrolls associated with Storm God symbolism. Drawing: Kumiko Sugiyama. a Tepantitla mural of the Storm God holding "Tlaloc" jars, from which three shells and watery scrolls are popping up (from Pasztory 1974: 5); b Tepantitla mural of the Storm God with a "waterlily" hanging out of his mouth (from Pasztory 1974: 17).

parts of this Storm God complex, although they also could have been parts of other motifs.

Feathered disks

A double-edged disk with feather fringe (Fig. 36) was represented in the collection; its outside circle measured about 25 cm in diameter. It is found in many contexts in Teotihuacan, including those with the Storm God (Fig. 35b: the disk is depicted partially with feathers here). Feathered disks are represented as a headdress ornament, medallion, pectoral, shield, mirror, etc. (Langley 1986: 259–60, 318; Taube 1992b). The feathered disk motif also appears as a cartouche containing symbols such as the Reptile Eye sign and animal heads (Múnera and Sugiyama 1993).

Punctuation panels

Long panels filled with small, irregular punctations were represented on several fragments (Fig. 37). All panels are 12–13 cm wide and at least 23 cm long. Since no

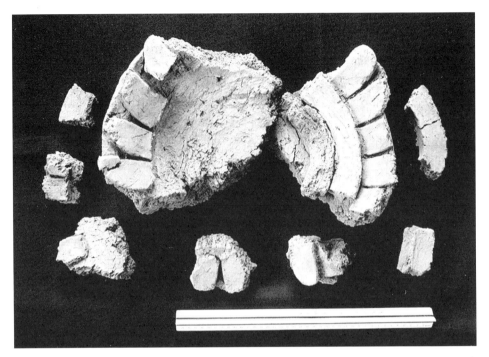

Fig. 36 Burned clay fragments with representation of "feathered disk" in low relief, found in the Adosada platform. Photo: author.

Fig. 37 Burned clay fragments with representation of "punctuation panel" in low relief, found in the Adosada Platform. Photo: author.

fragment had an edge line or other motif on either side of the panel, it is likely that they were originally long, flat, plain panels in a square shape, filled with punctuations and without other motifs. In Teotihuacan iconography, punctuations appear in different contexts: in cotton flowers, liquid, headdress ornaments, and panels falling from the hands of priests (see also Langley 1986: 315). However, they were usually accompanied with borderlines in various shapes. Long, flat, square panels with punctuations can be found in only a few cases. A striking analogous case can be found in a bow and knot element of, again, the Storm-God-associated three-"mountain" complex (Fig. 34). Outside of Teotihuacan, another analogy is the dotted band in the headdress worn by the "Teotihuacan ambassador" in Stela 31 from Tikal (Jones and Satterthwaite 1982: fig. 52). Although small fragments could still have been parts of any motif, homogeneity in punctuation use suggests that they were parts of a motif, possibly associated with the Storm God.

Circles
Two types of circle were detected in the collection: a hemispherical, convex circle with a smoothly curved surface, and a high-relief, sharp-edged circle or low column. Because the elements are so simple, their context is difficult to determine. Repeated circles often represented the eyes of various entities, beads, disks in headdresses, or other round ornaments on the bodies; or they appeared simply as abstract geometric motifs.

Possible plants
Relatively small, stalk-like elements were found in the fragment collection (Fig. 31). Some may have been branching parts of plants, although this identification is not conclusive. One of many possibilities is the so-called "waterlily" that often appears with the Storm God (Fig. 35).

Half-oval pieces
Nine fragments of oval form in cross-section have been found. They have a plain convex surface, but no information about their limits has been preserved. The two largest pieces, at least 25 cm and 30 cm wide, could have been body parts of anthropomorphic figures, although a plain surface would be rare on the trunk of an anthropomorphic figure. They also might have been parts of extremities or parts of other motifs.

Other pieces, too fragmentary to reconstruct motifs, could have been parts of many unidentifiable elements. All indicate that the temple's iconographic contents were significantly different from those of the pyramid's facades, although the data recovered were too small a portion and too fragmented to reconstruct the temple's imagery adequately. Since the scale of the motifs is comparable to those of the FSP facades, they may have been equally important and complementary to the facades.

The data seem to indicate that this possible temple frieze symbolized the water complex associated with the Storm God, with shell triplets, scrolls, headdress, feathered disks, and possibly waterlilies and other water-related elements. The Storm God himself might have been represented at the temple. While this reconstruction is still highly speculative, given that Feathered Serpents were often associated with the Storm God in Teotihuacan works of art, the existence of a Storm God complex at the temple may make sense. Although no written record of the old excavation is available today, it is logical to assume that the extensive excavation carried out between the FSP and the Adosada after 1917 found significant amounts of these and other materials from the temple, and it is probable that further excavation of the Adosada fill will provide additional burned clay fragments to support or modify the hypothetical reconstruction presented here.

General discussion
Several analysts (Coe 1981: 168; Drucker 1974: 16; Millon 1976: 237, 238; Taube 1992a) have suggested that the two alternating sculptural images on the pyramid (Feathered Serpent and headdress head) symbolize duality. However, the idea is now less convincing in view of the newer interpretation of the significance of the FSP's imagery. The two alternating heads were not equally positioned in terms of contextual meanings, although volumetrically they give us an impression of jux-taposition of two equally situated entities. Both heads were equally important to the Teotihuacanos; as the somewhat subordinate position of the headdress head to the Feathered Serpent suggests, the headdress complex, however, seems to provide attributes the Feathered Serpent carried on its body. The headdress head is considerably bigger than the Feathered Serpent head; this may indicate that the planner of the monument wanted to emphasize the symbols conferred by the supreme divine authority more explicitly to the public.

López (1990: 321–39) identified the Postclassic Feathered Serpent as the great initiator of the calendric division and the extractor of the divine-temporal-destiny force. The Feathered Serpent at the FSP, the main figure on the facades, was probably the principal entity in the cosmogonic watery Underworld and seems to have embodied, with mass-mortuary programs analyzed later, the meanings of sacred warfare and sacrifice in Teotihuacan. Later representations of Feathered Serpents in Teotihuacan and Central Mexico seem to have manifested these properties in different social contexts. The Feathered Serpent at the FSP carries the headdress complex I hypothesized as having symbolic cosmological and calendrical meanings that may have structured later pictorial representations. In addition to these ritual meanings, this symbol set brought by the initiator of time probably had more relevant sociopolitical functions than we had thought.

Given the related archaeological data and iconographic contexts in Teotihuacan, it is possible to propose that the headdress and nose pendant at the FSP symbolized the identity and authority of a specific ruler, and that it was this ruler who manipulated the building of the FSP. His political proclamation evidently was stated in terms of domination of Teotihuacan's most important value system, the time-reckoning complex. The Feathered Serpent seems to have been the paramount divine entity

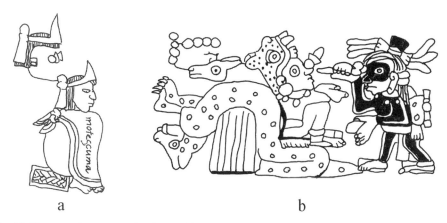

a   b

Fig. 38 Mesoamerican convention for manifestation of rulership by representations of headdresses and nose pendants. Drawing: Kumiko Sugiyama. a Aztec ruler, Moctezuma II, to which headdress and nose pendant were attached for identification (from Berdan and Anawalt 1992: vol. 3, 38, fo. 15v); b Accession scene of a Mixtec ruler, Eight Deer, by the nose piercing ceremony (from Caso 1977: pl. V).

conveying authority to the living bearer of this headdress and nose pendant, which were brought by the serpent itself.

This artistic, narrative expression of transferal of political authority by the most prestigious regalia granted by sacred entities was in fact a distinct convention commonly shared by Mesoamerican societies, including the Maya, Aztecs, Zapotecs, and Mixtecs. For example, a headdress and nose pendant were attached to images of Moctezuma II to identify him in Aztec codices (Fig. 38a). Among the Mixtecs, the ruler Eight Deer (Fig. 38b) was depicted in a holing ritual for a nose pendant, executed by Four Jaguar from Cholula. As John Pohl (1994) points out, this was a crucial moment in which rulers could gain divine power and status of royal kinship. Contemporaneous Maya rulers depicted their accession ceremonies by being given special headdresses by divine entities, ancestral rulers, or precedent royal family members (Fig. 23c). In Teotihuacan, headdresses and nose pendants used at the FSP probably became a conventional tool for an esoteric religious and political system and official iconographic communication programs. Headdress complexes and nose pendants without heads were the attire of ruling groups and depicted as royal emblems in Teotihuacan murals and ritual tripod vessels of later periods. The whole imagery at the FSP facade may have been an explicit governmental proclamation of the accession of a ruler who was to reign over the present world.

A peculiarity of the FSP is that this presumed accession was set up as a new period initiated in abstract form without a specific date sign. Nicholas Hopkins (1996) persuasively argues that Mayan languages have several built-in metaphors, such as "Space is (like) anatomy," "Time is (like) space," and "Kings are (like) gods," and that Classic Maya rulers metaphorically expressed "the succession of kings" as "the passage of time" (original quotations from Hopkins). At least since the Leiden Plaque (dated AD 320) onward, a king's accession was often stated in the same terms as the beginning of the month, Hopkins argues. The specific metaphors and metonyms of Mayan ritual language most likely had idiosyncratic roots common to other Mesoamerican societies.

If the ruler's succession at the FSP was part of the building of the pyramid, as suggested by the iconographic studies, a ruler may have proclaimed dynastic inheritance as a natural process or inevitable passage of time by depicting a headdress symbolizing time beginning, which was supposed to have been granted to him/her by a supreme creator of time and space. Thus, the ruler would have established his divine status in an overwhelmingly religious metaphor as contemporaneous Maya rulers did, though in a quite different artistic style.

It seems to me that the symbolic notation of the headdress of the possible Primordial Crocodile was a substantial part of the manifestation of warfare and sacrifice. James Langley (1991, 1992) points out that the Teotihuacan notational system in general was strongly associated with the imagery of war and sacrifice. Although we cannot find any martial objects or bloody elements in the iconography of the FSP, the Feathered Serpent itself seems to have carried the meaning of warfare and sacrifice integrally. The Feathered Serpent's martial attributes were evidenced materially by the graves of sacrificed people, many of whom were apparently buried as soldiers in a cosmological setting.

The excavation carried out at the Adosada has provided a new insight into the iconography of the temple of the FSP as well as the whole imagery of the Ciudadela. Although the FSP facades carry Feathered Serpent images as principal motifs, the main temple may have depicted a different deity. The recovered fragments suggest that a complex of watery symbols, often associated with the Storm God, probably adorned the temple. The excavation even raises the possibility that the Storm God itself was represented there as the principal deity in the Ciudadela. This proposition is supported by the fact that the Storm God was often associated with the Feathered Serpent in later periods, and seems to have carried the attributes of sacrifice and warfare suggested mythologically by the Feathered Serpent (Pasztory 1976; C. Millon 1988b; Parsons 1988; Taube 2000). Although this reading of FSP imagery is based on fragmented data, the information seems to confirm the divine symbol complex associated with warfare, sacrifice, and authority at the FSP.

In the following three chapters, I focus on the contexts of the FSP's symbolism through the mortuary program that took place at the start of the pyramid's construction, and I try to interpret ritual contents of the graves mainly based on burial patterns and associated offerings.

5

Burials

It is now known that the Teotihuacanos buried their dead mainly under floors in residential areas rather than in cemeteries. Differences in treatment of the dead buried under residences clearly indicate the society's hierarchical organization. However, people of the highest social status still have not been identified among these burials.

Drawing on previous work, the present study deals with particular grave patterns: burial complexes integrated into the city's monuments, which have not been clearly discerned as yet. The burials at the Feathered Serpent Pyramid (Fig. 5) form one of the most complicated complexes found to date, since it possibly contains both dedicatory and elite burials. Exceptionally rich offerings, intricately laid among the burials, add to its complexity. Moreover, Graves 12 and 13 – two multiple graves near the center of the pyramid – and a large pit in front of the staircase were heavily looted in pre-Columbian times, a fact which makes interpretation difficult. Additional postmortem activities have further complicated analyses and interpretation, though to a lesser extent. In addition, several burials that we believe still exist in the pyramid have not been excavated, and there are also limitations in the information available. Despite these problems, the data that I present in this chapter permit as close to a comprehensive analysis as possible of the entire FSP burial complex.

The skeletal collection found at the pyramid is still to be studied more comprehensively by Mexican physical anthropologists (see Chapter 1, note 3). Studies of bone from the FSP have not been made specifically and systematically from the point of view of human sacrifice, cannibalism, or other kinds of ritual behavior (compare with Darling 1995; Pijoan 1981; Schele 1984; Storey 1992: 129–30; Turner and Turner 1995), and no evidence as to cause of death has been reported, although obvious signs of injuries are absent. Ethnic identification of the buried individuals using bone analysis is ongoing and will likely provide more information on this subject. My objective here is to examine the excavation contexts more thoroughly and systematically, paying close attention to grave patterns.

The first FSP graves interpreted as sacrificial were four single graves found at the corners of the pyramid in 1925. Because of their association with the monument, they were considered part of a foundation program (Armillas 1950: 44; Reygadas 1930; Millon 1981: 213; Sempowski 1994: 49). When we found additional graves on the south side of the pyramid during the 1983–84 field season, I proposed that there was a single burial complex of more than sixty people dedicated to the erection of the pyramid (Sugiyama 1989a: 103). As a consequence of the excavations of 1988–89, we now believe that more than 200 people comprised this burial complex.

Although a mass sacrificial ritual was claimed to have taken place, based on the unusually high number of individuals included in the single structure (Cabrera, Sugiyama, and Cowgill 1991), interpretation of them as sacrificial victims still depends exclusively on excavation contexts, without any data concerning cause of death. Responsible in part for this claim, I now believe this initial interpretation needs to be examined in a more scientific manner, since it is possible that persons who died natural deaths were included in the complex, particularly a ruler or royal family members. Our tunnel excavation revealed the possibility that the pyramid included royal graves, which were looted in later Teotihuacan periods (Sugiyama 1998d). Cowgill (1992a: 106) and Millon (1992: 362) already suspected that the mass sacrificial burials were dedicated to a dead ruler or rulers and proposed that the most probable place of a royal grave was the looted Grave 13 (Fig. 8).

With this perspective, I begin my analyses with a review of the excavation contexts of the FSP burials. Since detailed descriptive information of the excavations is available in other publications, only a few relevant points are summarized here. I try to narrow possible interpretations of each grave or propose alternative explanations based on different treatment of the dead and the stratigraphy of the graves, and I argue that all graves except for 12 and 15, and the grave pit in front of the staircase, seem to have comprised a single program dedicated to the erection of the FSP. Stratigraphically, Graves 12 and 15 predate the others: Grave 12 originally may have been an elite grave associated with an earlier structure, which was reused as another sacrificial grave, after its looting, when the FSP was constructed. A grave pit found in front of the FSP staircase (pit 5 in Fig. 5) may have postdated the pyramid's erection. As explained in Chapter 7, I believe that this is one of the best candidates for an elite tomb (if any existed at the FSP) containing a person or people who died a natural death. Because of its exterior location and its grave form (analogous to those in Kaminaljuyú) and the evidence of subsequent looting activities, the grave's principal occupant may have been a ruler.

In the following section, the spatial arrangements of grave features are analyzed to examine the degree to which the burials were patterned, and detected patterning in mortuary treatment is further analyzed in conjunction with the distribution patterns of offerings associated with the burials, to test whether there were differences in mortuary treatment among individuals buried that may denote social hierarchy. As a consequence, cohesiveness among graves and four differentiated groups are suggested.

In the last section, I interpret some burial features revealed by previous analyses, using reconstruction of the bodies, and I argue that distribution of the graves seems to have been arranged in a collective form in accordance with ritual meanings. In particular, the central grave seems to represent the complexity of symbolism involved in this burial complex. The results are discussed further in terms of their sociopolitical implications in the final chapter.

Contextual interpretations

The discoveries of graves around the FSP were made by several projects; since I have adopted the original numbers used in each project, the identification numbering of graves is irregular. Numbers 153, 172, 190, 203, and 204 were given by PAT80–82, while numbers 1 to 17 were used in PTQ88–89. I describe the graves in what I believe is their chronological order, from the earliest to the most recent.

Grave 15

Grave 15 is the earliest burial associated with one of the substructures found in the FSP (Fig. 9); its stratigraphy indicates that it predates Grave 12. Skeletal remains consisted of the pelvis, vertebral column, and right ribs found in anatomical relationship; no other bones from the rest of the body or offerings were found. A partial cranium of an animal touched the vertebrae over the left chest of the incomplete skeleton, and was placed upside down like a receptacle. The meaning of this peculiar entity, which most probably resulted from a ritual, is unknown. Only the location of the associated object at the heart position of the individual suggests, among other possibilities, that sacrificial ritual was involved. The soil stratum in which the skeleton was found was compact, homogeneous, and apparently undisturbed. Unfortunately, specific features of the substructures and their temporal associations are unknown due to lack of excavation; the data suggest, however inconclusively, that the spot had been a place of human sacrifice, perhaps including removal of the heart, before mass sacrifice took place in association with the FSP.

Grave 12

The pit of Grave 12 was found at 3 m west-southwest of the pyramid's center. Stratigraphic data indicate that the grave was earlier than the FSP construction; in addition, this spatial deviation from the pyramid's axis suggests that it did not originally belong to the FSP complex, which shows a highly symmetric patterning of grave distribution (Fig. 5). The grave pit was square (3 m × 3 m) and dug into the subsoil to a depth of 0.9 m. A narrow bench or ledge was found at the southeast and southwest corners of the pit, perhaps indicating that a grave was dug twice in the same place. A posthole was found on the grave floor near the southwest corner of the pit.[1] These data suggest that the grave structure was different from other graves of the FSP complex. Although the stratigraphic data are largely disturbed by later looting activities, they suggest that Grave 12 had been used as an elite grave associated with an earlier structure. The grave seems to have been once disturbed and reused for one of the complex burials when the construction of the FSP began.

The grave was again seriously looted in a later Teotihuacan period, except for a small portion around the northeastern corner. The looters filled the pit with secondary fill after they had emptied nearly all the original contents. A few human bone fragments and offerings were found in the lowest levels of the pit's backfill, perhaps the remains of a multiple burial of the FSP. Impressions of human bones dispersed on the floor also confirm its function as a grave of a multiple burial. Several fragments of obsidian, shell, greenstone, slate, and bones suggest that it was a high-status burial.

Near the northeast corner of the pit, in the second fill, bones of a human adult in anatomical relationship were discovered. The second fill – rocks and mud with grass – is quite different from the original fill of gray soil, and is the same as the nucleus of the FSP. Although the skeleton was incomplete, the bones indicate that the individual was buried in a supine position with an east–west orientation, with hands tied behind the back. I believe that Grave 12, made by reusing an earlier grave, consisted of several individuals who were probably sacrificed for the FSP construction because the burial was covered when the formation of the FSP's nucleus began. However, it is an open question whether it included a person or persons of high social status who died natural deaths.

Grave 14
Discovered intact, Grave 14 was the pyramid's central grave. It contained twenty individuals and exceptionally rich offerings (Figs. 10 and 11). The individuals laid in this central area were not placed in a grave pit but on the hard subsoil and covered with rocks and mud, making the grave unlike any other found at the FSP. A roughly made, dome-like arrangement of rocks defined this central grave area. The stratigraphic data indicate that the individuals were placed in this location at the onset of construction of the FSP. Vertical walls forming the pyramid's nucleus were then built covering the dome-like construction. This was probably a continuous process because the dome (or dome-shaped pile of rocks) lacked facing and had no definitive form and because the materials used for the dome were the same as those of the nucleus.

It is evident that, along with associated offerings, all twenty people formed a single burial event. There is no evidence for reuse, alteration, or disturbance of the primary burial context after the completion of the burial, except for minimal disturbance caused by small animals which would have got in through spaces among rocks from the nearby looters' tunnel.

The positions and orientations of the twenty individuals were diverse and complicated. They were buried with little space between them, some partially overlapping others. Treatment of the individuals was uniform (to be examined in a later chapter), and the distribution of offerings did not provide clear evidence of differential status. Despite the outstanding richness of the burial offerings, I tentatively concluded that the occupants of the central grave were also victims of sacrifice performed on the occasion of the commencement of pyramid construction (Sugiyama 1991b). This interpretation is examined in detail in the following section.

Grave 13
A large, deep pit containing Grave 13 was encountered along the route of the looters' tunnel (Fig. 7), located approximately 9 m west of the pyramid's center and positioned exactly on its east–west centerline. Excavated into the subsoil in quadrangular form (Fig. 8), it was filled after the bodies were laid in it, apparently with no other

structure built in association with it. The roughly made vertical walls around and above it were built as part of the pyramid's nucleus structure after the pit was filled. The grave was later disturbed by looters and subsequently refilled by them as they continued their exploratory tunnels toward the north, south, and west. Only a small portion of the original fill was found, near the western edge; the material used was the same as the pyramid's rubble fill. This clearly suggests that grave preparation was integrated into the pyramid construction at its initial stage. No indication of the reuse of the grave was observed in this original fill.

The remains of one complete and one partial skeleton were uncovered in the pit's undisturbed fill, in anatomical relationship and in fairly good condition. Impressions of bones on the subsoil floor were faintly visible in the looted area, confirming that the pit had been used for a multiple burial. Above the floor was a layer of loosely laid rocks in which a large number of fragmented bones were recovered with grave offerings (Fig. 8).

This grave has been considered by Cowgill and Millon to be likely a royal grave. Their interpretation is based mainly on offerings of exceptionally high quality, the grave's size, and its location. The fact that the undisturbed individual, roughly protected by rock fill, wore unusual ornaments also seems to support their intuitive interpretation. I too believe that this grave contained individuals different from those buried in the other graves, in both social status and ritual treatment. However, as I will discuss in detail, my analyses suggest that the grave was another kind of multiple sacrificial burial rather than a royal burial.

The complete skeleton of a single individual, an unusually robust adult male, was discovered near the west edge of the pit, buried face down with extremely flexed knees tucked under the chest. He possessed outstanding ornaments, including a pair of greenstone ear spools of especially large size, twenty-one large greenstone beads, a "Tlaloc"-style nose pendant, and an obsidian eccentric. The other, incomplete individuals in Grave 13 were found without offerings, probably because they had been looted.

Apart from those found in Graves 12 and 13, a large number of bone fragments and offerings were found in the fill along the floors of the looters' tunnel. They were interpreted as originally belonging to individuals buried in Graves 12 and 13 according to the stratigraphy of the looters' tunnel. This interpretation was made on the supposition that the looters disturbed only these two graves, and that all artifacts found in the looters' tunnel originally belonged to the persons buried in Graves 12 and 13. However, it is also possible that a few artifacts, especially pottery, came from unknown caches that had been looted. These materials are included in offerings analyzed in Chapter 6.

South interior of the pyramid

Two multiple graves (Graves 2 and 4) were discovered during the excavation of the South Tunnel. Excavation profiles provide information about their stratigraphic relationships to the pyramid. Grave 2 was located 10 m from the south facade at subsoil level and consisted of a long, shallow pit in the subsoil and four roughly made, vertical stone walls which were, at the same time, part of the pyramid fill. The walls enclosing the burial space stood on the edge of the pit, and the tomb was unroofed and lacked an entrance. Stratigraphic data suggest that the interment was carried out as a single operation at the initial stage of construction of the FSP and that the chamber was neither reused nor disturbed in later periods. After the mortuary activities, the grave was completely filled with the same kinds of rocks and mud used to form the nucleus of the pyramid. In other words, the grave became part of the pyramid structure with no further access. The remains of eight people were found in Grave 2, evenly spaced and arranged in a row. Some of the individuals were found with arms and hands positioned as if tied behind the individuals' backs.

Grave 4 was found 13.5 m north of the pyramid's south facade. The grave pit and chamber walls were similar to those of Grave 2, except that the former was much longer than the latter. The buried persons were different from those of Grave 2 in several aspects: eighteen individuals, positioned in a row, were accompanied by a large number of ornaments and offerings. Burial types were similar to those of Graves 190, 204, 5, and 6, found outside the pyramid. Several individuals were found with arms positioned on their backs, as if the hands had been tied together.

Stratigraphy from the South Tunnel shows clearly that Graves 2 and 4 and the pyramid are related. The pyramid fill was homogeneous throughout, and numerous unfaced walls of rocks ran irregularly north–south and east–west, intersecting each other. The tunnel profile indicates that the nucleus was not always formed from the inside out. Instead, the formation of the nucleus at this southern portion began near Grave 4. After the chambers were completely filled, the formation of the walls of the nucleus continued outward. The two graves were evidently programmed simultaneously as a single unit: it is possible that they were prepared simultaneously to the central grave on the beginning of pyramid construction. However, whether the bodies in Graves 2 and 4 were placed at the same time as those in the central grave is unknown.

Upper part of the pyramid
At the beginning of Marquina's exploration in 1922, three burials of fragmented bones lacking apparent anatomical relationships were discovered on the top of the pyramid mound. The discoverer interpreted the burials as skeletal remains exhumed from other graves. It is also possible that they were remains of a primary or sacrificial burial altered after death by human and/or nonhuman agencies.

According to Marquina (1922: vol. 1, 159–61), two isolated, broken skulls were discovered at the southwest part of the summit, apparently within the platform nucleus, on which we also have information from our recent excavations. Several vertebrae, fragments of long bones, and ribs were found between the two skulls. Many offerings of high quality were found in a concentration with one of the skulls, and other offerings were found near another skull (Sugiyama 1989a: table 3).

Marquina concluded that these bones were exhumed from other burials and reburied at the top of the pyramid for the following reasons: (1) the sepulchers were not well constructed, the first two being formed by the walls of the construction system, while the third was said to have been placed in "an irregular pit which was filled with earth and loosely piled rocks after inhumation" (Marquina 1922: vol. 1, 161); (2) the poor condition in which the bones were found, absence of some bones, and the presence of old fractures; and (3) the association of ritual objects.

In my opinion, none of this evidence points to secondary burial. We obtained data indicating that some of the sacrificial burials at the pyramid were not protected by any grave structure (Grave 14). Concerning the third sepulcher, a pit could have been used for a primary burial. We also observed many skeletons in the fill that were heavily damaged by rocks of the pyramid nucleus, and bones found on the upper part of the platform may have incurred breakage by similar means. Old fractures do not necessarily mean that the bones were exhumed from other graves. We found bones that were very fragmented, and others, including long bones that had completely disintegrated. Those of Graves 2 and 4 were found in particularly poor condition although they had been located directly on the subsoil under rock fill of the same type. Based on my excavation experience, if the bodies of sacrificial victims were originally located in unstable fill and rocks at approximately 17 m above the subsoil, their bones would have been crushed, fragmented, and disarticulated. Poor bone preservation, which may have resulted from this postmortem process, apparently led Marquina to think that the skeletal materials were exhumed from another grave. He mentions that many parts of a body were actually found in Sepulcher I, including "cranium, fragments of mandibles, ... teeth and molars, ... a large quantity of vertebrae, fragments of long bones (extremities?), ribs, etc." (1922: vol. 1, 159). Moreover, if the victims had been dismembered, as in the case of Grave 15, identification of their partial bodies as sacrificial remains would have been difficult, given poor bone preservation.

Since no other detailed information is available, we cannot add to these speculations; however, I wish to point out that the human bones found at the top of the pyramid might have been a primary burial, possibly part of the sacrificial complex or an elite grave. The possibility remains open that the FSP burial complex was composed not only of graves prepared at ground level, but also of graves at higher levels.[2]

North and south sides

Two multiple graves were located on the south side of the pyramid exactly on its north–south central line (Fig. 5). Grave 190 contained a row of eighteen individuals, laid in a long pit parallel to the pyramid's south side. Grave 17 consisted of a row of eight individuals with fewer offerings, placed in a shorter pit located south of Grave 190. Two additional individual burials (Graves 153 and 203) were found in rectangular pits, one placed on each end of the Grave 190 pit in symmetric relationship to one another with respect to the same central line. All pits were made in the subsoil and sealed by the lowest floor of the FSP and there were no stratigraphic indications of later intrusion or reuse. Bones were found in anatomical relationships, although some parts of the skeletons had been fragmented and/or disarticulated by natural agencies. The graves found on the north side of the FSP (Graves 204, 16, 172, and 1) mirror the spatial pattern of the south complex with respect to the pyramid's east–west central line. Many individuals in these graves were found with arms crossed and positioned on the back as if they had been tied.

Stratigraphic data indicate that these graves dated to the same period as the FSP and adjacent complexes. It is evident that at least one substructure existed before the FSP, since the pit for Grave 190 was prepared by cutting into the wall of a substructure. The pit was used once and later filled with earth and sealed with the concrete floor of the FSP. It contained stone fragments and sand, which might have been derived from finishing or carving the FSP facades (Sugiyama 1991a: 289). A similar kind of sand was also found in PTQ88–89's test pits on the north side of the FSP (Martin Dudek 1988, personal communication), and in pits 3, 4, and 6 in the vicinity of the Adosada platform (Cowgill 1996, personal communication), suggesting that the pit for Grave 190 was made after, or while, the sculpturing work was taking place somewhere near the FSP. These data support the conjecture that the sacrifice for the burials mentioned here was executed toward the end of the construction program.

Additional evidence suggests later preparation of a pit during the pyramid's construction. The pits for Graves 1 and 203 cut through a low, roughly made platform, the foundation of the stone-block facade of the pyramid, indicating that the grave was made after the rock nucleus had been laid as a base for the sculptural heads. How much of the nucleus had been prepared before grave preparation is not clear; however, the data support the idea that not all the graves of the FSP were laid at the same time but were probably made intermittently, as construction work progressed. In particular, it is unlikely that inside and outside burials occurred simultaneously.

East (posterior) side

Excavation of Front A in our project located eight complete and incomplete graves (Graves 3, 5, 6, 7, 8, 9, 10, and 11) on the pyramid's east side, as well as one long narrow pit (pit 2 in Fig. 5). Six graves (Graves 3, 5, 6, 7, 10, and 11), found in grave pits made in subsoil and considered parts of the FSP burial complex, were symmetrically arranged with respect to the pyramid's east–west central line and covered by its concrete floor, the earliest surviving floor in this area.

An extensive excavation immediately east of the pyramid's base uncovered a small pit grave containing Grave 3. This had been heavily disturbed in post-Conquest times, but several bones from both hands of a person, in anatomical relationship, were recovered on the floor. The excavators interpreted them as the joined hands of possibly another sacrificial victim whose arms were crossed behind his back. Since many other buried persons recovered from the FSP exhibited such a position, our speculative interpretation may be valid.

Pit 2, located exactly on the east–west central line of the pyramid and without any burial contents (Fig. 5), apparently was part of the burial complex and may have been used as a depository of other kinds of material, perhaps perishable objects. Only three complete unworked shells were found within this long, narrow pit, near its floor and close to its west edge.

A pair of north–south pits, found on the north and south sides of pit 2 and each containing the well-preserved remains of nine individuals, were designated Graves 5 and 6 respectively. They were unearthed with stratigraphy similar to those on the pyramid's north and south sides. Forearms of all individuals were found behind the body, crossed at the wrists or with hands together.

Two more burial pits were found east of the north–south pits, again symmetrically aligned, one on each side of pit 2. Called Graves 10 and 11, each contained four individuals with offerings of poorer quality than those previously described. Positions of the individuals were also similar to those in Graves 5, and 6, suggesting that they were, likewise, victims of sacrifice.

Graves 5, 6, 10, and 11 were found intact with no evidence of reuse or alteration. Three later concrete floors were recognized by our extensive excavations, including one laid immediately after the grave pits were filled and serving as the first floor associated with the FSP. Stratigraphic data indicate that these graves were contemporaneous with those found on the pyramid's south and north sides. The locations of all these graves also indicate a strong association with the FSP.

One pit similar to that of Grave 3 was found east of pit 2 on the pyramid's east–west central line; its location suggests that it was also a grave pit (Grave 7) although no information about the original burial contents was available because of looting. Other small pits were found near, but slightly away from, the east–west central line. They seem to be remains from an earlier construction program that may have been associated with the substructures or earlier graves found inside the pyramid.

West (principal) side
Many offerings have been reported to have been found in an excavation in front of the staircase of the FSP. Others have been discovered further west under the Adosada (Pérez 1939; Rubín de la Borbolla 1947; Cowgill and Cabrera 1991). The intact objects of high quality, located in fill without clear evidence of association with burials, may have been independent caches, but some seem to have been part of offerings associated with a large pit discovered in 1988 in front of the pyramid's staircase.

This large pit was found 2 m west of the staircase exactly on the pyramid's east–west central line. According to limited excavation data, no skeletal materials or offerings have been found in it, since it had been thoroughly looted before it was sealed by the Adosada construction. However, a previous excavation report (Pérez 1939) mentions that bone fragments were recovered from this area. Excavation by Cowgill and Oralia Cabrera in 1988 revealed that a masonry wall of stones laid in mud mortar had been raised on the pit's south edge. Located in front of the pyramid's staircase, the structure may have been a low platform or altar covering the grave pit. These data lead me to suspect that the pit might have been made for a primary burial associated with the FSP. Its location, accessible after the completion of the pyramid's construction, suggests that it may once have contained the body of the person responsible for the FSP's construction.

The question may remain unanswered, because the pit had already been looted before, if not at the time of, the Adosada's construction. Lack of recorded excavations early in the twentieth century, and inconsistencies in later reports, make precise interpretation difficult (Sugiyama 1989a: 98–102). The 1988 excavation revealed that a further excavation and consolidation operation between the FSP and the Adosada took place sometime after Marquina's discovery in 1918–22 and before Pérez's excavation in 1939, although there is no record of such work. The operation must have removed the fill of the burial pit down to the grave floor. Our excavation (pit 5, Fig. 5) uncovered additional modern materials in the grave pit, including the stone and concrete base that supports the modern east wall of the Adosada. These serious limitations prevent detailed interpretation of the pit; however, another hypothetical interpretation is proposed later, based on other data.

The four corners of the pyramid
Four graves were discovered at the four corners of the pyramid's base (Dosal 1925a, 1925b), each containing an individual and associated offerings. Graves were found under various floors, within pits dug in subsoil. These stratigraphic and locational data suggest that the burials correspond to the construction of the FSP and were contemporaneous with other graves found on its four sides (discussed above). Associated offerings are similar among them, including 14 obsidian projectile points and some 400 pieces of shell beads worked into the form of human teeth (Siliceo 1925). According to the drawings attached to the excavation report, the hands of the individuals were not found crossed behind their backs; however, the burials were interpreted as dedication-sacrifices because of their apparent association with the monument.

Burial patterns
In this section, graves previously identified as part of the FSP burial complex are analyzed. Grave features, burial features, and characteristics of the deceased were examined to determine any spatial patterning. As discussed in Chapter 1, analyses were carried out mainly to detect ideological factors involved in the burials. The section examines the degree to which the graves were patterned and how the burials may have been related. Finally, the overall patterns are interpreted in terms of state symbolism.

Buried individuals may have been (1) captives from foreign enemies, (2) elites, soldiers, servants, or persons of other social categories chosen from within Teotihuacan society or related ethnic groups, or (3) a combination of these categories. They may have been killed, may have died voluntarily for this dedication ritual, or may have died a natural death and been brought to the pyramid. Analyses of osteological materials may provide biological information about the individuals and causes of death. The mortuary analyses presented here aim primarily to disclose ideational features involved in grave patterns rather than ethnic identification of the dead. However, they may also suggest certain social dimensions reflected in ritual terms. Chapter 8 discusses possible social implications following a search for what Teotihuacanos intended to manifest symbolically with the grave complex and offerings.

Grave forms at the FSP vary. Except for the central grave and those putatively in the upper part of the pyramid, all were laid in pits cut into the subsoil, and some had masonry walls. The hypothesis examined here is that varied sizes and forms of graves, positions of the individuals interred, and other burial features were not randomly or unconsciously chosen. Apparently, they were determined neither by the demands of the architecture nor by other practical reasons that surrounded them. It is proposed that symbolic meanings were the principal motive for these features. Cosmological, cosmogonical, calendrical, mythical, ritual, or other types of religious meanings may have been embodied in this ritual display, and social dimensions of the deceased would have been related to these ideological principles. The features I analyze indicate certain patterns with cohesive meanings that are unusual in mortuary practices known from other places at Teotihuacan.

In this section, I discuss burial patterns for each grave detected in the number of people buried, the form, depth, and total floor area of the grave occupied by the dead, position of the body, orientation of body-axis, direction in which the body faced, degree of body flexion, position of the arms, sex, age, and dental modification. In some cases, the pattern is not clear, while in others the regularity detected is useful to approach an emic conception of the burial program.

Distribution of bodies was diagrammed according to each feature. These data and some statistical generalizations are used for my interpretations of the grave complex. Since one feature is likely related to another, their correlation is also discussed.

Number of persons buried

The number of persons buried was evidently one of the principal features affecting other characteristics of the FSP grave complex. As shown in Figure 5, important numbers in the Mesoamerican calendar system and cosmology seem to have been applied to determine the grave form. Intricate numerical combinations of persons buried in each grave were found to have a symbolic spatial pattern. Since the entire burial complex has not yet been excavated, the decoding of the system is still hypothetical; however, I discuss here a few features to point out possible calendrical and cosmological associations.

Eight single and thirteen multiple graves (eleven intact, and two disturbed) have been excavated to date. The number of individuals found in each multiple grave was 4, 8, 9, 18, or 20. As suggested by their locations, the graves apparently were not independent of one another but clearly combined to form subsets. One typical combination, on both the south and north exteriors, is $18 + 8 + 1 + 1$ (Graves 190, 17, 153, 203 and Graves 204, 16, 1, 172 respectively). The $18 + 8$ combination was also found on the south interior in Graves 2 and 4. Although two additional individual graves $(1 + 1)$ have not been discovered yet, it is possible they will be found. On the pyramid's east (posterior) side, the configuration is different, but the combination of $18 + 8$ is evidently intended by Graves 5 and 6 $(9 + 9)$ and Graves 10 and 11 $(4 + 4)$ respectively. Two individual graves seem to have been involved, and

Mexican archaeologists dug for them without success in an area south of Grave 6.
I believe that the two disturbed burials found on the east–west axis (Graves 3 and 7)
were their equivalents; although the contents of these looted burials are unknown,
it is clear from their locations and sizes that they were part of this subset. The fact
that the west grave (Grave 3) was bigger than the east grave (Grave 7) supports this
interpretation, since it is a pattern found on the south and north sides. If this is
true, it indicates that the same combination, 18 + 8 + 1 + 1, was applied on the east
side.

Significant calendrical dates/numbers in this subset, such as 20, 18, and 13 (9 + 4
from the east side), can result from their combination. They are meaningful numbers
for the 260-day ritual calendar, called the Tonalpohualli in Nahuatl, which consisted
of the combination of twenty day signs with thirteen numbers. The solar calendar,
which consisted of eighteen months of twenty days plus five extra days, also appears
to have influenced this burial complex.

These numbers were related to specific Mesoamerican cosmologies and mythologies, with which the calendar system was closely tied. As described in Chapter 2
(Fig. 12), the Mesoamerican cosmos was divided into thirteen upper layers, nine
under layers, and four equal parts on the earth that corresponded to the cardinal
directions (Sahagún 1977: bk. 7). López (1990: 78) presents a version in which
the space was divided vertically into nine upper world and nine Underworld layers,
forming a universe of eighteen layers; the nine layers of the upper world were combined with four directions on earth to form thirteen layers. All these numbers can
be found in the burial complex, which was spatially distributed in an intriguing way.

Clemency Coggins (1980: 733; 1993: 144) proposes that the count of twenty,
which was basic to the calendar, was as fundamental to the organization and naming
of the Teotihuacan military as it was for the Maya, whose single word for war and
warrior signified a calendar unit of twenty. Although such associations have not been
identified in languages of the Mexican Highlands, Hassig (1988: 55–58) argues from
fragmentary ethnohistorical documentation that internal divisions in the Aztec army
were based on a vigesimal (base-20) numerical system. For his discussion, he cites
Bandelier (1880: 116, 118) who finds that paintings designated each unit of twenty
men for military organization by a banner, and that the Nahuatl word for flag or
banner was *pantli*, also the pictographic element indicating 20. At the FSP, the fact
that burial sets of twenty individuals (18 + 1 + 1) were most likely composed of
male soldiers suggests that the Mesoamerican calendrical and vigesimal system was
used in the grave complex as an organizational principle for the Teotihuacan state's
military units. The distribution of the mass-grave complex was made more intricate
by the fact that an eight-female grave (4 + 4) with martial objects was associated
with each twenty-male (18 + 1 + 1) grave set.

Location and form of graves
Although the form of each grave group differs significantly, certain uniformity exists.
Symmetry is a basic principle for this uniformity, in both grave form and grave
distribution (Fig. 5). Pits for multiple graves found on the exterior northern and

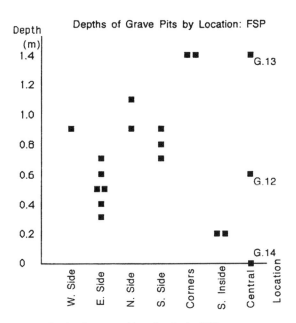

Fig. 39 Correlation between depth of grave and location in the FSP.

southern sides of the pyramid (Graves 190, 17, 204, and 16) share similar widths, forms, and depths, differing only in lengths; length varies by the number of people buried in each row. Graves 153 and 172 form a pair; Graves 203 and 1 form another pair. Each pair is in symmetric relationship to the other, sharing a similar form, depth, and size. Graves 5, 6, 10, and 11 form another subset of multiple graves, as indicated by their similar pit forms and depths, and Graves 3 and 7 could be an addition to the pattern, since they shared similar depths. Independent pits found at the pyramid's four corners appear to form a group, with shared forms and orientations. Grave 12's location was asymmetrical, originally corresponding to an earlier structure, and the form of the grave pit was quite different from the others, further supporting a chronological difference, indicated by a comparison of stratigraphic data between Grave 12 and the others.

Grave 13's pit was unusually large and deep and had no counterpart to the east of Grave 14, a fact proved by our tunnel excavation (Fig. 7). Although these unique features of grave form and the grave's unusual contents gave the impression that the burial was special, it is not sufficiently singular to demonstrate that it contained a ruler's body.

That the pit depth was deliberately controlled for all FSP burials is suggested by uniformity of depth. Except for graves inside the pyramid, grave depth is correlated with location (Fig. 39). Grave 13 was placed in the deepest pit, suggesting intentional differentiation. The grave pits at the four corners also had approximately the same depth, but since these were not among those with rich offerings, depth may not be a relevant feature to identify Grave 13 as a royal tomb. Neither was size an indication that Grave 13 was a royal interment, since it was smaller than the grave in front of the staircase. Rather, pit size may have been a consequence of the number of individuals buried in it.

Grave 14, located at the center of the pyramid, was the most distinctive grave, without any apparent counterpart. Yet, despite its centrality, it was the only one laid directly on subsoil, without any grave pit. The deliberateness of depth 0 (no pit) for the central burial may have had a specific ritual meaning, rather than indicating a lack of concern for those interred. In Grave 14, twenty people were directly covered with rocks and mud without protective chamber or walls. A roughly made, dome-like structure was apparently a stage of the fill process, which was immediately followed by the building of walls that formed the pyramid's nucleus. The apparently "careless" preparation of this grave contrasts with the exceptionally rich offerings found in it that suggest the extreme importance of the grave.

The pit found at the foot of the pyramid staircase was the largest in the burial complex, although its precise length is not yet known. Other features characterize it as a unique grave. Based on the proposed pattern of elite burials discussed in Chapter 7, I believe that a person of high status, who was not sacrificed, was included in this grave. This grave pit, differing from other burials found in and around the FSP (which were covered before the pyramid's completion), would have been built or used after the completion of the platform. This leaves open the possibility that someone responsible for construction of the pyramid was later buried there.

Burial area

Because of looting activities, the number of individuals buried in Graves 12 and 13 is unknown; however, measurements allow a range of possible numbers of people (Table 2). The fact that the dead were laid close to one another permits this calculation based on an assumption that the graves were used in a way similar to the others. Floor space used for the burials usually was not the full extent of the grave floors. Thus, the burial area was calculated as the area in which bones in anatomical relationship were recovered; the areas were divided by the number of persons interred in each grave in order to calculate the area per individual (column B.A./People in Table 2), and the areas correlated to the position of the dead. People in semi-extended positions (Graves 5, 6, 10, and 11) occupied a larger area than those in seated positions (Graves 190, 204, and 2). Grave 14 had people in both extended and seated positions. In addition, the bodies were deliberately overlapped to a certain degree, which made the average area of an interred individual in this central grave relatively small (0.36 m^2). These are the most reliable data for the calculation of the number of the individuals in Graves 12 and 13, since the central grave shares more features with these graves than with any others found at the FSP.

Grave 12 was heavily looted, so that the first stage of the burial in the substructure is completely unknown. At the latter level, corresponding to the FSP, in which the pit was reused as a part of the burial complex, there appears to have been a multiple grave of possibly sacrificed individuals. If the entire floor of the grave had been covered by bodies, about thirteen people would have been buried there; however, some of the original fill near the northeast corner, untouched by looters, indicates that this was an area also untouched by the burial. Based on this fact, the number of

Table 2 *Quantitative data from the graves at the Feathered Serpent Pyramid*

Burial No.	Indiv.	Burial Area	B.A./People	Depth(m)	Location
Pit #5	(looted)	?	?	0.9	W Side
5	9	3.91	0.43	0.4	E Side
6	9	3.71	0.41	0.5	E Side
10	4	1.94	0.49	0.6	E Side
11	4	1.88	0.47	0.7	E Side
3	1? (looted)	–	–	0.5	E Side
7	1? (looted)	–	–	0.3	E Side
1	1	–	–	1.1	N Side
204	18	6.27	0.35	0.9	N Side
190	18	4.58	0.25	0.9	S Side
153	1	–	–	0.7	S Side
203	1	–	–	0.8	S Side
SW	1	–	–	1.4	Corner
NW	1	–	–	1.4	Corner
4	18	7.2	0.4	0.2	S Inside
2	8	2.92	0.37	0.2	S Inside
12	(looted)	(4.62)floor	?	0.6	Central
13	(looted)	(9.87)floor	?	1.4	Central
14	20	7.29	0.36	0	Central
Average			0.39	0.71	

people interred in this grave probably was less than twelve, perhaps as few as eight to ten.

The looters left a larger quantity of original fill in Grave 13, from which we recovered valuable data. As I explain later, the grave form may have been similar to that of Grave 14, with floor space suggesting that twenty-seven people could have been laid in it, as in the case of Grave 14. In reality, the number of people buried would have been twenty or fewer than twenty, as indicated by vacant areas covered with original fill. Since twenty and eighteen are common numbers of sacrificial victims found interred in groups at the FSP, these are other possible numbers of individuals included in this grave.

General body position

The position of bodies was classified as follows: seated, supine (facing up), prone (facing down), right lateral, and left lateral. The judgment of body position was taken from the position of the trunk (thorax, vertebrae, and hip bones), rather than from the position of the head or inferior extremities. In the case of seated burials, the bones of upper bodies were found to have fallen down, partly losing anatomical relationship. In many cases, the classification was clear; in others (positions between seated and prone, seated and lateral, lateral and supine, and lateral and prone) categories were not evident. Many originally may have been laid in seated positions and fell over during the filling of the pit with earth and rocks. The upper bodies

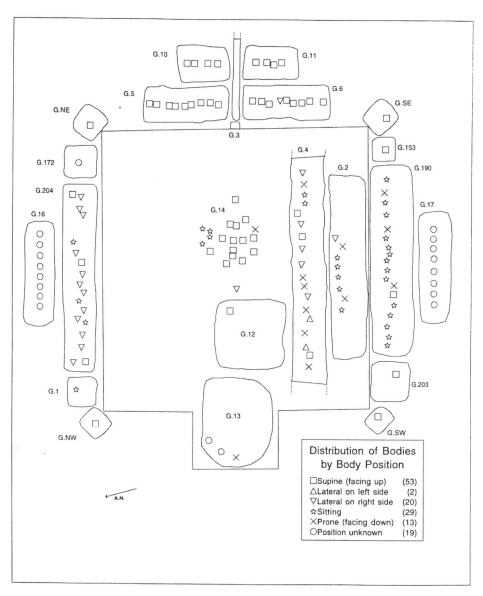

Fig. 40 Spatial distribution of the burials by general body position. The size of graves has been enlarged out of proportion to the pyramid so that individuals can be appreciated. GIS map: author.

slumped as the flesh decomposed; this was indicated by small spaces often found in the fill above the burials and floors above them that had sunk. Examples include the graves found on the pyramid's north–south axis (excepting the central grave). I took into account the position in which the bodies were actually discovered instead of presuming postmortem shifting, and I later interpreted the original positions contextually, through analyses of these factual data.

One position apparently predominated in each multiple grave (Fig. 40). The supine position was used for Graves 5, 6, 10, 11, and 14 and those found at the pyramid's corners. In the first four graves on the pyramid's east side, body position was homogeneous. In contrast, Grave 14 included bodies in other positions; four individuals in the northern part, in seated positions, and one individual on the west, in the right lateral position, stand out in this central grave. Body positions suggest that the four individuals buried on the north side (individuals 14-A, B, C, and D) were correlated with those found along the north–south axis whose predominant body position was seated. Associated offerings suggest that these are analogous to Graves 153 and 172.

In Graves 190 and 2, the seated position predominated. Although the positions in Graves 4 and 204 were less homogeneous than in others, there were certain trends. The prone and right lateral positions were prevalent in Grave 4, while the right lateral was predominant in Grave 204. The last two graves included bodies whose positions were difficult to assess because of the effects of postmortem agencies.

In general, the burials along the east–west axis of the pyramid were distinct from those along the north–south axis. Particularly, the supine position used in graves on the east side and those near the center, including Grave 12, contrasts strongly with those found on the south and north sides.

Orientation of body axis

In Figure 41, the distribution of bodies is shown by body-axis orientation; extreme points of the spinal column found in anatomical relationship were used to establish the alignment of each body. Alignment was calculated in relation to astronomical north. These numerical data were always measured clockwise from the north and the numbers later converted into eight directional categories: North, Northeast, East, Southeast, and so on, each with a range of 45 degrees. The category North measured from 353 to 38 degrees from astronomical north to reflect Teotihuacan North, which is 15.5 degrees east of astronomical north. In the same way, measurements between 38 and 83, 83 and 128, 128 and 173, 173 and 218, 218 and 263, 263 and 308, and 308 and 353 were expressed as Teotihuacan Northeast, East, Southeast, South, Southwest, West, and Northwest respectively, in order to examine the correspondence between the pyramid and body orientation. The distribution map was prepared by converting these categories into eight symbols, as indicated in the legend. In addition to these categories, all individuals whose body positions were identified as seated were assigned to the category Upward, since the tops of their heads were presumably pointing upward.

The variable Upward also shows certain subgroups which are similar to, but significantly different from, the pattern suggested by body position. As we have seen, burials on the east side show homogeneity among themselves, all individuals having been laid with the tops of their heads pointing toward the pyramid. Many individuals in the central grave had a body orientation toward Teotihuacan East. Again, four individuals on the north side and the far western individual in the central grave contrast strongly with this East–West directional trend, perhaps reflecting similarities to those on the North–South axis.

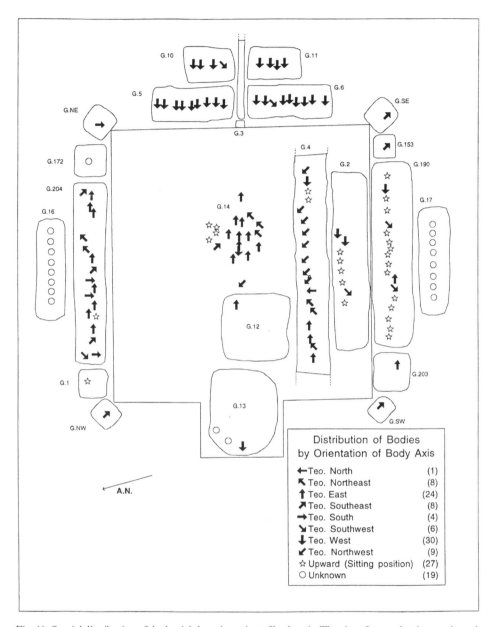

Fig. 41 Spatial distribution of the burials by orientation of body axis. The size of graves has been enlarged out of proportion to the pyramid. GIS map: author.

Grave 190 consisted primarily of people with Upward body-axes, the seated position. Grave 2 on the same side had a similar orientation. The orientation of the individuals in Grave 4 differed significantly from these two, consisting of individuals with a wider variety of orientations. Teotihuacan North (Northwest, North, and Northeast) was strongly represented in this grave, while no Teotihuacan South-oriented (Southeast, South, and Southwest) individuals were found. Grave 4 was divided into two groups, with the individual uniquely oriented to Teotihuacan North at the center: the East group consisted of Teotihuacan Northwest- and West-oriented persons, and the West group with Northeast- and East-oriented persons. In other words, individuals on both sides of the Teotihuacan North-oriented person were apparently set toward the center of the pyramid, according to their body orientations. However, this pattern is not indicated either by other variables or by associated offerings. The body orientations in Grave 204 contrast significantly with those of the southern group: the majority of bodies in this grave were oriented towards Teotihuacan Southeast (East, Southeast, and South), and no particular individuals stand out from the others.

In general, it seems that individuals in the multiple graves of the peripheral area (Graves 4, 5, 6, 10, 11, and 204) were intentionally oriented with their heads toward the pyramid. Graves 190 and 2 cannot be judged in this way because the predominant body-axis orientation of the individuals is Upward. However, the relationship of Graves 190 and 2 with the pyramid is clearly indicated by the orientation of body facing. This is not true for individual graves found around the pyramid (Graves 153, 203, 1, Northeast, Southeast, Southwest, and Northwest), where Teotihuacan Southeast was predominant for some reason.

In the central area, the pattern is quite different: the principal orientation of the burial was Teotihuacan East, as indicated by the majority of people oriented toward Teotihuacan East (10), Northeast (3), and Southeast (1). Although body orientation in Graves 12 and 13 is not known because of looting, two individuals found intact again show the primacy of an East–West orientation rather than a North–South one. Together, these data indicate that people in the peripheral area were deliberately buried in relation with the pyramid's center; in turn, those near the center of that pyramid were buried with an East–West orientation.

Orientation of body facing

The direction in which bodies faced was recorded in general descriptive terms: North, Northeast, East, Southeast, etc. (Fig. 42) relative to astronomical north, since no precise determination was possible. Body facing is clearly related to position and orientation: in cases of prone or supine positions, the orientation of body facing is automatically determined – facing-down or facing-up respectively. In cases of lateral position, the orientation of body face depends on the orientation of the body-axis. Only in the case of the seated position was body facing independent of the other variables.

Burials on the east side, those near the center, and those at the corners of the pyramid belong to the same up-facing group. Only four seated individuals in the central grave distinctively show orientation to the south. Three multiple graves on the south side (Graves 190, 2, and 4) strongly indicate south associations, particularly those seated. In contrast, Grave 204 on the north side is characterized by bodies facing generally North. In other words, individuals found on either the south or north sides were facing outside or away from the pyramid, as if guarding it. This is consistent with patterns of body axis orientation, which indicate that peripheral burials were positioned with reference to the pyramid.

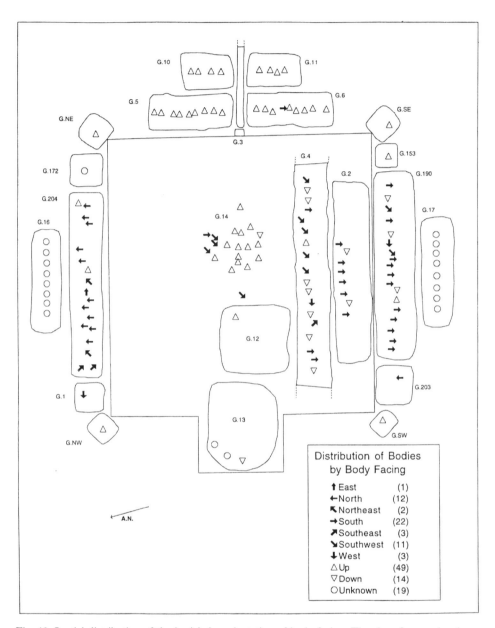

Fig. 42 Spatial distribution of the burials by orientation of body facing. The size of graves has been enlarged out of proportion to the pyramid. GIS map: author.

Body flexion

The degree of body flexion was measured at the point of articulation of the spinal column and the femur. These measurements were divided into five categories: extended, semiextended, semiflexed, flexed, and extremely flexed (Fig. 43). To a certain extent, this variable was related to the other variables: seated individuals were obviously not extended. Pit size may also have limited the degree of body extension.

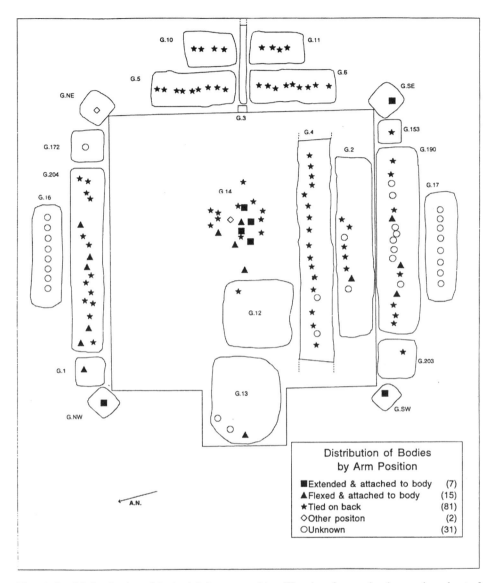

Fig. 43 Spatial distribution of the burials by arm position. The size of graves has been enlarged out of proportion to the pyramid. GIS map: author.

It is evident that flexed position was dominant in this burial complex and may reflect body preparation. As suggested by a few remains of fiber found with skeletons, bodies may have been tied into bundles. No clear, distinctive trends in body flexion exist among the burials found in the peripheral area, although some contained more flexed bodies than others. This may mean that the bodies found in flexed positions were prepared for burial in the same way.

Most distinct is the central grave, which contained nine individuals in extended or semiextended position, a highly unusual position in Teotihuacan (Sempowski 1994: 139–40). Eight of the individuals were among a group of twelve located close to the

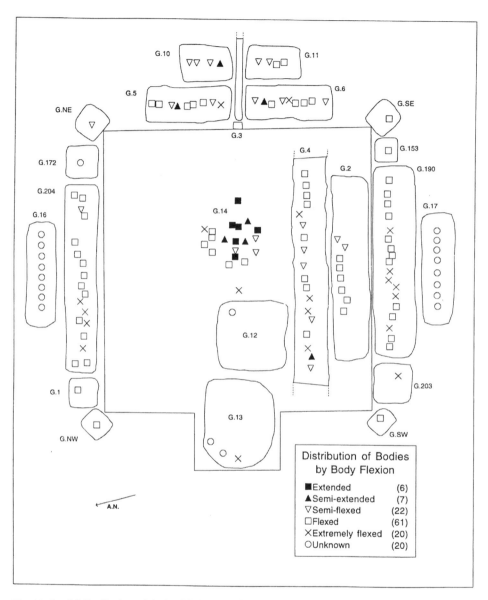

Fig. 44 Spatial distribution of the burials by body flexion posture. The size of graves has been enlarged out of proportion to the pyramid. GIS map: author.

east–west axis of the pyramid; five individuals with flexed bodies, found to the north in Grave 14, were similar to those located in the peripheral area. Also worth noting is that the westernmost individuals in Graves 13 and 14 were extremely flexed.

The contrast between extended and flexed positions is explicit in the burial complex. The distinctively different spatial distribution of these positions could have been related to several features: a distinction between burials prepared in different ways and/or in different places; circumstantial grave features which limited certain positions; or other technical, physical preconditions of the burials or graves. In any case, body flexion seems to have been arranged intentionally, and ritual meanings would have been attached to these positions, as suggested by symbolic forms (in particular those of Grave 14, discussed later) which otherwise would not have been necessary.

Arm position

Since the discovery in 1983 of Grave 190, which contained many individuals with their arms crossed behind their backs, special attention has been paid to the position of superior extremities. Arm positions have been classified into four categories: arms crossed or touching on the back, arms flexed and adjoining the body, arms extended and adjoining the body, and arms not adjoining (Fig. 44). The superior extremities of seated bodies have rarely been found in clear anatomical relationships, because the bodies collapsed upon decomposing.

Seventy-seven percent of all persons buried at the FSP whose arm positions are known had arms crossed on their backs as if they had been tied. This peculiar arm position was reported for at least some individuals in all intact, multiple graves. More than 81 percent of the individuals found in the nine multiple graves had arms crossed behind the back, which may indicate an unwilling death forced by others. Graves 5, 6, 10, and 11 contained only individuals whose arms appear to have been tied behind their backs. The position of flexed arms adjoining the body without being crossed behind the back is frequent in graves with a high percentage of people whose arms were crossed behind the back. This position may also be an indication of sacrifice, as the people in this position were perhaps also bound. Ninety-one percent of the persons in the burial complex were dealt with in one of these two ways: with arms crossed behind the back or arms flexed and adjoining the body.

This distribution suggests that all grave pits included sacrificial victims, and that this pattern was strongly and homogeneously manifested in the peripheral area.

In contrast, the central grave (Grave 14) was characterized by the lowest percentage of people with arms behind their backs (55 percent). This grave, together with those at the four corners of the pyramid, is also distinguished from the others by individuals with a rare arm position, arms extended and/or not close to the body, a position that may reflect differential treatment among the sacrificial burials that implies distinctiveness of a certain kind, involving only Grave 14.

Sex

Sex was determined by several Mexican physical anthropologists, and different opinions on the sex of deteriorated skeletons were proposed by various researchers (Sugiyama 1989a; Mercado 1987; Serrano et al. 1989, personal communication, and 1991). The designations of sex and age taken into account for my analyses are the final ones determined by Serrano et al. (1991). Although the sex of all individuals was determined, and the sex ratios seem to accord with cultural features, it would be safer to leave undetermined the sex of seriously damaged skeletons of young individuals, especially those of Grave 2 and a few of Grave 14. The sex identification of the persons recently discovered by Mexican students, in Graves 16 and 17 on the north and south sides of the pyramid, are preliminary (Gallardo 1994, personal communication).

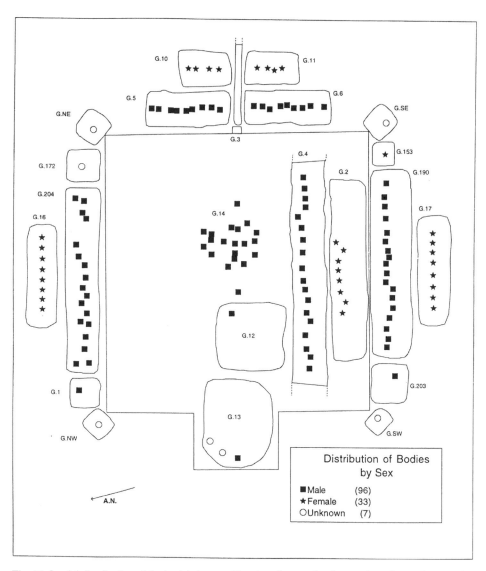

Fig. 45 Spatial distribution of the burials by sex. The size of graves has been enlarged out of proportion to the pyramid. GIS map: author.

Sex was a primary factor in the distribution of burials, as is evident in Figure 45. A pattern of eighteen males and eight females was a basic subset used repeatedly in and around the pyramid. The central grave was unique: twenty males without any apparent female counterparts, according to the most recent analysis.[3]

Age

Information on the ages of individuals found at the FSP was provided by Serrano et al. (1991). Ages were grouped into five ranges – thirteen to twenty, twenty to

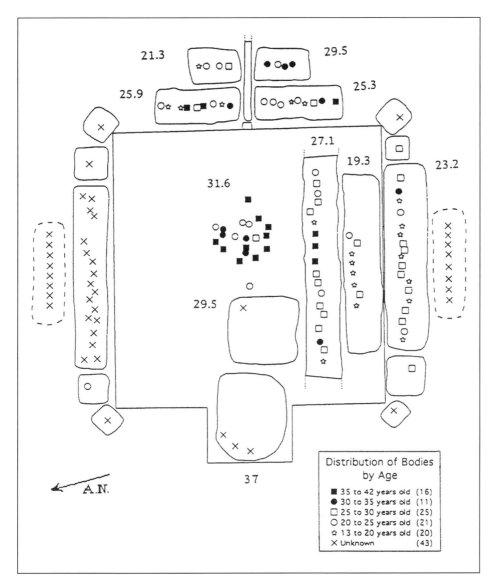

Fig. 46 Spatial distribution of the burials by age. Numbers in the diagram indicate the average ages of individuals at death. The size of graves has been enlarged out of proportion to the pyramid. GIS map: author.

twenty-five, twenty-five to thirty, thirty to thirty-five, and thirty-five to forty-two – and a distribution map of bodies by age was drawn using these ranges (Fig. 46).

The age of individuals varies with each grave. There was no clear intercorrespondence of age order among any multiple graves; in fact, the intragrave differences of age are larger than the intergrave differences, which may mean that age was not a primary component of burial distribution.

However, there is a general relationship among graves: the closer to the pyramid's center a male individual was located, the older he tended to be, though this is not the case for females. The central grave included ten persons who were more than thirty-five years old; no one less was than twenty years old. In contrast, Grave 190 consisted of seven teenagers, ten individuals in their twenties, and one individual older than thirty. The data indicate that a larger number of senior people were selected for the central grave – Grave 14 – than for other graves, which may imply that age distribution correlates with differential sociopolitical status or role of the people buried.

In contrast to this pattern of male burials, age differentiation among female burials is not reflected in their spatial distribution. Rather, older females were concentrated in exterior graves, particularly in Grave 11. It could be argued as a general trend that the closer to the center of the pyramid a female was located, the younger she was. However, age difference between two graves which form a pair (8.2 years between Graves 10 and 11) is larger than the difference of 6.1 years between the inner grave (Grave 2) and the average of the outside graves. This seems to imply that age differentiation of female burials is not correlated with location.

There is no age correlation or pattern between male and corresponding female graves. What kinds of relationships female burials had to male burials with which they were apparently associated should be addressed in terms other than age correlation (to be discussed in Chapter 8).

Dental modification

Dental modification is a feature that may have indicated sociocultural identities of people in Mesoamerica. Modification techniques normally included partial mutilation or incision on edges or frontal surfaces of incisors or canines, and inlay with precious gems on dental surfaces. However, little is known about the meaning and social function of dental modification. Some scholars believe it reflects social hierarchy, especially high status (Romero 1958). There are contradictory data from the Maya that people with modified teeth were often buried with poorer offerings than those whose teeth were not modified (Culbert 1994, personal communication).

The uncertainty of dental modification's meaning and function reduces its utility in identifying individuals buried at the FSP. Nonetheless, it may offer important insights into the nature of the burials. Since I used general data from ongoing studies of osteological materials by Mexican physical anthropologists (Serrano et al. 1993), I have analyzed only the spatial patterns of individuals whose teeth were modified, to discern differential burial treatment more clearly.

Javier Romero's 1986 classification recognizes fifty-nine types of dental modification and inlay. Eighteen of those types were found at the FSP, including a new one never before recorded in Mesoamerica. Among the eighteen, only three types had been reported in Teotihuacan before the discoveries at the FSP in the 1980s. Fifty percent of all men but only one woman showed some kind of dental modification (Fig. 47), indicating that there was a strong correlation between dental modification and sex. The percentage of men with modified teeth – exactly 50 percent – is intriguing (although the number may change as the analysis progresses and new

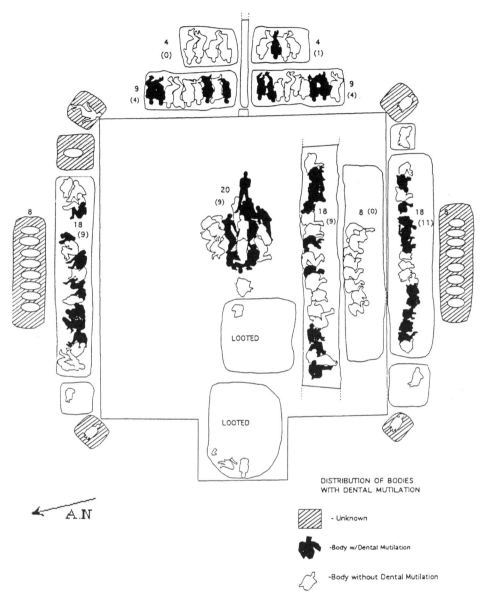

Fig. 47 Spatial distribution of the individuals with dental modification. The size of graves has been enlarged out of proportion to the pyramid. GIS map: author.

excavations increase our data). Contrary to my expectation of a certain concentration of individuals with dental modification, the data indicate even dispersal, with a certain intragrave irregularity, suggesting that dental modification was not correlated with other variables indicating differential patterns among graves. Somehow, dental modification seems to have been related to the entire burial complex, as indicated by unusual evenness of distribution, since there is no apparent pattern to this feature by row of interred persons, nor any correspondence among burials.

Additional plots of individuals by dental modification type were made in search of patterning, but even the additional plots indicate irregularity rather than patterned distribution of certain types. Twenty-three different combinations of dental modification in forty-seven individuals were distributed without any clear pattern, again confirming irregular intragrave distribution of those with dental modification.

Skeletal evidence

Cranial deformation occasionally has been reported in Teotihuacan (Rattray 1992: 51–52; Serrano and Lagunas 1975: table 8); three types have been suggested depending on types of pressure applied to the front and back of the skull in infancy (Sempowski 1994: 127–28). Although FSP burials are reported to have shown cranial deformation, the relationship between those buried and cranial deformation cannot be addressed at present, since the number of well-preserved crania is small.

According to Serrano et al. (1993, personal communication), little evidence of trauma has been found on bones from the FSP burial complex, suggesting that the buried individuals may not have been fighting soldiers. Good nutritional status and little evidence of pathological conditions characterize these individuals, which may indicate that they were of relatively high social status.

As we have seen, no evidence concerning the causes of death has been detected by physical anthropologists. Absence of inflicted trauma on bones suggests that, if these persons were sacrificed, they were killed in a way that left no evidence of cause of death.

General discussion

In previous sections, I discussed excavation contexts and burial patterns using etic categorization of burial features. In this final section, I attempt an emic perspective of this funerary event. For visual reference, I reconstructed the buried individuals, using skeletal data and showing features previously discussed. Figure 48 comprises seventy-three separate drawings made in the field, showing all osteological materials found in the central grave. Based on the composite drawing, photos, and descriptions, the bodies were hypothetically reconstructed as they lay in their original positions (Fig. 49). The same process was used for all other graves for which information was available (Fig. 50). In the case of the central grave (the most complicated because of the overlapping of bodies), each individual was reconstructed and a general diagram was created to assemble them. The following conclusions may be assisted by these drawings.

The central grave (Grave 14) was the most distinct and intricate. Its overall symbolic form is one of the most unusual ever recorded, not only in Teotihuacan but in all Mesoamerica. For this reason, the data should be interpreted in their own context. Discussion of specific ritual meanings is difficult and remains speculative, since we lack analogous instances in archaeological and ethnohistorical records.

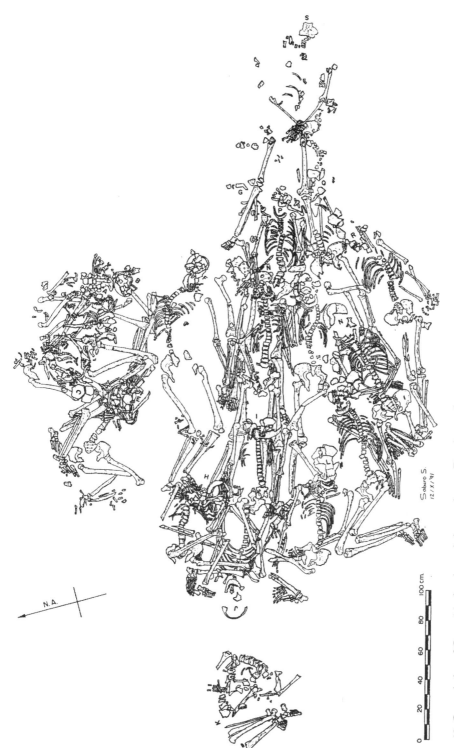

N.A.

Saburo S.
12/X/91

0 20 40 60 80 100 cm

Fig. 48 General plan of Grave 14, showing only human bones. Drawing: author.

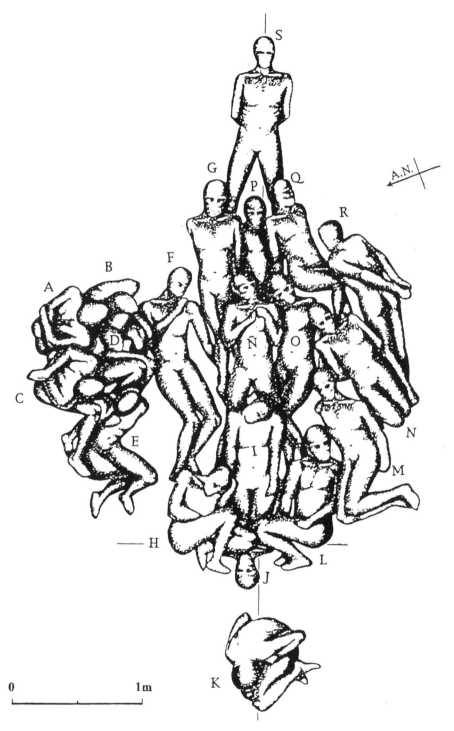

Fig. 49 Plan of the body positions in Grave 14, reconstructed from field drawings, photos, and notes. Interpretation: author; drawing: Jamie Borowicz.

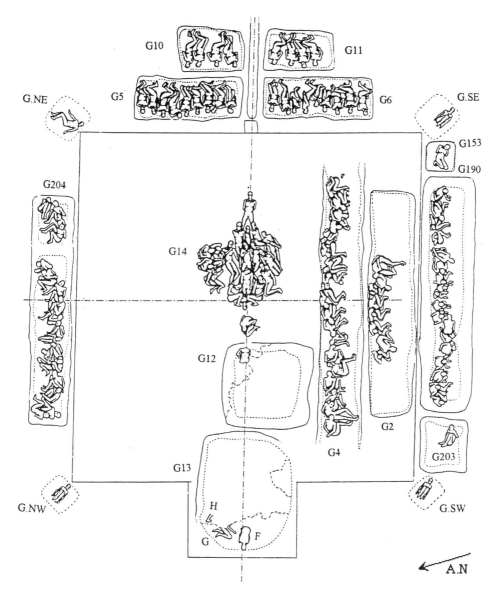

Fig. 50 General plan of reconstructed body positions of the FSP burials. The size of graves has been enlarged out of proportion to the pyramid. Interpretation: author; drawing: Jamie Borowicz.

The bodies of Grave 14 appear to have been deliberately placed to express specific ritual meanings, indicated by their unusual positions and symmetric relationships. Eight individuals (14-S, G, P, Q, F, Ñ, O, and J) were laid along the pyramid's east–west axis in extended or semiextended position, highly unusual in Teotihuacan.[4] Four of the eight (14-S, G, Q, and J) had arms crossed behind their backs. Seven of the eight were laid with their heads pointing east, suggesting primacy of direction. In contrast, 14-J was found with its head toward the west. This individual was one of the first bodies laid in the grave and may be connected with the persons found on the east side of the pyramid, with whom he shared the same position, orientation of body-axis, and arm position.

Individuals 14-S, P, Ñ, I, J, and K were evidently laid exactly on the pyramid's east–west axis (Fig. 49). Location and position of 14-G and Q, F and O, H and L, and probably E and M, were determined to be symmetrically related to each other with respect to the east–west axis. Three individuals on the south edge (14-R, N, and M) were found with arms crossed behind their backs and with orientations and positions similar to one another, although 14-R was unusual, in that it was laid facing down and extended. Asymmetrically opposed to them, individuals found on the north edge (14-A, B, C, and D) were placed in seated positions with their faces toward the south and with their arms crossed behind their backs. This clear asymmetric body position is reflected in their associated offerings. Individual 14-K, located at the western edge of the grave, was independent of the others and in an extremely flexed position, contrasting strongly in general position, body orientation, body flexion, and arm position with individual 14-S at the eastern edge.

The spatial arrangement of bodies described above indicates that ritual meanings were explicitly involved in this presentation, although the content of these meanings is difficult to decipher. At the same time, the pattern of the central grave seems to imply cohesion and anonymity, and the individuals who comprised it were likely elements of its collective presentation. Individual 14-S would have been the most distinct because of his location at the far east edge, toward which many others were oriented; however, this person would not have been the grave's principal occupant, since his arms were also crossed behind his back. Individual 14-K, found at the west edge, was also distinct from the others because of his location, body position, and body flexion, although these features may reflect treatment of the body (tied in a bundle, perhaps) rather than distinctiveness accompanying his social status, as was the case for individuals with similar conditions found in other graves (13-F, 190-F, 4F). In addition, 14-S and 14-K were associated with fairly common ornaments, shared by many others in the central grave. As we will see in Chapter 6, many offerings were concentrated around individuals 14-F, Ñ, I, and L; however, these seem to have been collective offerings later placed over and between the bodies.

No consistently conspicuous person was identified in this central grave: locations of offerings suggest that the individuals were elements in the formulation of a collective symbolic presentation. I therefore conclude that, despite the unusually rich offerings associated with the bodies, all twenty individuals found at the pyramid's center were victims of sacrifice.

As we have seen, Grave 12, originally a grave of one of the substructures, was later disturbed and reused as a sacrificial grave when the FSP was under construction. An incomplete skeleton found in the second fill would have been part of the second interment in the FSP burial complex. Since the hands of this skeleton were found crossed behind its back, this individual probably was also sacrificed (Fig. 50). The floor area suggests that eight to ten persons could have been buried in it if the space had contained only sacrificial victims. In contrast to this second use of the grave, the context of the first burial in a substructure is completely unknown because of two looting episodes.

Stratigraphy indicates that Grave 13 was part of the FSP burial complex, and its location on the east–west axis near the pyramid's center suggests the primacy of its position in the complex. The grave's size and form also indicate that it was special, as the grave pit was the second largest and one of the deepest. While these distinctive features might indicate social differentiation of the individuals buried, they would not necessarily have been indications of a royal grave since none is confirmed as a diagnostic variable for social differentiation. The burial features instead suggest that the grave contained a group of sacrificial victims distinct from the others.

Although Grave 13 was seriously disturbed, the looters left a larger amount of original fill than was left in Grave 12. Reconstruction of the bodies in Grave 13 indicates that their distribution may have been similar to that of the central grave (Fig. 50; compare to Fig. 49). Indicated by its position, and its location independent of others, the complete skeleton of 13-F, recovered from the original fill, seems to have been the counterpart of 14-K in the central grave. Although the general position of 13-F differs from the position of 14-K in our categorization, both may have been tied in bundles since both were extremely flexed. Half of individual 13-G, discovered north of 13-F in the original fill, may have been the counterpart of 14-H, as suggested by the position of its reconstructed extremities; and part of a leg of individual 13-H, found in the disturbed layer, also supports the similarity of these two graves, since it might have been the counterpart of individual 14-E of the central grave. Calculation of the floor space used for the burial suggests that about eighteen to twenty persons could have been laid in a manner like Grave 14, if the grave contained a sacrificial burial. These data, as well as data pertaining to offerings, support the interpretation that Grave 13 was a collective sacrificial grave rather than a royal tomb (with or without accompanying sacrificial victims), although this is still far from certain.

In contrast to graves found near the center, those in the peripheral area seem to have been more homogeneous, with clearer patterns, indicating that they represent collective sacrifices. Calendrical and/or cosmogonic numbers of individuals of determined sex were chosen to be buried symmetrically with respect to the east–west axis. Individuals buried on the south side were mainly seated facing south, while those on the north side were seated facing north, as if they guarded the pyramid behind them. People on the east side were laid on their backs with their heads toward the pyramid. These features also may indicate "subjugation" of the eastern burials to the pyramid.

The deliberate distinction among graves correlates with depth of the pits. Many victims had their hands crossed behind their backs or flexed and adjoining the body as if they were tied in bundles, and it can be argued that these victims were anonymously and collectively arranged in a row. The distribution of their offerings also indicates intragrave homogeneity and anonymity; intergrave differentiation was more clearly manifested by the patterned spatial distribution of the graves and by distinct mortuary variables.

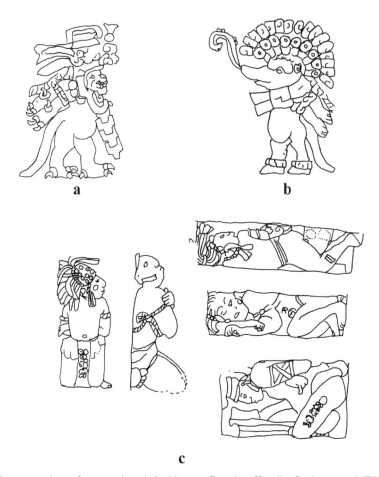

Fig. 51 Representations of war captives tied with rope. Drawing: Kumiko Sugiyama. a, b Elite captives commemorated in sculptures at Monte Albán (from Marcus 1983: 138); c Mayan captives, recorded in sculptures, at Classic Maya sites. The examples show that tied captives did not necessarily have their arms crossed on their backs (from Schele 1984: figs. 9 and 10).

The burials were most likely a collective ritual presentation prepared by the builders of this monumental work, in which hierarchical differentiation among groups seems to have been manifested to a certain degree. The overall mortuary form indicates that individuals buried in Graves 14, 13, 12, 4, 2, 190, 203, 153, 17, 204, 1, 172, 16, 5, 6, 10, 11, 3, and 7 (the graves at the northeast, northwest, southeast, and southwest corners, and others still undiscovered at the FSP) most likely comprised a dedication program. Cosmological and calendrical significance is apparently involved in these dedicatory burials.

The main factors determining the form of these dedicatory burials are apparently the number of individuals buried in a pit, symmetrical location with centrality toward the center of the pyramid, and sex. Anonymity is suggested by several types of body position and dental modification. In contrast, types of body flexion, arm position, and age suggest considerable difference in mortuary treatments, particularly of the central burial, that could have reflected social differentiation, in addition to ritual meanings. Among these types, a position of arms tied behind their backs is indicative of individuals' subjugated status; in fact, this position has been used in public contexts in Mesoamerica to represent conquered persons, often in contrast to conquerors or kings represented as standing on them (compare the reconstructed bodies of FSP burials with those in Fig. 51). The FSP suggests such a sociopolitical implication.

The grave pit found in front of the staircase, the largest in this burial complex, could have been later than the erection of the FSP. Sealed by a concrete floor before construction of the pyramid was complete, this grave is distinctly different from the others found outside the pyramid and could have been used after completion. It is possible that someone responsible for construction of the pyramid was later buried there. This issue is discussed in Chapter 7.

6

Offerings

Before the mass-sacrificial burial complex at the FSP was discovered in the 1980s, the uniqueness of the offerings associated with it was pointed out by Sempowski (1983, 1994: 47–50, 177–78). In her systematic mortuary analysis, which focused on social differentiation reflected in the variety and quantity of objects, Sempowski noted that offerings found at the pyramid early in the twentieth century were distinct from those found in residential areas, especially in quality.

Excavations in the 1980s substantially increased the number and variety of offerings known from the FSP. As we have seen, the cohesiveness of the graves in and around the pyramid indicates that they comprised a single burial complex dedicated to the pyramid. The offerings connected with the burials are exceptionally rich in quality, quantity, and diversity compared to any found to date in Teotihuacan. Their exceptional quality is only comparable to those being discovered recently in the Moon Pyramid.[1]

It was noted in 1989 that the offerings were combined quite differently from those previously known in Teotihuacan, and that some materials were highly unusual for Mesoamerica, consisting mainly of objects of personal adornment and ritual objects and not including pottery, except for some Storm God jars[2] and vessels that might have contained liquid or organic materials.

In this chapter, I describe and analyze these offerings, emphasizing their symbolic nature. I focus on the offerings' morphological features and spatial distribution to elucidate the meanings of the pyramid's burial contexts. Differences in patterns may also have been related to their functions, to craft divisions, or to other social variables. If specific types of certain objects were distributed by grave or group of graves, it could be that offerings found in each section were prepared by units of craftsmen who used significantly different raw materials, techniques, or other features of craft tradition. However, as I indicate in each section, specific types or features of objects are distributed with certain cross-grave patterns, as if a higher order structured the distribution over the entire grave complex. That the distribution patterns of certain kinds of offerings are correlated with grave variables indicates that an intention governed the entire presentation of the dedicatory complex; this in turn implies that offering differences were spatially arranged with meanings at the moment of placement. Intentionality is suggested by the cohesive and/or symmetrical patterns detected over the grave complex.

In this chapter, I aim at emic categorization of offerings and explore possible meanings embedded in ritual context through classifications and spatial distributional analyses. Offerings were first classified morphologically. In some cases, formal distinctions are discontinuous and obvious and may be considered as the classification by Teotihuacanos; in others, differences in form are complex and gradual. Therefore, quantitative data were also taken into account to form etic categorizations, plotted spatially in plans of graves and burials to see relationships with individuals interred and correlations among offerings. This procedure may help to reconstruct burial contexts in which ritual meanings and functions of objects were involved.

Objects are often discussed in terms of personal ornaments versus general offerings, since meanings involved may differ one from another. It may be appropriate to interpret individuals' status and roles from personal ornaments, while general offerings seem designed to express attributes of groups with which the objects were associated. The former can be used to distinguish individuals from each other (if any differentiations existed), while the latter seem to provide anonymity within a group and may be useful for intergroup distinction. Spatial distributions of general offerings are also discussed to discover if they were scattered or placed intentionally at particular spots. Distribution of offerings in Grave 14 especially was examined with this question in mind since this central grave contained a majority of general offerings which were evidently spread out.

After examining each category of offerings, I look at the associations of the offerings, concentrating on Grave 14 for this purpose since the other two graves found with a large variety of offerings had been looted. Postdepositional mobility in Grave 14 also seems to be possible. However, because the grave was covered with the pyramid's construction fill immediately after deposition, postdepositional mobility would not have been sufficient to disrupt the patterns discussed here. More careful consideration of the precision of locational information is necessary for multivariate analyses.

Computer-assisted analyses, using the GIS program MapInfo (MapInfo Corporation 1992–94), were produced for the reconstruction of the burials and the distribution patterns among offerings. Locational data were derived from seventy-three drawings made during the excavations. Offerings recorded in Microsoft Excel tables were spatially encoded in MapInfo. Only data on objects with precisely known locations were used. Ranges of possible error are specified in each section. A certain number of fragments was not located precisely in the field; this incompleteness, plus significant irregularity in records, hinders some confirmative arguments and further statistical data analyses. Nonetheless, distribution of a major portion of offerings in each category was mapped in relation to other variables, with or without body silhouettes representing the positions in which the deceased individuals were believed to have been laid. Patterns of distribution of the objects and their relationships to one another are discussed later in the final chapter.[3]

While many offerings were found intact, some were represented only by fragments. Missing parts of some fragmented objects could not be found in the excavations (also true of the exploration of Grave 14, although all earth from graves was transported to the laboratory and carefully screened); this may have been due to the fact that the tunnel excavation was limited to an area disclosing only the burial zone, which may not have been extensive enough to recover fragments of broken objects scattered around the burial area. I believe that, except for a few cases, almost all objects were originally complete. The number of complete objects was posited only when the data were sufficient for calculation. Fracture form, typology, applied techniques, color, and matrix of material were considered to reconstruct the fragmented objects theoretically.

Interpretations described here are based primarily on results of the above analyses. Results are also discussed in conjunction with field data, including photos, drawings, and excavators' notes. Figure 11 contains information not quantified for the analyses, particularly to explain complicated offering sets in Grave 14; it may provide data on excavation contexts of the offerings, intuitive views of their intentional arrangement, or the degree of their displacement by settling, which can be combined with the results of typological and spatial analyses of offerings for appropriate contextual interpretations.

Obsidian

Besides various forms of figurines, obsidian objects in the graves were used mainly for tools to cut or pierce with a sharp edge or point, like projectile points, prismatic blades, knives, or piercers. In this burial context, ritual meanings of figurines as well as these tools, perhaps designed for symbolic acts, will be explored.[4]

Projectile points
All projectile points, found in various sizes and forms in almost all graves at the FSP, were made of obsidian. Many were found in clusters above, below, and between individuals, and others were dispersed singly around persons interred close to one another. Because their association with individuals was often questionable, some points were registered in the field as general offerings. While projectile points found outside the pyramid were well preserved, those inside were often fragmented and dispersed, probably due to the placement of rocks over the burials, causing serious difficulty in determining exactly how many complete offerings were originally associated with the burials.

To search for a native classification of projectile point types, I first noted length and weight (Fig. 52); two major groups are clearly represented on the plot made by these basic quantitative variables. Length and weight of projectile points were also correlated with color. Gray obsidian is dominant among large projectile points while green obsidian was preferred for smaller-sized points. The group of large projectile points (>45 mm long and 4 g weight) was subdivided into three types (A, B, and C) by the shape of the lateral edge (Fig. 53). Type A points have concave lateral edges and barbed shoulders; type B points have convex lateral edges; and type C points have smoothly bowed lateral edges. Although the trait distinguishing type A from type B is subtle, it seems to have been recognized in practice, since the two were distributed in part on the basis of this characteristic and formed distinct

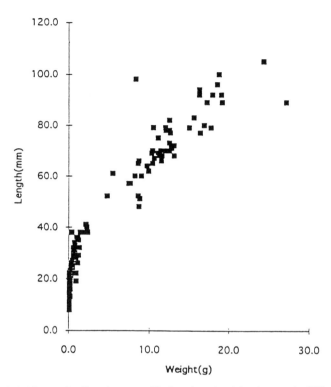

by Weight & Length

Fig. 52 Chart of obsidian projectile points sorted by length and weight. Among the 203 projectile points from Grave 14, only the complete pieces (148 pieces) are plotted. Projectile points from other graves also showed a similar trend.

spatial groups in Grave 14 (Fig. 54). Type C was distinguished from the other types by standardized lateral-edge form and the homogeneously fine technique with which examples were crafted. Only green obsidian was used for the production of type C projectile points although in general gray was preferred for large points. Form of the lateral edges is not a reliable diagnostic feature for small points (type D), since they are irregular and their differences are minimal; therefore, type D points were not subdivided for this general description although the group can be subdivided by other variables. All four projectile point types were reported previously in excavation reports and analyses of materials from Teotihuacan (e.g., Muller 1965) although typologies applied are different from the above categories.

More than 1,267 projectile points were recovered from graves at the FSP in the 1980s; 28 projectile points were discovered in front of the pyramid's staircase, as caches or as grave offerings removed from their original contexts.[5] Multiple graves of males contained numerous projectile points, and a similar number was discovered in graves containing twenty or eighteen males. Graves 14, 4, 190, and

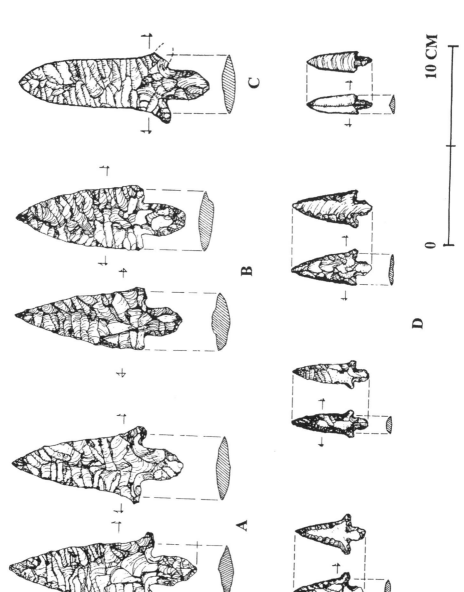

Fig. 53 Obsidian projectile points: types A, B, C, and D (miniature). Drawing: author.

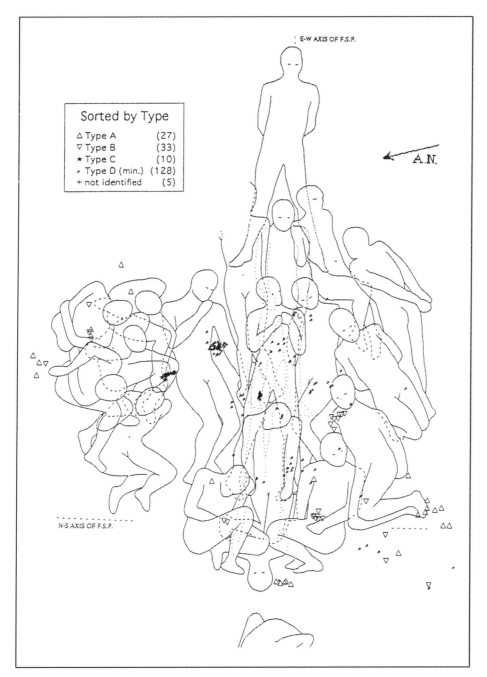

Fig. 54 Spatial distribution of projectile points by types in Grave 14: 175 pieces of 203 complete or incomplete points are shown. GIS map: author.

Graves 5 and 6 (if we consider these as a set), each containing twenty or eighteen individuals, generated approximately 200, 174, 169, and 205 projectile points respectively, with types A and B predominating. Interestingly, type C projectile points were found only in multiple graves inside the pyramid (Graves 2, 4, and 14), in individual graves (Graves 1 and 203), and in the pit in front of the pyramid staircase.

A close examination of distribution by type further suggests links among graves. Multiple graves containing females (Grave 2, and Graves 10 and 11 as a set) had projectile points but significantly fewer (47 and 56 points respectively) than graves of males (6.4 points/female vs. 10.1 points/male). Exterior graves had many miniatures (type D), and southern interior graves (Graves 2 and 4) have more projectile points made of green obsidian than those made of gray obsidian.

Individual graves contained fewer projectile points than group graves or none at all. Graves found at the northeast, southeast, southwest, and northwest corners contained 3, 3, 3, and 5 points respectively (Dosal 1925a, 1925b). Graves 203 and 1 on the south and north sides – respectively and mirroring one another – contained nine and ten projectile points. Among individual graves, only Graves 153 and 172 contained no projectile points.

The number of projectile points deposited in looted graves (Graves 12 and 13) is unknown; however, fragments found in disturbed grave layers and in the looters' tunnel indicate that both had contained an abundance of projectile points, Grave 13 with more than 100 points, and Grave 12, in the FSP's second burial context, at least tens of projectile points. In both graves, types A and B were predominant.

Studies of intragrave distribution of projectile points disclose further patterning. Generally speaking, types A and B were dispersed, while types C and D tended to be in clusters. In long pits, large projectile points were usually dispersed around the skulls or between skeletons and the pit walls close to the pyramid. The central grave shows a distinct spatial distribution (Fig. 54): almost all seem to have formed clusters of the same or similar projectile point types. Types A and B were found exclusively near the grave's northeast or southwest edges. Type C points were found only at the feet of individual 14-A, suggesting the distinctiveness of the person with whom they were associated. Unfortunately, the excavation context is not sufficient to determine which of three individuals – 14-A, D, or F – was associated with the type C points. Type D projectile points were found primarily in the grave's central section, some apparently deposited in tight clusters and others dispersed. As in the cases of other offerings, some of the dispersal may have been caused by postmortem activities, including covering the burials with rocks.

Although clustering by projectile point type is evident, whether the offerings in Grave 14 were directly associated with certain individuals is unclear, since there is no consistent spatial correlation between the clusters and body parts. For example, three clusters of types A and B projectile points were found behind the backs of individuals 14-A, B, and D, while clusters of the same types were located near the feet, head, or hands around the southwest edge of the grave. One cluster of type C points was found at the feet of 14-A and under the knees of 14-C, while clusters of type D points were found under the left upper arm of 14-F and on the thigh of 14-O. Since the clusters do not correlate consistently with body parts, the issue was examined later in relation to other offerings. However, since there is no correlation between clusters of projectile points and other types of offerings, at least some clusters were most likely offerings directly associated with these persons, despite the irregularity in their relationships to body parts; it is less likely that they were part of general offerings laid independently from other general offering clusters (discussed later).

Although almost all graves contained projectile points, the way in which they were intentionally selected and placed varied significantly in different places. Distribution patterns may have correlated with biological or social differences among individuals or may have reflected different ritual meanings. It is also possible that some projectile points, especially those found in clusters pointing in the same direction in Grave 14, may have been attached to perishable shafts. Formal homogeneity of each type, the absence of use marks (Sarabia 1993, personal communication), and exceptionally high quality and quantity also suggest that the projectile points may have been made exclusively for the dedication of the FSP burial complex. This may indicate that the burial complex was a ritualistic display of warfare rather than a reflection of real war.

Projectile points evidently symbolize warfare and seem to have been used as soldiers' insignia. Spears, represented in combination with spear-throwers and/or shields in Teotihuacan pictorial works (Fig. 21b and d), are carried not only by military figures but also by deities such as the Storm God, and by mythological animals such as birds (von Winning 1948) and butterflies (Berlo 1984). As discussed later in relation to obsidian figurines, projectile points are also associated with Feathered Serpents. At the FSP, projectile points were probably used as a diagnostic element for ritual warfare in association with the Feathered Serpent: the Feathered Serpent's martial aspects are established most prominently with projectile points with clear patterns distributed widely throughout the burials.

Prismatic blades

Blades are among the most commonly found obsidian objects in Teotihuacan, if not in all Mesoamerica; however, they were buried as offerings only in Grave 14 at the FSP.[6] In other FSP graves, blade fragments have been found in much smaller quantities. They were registered as intrusive since they were fragments and as dispersed as those normally in the rest of the pyramid fill.[7] Therefore, my discussion focuses on blades found in Grave 14.

It was observed during fieldwork that many large blades comprised a complex of offerings referred to as "bags," because in some cases long blades were arranged in parallel rows, often beneath remains of textiles or other organic materials. Many short, wide blades found near these complexes originally seem to have been part of the complexes (since long, wide obsidian blades were found in combination with other objects, they will be discussed in the section on offering associations). Besides these, short blades were found in some concentration in several spots.

As we have seen, blades were very fragmented. Despite Sarabia's painstaking efforts in the laboratory to reconstruct their original forms, it was difficult to figure out the total number of complete pieces in the offerings. Only approximate numbers

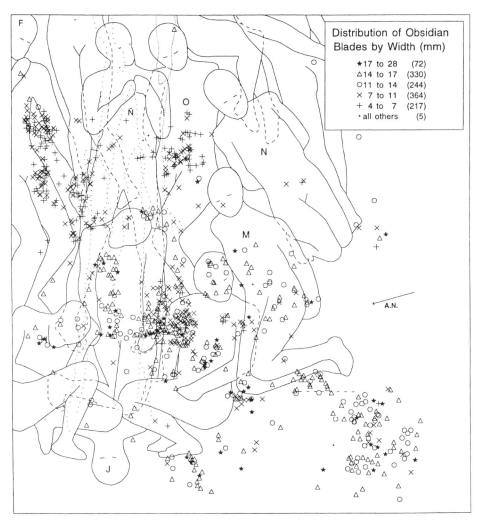

Fig. 55 Spatial distribution of obsidian blades by width (in mm): 840 of 1,230 pieces from Grave 14 were geocoded; the remainder (390 pieces, mainly fragments), whose precise locations are unknown, were not geocoded. The first three groups (11–28 mm width) were considered as type A, while the last two (4–11 mm width) comprised type B blades. GIS map: author.

can be suggested from the total number of fragments having a basal platform at one end. This calculation also takes into account blade color, size, form, and technology.

A total of 1,230 complete or incomplete prismatic blades was recorded for Grave 14. Among this number, 1,148 are green. Since a strong preference for green obsidian was common in production of prismatic blades in Teotihuacan, green color may not imply ritual meaning. Spatial distribution by color, and relationship with the bodies, does not indicate a clear pattern, suggesting again that color was not correlated with spatial ritual display.

Blade distribution was plotted by length, width, and number of notches. Distribution maps suggest that there were two basic types of obsidian blades (Fig. 55) located in two distinct zones of Grave 14: long, wide blades (type A), usually with blunt points and sharp edges without notches, were located in the central and south-western zone. Type B blades that were short (<122 mm), narrow (<10 mm), light (<6 g), and often possessing one sharp point and two or more side notches, were discovered primarily in the northeastern zone. Since these fragments were found with other objects on and between the partially overlapping bodies, they most likely comprised a general offering dedicated to the burial. Concentrations of blades were not consistently associated with any specific part of the individual's body but seem to have been deliberately laid collectively on the bodies.

Functions and meanings of the two distinct types of obsidian blades found in the grave are unclear, although evidently they were different. The large-blade group, possibly part of the offering complex, is interpreted in the section on offering as-sociations. Large blades may have been part of an offering complex scattered on the interred individuals or may have been parts of ornaments such as headdress complexes. As Parsons pointed out (1988: 24), some headdresses on priests' heads (Fig. 17b) seem to include obsidian blades; if this is true, sets of long blades found with organic fragments in the central grave might have been parts of headdresses. Since only a few of the organic fragments found in Grave 14 apparently were folded (see "Textiles"), this identification remains only a possibility.

Small blades in Grave 14 seem to have been tools; their thin, narrow bodies and sharp, fragile points suggest that they may have been designed for drilling soft ma-terial. One or more notches near their bases suggest that another material was at-tached to them. These objects may not have been mundane hafted drills or per-forators but rather used for auto-sacrifice, since they would have been ideal for pricking soft tissue, including the human body. Auto-sacrifice was fairly common in Mesoamerican societies outside of Teotihuacan (Klein 1987; Wilkerson 1984: 127) although, as far as I know, scenes of auto-sacrifice have not been identified in Teotihuacan iconography, except for Clara Millon (1988c: 199–200) and Lang-ley's claim (1996, personal communication) that an element in front of priests in a Maguey ritual mural (Fig. 18c) is composed of a tied bundle (Zacatapoalli, which in Nahuatl means "sacred bundle"), and implanted Maguey bloodletters. If the short blades with sharp points in Grave 14 were tools for auto-sacrifice, then the central grave may reflect its ritual importance at Teotihuacan. It is worth remembering that among Classic Maya, autosacrifice was performed especially by elites (Stuart 1988).

Bifaces

Most of the obsidian knives and other bifacial forms were found in the pyramid's central area: a total of 203 complete or semicomplete (>50 percent of a complete ob-ject) bifaces and twenty-six fragments (<50 percent complete) were found in Grave 14. Ten complete or semicomplete bifaces and two fragments were discovered in Grave 13, which had been disturbed by looters. Twenty-six complete or semicom-plete bifaces and fifteen fragments were found on the floor of the looters' tunnel. Most of the last group seem to have belonged originally to Grave 13, according to

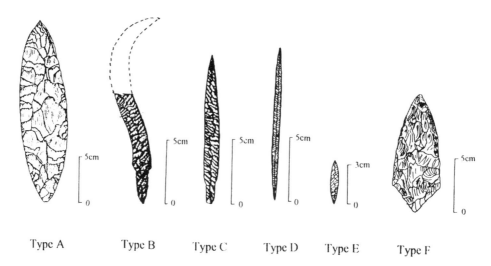

Type A   Type B   Type C   Type D   Type E   Type F

Fig. 56 Five types of obsidian biface. Drawing: Verónica Moreno, from the originals.

their stratigraphy and location near the grave. Another looted grave, Grave 12, from which some bifaces might have derived, contained only one fragment.

Besides bifaces in the central area, more than forty complete pieces were found outside the pyramid early in the twentieth century, sixteen uncovered by Marquina atop the pyramid (Marquina 1922); twenty-four bifaces and thirteen fragments were found at the foot of the pyramid's staircase, and several bifaces on the same side of the pyramid, under the Adosada construction (Pérez 1939; Rubín de la Borbolla 1947). Detailed data on the excavation contexts and morphology of these objects are unavailable.

The bifaces found by PTQ88–89 were classified into six types (Fig. 56). Because of clear morphological differences, five types (A, B, C, F, and D + E) were probably part of the original, native classification system. Only the distinctions between types D and E were not clear, since the classification was based on regular gradual quantitative differences. Type A consisted of large, wide bifacial knives with a point at each end. One complete example measured 20 cm long, 5.5 cm wide, and 1.2 cm thick. Type B is an S-curved, narrow bifacial knife with a point at one end and a stem at the other. Type C includes straight narrow bifacials with a point at one end and a stem at the other. Type D is composed of needle-like, straight, long, narrow bifacials with a sharp point at each end. Type E is a short version of type A and is defined by a width greater than type D (>8 mm maximum width). Type F is similar to a projectile point with a point at one end; however, their large size and heavy weight and the shape of their stems suggest their function as knives. Type E bifaces are similar to those of type D in form and applied technique; only spatial distribution in Grave 14 (Fig. 57) and the ratio of length to width of complete knives of these two types suggest that type E bifaces were likely differentiated from those of type D. One might expect that the length and width of bifaces in a single group would be correlated; in this case, however, length of the wider group (type E) ranges only from 44 mm to 60 mm (one

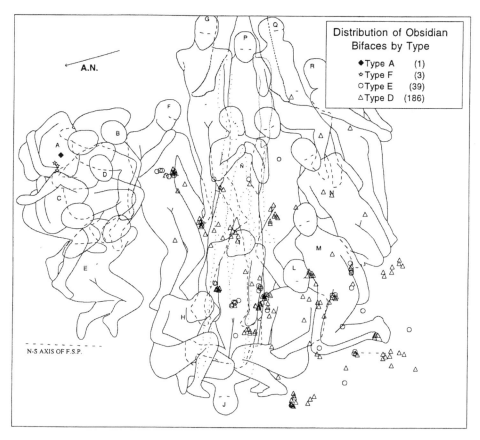

Fig. 57 Spatial distribution of obsidian knives in Grave 14: 193 of 226 pieces were mapped, while the precise locations of the remainder (33 pieces, mainly fragments) are unknown. GIS map: author.

exception measures 17 mm), while the length of the narrow group (type D) varies from 29 mm to 85 mm (with two exceptionally long examples measuring 113 and 120 mm).

These six biface types were concentrated in graves located near the center of the pyramid. Type A consisted of only one complete example from the central grave, in association with individual 14-A, and three incomplete pieces found in the looters' tunnel. Type B and C knives were completely absent from the central grave, type B having been found only on the floor of the looters' tunnel and in the disturbed layers of Graves 12 and 13. These graves seem to have been burials that contained knives only of type B as offerings. Only one complete type C knife and one fragment of the same type have been found at the pyramid so far, discovered in the looters' tunnel; they may also have come from Graves 12 and/or 13. A few type D and E bifaces were recovered from the looters' layers in Grave 13; however, they were dominant in the central grave – sharp-pointed "piercers" (type D) and "miniature bifaces of type A" (type E) originally laid in clusters, although the pattern of the clusters is not clear (Fig. 57). Neither is there an apparent correlation between the clusters and

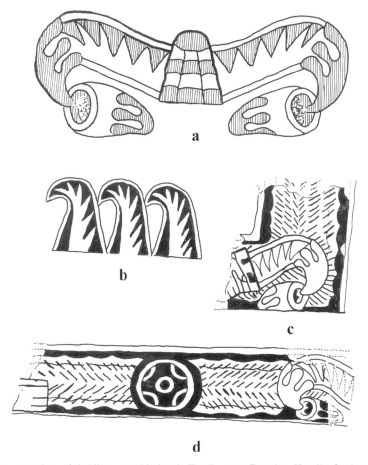

Fig. 58 Representations of obsidian curved knives in Teotihuacan. Drawing: Kumiko Sugiyama. a Knife motif in ceramic vessel from Zacuala (from Séjourné 1966a: fig. 82); b Knife motif in ceramic vessel from Teotihuacan (from Séjourné 1956: fig. 41); c Knife motif in a mural of Zacuala (from Miller 1973: fig. 218); d Knife motif in a mural of Zacuala (from Miller 1973: fig. 219).

the interred individuals. Rather, the clusters seem to have been associated with other kinds of objects as components of offering sets, as will be seen below. Type F consists of three bifaces found together with a type A knife, all apparently in association with individual 14-A.

Straight knives are not widely represented in Teotihuacan art. Type A, similar to the well-known Aztec sacrificial knife, has not been identified in Teotihuacan imagery. However, based on iconographic representations of this knife type in other Mesoamerican societies (Robicsek and Hales 1984: 67–69), it is logical to assume that one use may have been for human sacrificial ritual. The most frequently depicted knives at Teotihuacan were curved (type B) and usually appeared in martial or sacrificial contexts (Figs. 58 and 92a). Type D and E knives, with a sharp point at each end, were extremely fragile and, like the short blades, probably would have been reserved for auto-sacrifice.

Why these tools for sacrifice or auto-sacrifice were included in the sacrificial burial with certain patterns is puzzling. They may have been buried with persons killed by someone else or auto-sacrificed with these tools, added to symbolize ritual meanings of sacrifice, or used to classify or honor sacrificed individuals buried in the pyramid's central graves.

Figurines (eccentrics)

Obsidian figurines found at the FSP form a highly unusual set. Similar figurines were reported to have been discovered at the Sun Pyramid (Millon et al. 1965). A significant number of obsidian figurines of varied sizes was also uncovered recently in the graves at the Moon Pyramid (Sugiyama and Cabrera 2000). At the FSP, figurines were concentrated in the pyramid's central zones (Graves 14 and 13) and in front of the staircase.

These figurines were classified on the basis of what they appear to represent. Although their surfaces have no distinguishing traits, their silhouettes differ to the extent that they could be used in identification (Figs. 59 and 60). The figurines form three major groups: anthropomorphic figures (type A); representations of the Feathered Serpent (type B); and unidentified shapes (type C), with differences in morphology, technique, size, and spatial distribution within each group.

Sarabia divides type A (anthropomorphic figurines) into three subgroups based on the quality of retouching: thin figurines with high quality retouching (type A1); roughly retouched, robust figurines (type A2); and coarsely made figurines which appear to have been unfinished (type A3). Proportion of height to maximum width, thickness, and weight of these eccentrics supports his classification. Type A1 figurines always have a maximum width of less than half their height. In figurines of types A2 and A3, width is more than half of height. Figurines of the latter group also are usually thicker than those of the same size in the former group. Within each group, size and weight vary greatly.

Type B figurines have undulating-profile bodies characteristic of Feathered Serpents in Teotihuacan iconography. The shape of all type B eccentrics is of the entire undulating serpent body in profile, from its opened mouth to its tail. I do not subdivide this group, although they vary significantly in size.

The shapes of type C figurines are clearly distinct from the others, had been called simply eccentrics and often identified as lizards (Herrera 1922: vol. 1, 190). They also look like anthropomorphic representations; however, I identify them as half Feathered Serpent and half projectile point, an interpretation supported by the fact that these eccentrics represent both the combination of the upper portion of the serpent body and a projectile point (type C1), and the lower portion of the body and projectile point (type C2). Forms of the serpent head and tail are identical to type B obsidian figurines described above. The form of projectile point combined with them is also analogous to the points identified as type A or C (Fig. 53).[8] That the form of obsidian representations of Feathered Serpents and projectile points (which type C figurines resemble) is standardized at the FSP seems to support this interpretation. In turn, interpretations as lizards or human figures are weakened by

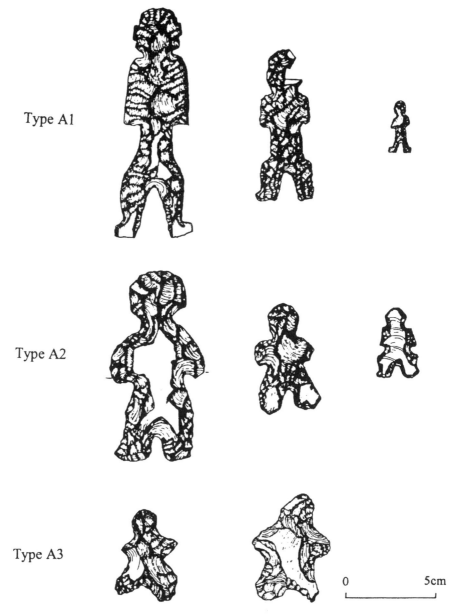

Type A1

Type A2

Type A3

0   5cm

Fig. 59 Anthropomorphic obsidian figurines (eccentrics), classified as type A1, A2, and A3. Drawing: Verónica Moreno, from the originals.

the fact that lizards or humans in such forms have not been identified in any kind of pictorial representations in Teotihuacan. Type C3 is represented by one eccentric, the form of which is unidentified.

These three types of obsidian figurine were distributed in only a few graves. Types A and B were found only in Graves 13 and 14 while type C was found in Graves 13 (one piece) and 14 (three pieces), and in Graves 3 (one), 5 (one), 6 (four),

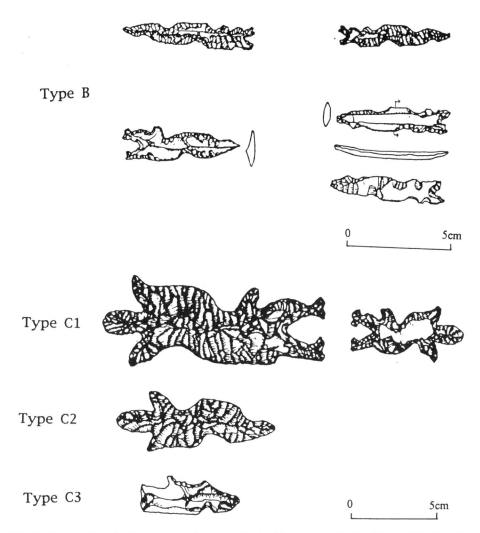

Type B

Type C1

Type C2

Type C3

Fig. 60 Zoomorphic obsidian figurines (eccentrics), classified as type B, C1, C2, and C3. Drawing: Verónica Moreno, from the originals.

10 (one), and 11 (two), located outside the FSP. Interestingly, type C figurines are concentrated in graves along the east–west centerline and are apparently associated with particular persons in Grave 13 and the graves outside the pyramid, although this is not certain in Grave 14 (Fig. 61).

Examples of types A and B figurines were concentrated primarily in specific areas of the central grave. Many were found in three clusters near the center; others were dispersed in the southwestern section. Two of the three clusters were located on each side of individual 14-Ñ, who was symmetrically aligned with the pyramid's east–west axis. Three clusters were composed exclusively of figurines of types A1 and B (Fig. 61). In contrast, all figurine types occurred in the southwestern part of the grave without any clear pattern of distribution. In summary,

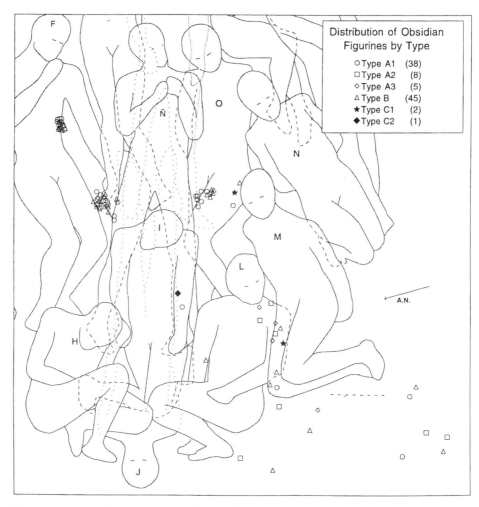

Fig. 61 Spatial distribution of obsidian figurines by type: 92 out of the 99 pieces from Grave 14 are shown; precise locations of the remainder (7 pieces) are unknown. GIS map: author.

the data indicate that the figurines in Grave 14 had not been associated directly with specific individuals but seem to have been a compositional element of a ritual display.

Besides those found as offerings, a small number of obsidian figurines were discovered in other places during the excavations of the pyramid. One fragment representing a large human leg was found on the surface of the east slope, its size and form suggesting that it was probably of the A1 type, and originally measured approximately 13 cm high. This suggests that offering caches including obsidian figurines had been located at the top of the pyramid, since other types of offerings were found there by Marquina's excavation in 1922. In addition, numerous obsidian figurines had been discovered earlier in front of the staircase (Pérez 1939; Rubín de la Borbolla 1947). Twenty-seven pieces of type A and four pieces of type B were found at the foot of the staircase, and more pieces were reported to have been discovered under the Adosada platform.

Obsidian figurines were discovered in limited places but were not exclusive to the FSP. Anthropomorphic figurines have also been found with burials in residential compounds (Linné 1934: 153), and the Adosada platform of the Sun Pyramid contained caches that included figurines of types A1 and B (Millon et al. 1965: figs. 93, 94). These probably were not associated with burials but seem to have formed caches dedicated to the pyramid. In contrast, figurines of types A and B were recently discovered in three grave complexes at the Moon Pyramid. It is believed that the Adosada of the Sun Pyramid and the substructures with which the burials were associated were roughly contemporaneous or coexisted with the FSP, suggesting a certain relationship, or shared ideational foundation, among Teotihuacan's three major monuments.

Outside of Teotihuacan figurines strikingly similar to those of the FSP have been discovered at Altun Ha, Belize. David Pendergast (1971, 1990: 266–70) reports that Teotihuacan-type obsidian figurines made of Mexican Highland green obsidian were discovered as postinterment offerings associated with an elite tomb; several figurines of types A1, A2, and B have also been discovered together with other Teotihuacan-type offerings. Obsidian figurines similar to those at the FSP have also been found at other Maya sites (Coe 1959: fig. 36e), though they are less similar than those of Altun Ha.

Chris Beekman reminded me that the roughly made anthropomorphic figurines from Teotihuacan were similar to those found in shaft tombs in the Valley of Atemajac, Jalisco (Galván 1991: 104, 153). However, they were made of local obsidian, and their manufacture and size (particularly thickness) are quite different from those found in Grave 14, although their front view is similar. These eccentrics may not have been related.

Although peculiar forms of the collection at the pyramid suggest their ritual use in mortuary programs, we do not know exactly what kinds of meanings were attached to them in this particular burial context. In many cases they do not appear to have been directly related spatially to individuals but suggest a mortuary program entailing other types of offerings laid in a specific arrangement.

Morphological differences within the figurines of types A may reflect different contexts associated with their production and may represent anonymous humans. Their distinctive differences also may indicate a hierarchical order. If so, clearly differentiated figurines might represent groups of individuals or ritual/social categories in an anonymous sense. They could have represented groups of sacrificed individuals, as they were included in dedication graves with strong significance of human sacrifice. In contrast, figures of type B take the form of a Feathered Serpent in profile, and their shapes are uniform although their sizes vary considerably from one to another. Since this uniformity in style is also shared with Feathered Serpents represented in murals, vessels, and sculptures, no clear subdivisions or distinct meanings are suggested other than emphasis on Feathered Serpent attributes in the central graves.

Fig. 62 Stylized head of an animal, possibly a Feathered Serpent: lower jaw is missing and replaced by a bundle of spears. Drawing: Kumiko Sugiyama, from Parsons 1988: 48; Séjourné 1966b: fig. 94.

Types C1 and C2 figurines indicate the martial nature of the Feathered Serpent in Teotihuacan dating back to the time of the pyramid's construction, since projectile points were represented as weapons in combination with shields in Teotihuacan iconography. The association of the Feathered Serpent with warfare, symbolized by type C figurines, is also indicated by its later pictorial representations (see Chapter 4). Parsons (1988: 48) points out that the stylized head of an animal, possibly a Feathered Serpent, lacks a lower jaw, which has been replaced by a bundle of spears (Fig. 62). This also suggests a direct association of the Feathered Serpent with projectile points, as in the case of type C eccentrics. Moreover, replacement of the lower jaw by a bundle of projectile points is reminiscent of the maxilla pendants found in this burial complex; these may have been an identification code for soldiers who were also carrying projectile points at the FSP. Thus, both Feathered Serpents and projectile points are metaphorically related to warfare and sacrifices.

Greenstone
Greenstone was used mainly for individual ornaments but also for ritual objects such as cones, figurines, headdress-like plaques called "resplandores," and other types of plaques. They are mainly concentrated in the pyramid's central zone.

Different qualities of greenstone were used to produce different types of objects. According to a preliminary microscopic analysis by Margaret Turner (1991, personal communication), Teotihuacanos deliberately employed different qualities of this material. This was indicated by quantitative data used to sort the objects by types, and Turner's preliminary identification of jadeite or serpentine, and was later supported by petrographic analyses by INAH's laboratory, which identified fuchsita in addition to jadeite and serpentine, used for the production of offerings. In the following section, my interpretation of general quantitative data, measured by Oralia Cabrera (1995), is provided in light of burial contexts and iconographic information.

Greenstone beads

A total of 538 greenstone beads was found with the burials during the FSP excavations in the 1980s and these were distributed in Graves 1, 5, 13, 14, and 203. In addition, 400 beads were found at the top of the pyramid (Marquina 1922) and, in 1988–89, 13 in the fill of the post-Teotihuacan layers on the pyramid's east side (which may have fallen from a burial or caches atop the pyramid) and 79 in caches in front of the staircase (Pérez 1939). The majority were recovered from Graves 14 and 13. They are approximately spherical, with single, central holes; shapes are often irregular, and sizes vary widely (0.4–1.9 cm in diameter). Only quantitative data – diameter, thickness, and weight – are used here.

In general, beads in the central grave show greater variation among themselves than do those of Grave 13. Almost all beads from Grave 13 (98 percent of 330 beads) are larger than 1.64 cm (in the sum of diameter and thickness), whereas the central grave included a larger number (226 of 330: 68 percent) of beads smaller than 1.64 cm (in the sum of diameter and thickness). In addition, the beads from Grave 13 tend to be thicker than those from Grave 14. These data clearly indicate differences between beads in Grave 13 and those in Grave 14, which may reflect differences in use, social status of individuals with whom they were associated, or production contexts (craftsman, origin of material, etc.).

The distribution of beads in disturbed layers of the burials (Graves 12 and 13) did not show clear patterning because of looting. However, the distribution of beads in Grave 14 by diameter indicates some patterning (Fig. 63). A majority were laid down in clusters, with high concentrations found around the abdominal region of individual 14-F, the waist of 14-Ñ, and the right upper arm of 14-L (locational data do not indicate that they were used as necklaces for these individuals); several small clusters were also detected in the central and southwestern areas. These objects were part of offering clusters.

Besides those forming clusters, beads were scattered individually and apparently irregularly throughout a wide area of the grave, several seeming to have been associated with the thorax region of individuals: individuals 14-E, F, H, I, J, K, L, N, Ñ, O, P (and/or Q), R, and S each had one bead near their chests or necks.[9] Plotting beads by diameter revealed that larger beads (1.7–2.3 cm) tended to have been selected for this purpose, while smaller beads (0.8–1.7 cm) were used for the clusters.

In Graves 1, 203, and 13-F, greenstone beads formed necklaces of personal ornament, contrasting with the central grave, in which no individuals wore bead necklaces. There, beads were used for other purposes. Smaller clusters had most likely been used as necklaces for greenstone figurines.

Individual beads found around the thorax region seem to have been located originally on the chests. It is even possible that some were put in the mouths of the dead, since the bead-in-mouth custom was widely diffused in Mesoamerica, and similar cases have been reported from Teotihuacan (Noguera and Leonard 1957: 8; Serrano 1993: 112). More than thirteen centuries after the burials at Teotihuacan, Spanish chronicles described this custom and interpreted beads in the mouths of the deceased as representing their soul (Sahagún 1978: bk. 3: 45). Individuals

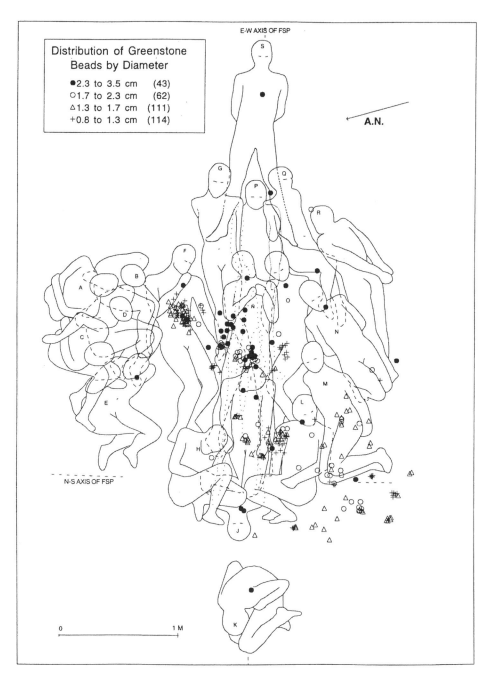

Fig. 63 Spatial distribution of greenstone beads by diameter: 314 of 330 pieces in total from Grave 14 were geocoded and plotted. GIS map: author.

in Graves 1 and 203 may have held one bead on their chests or in their mouths separately from twenty other beads. In Teotihuacan iconography, only anthropomorphic and zoomorphic figures wearing elaborate costumes wore greenstone bead necklaces, as if the necklaces were an emblem of high social status.

Greenstone earspools

A total of 139 earspools was found in Graves 1, 13, 14, and 203, along with some whole and fragmented examples in the looters' tunnel. Excavations indicate that earspools had been deposited in Grave 13 and were later removed. Twenty-four earspools were also discovered with burials at the top of the pyramid and more than eight in caches in front of it.

All greenstone earspools had a relatively standardized form but differed greatly in size (1.4–5.3 cm in diameter). Their circular form is like those worn by anthropomorphic figures in murals and on pottery (Figs. 18c, 20a–b, 21a–f, and 29b–c). Individual graves (Graves 1 and 203), symmetrically aligned to the pyramid's east–west axis, contained the same type of earspool. Two exceptionally large earspools were found in Grave 13 in association with the one individual undiscovered by looters, and one fragment in the disturbed layer of Grave 12 was even larger, suggesting that Graves 13 and 12 contained individuals who merited distinction in terms of their ornament associations. Other earspools in the disturbed layers were small, similar to those in the central grave.

The central grave yielded 123 earspools. The spatial distribution map (Fig. 64) shows that individuals 14-E, F, G, H, I, J, K, L, N, Ñ, O, P, Q, R, and S, approximately corresponding to those holding greenstone beads on their chests, each apparently wore a pair of earspools, while the others apparently did not.[10] Other earspools were dispersed, in no apparent association with individuals. A large concentration of earspools was discovered under the left upper arm of individual 14-F, and others were scattered throughout the southwestern part of the grave. Some earspools seem to have been associated with greenstone figurines, as I will discuss in the final section.

As we have seen, earspools found at the FSP are common to Teotihuacan's archaeological record and its iconography, and two similar types have been found in Grave 21 at La Ventilla B in Teotihuacan (Rattray 1992: pl. IV). More greenstone earspools including examplars similar to those in Grave 13 were recently found at the Moon Pyramid. Earspools were used in sets with other greenstone ornaments as regalia for elites, as depicted in anthropomorphic representations.

Greenstone nose pendants

Greenstone nose pendants were part of ornament sets associated with select individuals in the FSP burial complex: eighteen were found in the central grave (Grave 14); two were discovered in the looted pit of Grave 13; pendants were also found on individuals in Graves 1 and 203, which are symmetrically aligned with the pyramid's east–west axis; and at least two pendants were found at the pyramid's top (Marquina 1922: vol. 1, 158–61) .

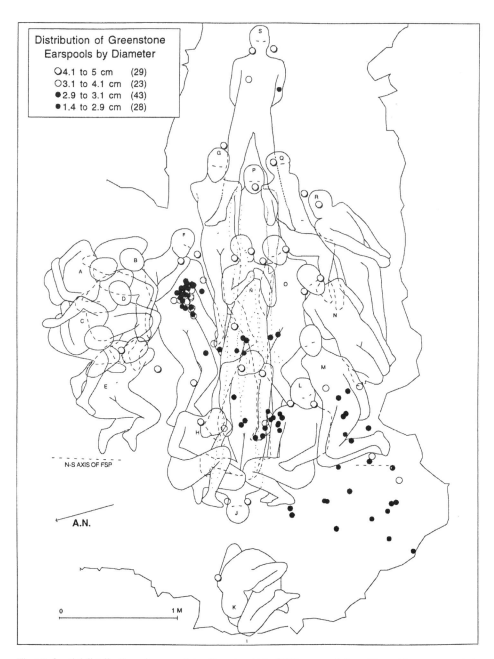

Fig. 64 Spatial distribution of earspools by diameter: 117 of 123 earspools from Grave 14 were geocoded. GIS map: author.

Nose pendants were classified by form into two basic types (Fig. 65), one the so-called "butterfly" type (type A), and the other (type B) a rectangular plaque with a distinctive bifurcated, tongue-like projection below it and distinguished from type A by three concentric circles carved on the frontal surface of its upper section. The

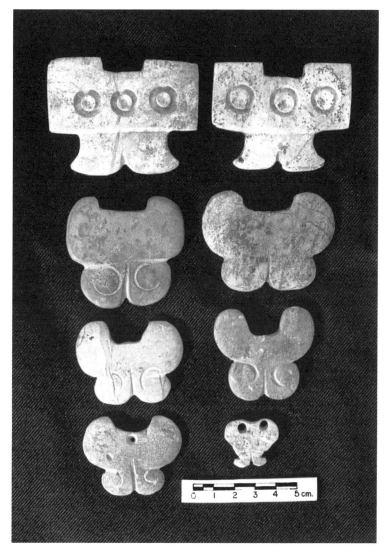

Fig. 65 Two types of greenstone nose pendant: type A (two upper pieces) and type B (others). Photo: author.

majority of nose pendants is type A and can be subdivided into additional groups mainly by size. Only two nearly identical nose pendants from Grave 13 were type B.

Eighteen nose pendants, all of type A, were discovered scattered throughout Grave 14 and lacked clear associations with specific individuals. However, the distribution map (Fig. 66) suggests that fourteen of the eighteen were originally attached to individuals 14-E, F, G, H, I, J, K, L, N, Ñ, O, P, R, and S, since each was found within a 25 cm radius of these individuals' noses. Four pendants were found too far from individuals to be confidently assigned to them. Persons nearest these pieces, who have not been assigned a nose pendant, are 14-B, Q, and M; the distances

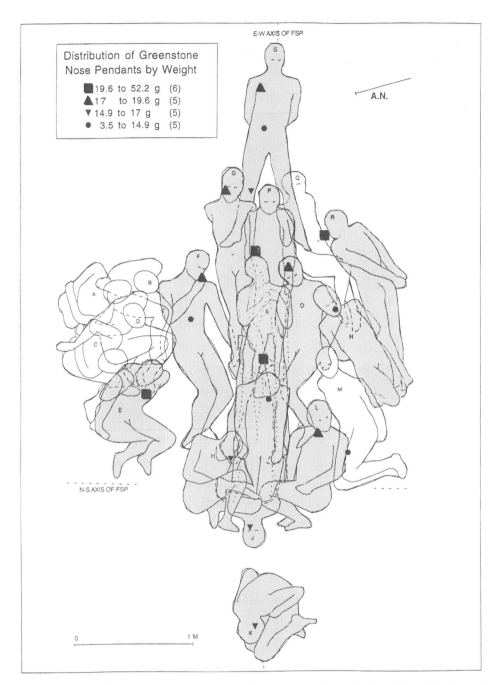

Fig. 66 Spatial distribution of all nose pendants (18 pieces) from Grave 14 plotted by weight. Shaded bodies are those who are thought to have had a nose pendant attached. GIS map: author.

between the pendants and noses of these reconstructed bodies are 40, 60, 55, and 70 cm, respectively (the last two distances are both from M). One piece, a single pendant of exceptionally small size with a distinctly different form, does not seem to have been attached to the individual nearest to it (14-M). Any direct association of the other three with individuals is unclear. However, ornament combinations suggest that individual 14-Q, wearing earspools and one bead, might also have had a nose pendant, although the spatial deviation is large and no immediately reasonable explanation for it can be offered. Individuals 14-M and B also could not be dismissed as individuals who wore the regalia set, since they might have been ornamented with earspools and one bead (location unknown). In brief, at least fifteen of twenty individuals in the central grave originally had type A nose pendants.

Type A nose pendants were also found attached to individuals of Graves 1 and 203. In these single graves, the excavation contexts indicate that the pendants, together with two earspools and twenty-one beads for each individual, were part of their ornaments. This suggests that Graves 1 and 203 were directly associated with the central grave rather than with the nearby graves with which they formed a subset.

Type B nose pendants were found only in Grave 13. One piece was attached to the individual in an undisturbed layer; another was discovered on the floor of the pit within the looters' layer.

Greenstone nose pendants of type B apparently have not been found before. In contrast, the "butterfly" form has been found in Early Tlamimilolpa Grave 21 in the residential compound called La Ventilla (Rattray 1992: 9; Rattray and Ruiz 1980), discovered with accompanying ornaments including greenstone beads, earspools, and pyrite/slate disks. This later-period burial may have been related to the FSP burial complex, since such analogies in morphologies of objects and their combination are unusual in Teotihuacan burials. The analogies may reflect ritual, social, or political affiliation with those wearing the same types of greenstone objects at the FSP, imply technological continuity in certain groups or the same production source, or suggest that offerings at the FSP were retrieved and buried again at La Ventilla. One nose pendant of type A was also found together with greenstone beads in association with a sacrificed individual in the Moon Pyramid, suggesting that this ornament set was used in other graves at major monuments.

The meanings of these two types of nose pendants are unclear. In Teotihuacan iconography, representations of butterflies, whose morphology is similar to type A nose pendants, are abundant, especially in incense burner complexes (Berlo 1984). In fact, a censer workshop was found in an area adjacent to the Ciudadela, suggesting that butterfly symbolism in Teotihuacan was linked to the Ciudadela (Múnera 1985; Sugiyama 1998a). Butterfly images in Teotihuacan have been referred to as the patron deity of merchants (von Winning 1987), as the predecessor of the Aztec Xochipilli (Séjourné 1961), as a notational sign (Langley 1986: 240), and as a symbol of soul, death, and warfare (Berlo 1983, 1984: 63–65). The mortuary and martial contexts in which the nose pendants were discovered at the FSP may support the identification of type A nose pendants with butterflies as a symbol of dead soldiers; however, this identification presents a problem, in that no representations identical to type A nose pendants have been found in the wide variety of butterfly images at Teotihuacan.

Oralia Cabrera (1995) pointed out that type A nose pendants may represent the end portion of a rattlesnake's rattle. Morphologically, a type A nose pendant is more similar to a rattle than to a butterfly in Teotihuacan iconography. Moreover, the contexts in which type A nose pendants were used strongly support Cabrera's idea since they were found at the pyramid dedicated to the Feathered Serpent. If the nose pendant was used as an identification element, individuals found with it would have been soldiers affiliated with the Feathered Serpent. In fact, the eighteen individuals who wore it, discovered at the pyramid's center with sumptuous offerings, would have been elite soldiers who played paramount roles: sacrificed in honor of the Feathered Serpent for the ideological and political foundation of the state.

Nose pendants similar to type B appear on the faces of individuals wearing elaborate costumes and ornaments in Teotihuacan iconography (Fig. 67a); they are also similar to those on Teotihuacan masks in censer complexes, worn as facial ornaments. Some of these anthropomorphic figures were identified as Tlaloc (Caso 1967a: 252) and, recently, as the Great Goddess (Pasztory 1988). Most intriguing are similar nose pendants below the sculptured heads of the Primordial Crocodile (Fig. 29a). The Primordial Crocodile is represented in the form of a headdress, probably with cosmological and calendrical meanings. Headdresses combined with nose pendants are found on the bodies of the Feathered Serpent, as if this mythical entity carries a regalia set of authority as a time bearer. In Petén Maya sites, nose pendants similar to types A and B, apparently introduced from Teotihuacan, were worn by warrior-kings (Fig. 67b and c); however, the exact form, with a bifurcated tongue-like projection in its lower section, has not been identified in any of these cases.

Although type B nose pendants were found only in Grave 13, it appears there were originally more than two of the same type in the grave. If this looted grave once contained a king's body, as proposed by Cowgill (1992a: 106), it is unlikely that nose pendants were used only by the king. If Grave 13 contained another sacrificial complex, as suggested by its burial pattern (similar to Grave 14), the type B nose pendants would have been used to identify the group sacrificed and buried there. Types A and B nose pendants, contrasting with each other, may have been identification codes of sacrificial victims belonging to two different ritual and/or political affiliations. Implications are discussed in Chapter 8.

Greenstone anthropomorphic figurines
Greenstone figurines have been found in only a few graves. Thirty-five were concentrated in the central grave (Grave 14), and at least six were uncovered in front of the FSP (Pérez 1939; Rubín de la Borbolla 1947; Cowgill and Cabrera 1991). Besides these body figurines, six small greenstone anthropomorphic heads, perhaps used as pendants, were uncovered at the top of the pyramid (Marquina 1922: vol. 1, 158–61). Here, only objects found in Grave 14 are discussed, since data about the objects discovered in previous excavations are not available.

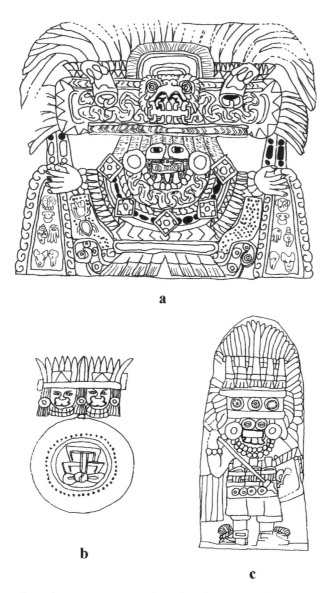

Fig. 67 Representations of greenstone nose pendants. Drawing: Kumiko Sugiyama. a Mural painting, "Green Tlaloc" at Tetitla compound (from Berrin and Pasztory 1993: 49); b Two human heads wearing type A nose pendants, sculptured on a stela called "ballgame marker" in Tikal, whose associated architecture and iconography indicate Teotihuacan influence (from Laporte and Fialko 1990: 53); c Soldier wearing Teotihuacan-influenced ornaments, including a type B nose pendant. Stela from Yaxha, Maya (from Schele and Grube 1994: 91).

A great variety of figurines was found in the central grave (Fig. 68). Figurines in various sizes, forms, and body proportions, carved in different techniques and elaborateness, were uncovered from the central and southwestern parts of the grave; they were apparently scattered on the bodies of the sacrificed victims. Their typological differences and similarities may have had ritual significance and/or social

Fig. 68 Greenstone figurines of types A1, A2, A3, B, C1, C2, D, E, F, G, H1, and H2 (from the upper left to the lower right). Photo: author.

implications; the differences also would have reflected variables not directly related to the mortuary program such as temporal variation in production or different craftsmen. Their variety may even indicate that each piece represented a specific individual or group. Because of this complexity, the figurines were classified according to detailed features, and variation in location was related to morphological differentiation. The underlying proposition is that, if certain patterns of spatial distribution or correlation with other objects are observed, intentionality of meanings in the wide variety throughout the mortuary program is more specifically suggested, whereas random distribution may indicate no deliberateness to the spatial patterns.

I took into account both quantitative data and presence of ornaments for classification of figurines. Plots of height and width indicated two basic groups, subdivided by headdress, earspool, pendant, *maxtlatl* (loincloth), inlaid teeth, groove on back, and other features. The resulting classification indicates that figurine size, and perhaps quality of material, are correlated with these variables. Teotihuacanos seem to have selected large pieces of greenstone to make figurines of special types (principally types C and D), while small, thin pieces were used for type A figurines.

Type A figurines (Fig. 68) are distinguished from other types by the presence of a headdress, necklace (with one exception), *maxtlatl*, and by a flat back with grooved lines, of a standardized size. Moreover, this group is distinguished by a higher quality of greenstone (Turner 1991, personal communication), and further subdivided into A1, A2, and A3 types. Three examples of type A1 figurines, forming a group of medium weight, have one hole on each side of the head for earspools; two figurines of type A2 do not have the holes for earspools, and are the heaviest of this group. One type A3 example, the only piece in this group without a pendant on the chest or grooved lines on its back surface, has a channel instead of holes for attaching earspools; its body is slimmer than the others in this collection, and it weighs the least.

Type B figurines are represented by two examples, each with a helmet-like ornament on the head. The back sides of the bodies have convex smooth surfaces. Type C figurines are characterized by large, heavy bodies with standardized proportions and grooved extremities. One channel on the back of the neck, possibly used to attach a "resplandor" (see below), makes these figurines distinct from other groups, and more inlay was found in this group. Two additional subgroups can be formed by the presence of head treatment. The four type C1 figurines do not have any special head treatment, while C2 figurines have horn-like objects or line grooves as head ornaments.

One figurine, distinguished from the others by its unique facial and body form, was classified as type D. It is the largest and heaviest of the collection and has a carved line on the top of the head, like typical Teotihuacan ceramic human figurines. Type E figurines are characterized by the high quality of their pure green jadeite, finely polished surfaces, and a different headdress. This figurine is not three-dimensional but is a thin, flat plaque cut in human form, with grooves representing parts of the body. Type F figurines are distinguished by earspools and *maxtlatl*.

Type G consists of one example, with its arms crossed over the chest, two holes representing eyes, and two more holes on its lateral sides, presumably for the attachment of earspools. On its head are three lines, possibly representing a head ornament. Type H figurines have few distinguishing characteristics, with none of the previously listed features and no inlay, but with distinctive diagonal lines delineating nose and cheek areas. They were tentatively subdivided simply by size and weight: H1 types are more than 4 cm in height, 1.85 cm in width, and 6 g in weight; H2 figurines measure less than these dimensions and are more crudely made than any of the other groups.

Contrary to expectations, a plot of these figurines by type (Fig. 69) does not reveal any special patterning among them or clear indication of their association with individuals. Rather, it indicates a wide, irregular dispersion of same-type figurines. This apparently unpatterned distribution is discussed later in connection with other offerings.

In Teotihuacan iconography, anthropomorphic figurines are seldom depicted, although small zoomorphic creatures were often shown, especially in association with water-related symbols and emerging from spiral and bivalve shells. Only a few cases of an apparent figurine head are known in Teotihuacan murals. In a Tetitla mural,

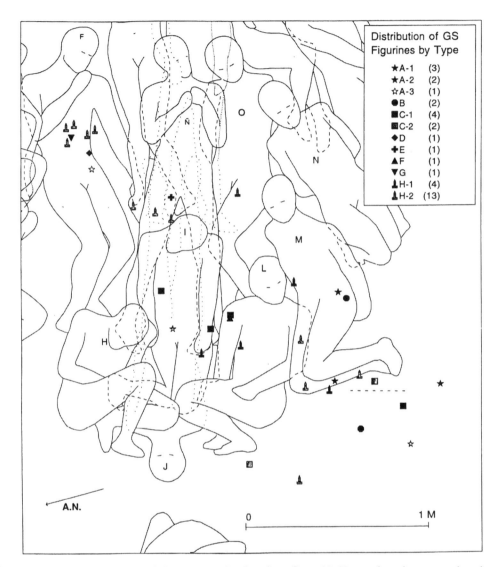

Fig. 69 Spatial distribution of all greenstone figurines from Grave 14: 35 complete pieces were plotted by type. GIS map: author.

the so-called "Green Tlaloc" (Fig. 67), two greenstone figurine heads are evidently shown with other kinds of offerings in the panels falling from the hands of anthro-pomorphic figures wearing type B nose pendants. Possible meanings are discussed in the section on offering associations.

Greenstone "resplandores"

Although there are significant differences in size, the forms of greenstone "resplan-dores" are fairly uniform, and distinguishing morphological features are considered minimal (Fig. 70); only size was taken into account to plot their spatial distribution (Fig. 71). The plots revealed that all large resplandores were concentrated in a small

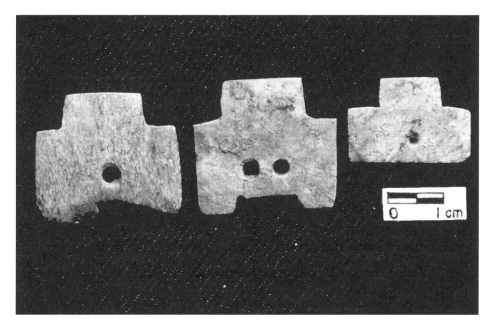

Fig. 70 Greenstone "resplandores" of various sizes found at the FSP. Photo: author.

area under the left upper arm of individual 14-F; several apparently formed part of offering clusters.

Although resplandores evidently had been attached to the figurines (Rubín de la Borbolla 1947; Cowgill and Cabrera 1991), what they represent is unknown. Their form is similar to a certain type of Teotihuacan headdress, and they had been attached on the back sides of figurine heads as if they were headdresses. However, resplandores were found with type A figurines which already wore headdresses, and their size was usually too large for a headdress. Taken together, they could have comprised a headdress complex of multilayered components. Their silhouette is similar to those of some headdresses associated with the Feathered Serpent, including the headdress worn by the Primordial Crocodile on the facades of the FSP (Chapter 4; Fig. 25a). Representations of headdresses which Langley (1986: 114) called the Feathered Headdress symbol, including the year-sign headdress, have a structure similar to the resplandor form. Therefore, resplandores might have had calendrical significance, as well as the ritual meaning of a bearer/burden that headdresses often represented in Teotihuacan (López et al. 1991: 102–3). Small, simple figurines without headdresses also carry large resplandores that apparently represented a burden borne on their backs.

Greenstone cones
Eighteen cones (Fig. 72) were found in a specific area of Grave 14: only under the left upper arm of individual 14-F, a location that suggests that all were associated with this individual. However, they may also have been parts of general offerings put over the bodies of several individuals in the central part of the grave.

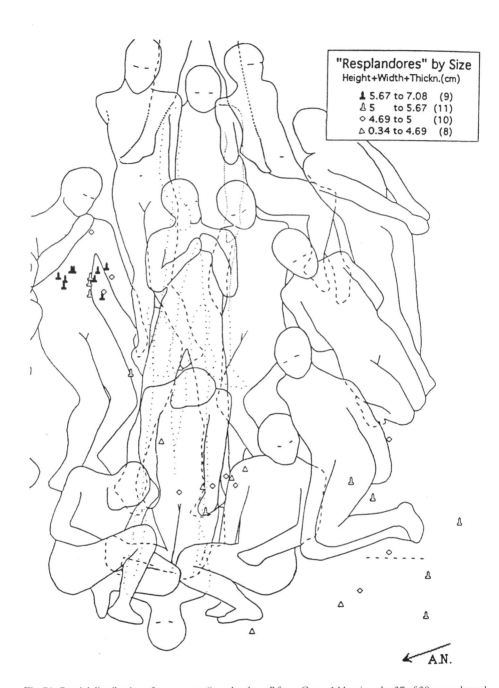

Fig. 71 Spatial distribution of greenstone "resplandores" from Grave 14 by size: the 37 of 38 were plotted by sum (cm) of height, width, and thickness. One piece found between two individuals, 14-I and 14-L, was not geocoded. Large "resplandores" were apparently concentrated on the upper body of individual 14-F. GIS map: author.

Fig. 72 Greenstone cones found in Grave 14. Photo: author.

They are homogeneous in material, form, and incised surface motif, except for one extremely small cone without incisions. Seventeen of the eighteen cones are decorated similarly, with triangle motifs in a row along the bottom edges of their sloped exterior surfaces. All surfaces of these cones are well polished except for the bottoms, and the summits are sharply pointed. Size of the cones and the number of triangle designs (ranging from seven to nine) vary from one to another. Based on these minor differences, the eighteen cones were classified into four groups.

Type A cones were represented by the one small, well-polished cone already mentioned (18 mm height × 16 mm diameter), whose size is extremely small; it might have had a different function from the others; a small area on the sloping wall near its bottom was apparently cut off, simulating the large cones (discussed in the section on slate and other stone). Type B cones, the largest (mean: 64.5 mm height × 51.5 mm diameter), consist of two examples, each with seven triangle motifs at the bottom of their sloping wall. Type C (mean: 55.3 mm height × 51.5 mm diameter) is represented by ten cones, each with eight triangle designs. Type D (mean: 47.0 mm height × 47.2 mm diameter) consists of five cones, each decorated with a row of nine triangle designs. The number of triangle designs is correlated with cone size. If the one type A cone is excluded, examples with nine triangles comprise the group of smallest and lightest cones, while two examples with seven triangles are those of the largest and heaviest. Although this correlation is clearly indicated, no attached meanings or functions are apparent. It was considered that their spatial relationships might suggest something about their function, particularly a possible usage for game-ritual (see below); however, plots by triangle design number, cone height, and cone diameter yielded no obvious distribution pattern (Fig. 73).

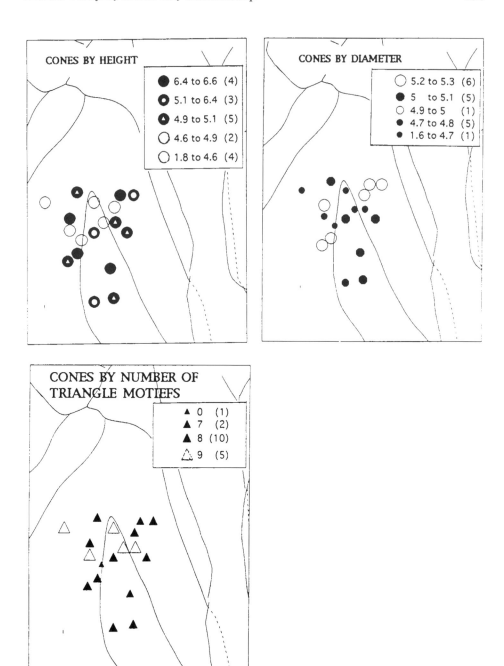

Fig. 73 Spatial distribution of greenstone cones in Grave 14: all 18 pieces were plotted by height, diameter (cm), and the number of triangle motifs. GIS map: author.

As far as I know, greenstone cones have not been found elsewhere in Teotihuacan, and they seem to have been rare in the rest of Mesoamerica. Only a few relevant references have been found. Mountjoy and Smith (1985) report the discovery of cones in Jalisco, which they believe were used for *patolli*. These are more similar to the FSP cones than any others although their materials, shapes, and archaeological contexts are different. *Patolli* was considered not only a game but also a sacred act by Mesoamericans (Sahagún 1954: bk. 8, ch. 10). Aveni (1980: 231–33) discusses possible calendrical and astrological meanings of *patolli* in the Mexican Highlands. The resemblance of *patolli* to the marks of pecked crosses, which were found in abundance in Teotihuacan, also supports this interpretation.

John Carlson has informed me that the collection of pre-Columbian art in Yale University Art Gallery contains an object (Kubler 1986: 221) comparable to the FSP cones: the triangle design on the bottom edge of the object is strikingly similar to that of the cones. However, this pottery object's shape is not really a cone but a flat plaque whose upper half represents two other objects, one a square form with two holes near the edge, the other resembling the distal end of a femur. Carlson thinks this indicates a ritual use of cones with human sacrifice because the entire object appears to represent the femur head stuck on the point of a cone. This interpretation corresponds well with the burial contexts of the object, which explicitly indicates human sacrifices, although significant differences of material, shape, and the uncertain identification of other added elements raise many questions about the interpretation. Since no other references to greenstone cones have been found, Carlson's interpretation awaits additional data and explanations.

Two of the interpretations mentioned above are not exclusive; therefore the cones could have been bloody ritual objects with calendrical astrological meanings, used for *patolli*. According to Christopher Carr (1995, personal communication), the Hopewell people of the eastern United States placed cones in the graves of some of their dead, some made of quartz and others made of copper (green) and sparkling stones. Carr has assumed that the cones were used in a divining game. This analogy might also be suggestive for the FSP cones, although the instances mentioned are too isolated to discuss possible relationships among them.

Miscellaneous

In addition to the objects discussed above, several other kinds of greenstone objects were found in the central area of the FSP, some from Grave 14, others from looted graves or the looters' tunnel. These unusual pieces distinguish the central graves from peripheral graves, although there is no clear indication of hierarchical distinction among the central graves (Graves 12, 13, and 14) in their offerings. Graves 14 and 13 contained their own unique objects; however, the data were not sufficient to differentiate them hierarchically from one another in quality, quantity, or variety, because Graves 12 and 13 were looted. According to stratigraphic data, certain pieces found in the looters' tunnel may have been offerings originally deposited in Grave 13. A small plaque in the form of a temple was found in the disturbed layer

Fig. 74 Various greenstone objects: a "resplandor," b nose pendant miniature, c and d plaque pendants, e miniature ax with sharp edge, f and g plaque fragments, h a "scroll" pendant with a perforation, i small temple plaque, j and k two button-like round objects. Photo: author.

near the floor of Grave 13 (Fig. 74i), incised with the same design on both sides to represent a temple platform. In the same layer of Grave 13, two small button-like round objects were found (Fig. 74j and k) and another, very similar round plaque was found in a layer covering Grave 13. They formed parts of the same type of object, as their identical location (in different layers) and morphological similarities suggest. One greenstone pendant in the form of a scroll with a perforation (Fig. 74h) was found in the lowest disturbed layer of Grave 13. Although this was a motif used frequently, what the piece specifically represents is unknown. The presence of a hole indicates that it functioned as a pendant, and it could have been used with other pendants. If a counterpart had the same form, they may have represented a bifurcated tongue.

Grave 14 also contained unique greenstone objects. One miniature ax was found near the cranium of individual 14-B (Fig. 74e), its surface smoothed and one end with a long, sharp edge. Several unique beads and plaques were also found among many other offerings, including simple greenstone beads that would have been variations of beads or pendants deposited as general offerings. Other unidentified greenstone objects, mostly fragments, are not included here.

The varieties of unique greenstone offerings, together with unusual objects made of other materials, stress the special qualities of Graves 13 and 14. Yet the data do not seem to indicate the superiority of either of these two graves.

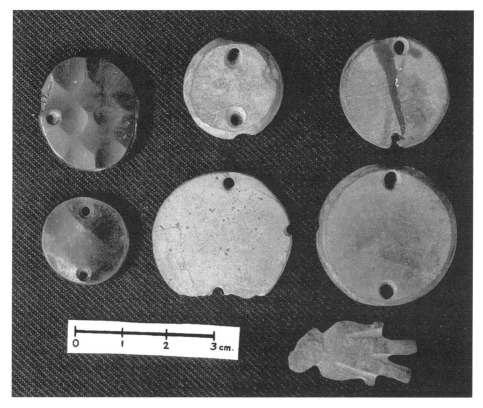

Fig. 75 Slate disks of various sizes from the FSP graves. Two disks to the left are classified as small, while four pieces to the right belong to a third group of medium size. The human figure made of slate was also found at the FSP. Photo: author.

Slate and other stones

Disks

More than 185 stone disks, mainly of slate and varying considerably in size (Fig. 75), were found in many graves at the FSP. Those found in the 1980s were classified into three groups, basically by size and provenance. It had been noticed that disks found in peripheral areas comprise two groups of distinct sizes: large (>4 cm diameter and 0.24 cm thick) and small (<2.4 cm diameter and 0.2 cm thick) respectively. Disks found in Graves 190, 4, 5, and 6 consistently belong to either group; however, many disks discovered in the central grave do not belong to either of the two well-defined groups, being thicker than the small disks, with diameters between 2 and 4 cm. I defined these disks as a third group of medium size.

Large slate disks, except for those found in Grave 14, were always discovered in peripheral areas, at the posterior part of the hipbones of male individuals found with maxilla pendants. They have been identified as the rear waist ornament known as *tezcacuitlapilli* in Postclassic Nahuatl, and were a diagnostic element for the identification of soldiers. Disks were also worn as back ornaments by priests or military figures in Teotihuacan iconography that have been dated to the fourth to sixth centuries AD (Fig. 18c; Miller 1973: figs. 149, 317; Taube 1992b: 172–77). Excavation contexts confirm that back disks already symbolized martial affairs from the early third century in Teotihuacan.

Large slate disks normally had two holes near their edges, and the forms were quite homogeneous. They were often found with a yellow substance on them, suggesting that now-disintegrated pyrite had been attached to them (pyrite is a pale brass-yellow mineral with metallic luster, used mainly for mirrors in Mesoamerica). Other, unidentified mineral and organic remains were recognized around the disks in the field. Perhaps they were originally parts of ornaments attached to the disks, as suggested by the back disk representations in Teotihuacan murals.

At the FSP, only individuals found in peripheral areas wore back disks. Figure 76 shows distribution of individuals wearing back disks by size of disk. A strong correlation of back disk with male is indicated by the fact that all back-disk wearers were male although all males did not wear back disks (Compare Fig. 76 with Fig. 45). Positive correlation of disks with maxilla pendants (see below) is also clear, since 87 percent of males wearing maxilla pendants (Graves 190, 4, 5, and 6) had back disks, and all individuals wearing back disks were ornamented with maxilla pendants. The figure also indicates that there was no apparent regularity in the order of the individuals by size of back disk.

The second group of small disks was found only in peripheral graves (Graves 190, 4, 5, and 6). They were <2.4 cm in diameter and <2.2 mm in thickness and usually had one hole, suggesting that they were pendants. Excavation contexts also support the theory that they functioned as pendants, since they were found at the thoracic region of individuals wearing large back disks. Individuals 190-N, 4-J, 4-P, and 6-C wore four, three, one, and three small disks respectively. There is no apparent locational pattern of individuals wearing small disks, although the fact that each multiple grave contained three or four small disks might be significant.

The central graves (Graves 12, 13, and 14) included, besides twelve fragments of disks (<30 percent of complete piece), twenty-five complete or incomplete disks (>30 percent of complete piece) of medium size, and nine complete or incomplete disks of large size. Their spatial distribution is different from the others. As shown in Figure 77, disks measuring >4 cm, which could have been used as back disks, were not found on the back of the waist of any individuals. This is also consistent with the strong positive correlation of large disks with maxilla pendants, since the central grave did not contain maxilla pendants. The function of large disks in the central grave would have been different from that in peripheral graves. Nor have the medium-sized disks been found in clear association with specific individuals, but seem to have been parts of general offerings, although they were not likely components of offering clusters.

In the looters' tunnel, eight complete or incomplete disks were found. Grave 12 contained one piece of a large disk, two pieces of small disks, and four pieces of medium-sized disks, while Grave 13 included only one medium-sized piece. The data again indicate similarity among the offerings of the central graves (Graves 12,

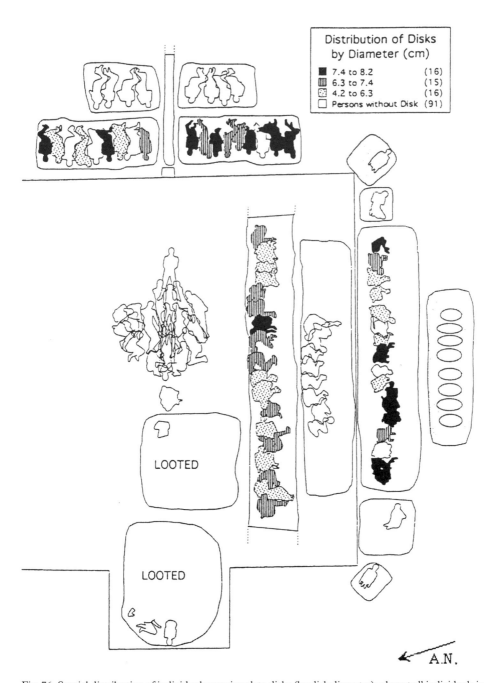

Fig. 76 Spatial distribution of individuals wearing slate disks (by disk diameter): almost all individuals in Graves 190, 4, 5, and 6 had back disks. Individuals in Grave 204 on the FSP's north side, also ornamented with slate disks, are not shown; Grave 14 also contained disks, which are not indicated, since they were not directly associated with individuals. GIS map: author.

small or fragmented disks

disks more than 4 cm diameter

Fig. 77 Spatial distribution of disks in Grave 14; these were not worn as back ornaments. Disks of all sizes seem to comprise general offerings. Among 46 complete or incomplete disks, 42 pieces were geocoded; precise locations of 4 fragments of disks were unknown. GIS map: author.

13, and 14). Besides those found in the 1980s, Pérez reports that slate fragments were recovered in front of the FSP stairway, while Marquina mentions that at least fifteen slate disks were discovered at the top of the pyramid. The excavation contexts and the details of these disks are unknown.

In summary, disks of large size can be identified as back disks diagnostic of soldiers. Small disks may have comprised small pendant clusters on interred individuals. The

Fig. 78 Large cones with stems: materials for construction fill in the FSP's central zone. Size, proportion, and wear marks vary significantly from one to another. Photo: author.

function of disks of medium size cannot be inferred from the excavation contexts, since they were not found in consistent association with specific body parts. In Teotihuacan iconography, representations of disks are abundant, depicted as waist disks, mirrors, chest disks, disks on headdresses, and other ornaments (Taube 1992b). Small disks are inlaid in stone anthropomorphic figures in Teotihuacan; some may have been parts of ornaments associated with greenstone figurines, although their spatial relations with other types of offerings do not suggest a clear association.

Large cones

During the exploration of the FSP's central zone, forty-six large stone cones with stems (Fig. 78) were discovered in the fill. Cone form is rather uniform, although the ratio of height to width (maximum diameter) varies from one to another, and size also varies considerably. The largest one measures 30.7 cm high and 17.7 cm width (maximum), while the smallest is 15.7 cm high and 14.9 cm wide. Stems measure approximately one-fifth to one-quarter their total length, and points are usually somewhat rounded or worn. Many cones were broken, some with stems cut off at their bases; seven had been cut off vertically (Fig. 79); in five, one part was cut off vertically at the stem edge, and in two, part of both the cone and the stem were cut off. Several have smoothed surfaces.

The cones were found at various stratigraphic depths, without apparent patterning in position. Excavation contexts indicate that they were thrown into the fill with other rocks to make the nucleus of the pyramid and that they were not intended to be part

Fig. 79 Seven large, stemmed cones with portions of surface partially cut off, in some cases (two at lower right) as far as the stem. Photo: author.

of the offerings of the dedicatory complex. However, I considered them as another element intentionally incorporated into the construction of the monument, because they are objects unique to Teotihuacan, and because the form suggested that cones have a symbolic meaning much like that posited for greenstone cones. In addition, the cones were found exclusively in the pyramid's central zone, which may indicate that the large cones were deliberately buried with certain functions and/or meanings, as in the case of greenstone cones, which were found exclusively in the central grave. It may also be that they were thrown in during the construction process, after their original function was lost.

The spatial distribution of the cones is irregular, strongly concentrated in an area to the west of the central grave, and limited to the zone defined by the looters' tunnel and a small portion of the central tunnel. Although we found several in the walls of the looters' tunnel, we do not know how many had been removed by looters or how many remain in the pyramid's unexcavated fill. Only the central tunnel has provided data on the density and area into which the cones were thrown, and it is therefore difficult to tell if there was an overall distribution pattern.

Three of the thirty-nine recovered cones (seven remained in situ) had separate stems. They could have been made originally in two parts, or broken stems might have been replaced with new ones. In these cases, a pillar (or stem) would have been inserted in a hole of the same diameter with stucco used to glue it in place, suggesting that stems were replaceable and that cones may have been used with force.

The functions of these large cones are unknown, since they have been neither reported nor discussed previously. I propose two hypotheses, one of which excludes the other. First, because of the presence of stems, they might have been architectural elements. Stems give the impression that they were inserted in holes like the composite stelae found in La Ventilla (Arroyo de Andla 1963: figs. 1–3) and "Quetzalpapalotl Palace" (Acosta 1964: figs. 21, 35). An analogy with the greenstone cones found in the central grave suggests that large cones also possessed a symbolic quality. These interpretations mutually support the theory that they were symbolic architectural elements, and excavation contexts also support the idea, since remains of substructures were found around the central part of the FSP, where the cones were discovered.

However, some questions remain. First, no Teotihuacan architecture incorporates this type of cone, nor is there any representation as yet identified in the city. The cones could have been unique architectural elements that were never used again; however, if they were part of architectural elements used at some place in a unique substructure, why did the size and proportions of all cones vary significantly from one to another? This interpretation also does not explain coarsely finished surfaces, vertically cut-off portions, or partially smoothed surfaces (possibly wear marks).

The second hypothesis is that the large cones were tools, possibly used to dig burial pits in the hard subsoil. Herb Sallet has offered an explanation for the cut portions of the cones, pointing out their similarity to a certain type of "bit," a modern tool for making holes. Both large cones and stems have vertically cut portions near the point, through which dug-out material might pass. Size, weight, form, suitability for digging, surface wear marks, replaceable stem, and rough surfaces of the vertically cut portions without wear marks support the theory that the cones functioned as digging tools.

Excavation contexts also fit well with the second interpretation. The cones were found in an area surrounded by more than twenty-four pits dug into hard subsoil by the Teotihuacanos, some exceptionally large and deep. Stratigraphic data indicate that these possible stone tools were buried immediately after the pits were made or during the construction process. However, it is strange that cones of this type have not previously been reported elsewhere in Teotihuacan if they had been used as digging tools. Specific technical questions about how to dig pits with these tools are a matter for experimental archaeology, in order to support either one of the explanations presented here.

Shell

Shell artifacts comprise one of the main offerings in the FSP burial complex, having been found in almost all graves. They include beads, pendants, teeth imitations used for maxilla pendants, and unworked shell, and the majority were ornaments found in association with individuals. Besides those found in the 1980s on the north, south, and east sides and inside the pyramid, Marquina (1922: vol. 1, 158–61) reported discoveries of shell offerings at the top of the pyramid. Pérez (1939) and Rubín de la Borbolla (1947) also state that spiral and conch shells were discovered in front of the pyramid stairway. These offerings might have been part of offerings interred with burials, or independent caches. Their precise quantities and forms are unknown. I briefly describe analyses and interpretation of the materials discovered in 1980s. Many shell objects were correlated with sex (a principal variable for the distribution of bodies) and were distributed in patterned ways in the burial complex.[11] Logically, they were correlated with other offerings that reflected sex distribution, such as greenstone artifacts and slate disks.

Unworked shell

Unworked shells were limited to only a few graves, the majority in the central grave (Grave 14), and a few in looted graves (Graves 12 and 13). Others were found at the pyramid's front and back sides; several spiral and conch shells of different sizes were found at the top of the pyramid (Marquina 1922) and in front of its stairway (Pérez 1939; Rubín de la Borbolla 1947). Sixty-six complete or semicomplete unworked shells were discovered as general offerings in the central and southwestern parts of Grave 14. Their direct associations with individuals were not recognized in the field since they were found on and between the bodies with many other kinds of offerings.

Unworked shells were identified taxonomically by Clara Paz based on sample identification by INAH biologist Oscar Polaco. Within the family Gastropoda (univalve shells), genus *Oliva* and *Turbinella* were identified, and in the family Pelecypoda (bivalve shells), genus *Argopecten*, *Ostrea*, *Pecten*, *Pinctada*, and *Spondylus* were identified. They had been brought from both the Pacific and Atlantic Oceans.

Spatial distribution of shells by species indicates that the offerings were intentionally located by type (Fig. 80). One *Oliva* was found on the head of individual fourteen-I near the center of the grave and the center of the pyramid. *Turbinella*, so-called trumpet shells, may have formed three or four clusters. Seven pieces were apparently arranged in the form of an upside-down V on the body of individual 14-Ñ, and another cluster of seven pieces was located around the right shoulder of individual 14-I. Ten pieces of the same group were found on the thoracic region of individual 14-L, four pieces were dispersed around individual 14-M; these fourteen pieces might have been associated with individual 14-L, or they might have been derived from two clusters of seven pieces associated with individuals 14-L and M. Genus *Argopecten*, *Ostrea*, and *Pecten* were discovered around the individuals F, Ñ, I, L, M, and N. Pieces of *Pinctada* and *Spondylus* were also found in limited areas of the grave, in the southwestern and central zones respectively, and appear to have been laid down as general offerings. Some species could have been associated with specific individuals.

Shells appear frequently in Teotihuacan iconography, often with various water symbols; therefore, one essential quality is association with water. In extension, they may also have been used as a backdrop to the watery Underworld in which mythological entities are represented. Shell representations on FSP facades were probably one such case, as discussed in Chapter 4 (Fig. 17a). It would not have been accidental that the same types of shells depicted on the facades (trumpets, *Oliva*, bivalves, etc.) were actually buried with the individuals of the central grave. The same types

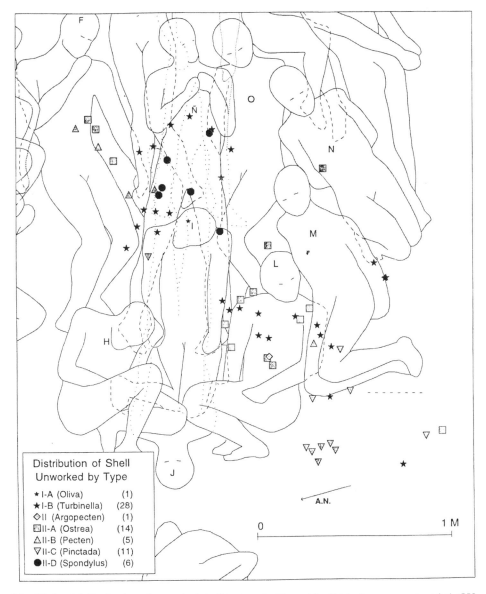

Fig. 80 Spatial distribution of unworked shell by type in Grave 14: all 66 pieces were geocoded. GIS map: author.

of marine shells were also represented extensively in murals as objects being scattered from the hands of anthropomorphic figures (see discussion in the section on "Offering associations"). In scroll panels, shell objects were also often represented as emerging from the mouths of priests, as if the priests were chanting about shells and the other objects depicted (e.g., Fig. 18c). Thus, marine shells, represented both in art and in the dedication burial, would have been objects symbolizing water, the watery Underworld, or ritual tools handled or chanted about by priests. In the FSP

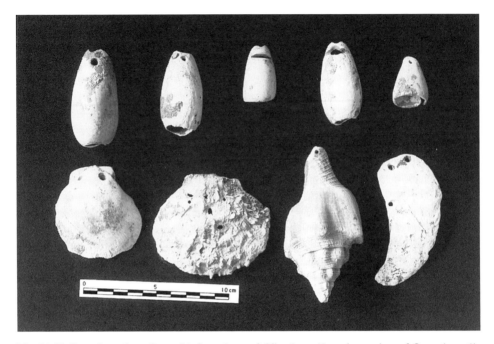

Fig. 81 Shell pendants from Grave 14: four pieces of *Oliva* (type 1), and one piece of *Conus* (type 2), *Pecten* (type 3), *Spondylus* (type 4), *Turbinella angulata* (type 5), and *Siliqua* (type 6), from top left to lower right. Photo: author.

burial complex, shells were one of the principal objects accompanying a sacrificial ritual with unknown intention, as reflected in spatial patterns.

Shell pendants

Shell pendants, consisting of complete or semicomplete shells with one or more holes near the edges, were found only in the central grave and in front of the pyramid's principal facade. Six different kinds of shell pendants were found in Grave 14. Type 1 (Fig. 81: four pieces at upper left) is worked *Oliva* with holes, and type 2 (upper right) is worked *Conus* with holes; the lower parts of these two types were usually cut off. Type 3 (lower left) is an entire *Pecten* shell, usually with two holes. Type 4 (second from left, lower row) is an entire *Spondylus* shell with two holes. Type 5 (the third) represents so-called trumpets, *Turbinella angulata*, with one hole near one end. Type 6 (lower right) consists of six *Siliqua* worked into a chili-shaped form, with two holes near the top.

The general spatial distribution of shell pendants (Fig. 82) indicates that they were dispersed widely in the grave with three spots of concentration: under the left upper arm of individual 14-F, between the legs of individuals 14-F and Ñ, and around the right shoulder of individual 14-L. Spatial distribution by type, however, indicates that two of the three clusters were composed of pendants of types 1 and 2; it is notable that type 2 pendants were not used for the third cluster. The clusters might have been associated with specific individuals as their ornaments, but again, because

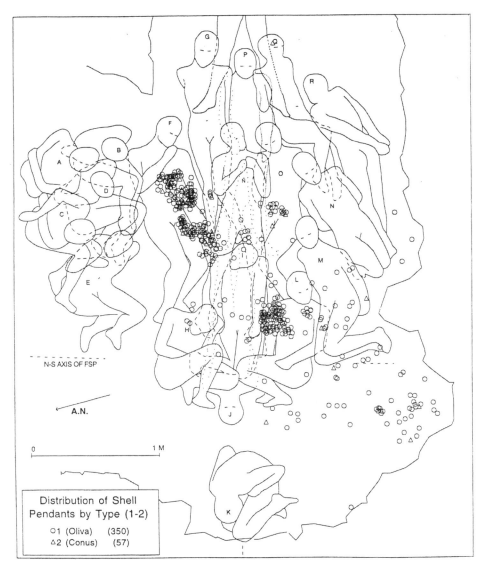

N-S AXIS OF FSP

A.N.

0   1 M

Distribution of Shell
Pendants by Type (1-2)

○1 (Oliva)   (350)
△2 (Conus)   (57)

Fig. 82 Spatial distribution of shell pendants in Grave 14: types 1 and 2. Among 464 pieces, 455 were geocoded. GIS map: author.

of their lack of correspondence with any part of the bodies, they seem to have been parts of general offerings. The same types of *Oliva* pendants (type 1) have been found in mortuary contexts at many Mesoamerican sites, including Tombs A-I, A-III, and B-II in Kaminaljuyú (Kidder et al. 1946: fig. 164). In these cases, the pendants were found as clustered offerings apart from the individual interred, as was the case in Grave 14 at the FSP.

Pendants made with bivalves, *Pecten* (type 3) and *Spondylus* (type 4), were dispersed along a northeast-to-southwest direction over several bodies without a strong

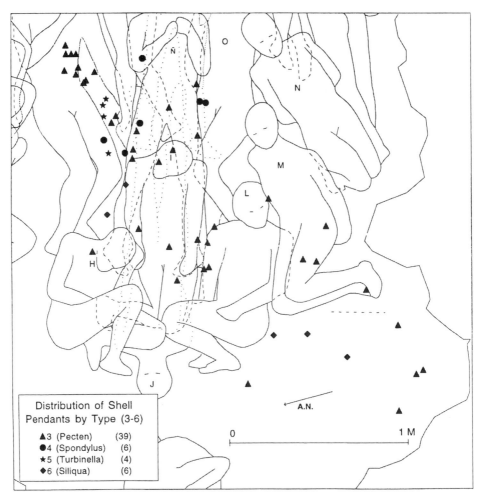

Fig. 83 Spatial distribution of shell pendants in Grave 14: types 3, 4, 5, and 6. GIS map: author.

concentration (Fig. 83). Type 4 pendants were located only around the body of individual 14-Ñ. Four type 5 (trumpet) pendants were discovered only in a small area between individuals F and Ñ. *Siliqua* pendants (type 6) were also found in two limited areas, but they also may not have been associated with any particular part of the bodies. It is noteworthy that the distribution area of *Spondylus* pendants (type 4) corresponds to that of unworked *Spondylus* (II-D in Fig. 80). This suggests that both categories of *Spondylus* were used in relation to each other, and that the function of *Spondylus* pendants might have been secondary to their meanings.

In Teotihuacan iconography, shell pendants are often associated with anthropomorphic (Miller 1973: 100) and zoomorphic (Miller 1973: 50, 109) figurines; they were presumably suspended by strings through holes. All are bivalves similar to type 3 pendants. *Spondylus*-like pendants apparently are not represented in Teotihuacan, although they were depicted by the Lowland Maya. So-called shell trumpets were often represented in Teotihuacan iconography (Miller 1973: 50), although it is uncertain whether they had holes for use as pendants, since holes are not usually shown.

Oliva pendants, found abundantly in Grave 14, were not common in Teotihuacan works of art. As suggested by the Oaxaca statues mentioned later (Fig. 89), they may have been used as body ornaments attached to the waist. Ceramic sculptures from Classic-period Veracruz and many other representations from different regions also display *Oliva* waistbands or bracelet tinklers (Medellín 1983: 108). As we have seen, excavation contexts in the central grave indicate that shells with holes had not been attached as necklaces to the persons interred, and the distribution of the pendants in relation to reconstructed bodies again does not support such use. Although association of certain types of shell pendants with other kinds of offerings can be suggested, the functions of other pendants in Grave 14 are not clear.

Maxilla necklace complexes
Shell beads, small pendants, plaques, or tooth imitations were found in almost all graves at the FSP. Their original natural forms were completely transformed into plaque, cylinder, or tooth shapes, and they vary greatly in size and form. Most shell beads were associated with individuals interred in the peripheral areas, and most were considered parts of necklace complexes. In this section, shell objects imitating human teeth also are discussed, since they formed parts of necklaces. Excavation contexts indicate that tooth imitations formed maxilla attached to the necklace complexes. Also discussed here are the data on real human and animal maxillae, which had been integrated in the necklace complexes.

Four large categories – shell beads, small pendants, teeth imitations, and others – were subdivided into 122 types by form and size (Fig. 84). This typology can further be subdivided if further detailed differences are taken into account. Beads consist of shell modified into cylinders, rectangles, or human teeth, each with one hole at their center. Pendants were defined as worked shell objects with one or more holes near the edge. Tooth imitations had shapes similar to human or animal teeth and were used exclusively to compose maxilla imitations; they are grouped into incisors, canines, premolars, and molars. Some types present quite realistic shapes of human teeth, but others were too stylized to distinguish canines from incisors or premolars from molars. Although certain types do not look like teeth, they were often classified as tooth imitations based on excavation contexts, in which they formed maxilla pendants.

Subdivision (122 types) was based mainly on morphological features. A cuspid form was apparently produced distinguishably from other types and used for a few individuals. These standard forms were taken into consideration for classification, since they seem to represent native categorization. Differences may reflect distinct production processes and may not have been significant for rituals executed at the FSP; however, if certain distribution patterns are formed with other burial and/or offertory variables, the distinctiveness of tooth forms may have been embedded with certain ritual and social distinctions of the burials.

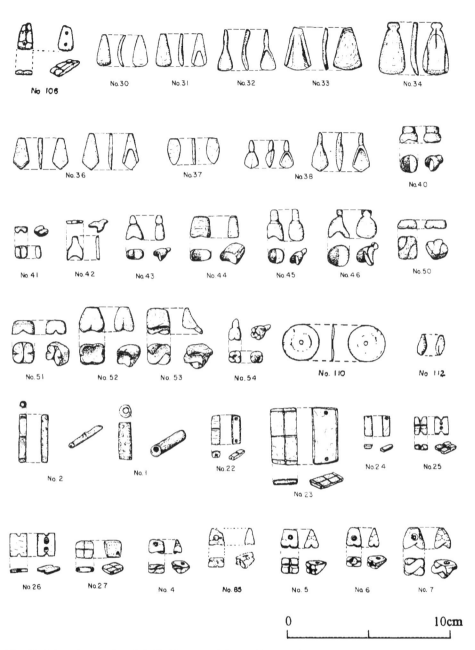

Fig. 84 Selected examples of shell objects used for necklaces and maxilla pendants, divided into four categories: shell beads (Nos. 1, 2, 4–7, 85, 110, 112), small pendants (Nos. 22–27, 106), teeth imitations (Nos. 30–34, 36–38, 40–46, 50–54), and others. Drawing: author and Verónica Moreno, from the originals.

The original forms of necklaces and maxilla pendants were better preserved in Graves 5 and 6 than in other graves because of their upward-facing body positions, the soft earth in the pits, and concrete floors sealing the burial pits. The upper bodies of individuals found in seated positions on the pyramid's south side (Grave 190) fell down with their shell ornaments on their chests, and the original forms were not preserved in most cases. Grave 4, inside the pyramid, contained badly preserved individuals because rock fill pressed on the bodies, often in a seated position, causing the original structure of necklaces and maxilla pendants associated with them to be altered.

The original forms of necklaces and maxilla pendants are here reconstructed individually based as closely as possible on typology and field data, in order to show spatial correlation by types of necklaces among the individuals interred. Numbers of maxillae may have been orderly and meaningfully arranged. Since the original forms were lost in many cases, the better-preserved Graves 5 and 6 served as a base from which to reconstruct the maxilla pendants in Graves 190 and 4. It was supposed, unless indicated by excavation context, that the maxillae had basically the same compositional structure as that of an adult human (fourteen or sixteen teeth). Calculation of the possible number of maxilla imitations was based on tables made by types and individuals, using field notes, drawings, and photos. Consequently, it was observed that an individual most likely had a necklace complex composed of a limited variety of beads and tooth imitations and that the same types of tooth imitations were consistently used for all maxilla imitations of an individual. Since analyses and results will be discussed in detail in separate reports, some results relevant to this volume are summarized here.

All maxilla necklace complexes found in peripheral graves (Graves 190, 4, 5, and 6) shared the same compositional structure, consisting of upper and lower sections (Fig. 85). The upper sections were subdivided into left, center, and right parts, and the lower sections were composed of a series of real or false maxillae. All beads, pendants, and certain types of tooth imitations with holes were used only for the upper section, while other types of tooth imitations with or without holes comprised maxilla pendants exclusively. Some types were widely shared by many individuals, others associated with a limited number of persons. No individuals shared maxilla necklace complexes of the same composition, suggesting that persons interred as soldiers were adorned with maxilla complexes combined differently from the others. The results cause one to suspect that maxilla pendants may have functioned as emblems, although it is also possible that differences in types reflected personal preference or style of individuals and had no social implications.

Maxilla pendants or imitation teeth made with shell had not been found outside the FSP until two sacrificial grave complexes containing identical maxilla pendants were recently discovered at the Moon Pyramid (Sugiyama and Cabrera 2000). This may weaken the idea that they were part of traditional garb worn widely in the city and mobilized for the offerings. The absence of these pieces beyond the Ciudadela and the Moon Pyramid suggests that maxilla pendants were quite special and might have been foreign products brought from the coastal areas, or that all

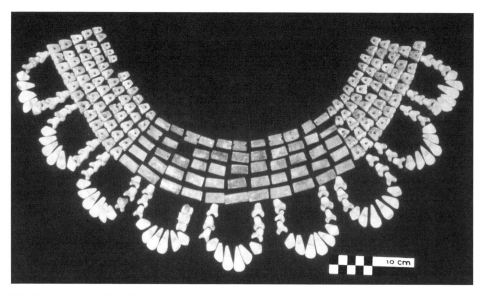

Fig. 85 An example of a shell necklace complex with maxilla imitation pendants: a common compositional structure was consistently used for all maxilla collars, though numbers of beads, tooth imitations, or maxilla imitations, width and length of collar, or types of pieces used vary significantly from person to person. Photo: author.

tooth imitations were manufactured for these special burial complexes by a group of craftsmen at Teotihuacan within a relatively short period. At any rate, the complexity of the combinations suggests that tooth imitations were not assembled as a simple reproduction of standard types to attach homogeneously to sacrificial victims. Great care was taken to express diverse types and to distinguish each maxilla complex from the others, and they may have been distributed meaningfully rather than at random.

A total of more than 21,383 shell pieces worked into beads, pendants, teeth, and other forms was found at the FSP. Inter- and intragrave distinctions were clearly indicated among burials containing maxilla pendants (Graves 190, 4, 5, and 6); however, whether political implications were involved in maxilla complexes is not clear. Persons distinguished by wearing maxilla imitations in larger quantity than others apparently were not spatially patterned, although some distinctiveness in type may have implied ritual and/or political differences.

Among distinctly different types of maxilla pendants, a few were of real humans (used for individuals 190-A, F; 5-H; and 4-Ñ: Fig. 86), real canids (4-A and 4-O), and false maxillae of canids made with shell (6-H: Fig. 87) that may have had meanings and functions different from those of human maxilla pendants made with shell. Spatial distribution indicates that the individuals wearing them were rather randomly buried among Graves 4, 5, 6, and 190, without significant spatial patterning or correlation with other variables.

Whether real or false maxilla pendants were of dogs or coyotes is unknown, but it is worth noting that coyotes seem to have had a special status, according to Teotihuacan iconographic studies (C. Millon 1988b). Coyote representations or coyote elements

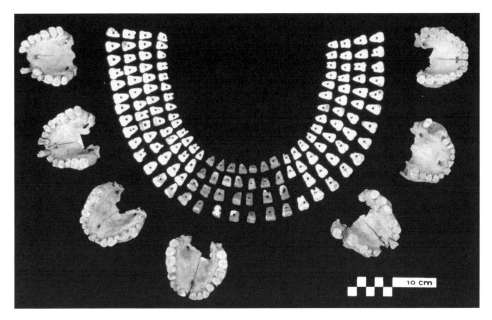

Fig. 86 Collar of real human maxillae, associated with individual 5-H. Photo: author.

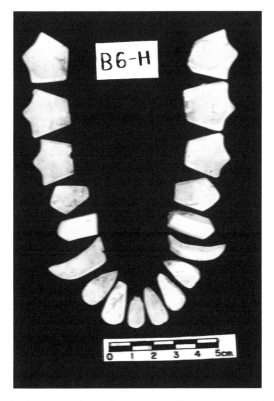

Fig. 87 Canid tooth imitations made of shell, forming a maxilla pendant associated with individual 6-H. Photo: author.

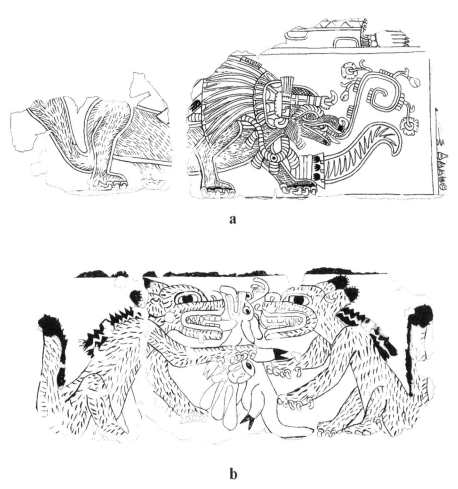

Fig. 88 Coyote representations in Teotihuacan murals. Drawing: author, from the original. a Coyote with a sacrificial knife; from a mural in the Wagner collection, San Francisco Fine Art Museum (after Berrin 1988: 123); b Two coyotes sacrificing a deer by heart extraction; from a mural in the Wagner collection, San Francisco Fine Art Museum (after Berrin 1988: 123).

are frequently associated with soldiers or human sacrificial rituals. Figure 88a shows a mural of a coyote with a sacrificial knife, the shape of which is identical to the obsidian bifacial knives of type B found in Grave 13 (Fig. 56, see also Fig. 58). Figure 88b represents two coyotes sacrificing a deer by heart extraction, a scene that seems to be a metaphor for human heart sacrifice. Thus, coyotes evidently symbolize soldiers and/or sacrificers in Teotihuacan.

Maxilla pendants were limited to multiple male burials containing martial offerings. In contrast, female individuals found near the soldier graves had fewer pendants of certain other types used for male individuals (6.9 pieces/female, against 354.5 pieces/male), and none had tooth imitations.[12] Individuals in Graves 1 and 153 and seven individuals (14-B, C, D, H, L, M, and N) in the central grave, all identified as male, were ornamented with extremely abundant beads of type 112

(Fig. 84) possessed by no other persons. Individual 14-E had a large number of another unique bead type (110). The same types of beads were also found in Kaminaljuyú (Kidder et al. 1946: fig. 163e), discovered, like those at the FSP, around the thoracic regions of the individuals.

In summary, it is evident that shell necklaces and maxilla pendants were strongly correlated with sex. Although not all males were associated with maxilla pendants, all eighteen or nine males interred with martial objects in Graves 190, 4, 5, and 6 were adorned with maxilla pendants. To other male burials without maxilla pendants, other types of shell beads, which were not used for females, were often attached. This spatial pattern supports the interpretation of maxilla pendants discussed below.

Although meanings attached to human maxilla pendants in Teotihuacan are unknown, ethnohistorical records from Yucatán suggest that they may have functioned as war trophies and/or as counting tools. Tozzer (1941: 120), citing Landa's *Relación de las cosas de Yucatán*, mentioned that people sacrificed were buried in the court of the temple, and that "if the victims were slaves captured in war, their master took their bones, to use them as a trophy in their dances as tokens of victory." Roys (1943: 67) describes the removal of real human mandibles of those killed in war for armlets or as symbols of honor. "After the victory they took the jaws off the dead bodies and with the flesh cleaned off, they put them on their arms" (Tozzer 1941: 123; Welsh 1988a: 171). In those found at the FSP, the interpretation of maxilla pendants as war trophies is supported by other kinds of martial objects associated with the individuals wearing maxilla pendants.

Tozzer (1941: 123) noted that "the Lacandones preserve in their idol houses the lower jaws, especially of the deer, the monkey, and the wild boar. These may serve as counts of sacrifices." The proposition about the jaw's function as a counting tool was also put forth by Schele and Parsons (Parsons 1988: 56). At the FSP, the number of the maxillae attached to each individual also might have reflected counts of sacrifices in which he was involved; however, the fact that the individuals with maxilla pendants apparently wore similar numbers of maxilla (usually seven to nine) weakens this possibility. It was hypothesized below that numbers of maxillae would have had ritual meanings. But the function as counting tools for ritual purposes can hardy be proved or disproved since precise reconstruction of maxilla pendants by individual was impossible. Any possible numbers of maxillae or tooth imitations meaningful for calendar systems or vigesimal counting were not suggested even by the data from better-preserved Graves 5 and 6.

Despite Postclassic accounts of war trophies, there are few archaeological or iconographic references to maxilla pendants in the Classic period. Pendants of real or false human maxillae have been discovered only in association with the FSP and the Moon Pyramid in Teotihuacan. As far as I know, in all of Mesoamerica there are only four documented cases of figures definitely wearing maxilla pendants (Fig. 89); all derive from the Oaxaca region and date vaguely to the Classic or early Postclassic periods (Scott 1993: 31–34; Urcid 1995, personal communication). Attributes attached to these figures, such as the pendant of a decapitated head, suggest sacrificial ritual. The data may suggest a certain relationship between these two cultural areas (discussed

Fig. 89 Ceramic statue with maxilla pendants from the Oaxaca region (present location: National Museum of the American Indian, Smithsonian Institution). Drawing: Kuniko Naruse, from Scott 1993: pl. 17).

in the final chapter); on the other hand, Schele and Miller (1986: 54, 61) note that Maya iconography also depicted a method of sacrifice that involved the removal of the jaw of a living victim. Certain types of shell tooth imitations similar to those at the FSP have been found in Piedras Negras (Coe 1959: fig. 52p, s, t, x, and perhaps b′ and m). Mandible-only burials have also been found in the Maya area (Welsh 1988a: 172). Thus, although the instances are few, mandibles and maxillae had special ritual meanings since the Classic period in Mesoamerica.

In Teotihuacan iconography, there is no clear representation of maxilla pendants. Cynthia Conides (1998) pointed out that a stuccoed tripod vessel is painted with the image of a disembodied garment, including seven U-shaped pendants that may represent maxilla pendants. Although details are insufficient for identification, the contexts in which the garment is displayed (with strong connotations of human sacrifice) support Conides's identification. A Teotihuacan-style figurine from the Tiquisate region in Guatemala wears U-shaped objects in rows (Hellmuth 1975: 58), which might represent a maxilla pendant, otherwise a unique ornament of Teotihuacan iconographic variety. That the figure evidently represented a Teotihuacan priest-warrior with butterfly symbols may support this idea. As suggested by Parsons (1988), some Storm God representations seem to lack mandibles and often have symbols of blood below the maxilla instead (Berrin 1988: 114). These might have symbolized the sacrifice of gods by removing their jaws, as in the Maya cases. Although we found in the FSP graves mostly maxillae worn by sacrificed victims, the association of removal of mandibles with the Storm God at the FSP may be suggested, since the temple may have been dedicated to that deity (Chapter 4). Thus, mandible pendants seem to have represented warfare and sacrifice both as reality and as metaphor. Strong association of maxilla necklace with male and martial offerings at the FSP supports this idea.

In Grave 190, four human mandibles were included in maxilla pendants for individual 190-F, their ascending rami cut off so that they resembled maxillae. This may indicate that pendants were required to be "maxillae," perhaps because of ritual meanings attached to maxillae rather than to mandibles. Alfredo López Austin (personal communication 1989) suggested that maxilla pendants may have been related to an attribute of Cipactli, which often appears without a mandible (López et al. 1991: 102–3). As discussed in Chapter 4 ("Sculpture of the facades"), one of the two sculptural heads on the facades of the FSP seems to represent an inherited form of Preclassic Olmec Dragon or an ancestral form of Postclassic Cipactli, which I call Teotihuacan Primordial Crocodile. The maxilla pendants may have provided symbolic status of this calender-related creature.

In conclusion, the maxilla pendants would not only have symbolized warfare but may also have possessed mythological/calendrical meanings, including attributes of the Storm God or the Primordial Crocodile represented on the facades of the FSP. The people wearing the maxilla necklace may have been disguised as sacred soldiers related to the creation myth in Teotihuacan cosmogony.

Shell earplugs
Shell earplugs were found only in female burials (Graves 2, 10, and 11) and in the central grave (Grave 14). All had a standard form (except for one piece found in Grave 14, whose form is similar to that of a greenstone earspool), although detailed features make subgrouping possible (Fig. 90). An earplug of the standard form consists of a round flat plaque with a small hole in its center and a supplemental appendage that seems to have been used to attach it to the ear. All females in all graves had earplugs of this type, with corresponding appendages. The appendages were often very fragmented, because they were composed of organic materials covered with stucco. It can be argued, on the basis of sex identification by physical anthropologists, that the shell earplugs were strongly correlated with sex in the FSP burial complex since they seem to have been used only for females. This correlation complements in part the association of greenstone earspools with males.

Fig. 90 Shell earplugs found at the FSP. Photo: author.

In the central grave (Grave 14), five shell earplugs were found with no clear association with individuals (Fig. 91). One unusual piece was discovered near the grave's
southwest edge, and four other pieces were found near individuals, a suggestion that
they might have been worn. Two pieces were found near the cranium of individual 14-I, who certainly wore greenstone earplugs; the other two were found on the
thorax region of individual 14-L, who also had greenstone earplugs. The person
nearest these shell earplugs, who apparently did not have greenstone earplugs, is individual 14-M; however, since the cranium of 14-M was located about 60 cm from
these shell earplugs, it is unlikely that the individual wore them. Spatial distributions
of greenstone beads, earplugs, and nose pendants suggest that individual 14-M in
Grave 14 was unusual in apparently not bearing those ornaments worn only by male
individuals. Although 14-M was identified as a male in the final analysis of the physical anthropologists, the data of the offerings described suggest that 14-M may have
been involved in female symbolism.

Other items

Pottery

The FSP burial complex and caches did not include a wide variety of ceramic offerings. Offerings were limited to Storm God jars (Fig. 92) and a few other vessels.
In some cases, the contents of the vessels, rather than the receptacles themselves,
may have been the principal offerings. At least four Storm God jars have been found
on the top of the pyramid, and two Storm God jars were discovered in Grave 14.
Excavation contexts suggest that, although some fragments may still be in nearby

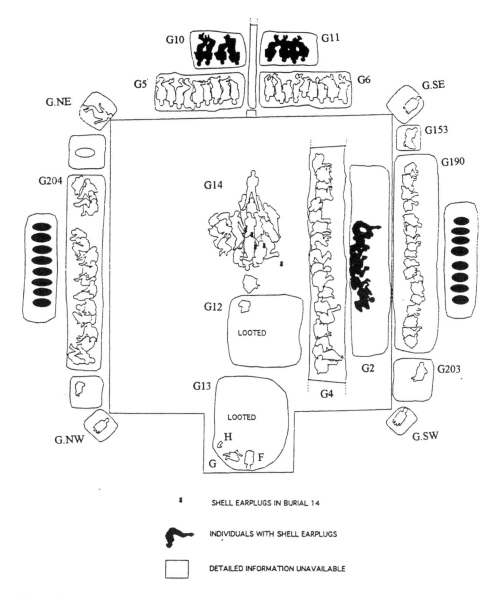

Fig. 91 Spatial distribution of individuals wearing shell earplugs in the FSP burial complex. Except for Grave 14, shell earplugs are correlated with female burials. GIS map: author.

parts of the pyramid fill, the jars might have been broken intentionally before the interment, and incomplete ones buried.

Storm God jars seem to have been among the principal elements of burials or dedication caches in other parts of the city (Linné 1934: fig. 34; Manzanilla et al. 1993: 216–17; Séjourné 1966b: 97; Rattray 1992: fig. 3). They were often discovered in monuments (Chapter 7), and were also found with similar burial contexts at Teotihuacan-related sites, such as Monte Albán and Kaminaljuyú (Caso and Bernal

Fig. 92 Storm God vessel found in Grave 14. The vessel lacks its lower portion, suggesting that it was intentionally broken before being buried. Photo: author.

1952: 36–37; Kidder et al. 1946: figs. 199–200). At the FSP, the jars were obviously integrated into the monument's erection program. Since they were not exclusive to the FSP, ritual meanings of Storm God jars at the FSP may not have been unique.

Effigies on the vessels evidently represented the Storm God. Although rings on eyes, often cited as a Storm God element, are missing, the "Tlaloc mustache," curving fangs, feathers, lightning, and three "mountains" on jars support its identification as the Storm God. However, specific functions of Storm God jars in the FSP burial complex are not well understood (Bracamontes 2002).

Wood baton or scepter

A complete wood baton or scepter, with its curved end depicting a Feathered Serpent head (Fig. 93a) was found in a disturbed layer of Grave 13. Although stratigraphic

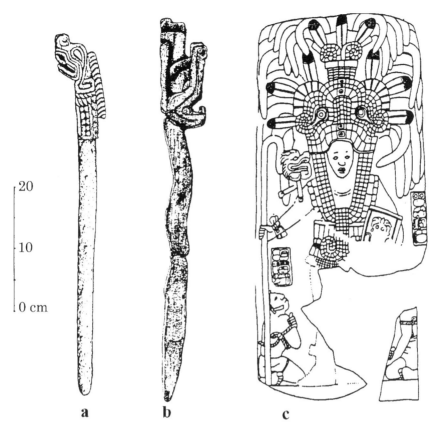

Fig. 93 Varieties of baton in the form of a Feathered Serpent. a Carved wooden baton (complete) from redeposited fill of Grave 13 pit; the Feathered Serpent head is duplicated on reverse side (Cabrera et al. 1991: fig. 7) (drawing: Maa-ling Chen, from the original); b Feathered Serpent baton/scepter from the Cenote of Sacrifice, Chichen Itzá, Yucatán (drawing: Nawa Sugiyama, from Coggins 1992: 266–68); c Maya stela showing a ruler grasping a Feathered Serpent baton/scepter: stela 26 from Piedras Negras, Maya (drawing: Kumiko Sugiyama, from Schele and Grube 1994: 111).

data were not conclusive as to its original provenance, its antiquity (about AD 70: calibrated date indicated by accelerator mass spectrometry C14 dating of a sample from the baton: Beta-37833 and Beta-37834) suggests that the baton was part of the original burial offering of Grave 13.

Similar objects have not been reported previously in Teotihuacan. Analogous types of batons with Feathered Serpent representations at their ends are found widely in archaeological and epigraphic records in Mesoamerica: Coggins (1992: 266 68) reports a serpent baton/scepter recovered from the Cenote of Sacrifice, Chichén Itzá, Yucatán (Fig. 93b); in the Petén Maya region, a baton/scepter with a representation of the Feathered Serpent was depicted on a stela and on ceramic vessels associated with king-warrior representations (Fig. 93c). Feathered Serpent batons are also comparable to royal "manikin scepters" of the Maya that represent God K/GII (Schele and Miller 1986: 49); this zoomorphic entity frequently had a serpent-headed foot and appeared on many different official occasions including accession of rulers.

Fig. 94 Tlaloc (Storm God) holding lightning. Drawing: Kumiko Sugiyama. a Tlaloc holding a spear-thrower and an undulating spear resembling lightning: mural in Tetitla (from von Winning 1987: vol. 1, 72–73); b Plumbate vessel depicting Tlaloc with a lightning snake (from Taube 1988: fig. 13-a); c Aztec representation of Tlaloc with a lightning serpent (from *Códice Borbónico* 1979: 7).

As we have seen, in the meanings and implications associated with the Feathered Serpent, the baton with that image seems to have been used in Teotihuacan as regalia of rulership and also may have represented metaphorically the lightning grasped by Storm Gods (Fig. 94). It seems that the lighting carried by Storm Gods was, in a sense, conceived as spears into which Feathered Serpents were often transformed, as indicated by the obsidian figurines (type C discussed above) whose forms are combined with the Feathered Serpent and a projectile point (Fig. 60). Thus, the baton would have connoted martial attributes in addition to divine rulership.

Textiles
During the excavation of Grave 14, remains of textiles were uncovered at nine spots, in some cases attached to other kinds of organic materials including paper-like pieces that were clearly folded. Certain types of offerings were located around these textile

remains, as if they were contents of bags. These sets were apparently put on the bodies of persons buried in the central grave, and I nicknamed them "bags" in the field, having in mind mural representations of priests with bags in their hands (Figs. 17b, 18c). Although the question whether they were originally bags cannot be confirmed by reconstructing their fragmented remains, the offering combinations with iconographic references, discussed in the following sections, seem to support the validity of the nickname.

Plants and animals

Grave 14 contained rich organic materials; abundant remains of plants were recovered from the grave's central zone. The strong concentration of stem remains appears to have been offerings of plants, possibly including flowers. Many fragments of wooden sticks, which could have been parts of wooden artifacts, were also found in Grave 14, and remains of fibers were recovered near the cranium of individual 14-I. Canid bones in anatomical relationship were discovered near individual 14-F.

Compared with the central grave, Graves 12 and 13 contained much less evidence of organic materials, perhaps because of looting activities. The remains of fiber forming a possible basket were found on the floor of Grave 13.

Although many plant and faunal remains were discovered, the studies for their identification have not yet been concluded except for some samples of animal bones. The question of postdepositional contamination, particularly that caused by looting activities, must be considered carefully in the interpretations of organic materials, and excavation contexts in which they appeared cannot properly be discussed here.

Offering associations

In previous sections, I described and analyzed offerings separately by material and type in order to search for possible ritual meanings. In this section, probable combinations of offerings are sought to discuss further the ritual contexts of uniquely executed mortuary practices. Excavation data suggest that some offerings were possibly placed with others so as to constitute material symbol complexes and, although specific ritual meanings perhaps have been lost, archaeological records of spatial patterns might still capture part of such symbolic behavior.

During fieldwork, we realized that the spatial distribution of the offerings dedicated to the FSP was exceptionally complex, consisting of various kinds of artifacts made with different materials. In addition, they seem to have been distributed in correlation with grave patterns. As discussed in an overview of interburial correlation in the final chapter, a principal variable for the distribution of bodies was sex; various kinds of offerings seem to have correlated with this variable. In the peripheral areas, male individuals of multiple graves wore maxilla pendants composed of small shell beads, and back disks were related to them with abundant projectile points (10.5 pieces/person). These objects were most likely diagnostic elements of male soldiers or warfare-related status. In contrast, females buried near the male graves bore two shell earplugs as a female identification code. Small numbers of cylindrical shell beads and projectile points (mean: 6.4 pieces/person) were associated consistently with female individuals. Although beads and projectile points were not exclusive to female graves, specific combinations of these three items (shell earplugs, shell beads, and projectile points) in certain quantities seem to have constituted a diagnostic feature for female individuals at the FSP.

The most complicated combinations of offerings were those of the central grave. This grave contained one of the richest offerings in quantity, quality, and variety of any found to date in Teotihuacan. In the following section, I focus on possible small clusters of various objects that we began to discern during fieldwork; the analyses presented here confirm the field observations, suggesting further complicated patterns of offering combinations.

Figure 95 is a plot of 2,407 offering pieces which had previously been geocoded separately (83 percent of all offerings or 2,905 pieces, except for fragments of animal bones, ceramics, textile, and other organic materials, and the 3,443 pieces of small shell beads associated with individuals 14-B, C, D, and E). The locations of many objects were apparently random, some perhaps displaced by settling. There were several strong concentrations of the offerings in certain areas, especially under the left upper arm of individual 14-F, around the right thigh of 14-Ñ, and on the right shoulder of 14-L; these were three spots where we found piles of small artifacts. These places of high concentration of offerings are not delimited clearly, but expand loosely and irregularly as shown in the figure; thus, clear associations of these piles with individuals cannot be determined. Only the first pile may have been associated with an individual, 14-F, the person closest to the pile. The other two piles were found between various individuals, and no associations with particular persons can be suggested. Moreover, as discussed in dealing with grave patterns, persons around whom piles of offerings were found do not seem to have been distinguished from others in terms of mortuary variables. Therefore, my preliminary conclusion is that they were general offerings dedicated anonymously to the erection of the FSP, along with the burials of sacrificed victims.

In order to understand the spatial distribution of the ritual objects in Grave 14, I first separated possible personal ornaments from general offerings. Aforementioned studies of spatial contexts indicated that some artifacts seem to have been attached to individuals. I included in this category some earspools, nose pendants, and beads found around the skull and thoracic region of sixteen individuals in Grave 14 (Fig. 96). I also tentatively classified as personal objects projectile points clustered without apparent correlation with other objects but probably with individuals; correlation of the projectile points will be tested again with data of clusters described below. Greenstone cones and unusual types of obsidian knives and eccentrics were also included tentatively in this category since they were exclusively found in very limited areas, as if they were associated with particular individuals. Although they provide particularity to certain individuals, the individual offerings are not concentrated on one or a few persons, nor are they correlated with burial variables including arm position that suggests sacrifice; in other words, the spatial distribution of the individual offerings did not show a royal grave pattern – a distinguished person with rich ornament, accompanied by subjugated (sacrificed) individuals.

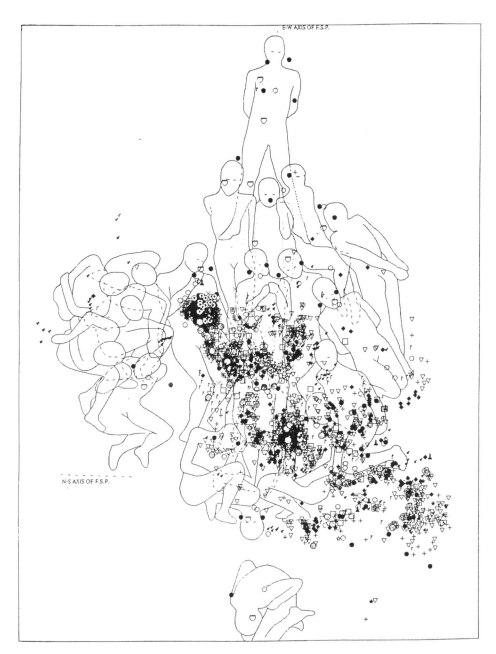

Fig. 95 Spatial distribution of offerings in Grave 14: all geocoded objects were plotted. GIS map: author.

Therefore, I concluded that the central grave consisted of anonymously sacrificed people.

The abovementioned objects were removed from Figure 95 to show only general offerings (Fig. 97). Greenstone cones, pottery, and one type A obsidian knife also were not included in this map because they were located in only one place and

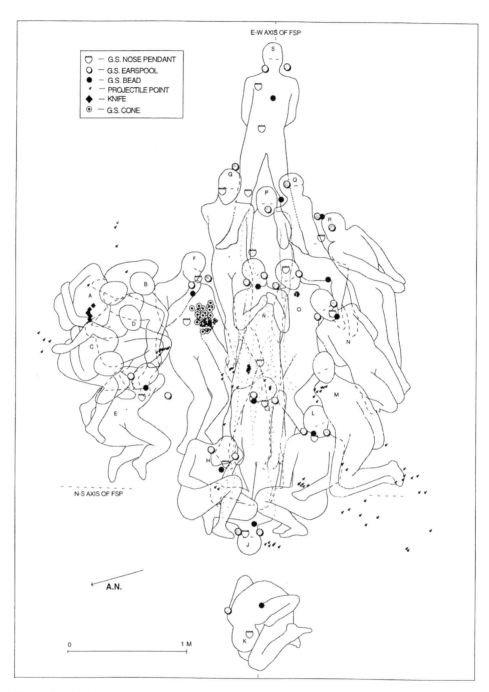

Fig. 96 Spatial distribution of objects thought to be personal ornaments in Grave 14. They consist of nose pendants (except for the smallest one), earspools, and beads – greenstone ornaments apparently worn by individuals; clustered obsidian projectile points, types A and F knives, and greenstone cones. GIS map: author.

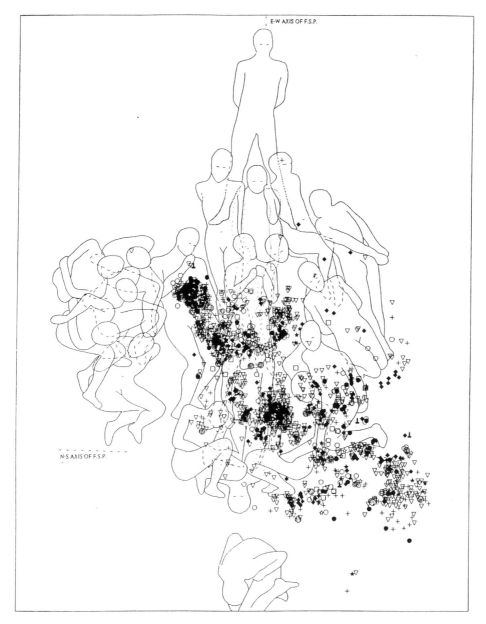

Fig. 97 Spatial distribution of objects thought to be general offerings in Grave 14. GIS map: author.

therefore cannot be interpreted as elements of patterned clusters although they could have been unique general offerings.

Figure 97 shows general offerings that may have been composed of clusters of different types and/or independent offerings, placed above nine of the twenty individuals and occupying the central and southern areas of Grave 14. Five individuals on the north (14-A, B, C, D, and E), five on the east (14-G, P, Q, R, and S), and another on the west (14-K) were virtually free from general offerings. After the area of general offerings was defined, I searched for small clusters of offerings composed of objects of specific types.

Because of limitations in data recording (incompleteness of locational data of offerings, particularly of fragments, and irregular precision of field drawings), I focus only on maps of a certain magnitude, based on error ranges specified in each section. In a focused view of spatial distribution, greenstone objects were first chosen in searching for sets (Figs. 98 and 99). Intuitive observations of offering sets in the field are supported by the data systematically recorded and graphically illustrated. The set is generally composed of one greenstone figurine, two (or one) earspools, one "resplandor," and seven beads (Fig. 107; See also Fig. 11). Small beads tend to have been selected for the sets. This would make sense if they were for necklaces associated with miniature figurines.

Apart from these set objects, many greenstone objects in these categories were dispersed without apparent correlation with others; however, they could have been components of the sets if the wider areas around the clusters are considered (Fig. 100). In fact, the three piles mentioned also contained the same types of elements for several sets. Therefore, it is possible that the dense piles included several sets of the same type.

The greenstone sets proposed here seem to have been parts of complexes larger than only the sets of greenstone objects since they could have been integrated with other kinds of materials. Some of their locations correspond to the spots of textile remains recorded in the field as "bags" (Fig. 101). Because the condition of their preservation was very bad, organic materials in some cases might have disintegrated completely; therefore, it is unknown whether all greenstone sets were associated with the same types of organic materials.

Miniature obsidian bifacial knives were also among the possible components of greenstone sets (Figs. 101, 102). As previously discussed, bifacial knives were distributed in clusters, some corresponding to the locations of greenstone sets. They usually appear to have been composed of six to eight knives. Many bifacial clusters were within the ranges that I preliminarily defined as greenstone sets although in a few cases the degree of deviation was significant. The data suggest that there may have been other types of greenstone sets with which some bifacial clusters were associated.

Prismatic obsidian blades also appear to have formed parts of greenstone clusters. In particular, long, wide blades seem to have lain under the cluster complex (including obsidian objects and textiles). Their correlation with the greenstone sets was not clearly indicated in all cases, probably because the blades were badly fragmented and only 68 percent of the total number of pieces were geocoded. It is also possible that some blades were distributed differently from the pattern of the greenstone sets.

One type of shell pendant also seems to have been associated with the greenstone clusters. In many cases, the locations of type 3 (*Pecten*) pendants were in or close to greenstone sets. The data suggest that all pieces found in the south and central sections originally might have been components of the greenstone sets, since their

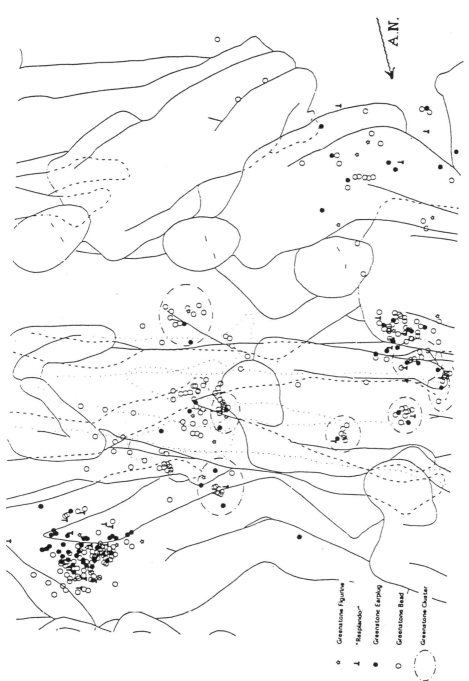

Fig. 98 Locations of greenstone clusters (circles with dot-and-dash line) in central section of Grave 14. GIS map: author.

Greenstone Figurine
"Resplandor"
Greenstone Earplug
Greenstone Bead
Greenstone Cluster

A.N.

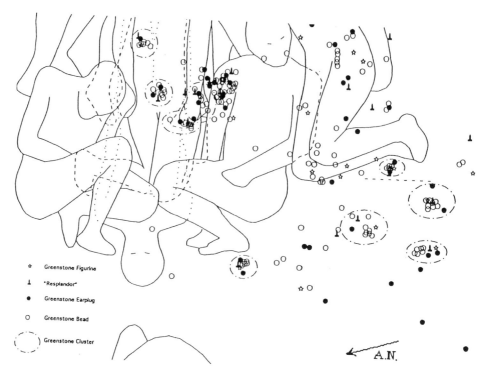

Fig. 99 Locations of greenstone clusters (circles with dot-and-dash line) in southwestern section of Grave 14. GIS map: author.

placement and quantity corresponds approximately to that of the proposed green-stone sets.

Other types of general offerings not previously mentioned may have formed other clusters or independent offering sets. After we examine their lack of involvement in the greenstone sets, we can reconsider some offerings as materials associated with individuals. For example, many obsidian projectile points were found in clusters, but their spatial distribution was evidently unrelated to the greenstone sets. Instead, the data support their association with individuals. The disks were also most likely unrelated to the greenstone sets (Fig. 103) although in a few cases they might have been associated with greenstone figurines.

Under field conditions, a greenstone set can be reconstructed as a combination of the following objects (although variations are possible): one greenstone figurine, two earspools, one "resplandor," six to eight greenstone beads, six to eight obsidian miniature bifacial knives, and one *Pecten* pendant. At least eighteen instances of such clusters seem to have been involved as general offerings in the central grave, and in at least nine cases, they were likely placed on or in a textile object, under which a series of wide prismatic obsidian blades had been set side by side. All objects seem originally to have composed offering complexes placed on the bodies of sacrificial victims. It is also possible that greenstone sets of similar combination were placed within the offering pile under the left upper arm of individual 14-F; however, they are

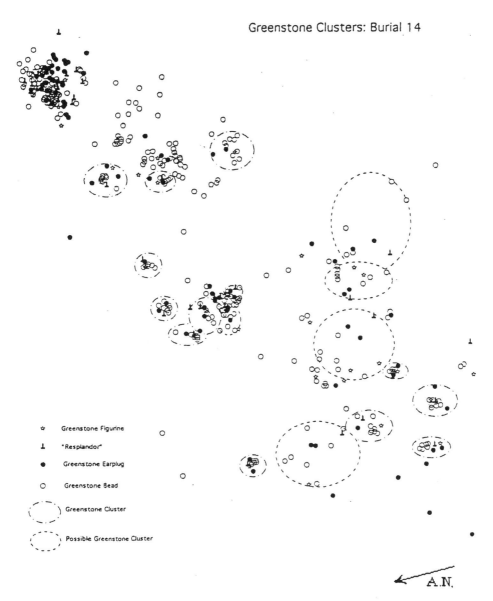

Fig. 100 Well-defined offering sets from Grave 14, composed of one greenstone figurine, two (or ±1) earspools, one "resplandor," and seven (or ±1) beads. GIS map: author.

not discernible since the objects were too densely located. The greenstone sets might also have been placed in the southwestern part of the grave, where the displacement of offerings appears to have been larger than in other sections, although in that area no clear evidence of textile forming "bags" was found.

Independent of the greenstone sets, other types of offering sets were observed in Grave 14. In one instance, different kinds of artifacts were found inside of a trumpet shell sealed with yellow pigment. They consisted of an anthropomorphic

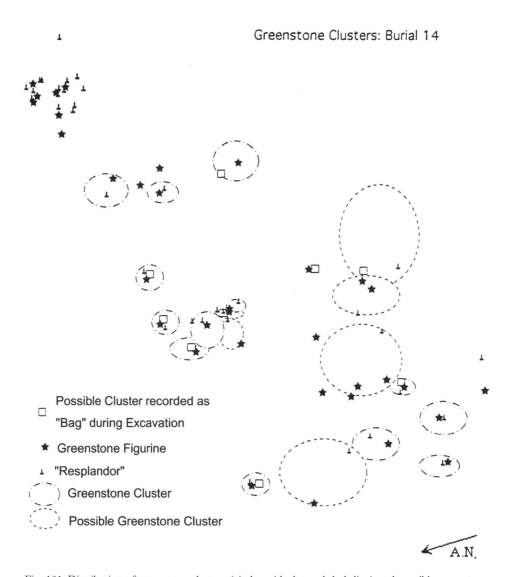

Greenstone Clusters: Burial 14

Possible Cluster recorded as
"Bag" during Excavation

★ Greenstone Figurine

⊥ "Resplandor"

( ) Greenstone Cluster

( ) Possible Greenstone Cluster

A.N.

Fig. 101 Distribution of greenstone clusters (circles with dot-and-dash line) and possible greenstone clusters (circles with dash line) in Grave 14. GIS map: author.

obsidian figurine, one obsidian projectile point, two bifacial obsidian knives, seven fragments of prismatic obsidian blades, one fragmented slate disk, one greenstone bead, one fragment of a worked stone, two spiral shells, remains of white fiber, and fragments of human bones. In other cases, precise cluster components were unclear, since objects seem to have fallen out of the trumpet shell. Components of the sets were significantly different from those of the greenstone sets. Apparently, the ritual meanings involved differed from one another.

Instances similar to the clusters described above have not been found elsewhere in Teotihuacan. A few similar instances observed in the graves found recently at the

Fig. 102 Spatial correlation of "bags," greenstone figurines, and "resplandores" with the greenstone clusters in Grave 14. Photo: author.

Moon Pyramid may be exceptions that need analytical and comparative studies in the near future. Those discovered previously in front of the staircase of the FSP would have formed an integral variation of the offering set since the object types were similar to those described here (Rubín de la Borbolla 1947). In addition, in 1988 Oralia Cabrera found a set of offerings composed of items similar to the types discussed here in pit 3 under the Adosada platform. The data confirm that the greenstone sets extended beyond Grave 14 on the east–west axis of the pyramid.

Ritual meanings involved in these clusters cannot be discussed to a large extent archaeologically. However, the ritual behaviors can be discussed through these archaeological data in reference to iconographic representations. In Teotihuacan, analogous clusters were represented in several murals of priestly processions in which anthropomorphic figures are scattering ritual objects (Figs. 17b, 18c, 67a, and 104a). Objects are depicted in enclosures, called Panel Fallings or Scroll Panels by Langley (1986). In some cases, objects in scroll panels seem to indicate chanting or speaking. Ritual chantings or orations in Mesoamerica were often accompanied by scattering; in fact, ethnohistorical records indicate that, among Aztecs, ritual scatterings of jades were equated with orations, *huehuetlatoll*: "the words of the elders, the wise men, the possessors of the books" (Sullivan 1986).

Teotihuacan panel elements vary significantly from figure to figure, and their contexts are not exactly the same as those found in Grave 14; however, some clusters analogous to those of Grave 14 seem to indicate that they refer to similar ritual behaviors. For example, priests in Tepantitla or Techinantitla (Figs. 17b, 18c, 20e, 104b) seem to be chanting over various kinds of shells, greenstone earspools, and miniature

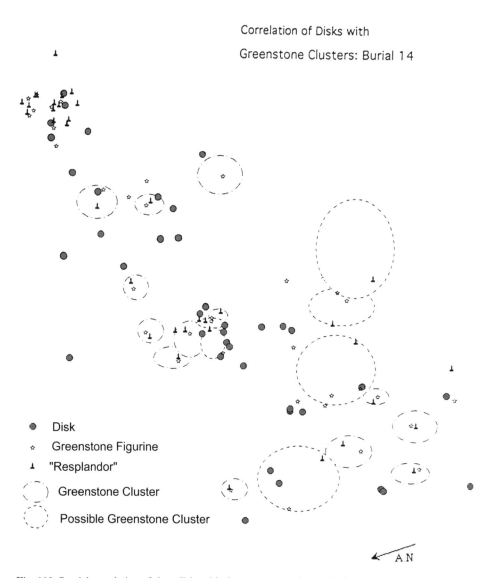

Fig. 103 Spatial correlation of slate disks with the greenstone clusters in Grave 14. GIS map: author.

animal heads, together with flower symbols. Objects scattered by anthropomorphic figures in a Tetitla mural – the so-called Green Tlalocs – include type B nose pendants and possibly greenstone figurines of human heads, which are unusual in Teotihuacan pictorial works (Figs. 67a and 104a). Moreover, the scattering ritual displayed in Tepantitla takes place under Feathered Serpent representations with headdresses on their bodies, while the figures in the Tetitla mural are bordered by unidentified snaking bodies. The burials under discussion are located under the pyramid covered with Feathered Serpent representations with the same type of headdresses on its body. These analogies in ritual components and structural setting suggest that

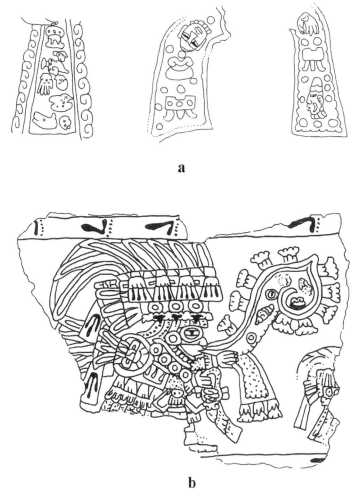

Fig. 104 Representations of scattering ritual in Teotihuacan murals. Drawing: Kumiko Sugiyama. a Various objects scattered from the hands of priests (from Miller 1973: 148–49); b A priest or general scattering and chanting over ritual objects (from Berrin 1988: 118).

the sacrificial mortuary program at the FSP involved a specific type of scattering ritual that was most likely referred to or linked with the murals in later periods at Teotihuacan.

Priests in the Tepantitla murals (Fig. 17b) carry bags decorated with knots, animal heads, serpent rattles, and fur (possibly of coyote). Textile fragments with the greenstone sets which we discovered might have been such bags. The priests wear headdresses of an animal head adorned with curved sacrificial knives, suggesting that the action was related to sacrificial rituals, and the headdresses themselves may represent coyotes, as the specific forms of snout, teeth, earlobes, and fur suggest. The remains of coyotes or dogs were also involved in the sacrificial burial complex, indicating their association with warfare and human sacrifice as was the case in the murals. This does not necessarily mean that the representation refers directly to the sacrificial rituals carried out specifically at the FSP; however, these structural analogies of the mural representing priests' actions of scattering with the symbolism discovered archaeologically at the FSP would not have been accidental. The mortuary ritual carried out at the pyramid's center seems to have established a religious canon of the Feathered Serpent symbolism and structured artistic presentations in later periods at Teotihuacan.

General discussion

In this chapter, offerings associated with the FSP burial complex were discussed. The offerings seem to have comprised a major factor of the burial/cache complex. Through analyses and interpretations, I have tried to explore the nature of this unique set of offerings. The following are brief remarks on the offerings that lead to the final chapter discussing the symbolism of the FSP together with results from other chapters.

I categorized and interpreted offerings on the basis of their morphological features and the spatial information that may have been related to embedded ritual meanings. An outcome of the study is a specification of meanings coherently attached to the burial complex. Certain objects indicate martial aspects, others suggest association with sacrifice, while some exceptional objects seem to symbolize divine authority. These apparently were elements that composed a mythical presentation of sacred soldiers associated with the Feathered Serpent. I discuss them extensively in the final chapter.

The offerings are distributed over various graves in certain patterns, indicating strong cohesiveness among graves, as if they were laid precisely according to a master mortuary program. The patterns are also strongly correlated with mortuary variables that indicate patterned distribution of the individuals. The correlations suggest that a whole process, from the production of offerings to their placement with particular burials, was systematically prepared under the strong control of prosecutors of the mortuary project.

Offerings included in the graves were not only associated with interred individuals, although most materials were found in the graves. Previous excavation reports demonstrate that similar types of artifacts were buried independently of FSP burials at the FSP. Caches found at the superior part of the platform, in front of the staircase, and under the Adosada platform comprised the sacrificial burial/cache complex. The central burial included a large number of objects scattered on the bodies of anonymous individuals and interpreted as general offerings. They can be called a cache placed on a multiple burial; in fact, both the individuals and the artifacts were integrated into the monument as parts of a dedicatory program (Becker 1988), components of a ritual process for a long-term dedication program integrated into the erection of the FSP. The execution of both dedicatory and constructive processes must have been carried out by a large administrative unit that programmed and executed the erection of the major monument at Teotihuacan. As we have seen, the significance of the FSP in the city's sacred geography, visual messages on the facade, scale of sacrificial burial complex, and large quantity and exceptional quality of associated offerings suggest that a powerful state office was responsible for these construction and dedication programs and that a divine ruler would have been the supreme authority of this state project.

Before implications are discussed in the final chapter, I provide information about sacrificial and elite burials in Teotihuacan and abroad, to assist in concluding our discussion of the dedication program that conveyed the symbolism of the FSP.

7

Overview: sacrificial and elite burials

An overview of several burial patterns found in Teotihuacan or Teotihuacan-related sites may be relevant to my conclusions in the final chapter of this volume. First, I briefly discuss sacrificial burials found elsewhere in Teotihuacan besides the Feathered Serpent Pyramid since several examples of this burial type have been reported previously from the city, primarily in residential areas; they include the remains of possible infanticides, decapitations, and other types of dismemberment. The Sun Pyramid and platforms at Oztoyahualco also seem to have contained sacrificial burials, somewhat similar to those of the FSP, as they were discovered in association with monuments. Recent discoveries at the Moon Pyramid are providing new insights about the meanings and functions of sacrificial burials associated with monuments. However, since the fieldwork is still underway, I only summarize the data from the Moon Pyramid very briefly here, citing preliminary excavation reports. I describe and discuss available information from these previous excavations to elucidate some features of the FSP burials through comparison.

In the following section, I review elite graves found in Teotihuacan and Teotihuacan-related sites to ask whether any FSP graves can be designated elite burials through comparison. Special attention is paid to graves discovered at Mounds A and B in Kaminaljuyú, Guatemala. At this urban center of the highland Maya, elite burials have been uncovered in association with Teotihuacan-type pyramids, and abundant offerings have also indicated strong Teotihuacan influence. Elite status has been attributed to the principal occupants in the graves on the basis of direct associations with the monuments and remnants of offerings found with them. In spite of analogies in various kinds of materials, the mortuary programs at Kaminaljuyú, including those at Mounds A and B, have been interpreted as a regional tradition rather than an importation from Teotihuacan, mainly because no counterpart had been reported in Teotihuacan (Brown 1977: 426–27). Some recently discovered burials at the FSP, however, share traits with these burials, perhaps more than with any other burials in Teotihuacan. Because the Kaminaljuyú pyramid complex also contained sacrificial burials, the data from the FSP make it necessary to reconsider the relationship between the two sites. It is proposed that the grave pattern indicated at the Kaminaljuyú monuments may have been derived from Teotihuacan. Recent discoveries of sacrificial and elite burials at the Moon Pyramid consequently indicate a strong relationship between the two sites (Sugiyama and Cabrera 2003).

Sacrificial burials in Teotihuacan

I have classified possible sacrificial and dedicatory burials reported in published and unpublished documents into two categories: sacrificial burials in residential areas and those in ceremonial zones. Many burials included in this discussion are ones which their excavators or others interpreted as sacrificial in their burial contexts, but not because of their physical characteristics, and the information is often insufficient for appropriate interpretation. Therefore, the burials listed below should not be considered definitive cases of human sacrifice. Despite the limitations of the data, nevertheless, it is possible that the instances reflect to a certain degree the range of variability of possible sacrificial burials in Teotihuacan and can help us to categorize the burials at the FSP.

Dismemberment

After 1990, a large area of Teotihuacan north of the Oaxaca Barrio was excavated by salvage archaeological projects prior to construction of new national army facilities. In the patio of a residential apartment complex, Rodolfo Cid (1993, personal communication) discovered the remains of four dismembered persons associated with an altar. According to Cid, the bones of two individuals showed sharp cut marks, probably made by prismatic blades. These patterned cut marks were identified through microscopic inspection.

Another salvage project carried out by Sergio Gómez (1992, personal communication), also near the modern national army complex adjacent to the Oaxaca Barrio, discovered the dismembered remains of more than eight adults placed in a well. Luis González was in charge of the excavation and laboratory analyses of the osteological materials; the exploration was suspended in 1992.

Decapitation

In Compound 2: N1E1 (Millon et al. 1973), north of the Ciudadela, four skulls without bodies were found in a circular structure by members of a Mexican project in 1980–82 (González and Fuentes 1982; Rodríguez 1982); according to Luis González and David Fuentes, two were males and two were females. Since the structure has not been dated, construction materials and relevant stratigraphy indicate only that it was built during the Teotihuacan period. The skulls were found with several upper cervical vertebrae still in anatomical relationship, indicating that they were cut off while flesh remained on the body. González (1993) has recently detected microscopic cut marks on one of these cervical vertebrae; this suggests a decapitation ritual associated with the circular structure.

A salvage excavation carried out by Enrique Martínez and Luis González (1991) in the town of San Francisco Mazapa (N3E3) unearthed eight burials, which they attributed to the Early Xolalpan phase. The burials were interpreted as sacrificed individuals because some apparently were decapitated (González 1993).

Decapitations were also found at the La Ventilla B compound (Serrano and Lagunas 1975; Rattray 1992: 12); two human skulls had been linked to an adult male buried with a large amount of Early Tlamimilolpa pottery (salvage grave III from Patio 1). The skulls may have been sacrificial remains accompanying the principal occupant of the grave.

These sacrificial burials, known from excavation contexts and laboratory analyses, are more diagnostically reliable than the examples I mention below, which lack sufficient data for determining whether the persons were victims of sacrifice. It is possible that the skulls mentioned in the following list were prepared either immediately after death or in skeletal condition. Chronologically, it is also possible that they were graves from post-Teotihuacan periods.

In an unpublished field report, Mogor (1966) mentions burials of six individuals, several of whom were buried in a common grave. One of the single graves contained only an isolated skull accompanied by a censer. Almaráz (1865) reports information received from local people in Teotihuacan about the discovery of a stone box containing a skull, obsidian, a "blood stone," beads, and beryl relics, which might have been an Aztec rather than Teotihuacan burial, given Aztec instances of stone boxes. Armillas (1950) mentions the discovery at Tetitla of a skeleton in fetal position (extremely flexed?) and an isolated skull. Bastien (1946) refers to a discovery of approximately thirty-five human skulls in a cave; according to Armillas (1950: 59), the cave contained ceramics dating to the Miccaotli phase, obsidian blades, figurines, and an intentionally cut human skull placed like a cap on another skull.

Infanticide

Possible human sacrifices were associated with altar construction in residential compounds. Rattray (1992: 12) has noted that four of the five altars at La Ventilla B contained infant burials, suggesting a custom of sacrifice with altar construction. Serrano and Lagunas (1975) interpreted them as burials of infants who died from natural causes or abortion.

Infants and fetuses were also found under altars in the Tlajinga 33 compound. Rattray (1992: 27) and Storey (1992: 154) do not think they were sacrificial victims but died from natural causes and were interred there perhaps because of their families' importance within the compound hierarchy. Infant burials dedicated to a new building were also reported from other residential areas. Rattray (1992: 53) excavated infant burials located in a residential room adjacent to Linné's excavation at the Tlamimilolpa compound. She believes they were dedicatory burials made when the new building level was constructed during the Late Xolalpan phase.

A salvage excavation by Jarquín and Martínez (1991) uncovered burials of eighteen children, considered by the excavators as sacrificed. Recent extensive excavations at La Ventilla by Gómez (2000) uncovered a large number of infant burials in one of three residential compounds explored in the 1990s. These and other recent excavation reports brought new insights into the deaths, and particularly the sacrifices, of children at Teotihuacan.

Sacrificial burials at monuments

The sacrificial graves discovered at the FSP contrast with those found in residential compounds in terms of complexity, scale, and, perhaps, ritual meanings. I use the terms "sacrificial burials at monuments" in order to highlight various degrees to which the state was involved in mortuary programs dedicated to monumental construction. Along with those of the FSP, Teotihuacan's strongest "candidates" in this category are burials found at the Sun Pyramid and the Moon Pyramid. Burials found at Oztoyahualco might also belong to this category. Rattray (1992: 6) suggests that several three-temple complexes, constructed in an early period, may also have contained sacrificial burials in this category.

In these cases, sacrifices have not yet been verified, since osteological materials did not show evidence of possible cause of death or were not microscopically examined from the point of view of human sacrifice. The circumstances in which the skeletons were found, however, indicate that individuals, either killed or naturally dead, were ritually buried in dedication to the monuments. Although limited information leaves unspecified the question of whether they were sacrificed, some analogies may help to understand shared ideas about dedicatory burials and to formulate certain spatial patterns in the relationships between the monuments and the graves in Teotihuacan. In the following paragraphs, I discuss mortuary features that suggest the possibility of sacrifices dedicated to monuments.

Cook de Leonard (1971: 191) excavated "Plaza One," a three-temple complex in Oztoyahualco, by means of a tunnel dug into the central mound (1B: N5W2 in Millon et al. 1973). Inside, twelve adult burials were unearthed, in flexed positions and many associated with Tlaloc vessels. They were wrapped mummy-style in cotton cloth and, in one instance, placed on the steps of the substructure. The spatial relationship of the graves to monumental architecture is reminiscent of those found at the FSP and the Kaminaljuyú tombs. Although excavation contexts in the reports are brief, they do not exclude the possibility that the dead may have been either elites or sacrificial victims buried in association with the monument. Rattray (1992) dates them to the Early Tzacualli phase, although Cook de Leonard initially dated them to the Miccaotli phase.

Cook de Leonard (1971: 191) found, in a low platform of Plaza One at Oztoyahualco, an infant burial she interpreted as a possible sacrifice made in dedication to the structure (Cook de Leonard 1957a: 1). The erection of the Plaza One complex was dated to the Early Tzacualli phase by associated ceramics (Cook de Leonard 1957b; Millon 1957). Again, lack of detailed information makes further contextual discussion of the sacrificial burial difficult; however, this does seem to have been another case of an early dedication burial associated with a monumental construction.

A similar pattern of sacrificial burial was found at the Sun Pyramid. Batres (1906) encountered the burial of a young child in each of the four corners of the three lower pyramidal platforms, presumably a total of twelve children. Although detailed excavation contexts are not available, the bodies seem to have been incorporated into the construction matrix. They could have been children who died by causes other than sacrifice, but they were most likely sacrificed (Millon 1992: 363) and dedicated to the monument, exactly like those found at the corners of the FSP. This discovery suggests that other sacrificial burials may exist, undiscovered, in the Sun Pyramid.

Krotser (1968) describes a burial at the southeast corner of the Sun Pyramid (the second construction level) that Millon (1981: 213; 1992) suspects was a sacrificed victim. It consisted of an adult male in an oval pit cut into the talud of the pyramid's lowest platform and may postdate the child burials reported by Batres, as argued by Millon (1992: 395). Its location suggests that it also may have been a sacrificial burial associated with one of the modification levels.

Brief reports by Batres include the description of architectural features of the Sun Pyramid complex and some artifacts discovered in the vicinity of the pyramid during its excavation. There is no mention of offerings or caches associated with the sacrificial burials or the pyramid; only an unpublished inventory of objects stored in the local museum may complement these brief excavation reports. The inventory, written in 1934 by Enrique Díaz Lozano and Eduardo Noguera, states that the objects listed were found at the Sun Pyramid: projectile points, blades, knives, and figurines made of obsidian; disks of slate, serpentine, pyrite, and other stones; stone masks, polishers, balls, Yugos, and sculptures; greenstone earplugs, figurines, and masks; mica sheets; different classes of worked and unworked shell objects of both Gastropoda and Pelecypoda; bone artifacts; ceramic figurines, heads, beads, vessels, spindle wheels, and ornaments; and other artifacts whose descriptions are vague.

It is not clear at all whether this list includes most or only a portion of the objects found by Batres at the Sun Pyramid. There are no detailed descriptions of the objects and no clear indication of their quantity, since collective terms were used in the inventory. The objects were stored in a local storehouse for about thirty years, and it is possible that some were taken to other museums or other facilities during this time. Nonetheless, the list informs us that some of the objects found around the Sun Pyramid may originally have been parts of offerings or caches buried in the pyramid, as the high quality of some objects suggests. The information in this inventory, together with information published elsewhere about objects found in the pyramid (Millon et al. 1965), suggests that child burials found at the corners were a part of a larger dedication program associated with the construction of the Sun Pyramid. The information also provides a reference for comparison of offerings found at the FSP, as cited in Chapter 6.

Three grave complexes recently excavated at the Moon Pyramid added substantial amounts of new data pertaining to this burial category. As a result of extensive tunnel excavations into the pyramid, the long modification process of the monument has been revealed; seven overlapping pyramidal platforms and three dedicatory burials were detected inside. Each new building was constructed larger than and covered earlier constructions, therefore we called the smallest pyramidal structure found under the Adosada platform Building 1, and the last and largest structure, known today as the Moon Pyramid, was named Building 7. Three sacrificial burial complexes, called Burials 2, 3, and 4, found with exceptionally rich offerings, had been associated with Buildings 4, 5, and 6, respectively.

Burial 2 was found in 1998 in the nucleus of Building 4. The grave, measuring 3.5 meters square, was bordered on four sides by roughly made stone walls with no outside access or roof, just like those of Graves 2 and 4 of the FSP. The inside space was filled completely with a homogeneous earth layer after a single body and a large number of offerings had been set carefully and symmetrically on the floor. Careful excavation revealed that the person was buried in a seated position near the eastern edge with his hands crossed behind his back as if they were tied together. Therefore we believe that this person, a male of forty to fifty years at the time of death, was a sacrificial victim buried alongside offerings in dedication to the monument.

The associated material comprises one of the highest quality offerings in a single grave excavated to date in Teotihuacan. It includes two greenstone anthropomorphic sculptures; several obsidian human figures; knives of exceptionally large size, projectile points, and prismatic blades of the same material; many shells, both unworked and worked in the form of ear spools, pendants, and beads; slate disks; and ceramics called Tlaloc vessels, among other items. Most impressive were the skeletons of sacrificed animals: two pumas and one wolf (each found in an individual wooden cage), nine eagles, one falcon, one owl, and three small rattlesnakes. The many militaristic objects and the animals, most probably buried alive during a mortuary ritual (since excrement was found in a cage), evidently symbolized military institutions, as iconographic data from later periods suggest.

Burial 3 discovered in 1999 also constitutes another unique dedicatory burial complex, although its contents are significantly different from those of Burial 2. Four individuals, possibly all males of about fourteen, nineteen, twenty-two, and forty-two years, evidently tied with their hands crossed behind their backs, were laid down carefully with offerings in a large pit. They were probably buried alive with stones, rocks, and earth, to form the nucleus of Building 5. Quite different types of ornaments have been associated directly with each of them, as if each person represented a different origin or social category. General offerings scattered around them include so-called shell trumpets, several clusters of obsidian projectile points, a large disk, and an organic sheet forming a mat-like object, which may have symbolized authority. Two clusters of offerings composed of many symbolic items were found in the central area. The most intriguing offerings were fourteen wolf skulls, four puma skulls, and one incomplete young owl skull. According to iconographic studies, representations of wolves, coyotes, or canines were symbols used to identify individuals or social groups related to sacrifice and warfare.

Burial 4 found in 2000 in association with Building 6 contrasted strongly with the previously uncovered burials from the Moon Pyramid. The builders apparently put or threw in seventeen severed human heads without pattern along with rocks, while constructing the north wall of Building 6. No offering was associated with them, except for the atlas of the eighteenth individual; this may suggest calendrical meanings attached to this dedication burial.

This long modification process revealed at the Moon Pyramid appears to have reflected changing state governance and increasing political power, and the contents of the burials would have represented the underlying state ideology and characteristics of its government as well. I don't here discuss the implications of the last discoveries because of the insufficiency of the data and analyses; however, the instances clearly indicate the major monuments in Teotihuacan contained sacrificial graves with certain patterns.

Discussion

Thanks to the abovementioned discoveries and recent iconographic studies that have shown the pervasive representation of symbols of sacrificial rituals in Teotihuacan, it is becoming clear that human sacrifice was widely practiced in Teotihuacan society, at least more so than was thought before the 1980s. Although there are not yet many instances identified clearly as sacrificial burials at Teotihuacan, I make the following points based on the preceding archaeological references.

The data indicate that human sacrifice was a ritual behavior linked to both apartment compounds and monuments, and they suggest that sacrificial rituals were not exclusive to persons of the highest social status but also involved people of various levels in different ways. This association has been archaeologically demonstrated by Ruz (1965, 1968) and Welsh (1988a, 1988b) for the Maya Lowlands and contrasts with what is recorded in epigraphy. Welsh (1988b: 144) believes that about 11 percent of all burials found in the Maya Lowlands suggest that the interred were sacrificed or at least suffered a sudden and unnatural end. In Teotihuacan, the percentage of sacrificial burials identified to date is far less; however, the data indicate convincingly that sacrificial rituals were also executed by different social units. Iconographic representations painted in these living areas with emphasis on bloody rituals also imply a strong concern of the residents with sacrifice.

Some sacrificial burials in residential compounds seem to have been associated with specific constructions, particularly altars in patios. The persons might have been buried there preferentially, but it is also possible that some burials found at altars were placed as dedicatory offerings. The data indicate several types of sacrificial burials in apartment compounds: dismemberment (particularly by decapitation) and possible infanticide. Burial forms, complexity, type of individuals involved, and possible ritual meanings seem to contrast with, rather than mirror, those of the FSP burial complex.

The sacrificial complex at the FSP can be distinguished from those of residential compounds primarily by its association with the monument, the grand scale of the grave complex, and types of associated offerings. Graves found at the Sun Pyramid and the Moon Pyramid, and perhaps the Oztoyahualco pyramid (Plaza One), together with those of the FSP, comprised this category of state-sponsored funeral practices taking place at major public buildings. This allows us to recognize for the first time characteristics of sacrificial burial complexes executed at the erection of major monuments in Teotihuacan. The burials were typically located on the axes or in symmetrical relationships either in the interior or on the exterior of the monuments at ground level. The interior space of the graves was always filled up with the construction materials inside the pyramids or below the floors corresponding to the monuments; thus, the graves can be interpreted as parts of the foundation program of new monumental construction.

Although many features of the burials at the Sun Pyramid, the Moon Pyramid, and the Oztoyahualco complex are far from completely known, a comparison may provide suggestions on the nature of the burials at the FSP. The fact that a major portion of the burials found at the Sun Pyramid were children highly contrasts with those of the FSP and the Moon Pyramid. Since child burials (possibly sacrificed and buried in altars) were also found in residential compounds, children seem to have been preferred for distinct types of dedication programs in Teotihuacan.

The burials discovered inside the Moon Pyramid are more analogous to those found at the FSP although differences were also presented. Like graves found at the FSP, Burials 2 and 3 at the Moon Pyramid contained individuals evidently sacrificed and buried in tied position with symbolic objects, some of which were quite similar to those of the FSP like greenstone ornaments, abundant shells, obsidian projectile points, and eccentrics; this would indicate certain kinds of links between, or ideas shared by, people associated with the two monuments, namely groups who orchestrated the events.

The distinctiveness of the FSP is also clear at the same time. The number of interred people at the FSP was much greater than those interred at the Moon Pyramid, and both monuments contained characteristic grave features with unique objects. The complex of mass-sacrificed adults buried with abundant martial objects at the FSP seems to have been distinctively different from other burial complexes found at the monuments. The erection of the FSP with a highly singular mortuary program may have derived from quite distinctive functions and ritual meanings different from those of other major monuments in Teotihuacan.

Elite burials in Teotihuacan and Teotihuacan provinces

Elite burials in Teotihuacan

Data on differential burial treatments derive mainly from residential compounds. Locational variability of burials in residential compounds may have been significant as an index of social differentiation (Sempowski 1994: 237–47), and the discussion of social status of burials is based mainly on associated offerings and biological features (Storey 1992). Sempowski (1994) indicates that, in terms of quantity, diversity, and quality of associated offerings, mortuary practices in residences seem to reflect social differentiation among buried individuals; the argument is that specific types of artifacts, personal adornment, diversity of ceramic vessels, and other variables are correlated with the social identity of the buried individuals.

Cremations were among the variables correlated with higher offering complexity (Sempowski 1994: 251; Serrano 1993: 112). Positive correlation between incinerated burials and offering complexity was found in Xolalpan, Tetitla, Yayahuala, La Ventilla, and other compounds. On the other hand, Spence (1994: 378–79) proposes, based on the data from a crematory area, that incineration may have been a distinctive mortuary ritual to identify the group who practiced it during a certain period. In Postclassic periods, the bodies of elites, including Aztec kings, were incinerated and buried in association with monuments (Umberger 1987b).

Fig. 105 Offering scene on the mural of the "Temple of Agriculture." Behind the cremation complex of mortuary bundles sitting on stone braziers (bold lines), anthropomorphic figures wearing a headdress and type B nose pendant (bold lines) are depicted as a vision associated with the individuals cremated. Drawing: Kumiko Sugiyama, from Miller 1973: 63.

Cremation was also shown in a Teotihuacan mural, the so-called Temple of Agriculture near the Sun Pyramid (Fig. 105). Beyer (1922b: 285–89) interpreted the mural for the first time as a cremation scene of two persons, using analogy with representations in codices. Múnera (1991: 341) followed his interpretation by adding new information of a ceramic figurine probably representing a mortuary human bundle. The silhouette of the figurine is identical to the mortuary bundles represented in the Temple of Agriculture mural. The figurine was discovered in mortuary context wearing a ceramic mask. In the mural, a burning mortuary bundle was represented with fire and smoke on the incense burner at each side of the scene. The identification of the censer is unmistakable as its form is identical to large Teotihuacan stone censers, like that found near the Sun Pyramid (Batres 1906: 26). Anthropomorphic figures are represented behind the burning bundles, as if they were visions of the deceased. Each one, without face and identical to the other, wears a headdress, a nose pendant, two earspools, and necklaces, probably identifying his/her high social status (see discussion on rulership and headdress in Chapter 4; Fig. 29). As the scene suggests – commoners with a variety of offerings worshipping the deceased – cremations seem to have been practiced for individuals of high social status in Teotihuacan.

Elite graves in residential compounds may be identified by burial location, offering complexity, evidence of incineration, and other variables. However, particular grave patterns for the highest social level have not been identified in residential zones at Teotihuacan. As analyses by Sempowski and Spence (1994) indicate, burial patterns in residential compounds seem to contrast strongly with burials found at monuments. Offerings in residences consist predominantly of ceramic vessels, while graves at monuments contain fewer ceramic vessels and more personal ornaments or ritual objects of exotic materials; and graves in residences seem to have been relatively simple and homogeneous (pit graves and no tombs under the floors of residences), without strong indication of outstanding individuals. These data suggest that burials for persons of highest social status might have been associated with temple-pyramid constructions; however, tombs for elites have not been identified in definitive form in monuments at Teotihuacan.

A burial complex found in 2002 at a middle level of the Moon Pyramid may become the first case, but the bones and offerings associated must be studied to identify people buried inside as Teotihuacan elites (Sugiyama and Cabrera 2003). Burial 5 was discovered at the top of Building 5 covered later by the Moon Pyramid. The grave pit was filled completely with rocks and earth, which were covered directly with the nucleus of Building 6. Therefore, it is clear that the grave was made when Building 5 was being abandoned, and when Building 6 was to be constructed covering it. Burial 5 was prepared in quite a different context in terms of its location, the form of the grave, and its contents. The remains of three individuals were found facing west in a cross-legged seating position with rich offerings around them. In contrast to the burials found below the pyramid, their hands were not found crossed behind the back, but were set together in front of their hip bones. The position is unique within the large variety of mortuary arrangements found to date at Teotihuacan, suggesting that they were foreigners or high dignitaries whom we never have excavated in the city before. We know similar cases in Mesoamerica, not many, but more frequently in contemporaneous Maya sites than in the Mexican Highlands, like the cases in elite tombs that have Teotihuacan-related offerings in Kaminaljuyú that I discuss below. At the same time, this cross-legged position can be observed in many representations of elites inside and outside Teotihuacan, suggesting that the three persons were buried in a high-status manner. They were determined to be males of fifty to fifty-five, forty-five to fifty, and forty to forty-five years old.

The associated materials also support the interpretation of Burial 5 as an elite grave. The offerings include those of greenstone, obsidian, other stones, shell, ceramic, organic materials, and animal bones. They were found as ornaments of the individuals, while others were discovered in groups or independently in the grave with certain spatial patterns. Many of them were of typically Teotihuacan style, and some were similar to those found at the FSP. Certain objects were contrastingly unique at Teotihuacan, especially jadeite pendants associated with two individuals, which have never been found before at Teotihuacan nor depicted in Teotihuacan imagery, but were frequently represented on the bodies of Maya rulers or elites as symbol of rulership. This indicates that these individuals may have had a direct relationship of some kind with contemporaneous Maya elites. The questions whether they were Teotihuacan rulers or elites or Maya dignitaries, and whether they died naturally or were sacrificed, should be discussed with the results of ongoing comprehensive studies in near future. At any rate, the implication of the discovery is that the FSP also might have had an elite burial at the top level of the pyramid. Aforementioned fragmented bones and offerings recovered from the upper fill of the FSP might have been remains of an elite grave already destroyed, as argued below in the discussion at the end of this chapter (see also Chapter 5, note 2).

Millon et al. (1965: 10, 13, 18, 19, and 90) discuss the possibility of a great tomb at the subsoil level near the center of the Sun Pyramid. Although the interpretation is weakly based on data from the archaeological tunnel, new information from other monuments discussed here suggests that a royal tomb or dedicatory burial/cache may be located at the proposed spot. Besides this, another candidate for a royal grave is suggested by results of research by personnel of the National Autonomous University of Mexico around the Sun Pyramid, providing new information and insights about the city plan and monuments in Teotihuacan (Manzanilla 1994; Manzanilla et al. 1989; Manzanilla et al. 1994). The most likely place for the royal tomb is in the tunnel under the Sun Pyramid, accidentally found in 1971 and excavated by Jorge Acosta of INAH immediately following the discovery.

A cave beneath the Sun Pyramid has been interpreted as originally a natural cave and later modified by Teotihuacanos to function as a sacred place for rituals (Heyden 1975: 131, 1981; Millon 1981: 231; Taube 1986). Because no clear evidence for royal tombs, such as sarcophagi, human skeletons, or rich offerings, was found inside by the intensive excavation, the cave was interpreted as a long-used holy ceremonial place even before the construction of the Sun Pyramid. Influenced by references in Postclassic and Colonial mythologies to the sacredness of caves in Mesoamerica, the tunnel has been explained primarily as a legendary cave of origins from which tribal groups were believed to have emerged (Heyden 1981; Millon 1981; Manzanilla 1994). Although this interpretation was widely accepted among scholars, the interpretation is very weakly grounded on the archaeological data, and the fact that the tunnel was exhaustively looted in ancient times does not seem to have been taken into account appropriately. New information and additional research conducted around the pyramid instead supports the proposition that the tunnel was originally a royal tomb integrated into the monument in a way distinctly different from the sacrificial burials described above (Sugiyama 1996).

Linda Manzanilla and her associates, in collaboration with the Institute of Geophysics and the Faculty of Engineering of the National Autonomous University of Mexico, propose that virtually all the caves around the Sun Pyramid were completely manmade, primarily for the quarrying of construction materials at the level of a volcanic flow (Manzanilla 1994; Manzanilla et al. 1994). Manzanilla further believes that the cave under the Sun Pyramid is one that was completely created for quarrying. The idea that the cave was completely manmade fits well with my interpretation of a unified plan for the city at an early stage of urban formation (Chapter 3). I further suspect – on the basis of its location, form, orientation, and the evidence of looting – that the tunnel was created not just for quarrying, but mainly for depositing a royal burial.

The entrance to the tunnel was found at the first step of the main staircase of the Adosada platform, exactly on the east–west axis of the Sun Pyramid. Since the

Adosada platform was a later addition to the main pyramid, built during the Miccaotli phase (R. Millon 1973), the tunnel was probably accessible from the outside after the completion of the construction of the pyramid. In other words, the tunnel was made with the intention of being used either for ritual or for burial use after the pyramid, and/or the Adosada platform, was completed. The "crypt" goes down vertically about 6 m, just as part of the shaft in shaft tombs descends; then, it continues horizontally toward the center of the pyramid, curving somewhat irregularly. Solid basaltic flows seem to have forced the excavators to proceed irregularly around them, resulting in the appearance of a natural tunnel.[1]

Two antechamber-like rooms were located about one-third of the way from the crypt's entrance. These spaces were evidently artificial and bear a symmetric relation to each other. If the end of the tunnel once contained a royal burial, the two opposing chambers may have served to store offerings or sacrifices dedicated to the people buried inside, as other Mesoamerican royal tombs, particularly in the Maya region, were accompanied by dedicatory burials/caches (e.g., Ruz 1965). The form is also reminiscent of the conceptual layout of Oaxacan tombs, although the architectural style and the scale differ from the tunnel under the Sun Pyramid. Between the paired chambers and the center of the pyramid with a single central room and four lobe-like chambers surrounding it, the tunnel was once blocked with nineteen stone walls sometime during the late Teotihuacan period. All the walls were broken down by later looting activities (Heyden 1975; Millon 1981).

This final room had also been heavily looted, probably when the wall-blockages were deliberately destroyed. Possibly Teotihuacanos in the fourth century and Aztecs in the fifteenth and sixteenth centuries were among those responsible for looting, as suggested by materials found inside (Millon 1993: 22). I suspect that the fourth-century looters knew that the tunnel contained a royal grave and therefore looted it. Thus, I conjecture from a purely archaeological point of view that the manmade tunnel was originally created to bury an important individual, probably a ruler, who died after the construction of the Sun Pyramid, and that the crypt with multichambers was perhaps used repeatedly until the passage was completely blocked. After the tunnel was sealed, new ritual meanings and sociopolitical functions were likely attached to it by Teotihuacanos and post-Teotihuacan visitors. The tunnel most likely later became a legendary or ritual cave for ancestral worship, as well as a sacred place in the search for legacy items by subsequent ruling groups, who may have looted the original offerings and coopted the bones of their predecessors. Since the information of the intensive excavations by INAH inside the cave has not been published, this speculative proposition can be neither confirmed nor rejected.

Although new data suggest the existence of royal graves at Teotihuacan, still their evidence contrasts with royal burials integrated into monuments in other Mesoamerican urban centers. As described in previous chapters, the excavations at the FSP provided data suggesting that elite burials had been associated with the monument. Unfortunately, the candidates for elite burials were almost completely looted in ancient times, making definitive confirmation of the presence of royal tombs difficult.

I further compare below the FSP's fragmented data and grave patterns with those of elite burials in Kaminaljuyú, which I consider the most similar of any instances of elite burials in Teotihuacan and abroad. I stress an analogy between the grave pits at the FSP, particularly one in front of the staircase (pit 5 in Fig. 5), and the elite graves found at Structures A and B in Kaminaljuyú. Chronologically, the graves at Kaminaljuyú can be understood as a mortuary practice influenced directly by Teotihuacan burial tradition, since graves at Structures A and B immediately followed the Adosada construction in Teotihuacan.

Elite burials in Kaminaljuyú
Kaminaljuyú was the largest pre-Columbian city of those known in the Guatemalan Highlands. This center, located in a suburb of present-day Guatemala City, was occupied from the Formative to the Early Postclassic periods (Table 1). The first controlled excavations of the site were carried out by Gamio (1926–27) and Villacorta and Villacorta (1930). Later, scholars from the Carnegie Institution of Washington, D.C. (Kidder et al. 1946; Shook and Kidder 1952; Shook 1951) and from the Pennsylvania State University (Sanders and Michels 1969; Cheek 1971) investigated the site, applying more scientific and systematic approaches from multiple perspectives. One important discovery was Teotihuacan's influence on Kaminaljuyú, which was revealed to a great extent by the groundbreaking excavations of Kidder et al. (1946). As a consequence of these studies, Kaminaljuyú has been interpreted to have been conquered, colonized, intruded with an enclave, and/or converted into a Guatemalan trade center by Teotihuacanos (Sanders and Michels 1977; Coggins 1975; Sanders 1978; Cheek 1971).

Many of the data substantiating a Teotihuacan–Kaminaljuyú connection are associated with mortuary practices at major monuments. Teotihuacan-type offerings found in Kaminaljuyú, especially pottery and green obsidian objects (Spence 1977) in the tombs of Structures A and B and their associated iconography, indicate unquestionable relations of the site with Teotihuacan and lowland Maya centers (Coggins 1975). Tablero-talud profiles (a Teotihuacan architectural feature) used at the pyramids containing these graves likewise support the proposition of a connection between the two sites.

Teotihuacan-influenced grave patterns are suggested by several other mortuary features beside offerings. In contrast to royal tombs in the Maya Lowlands, where graves of important personages were often placed in specially constructed masonry chambers in pyramids or under temples (Freidel and Suhler 1999; Ruz 1965, 1973; Welsh 1988a), the elites of Kaminaljuyú in the period of cultural contact were buried in simple earth-walled pits at ground level, a typical Teotihuacan grave form. The position of the dead also points to a Teotihuacan connection, specifically with graves found at the major monuments. While early burials of Structures A and B at Kaminaljuyú (Tombs A-I and A-II) contained the dead in extended position as many other Maya burials did (note also that those of Grave 14 of the FSP and Grave 4 of the Moon Pyramid had the same position), the majority of the dead in the structures were in a seated position, which was a common feature of Teotihuacan graves. Particularly, the cross-legged seating position applied to the later burials of Structures A and B (after Tomb A-III) was rare at Kaminaljuyú and elsewhere in Mesoamerica; the only instances known in Teotihuacan were individuals found with Maya-type ornaments at the Moon Pyramid (Grave 5) as discussed above. The fact that earlier interments at Kaminaljuyú (Mound E-III-3) included richly elaborate Maya tombs with local mortuary traits strengthens the idea that the Teotihuacanos influenced Maya mortuary practices for elites at certain times during the city's long history (Shook and Kidder 1952; Stuart 2000).

Among several burial features analogous to Teotihuacan burials, I concentrate on the location of elite graves in relation to the pyramid at Kaminaljuyú. A review of patterned spatial correlation may help differentiate elite graves from those of sacrificial victims at the FSP, if there was in fact any real distinction between them. At least six elite tombs were built during eight construction stages at Structure A (Fig. 106), while six tombs were prepared during seven construction stages at Structure B (Fig. 107). Figures were made by myself, taking into account the data and interpretations of Kidder et al. (1946), to show the chronological sequence of the spatial relationships between the structures and corresponding tombs. Except for the graves of Structures A-1, A-5, and B-1 to B-3, a distinct grave pattern was followed at each stage of architectural renovation; elite tombs were consistently located under the staircase or in front of it, evidently placed there at the time of the pyramid's modification.

Mound A contained eight structures, built one upon another. According to Kidder et al. (1946: 10), "Each one, except the earliest and perhaps one other, seems to have been erected after, and presumably in connection with, the entombment of an important personage." They appear to have been elite tombs, as suggested by high quality, quantity, and variety of the associated offerings and monumental architecture. Each grave was evidently prepared in relation to a new construction and on the main axis of the pyramid.

The excavators believed that the earliest structure (A-1) may have stood completely on solid ground or partly upon the roofed pit of a tomb later reused as Tomb A-III (Kidder et al. 1946: 11). This is the only structure that may have contained a tomb at the center, if one actually existed. Structures A-2 and A-3 were built consecutively, with the main facade facing west. It seems that the grave pits were dug on this side, at the foot of the pyramid, because the staircases were to be constructed on the same side. Tomb A-I was covered completely with the staircase and a low platform in front of it. Tomb A-II was also located under the corresponding staircase.

For some reason, the orientation of the building changed from west to east when Structure A-4 was constructed. A grave pit for Tomb A-III was made on the east side near the structure's edge, and the staircase was then built, covering the tomb on the same side. The modifications of Structures A-3 and A-4 demonstrate the close association of the graves with staircases at this Teotihuacan-influenced monument. The excavators (Kidder et al. 1946: 17–19) did not find tombs associated with Structure A-5; however, they proposed that a tomb may still lie to the west, beyond the limit of their excavations. During construction of Structure A-6, the grave pit of

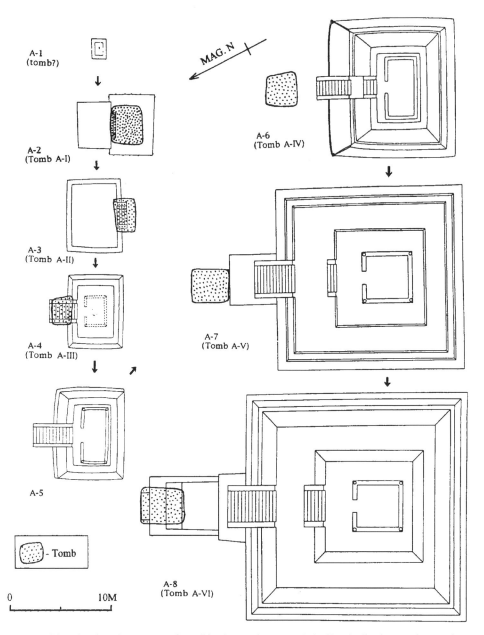

A-1
(tomb?)

A-2
(Tomb A-I)

A-3
(Tomb A-II)

A-4
(Tomb A-III)

A-5

MAG. N

A-6
(Tomb A-IV)

A-7
(Tomb A-V)

A-8
(Tomb A-VI)

- Tomb

0   10M

Fig. 106 Plan showing the process of modification at Structure A in Kaminaljuyú. Drawing: author, adapted from Kidder et al. 1946: figs. 103 and 106–9.

Tomb A-IV was laid about 2 m east of the staircase. The excavators believe that the tomb had been covered by a low platform, which was removed when Structure A-7 was erected.

Tomb A-V is believed to have been prepared in association with Structure A-7, which had tablero-talud facades. Again, the grave pit was located in front of the

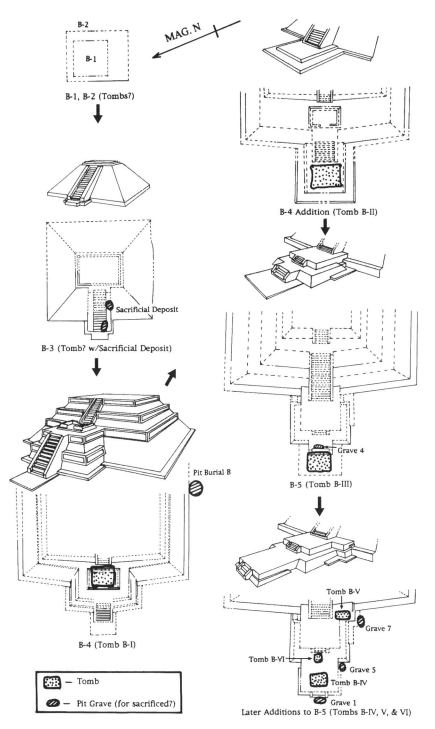

B-1, B-2 (Tombs?)

B-3 (Tomb? w/Sacrificial Deposit)

Sacrificial Deposit

B-4 (Tomb B-I)

Pit Burial B

B-4 Addition (Tomb B-II)

B-5 (Tomb B-III)

Grave 4

Later Additions to B-5 (Tombs B-IV, V, & VI)

Tomb B-V

Grave 7

Tomb B-VI

Grave 5

Tomb B-IV

Grave 1

▦ — Tomb

⬭ — Pit Grave (for sacrificed?)

MAG. N

Fig. 107 Plan showing the process of modification at Structure B in Kaminaljuyú. Drawing: Kuniko Naruse, adapted from Kidder et al. 1946: figs. 110 and 112–16.

staircase on the pyramid's east–west axis. The excavators believed the tomb was covered with a lower extension of its low platform oriented to the east. The last grave pit for Tomb A-VI was prepared further east of the staircase when the final modification program, the construction of Structure A-8, took place. Again, the grave pit was sealed with stepped platforms that ascend the pyramid.

In the case of Mound B, no burial was found in association with Structures B-1 and B-2, but the excavations leave open the possibility that one existed, since the reduced trench excavation did not follow the axial line of the mounds and may have missed it. The excavators suggested that the structures faced either north or south and that tombs may have been laid on this axis instead of its east–west axis. Structure B-3 also did not contain an elite tomb, at least not on the east–west axis; however, Kidder et al. (1946: 32–34) believed that fragments of funeral furniture (registered as Tomb X), found dispersed in the fill of Tomb B-I, had originally belonged to Structure B-3. In addition, the decapitated head of a young child, its body found in a separate location, was associated with this structure.

Tomb B-I was associated with Structure B-4, which is characterized by Teotihuacan-influenced "Adosada" construction. This form displays the tablero-talud profile, a unique architectural feature of Teotihuacan. The Adosada construction covered the tomb just as it did at the FSP. According to the excavators (Kidder et al. 1946: 34), "the individual interred in Tomb B-I was a very important personage because of the great size of his grave-pit and the richness of his funeral equipment." He was buried with three adolescents, thought to have been sacrificial victims.

Later, during the construction of the Structure B-4 Addition, the staircase and principal facade were modified "in connection with the burial of an important individual in Tomb B-II, the largest and one of the most richly furnished graves found at either mound" (Kidder et al. 1946: 38). In addition, a woman, who was interpreted to be a foreign captive (Kidder et al. 1946: 83–84), was buried as part of this construction stage, accompanied by odd skeletal materials and animal and bird bones. This possible sacrificial burial was located in Pit Grave B at the foot of the south facade of Structure B-4; its spatial relationship to the corresponding pyramid was somewhat similar to those found on the north and south sides of the FSP.

A new modification program, Structure B-5, took place with the preparation of Tomb B-III. The excavators believed that the grave's occupant was associated with the erection of the structure. A later addition to the platform was carried out by creating Tomb B-IV, built in the same place as Tomb B-III. The former was cut directly into the latter but to a much greater depth, and its shaft was made smaller so that it left portions of B-III's floor as a narrow bench or ledge. At the FSP, a similar case was recorded for Grave 12 in the looters' tunnel, which I interpreted similarly as a grave pit excavated twice (see Chapter 5).

Some time later, two small tombs, B-V and B-VI, were added, B-V being the only tomb in either mound situated off the central east–west axis; its principal occupant was well equipped with offerings (Kidder et al. 1946: 81). The final architectural modification program took place with the preparation of Tomb B-VI, which again was prepared in front of the small interior platform on the east–west axis.

In addition to these major tombs, a series of minor graves containing skeletons and simple offerings was located around Structure B near its major tomb or the monument's edges. These graves are thought to have been laid out in dedication to the monuments and more central tombs.

Discussion

The following interpretations can be offered for the grave patterns of Mounds A and B. As Kidder et al. (1946: 86) concluded, a major grave accompanied the construction phases of each mound, indicating direct association of the principal occupant in each grave with a corresponding architectural program. In other words, architectural renovation likely took place because of the death of the principal occupant buried in the grave, rather than in association with periodical calendrical significance or other type of sociopolitical events.

In the case of both Structures A and B, simple pit graves for elites were located under the staircase or in front of it, along the axis of the corresponding pyramid. As we have seen, this architectural association of graves with the staircase is especially clear in the transition from Structure A-3 to A-4. Since the staircase was moved from the east side to the west, the location of the grave shifted correspondingly. In every case (with the exception of Structure A-6, for which there are insufficient data), elite burials were covered by either Adosada construction, a staircase, or a low platform attached to it, and always located on the front facade.

It was a general trend to locate the graves under the staircase in the earlier construction stages of both mounds. In later periods, graves moved from the interior of the staircase to the front of the corresponding staircase, as construction of a low platform or footpath leading to the staircase became common. The location of graves under the low platform, footpath (or banquette), or Adosada gives the impression that a principal motive of these additional constructions was to cover graves containing elites.

At the FSP, a somewhat parallel architectural trend can be suggested from the field data. As we have seen, a grave pit was associated with a substructure inside the pyramid (Grave 12). At the construction level of the FSP, I believe that a grave pit might still exist under the pyramid's staircase, as in the cases of Tombs A-II and A-III at Kaminaljuyú, because the upper part of the staircase and its lateral walls were once damaged by the extraction of stone blocks and later repaired with small lava stones and typical Teotihuacan concrete (Sugiyama 1998c). The destruction evidence seems to indicate that a grave pit was prepared under the staircase after the completion of construction of the pyramid, or that a grave pit covered by the pyramid was originally located under the staircase and was later looted. The staircase would have been repaired as a new addition to it was made (Sugiyama 1989a). Sometime during the construction of the FSP or in a later period, a large pit was prepared in front of the staircase (pit 5 in Fig. 5), which probably served as a grave at one time and was covered with a masonry construction, perhaps a low platform or altar, possibly like Tombs A-I, A-IV, A-V, A-VI, B-III, and B-IV at Kaminaljuyú. After the pit was looted, it was finally covered by the Adosada platform, as in the cases of

Tombs B-I and B-II. This parallel architectural coincidence between the two sites seems not to be accidental, given the detailed architectural and offertory similarities at both sites and their approximate contemporaneousness.

At Kaminaljuyú, sacrificial burials were also discovered (Kidder et al. 1946: 86), usually located in the graves of elites (their principal occupants). They were often children, adolescents, or women, accompanied by poor offerings, and placed in marginal locations in the graves. These burial features are highly distinctive of the sacrificial burials found at the FSP. Independent minor graves at Kaminaljuyú, which the excavators interpreted as sacrifices, were also located at the edges of the pyramid, often off to the side of its axes. Perhaps dedicated to the monument or attendants to entombed elites, these graves and their locations are reminiscent of some FSP burials.

It is clear that elite graves at Kaminaljuyú were located conventionally, associated with a pyramid's staircase, probably at the death of the main individual in each tomb. As evidenced by the data (Cheek 1971: 238), these programmatic trends lasted from about AD 400 to 600, the period immediately following the construction of the Adosada of the FSP in Teotihuacan (about AD 350).[2] If the practice of renovating monuments in conjunction with elite graves in Kaminaljuyú is confirmed to have derived from Teotihuacan, analogies would support the idea that pits found in front of the FSP, and a possible grave under the staircase, were elite tombs rather than a part of the sacrificial burial complex.

Since this comparison is based on the proposition of a strong relationship between the two sites, supported by archaeological evidence, the proposition of elite burials associated with the FSP staircase should be investigated in more depth, at both sites. The proposition may be valid however, since the graves at Mounds A and B in Kaminaljuyú are the only cases known to date of elite burials directly associated with tablero-talud monumental architecture either in Teotihuacan or abroad.

A similar spatial relationship between monuments and elite graves in Teotihuacan is independently suggested by the data from the Sun Pyramid and perhaps from the Oztoyahualco monument, although interpretations are still conjectural. In the case of the tunnel under the Sun Pyramid, the way to prepare a royal grave (a tunnel in the form of a shaft tomb with an exceptionally long horizontal portion) is quite different from the case at the FSP (vertical pit). However, analogy in the spatial relationship of elite graves with the staircase at both monuments seems to indicate that a shared concept was applied to these two major monuments in Teotihuacan.

Another possible place for elite burial was recently suggested by the discovery of Burial 5 at the top of Building 5 in the Moon Pyramid. Individuals of high social status might have been buried under the upper floor of the monument being abandoned or near the three-dimensional center of the new building to be constructed. If the same pattern can be found at other monuments, bone fragments and offerings of unusual quality found dispersed in the upper portion of the FSP seem to be indicative that there was also an elite burial near the top of the monument, although such a grave would have been completely destroyed.

Like Mounds A and B in Kaminaljuyú, the Sun Pyramid, the Moon Pyramid, and the FSP evidently coexisted for several generations (as their modification phases and chronologies indicate), and the relationships among elite graves at three monuments would have been complex and difficult to understand without analytical, comparative studies of relevant archaeological data from all three. The relationships of elite graves at residences and monuments, as well as special meanings of cremation rituals, also make an explanation of royal graves even more complex. At any rate, the data discussed here suggest that certain patterns of elite graves and continuity of elite mortuary practices existed at the major monuments in Teotihuacan; the graves at the FSP should be interpreted contextually and historically with the patterns discussed above.

8

Conclusion: the Feathered Serpent Pyramid as symbol of sacrifice, militarism, and rulership

Symbolism

In previous chapters, I have presented analyses and interpretations of a series of programs associated with the construction of the Feathered Serpent Pyramid in the Ciudadela of Teotihuacan. This set of programs appears to have been one of many events carried out by the state for centuries at different places in the city; a dominant theme among them was probably sacrificial rites associated with large monumental constructions. To date, we still need substantial data for other cases, especially from the Sun Pyramid, to compare with those of the FSP; however, I do not believe that the events of the FSP were sector-specific, or that they were historically repeated ritual events in Teotihuacan. They most likely had a unique significance and function in the state program of consecration of the entire site. In this final chapter, my reasoning for this argument is summarized by consideration of meanings involved in these events. Finally, I discuss the events' sociopolitical implications, which centered on human sacrifice, militarism, and rulership.

Aveni (1980) and other archaeoastronomers have demonstrated that many aspects of the ancient Mesoamerican calendar system were clearly linked to astronomical observations. Astronomical objects that move with regularity and divide the sky (space) seem to have been fundamental to the Mesoamerican time-cognitive system and for symbolic conceptualization of space. Studies of Teotihuacan architectural orientation by Dow (1967), Drucker (1977b), and Aveni (1980) argue that astronomical bodies were a principal factor in the planning of the Teotihuacan city layout (see also Millon 1993: 35–36). My study of Teotihuacan measurement units (TMU) also suggests that the city's sacred space was planned with calendrical numbers that were apparently related to astronomical cycles (Chapter 3). Each monument in Teotihuacan, presumably dedicated to specific deities and ancestral worship, may have been located according to its astronomical significance. Since Mesoamerican deities were closely linked with astronomy (Milbrath 1997; Townsend 1979), Teotihuacan's ceremonial zone would have been a place where religious and astrological conceptions of time and space were realized in relationship to a deity complex. I believe that the city represented a version of Mesoamerican cosmology materialized in a master plan of exceptionally large scale.

As we have seen, this view is considerably different from current explanations by several Teotihuacan Mapping Project personnel, who have developed a function-sensitive view of modifications in the city layout over time, based on ceramic chronology. In their view, a major monument is explained as a manifestation of a political authority that was replaced or shifted by a new leadership and represented by another monument in a different style. I have tried to integrate meanings of the major monuments and the city layout into a contemporaneous chronological framework to detect cohesiveness among monuments that may have underlain the process creating the sacred center. As in many other ancient cities of the world, realization of a master plan may have taken several generations or perhaps more than a century; thus, materials in the construction fill may reflect chronological differences among monuments. However, chronological differences implied by differences in unearthed ceramics, often with distinct architectural styles, do not necessarily mean that the political units in charge of each phase of monumental construction were discontinuous, were unrelated, or had shifted. Although analyses are still preliminary because of the limitation of available data, the TMU study seems to support meaning-focused propositions of a coherent city plan such as are presented here.

I suggest that the erection of the FSP was imbued with meanings and functions relating to this entire city plan. The Ciudadela was probably an integral element of the original city layout, linked in particular to the Sun Pyramid compound (see Chapter 3), and the FSP was its principal pyramid. After completion of the pyramid, various kinds of sacrificial rituals at monuments, such as those of the Aztecs known from sixteenth-century Spanish chronicles, presumably took place at the temple. However, the burial complex I have discussed was carried out only once during the construction period of this unique monument in Teotihuacan. The FSP burial complex also may have been integrated into the long-term city program.

In my interpretation of the city's sacred geography, the north–south direction along the Avenue of the Dead seems to have been conceived as a horizontal reflection of the upper world and the Underworld. Teotihuacanos seem to have integrated topography as a crucial factor for the realization of the city's cosmological layout. Cerro Gordo, the San Juan and San Lorenzo rivers, and the natural slope of the valley appear to have been the key topographical features determining the distribution of major monuments. I suggest that the Ciudadela and the FSP, placed near the original natural course of the San Juan river near the lowest part of the Avenue of the Dead, were conceptually located in the watery Underworld associated with the south. The sacrificial ritual probably took place at this special watery spot in accordance with these underlying meanings.

In this volume, I interpret different kinds of programs for the construction of the FSP as a continuous process that proceeded with coherent meanings. The city's layout was traced reflecting cosmological calendrical significance; in particular, the Ciudadela seems to have been constructed in association with the Venus almanac. Iconographic studies suggest that the FSP was built to commemorate the Feathered Serpent, who carried on its body the Primordial Crocodile headdress, an image of cosmogonic and calendrical significance. The FSP was surmounted by a temple, which may have been adorned with Storm God imagery, another of Teotihuacan's major deities. The mass-sacrificial burial, taking place during the pyramid's construction phase, seems to have been dedicated to these deities. Studies of burial patterns and offerings indicate that cosmological, mythological, and calendrical meanings were again principal factors that structured this official mortuary act. The meanings were expressed in numbers of individuals interred in the graves and in numbers of some symbolic materials associated with them. Basically, the burial complex comprised collective, anonymous, and symbolic representations of sacrificed elite soldiers (see Chapters 5 and 6). The association of ritual warfare and human sacrifice with the Ciudadela may have symbolized fights or journeys of divine soldiers in the watery Underworld, as recounted in Classic and Postclassic Mesoamerican mythologies (Coe 1978; *Popol Vuh* 1985; Schele and Miller 1986: 265–88).

Ethnohistorical records demonstrate that human sacrifice was a widespread institution at the time of the Spanish conquest. Abundant epigraphic and iconographic studies indicate that human sacrifice was a fundamental sociopolitical institution in many Mesoamerican societies, at least since Preclassic periods. An increasing number of archaeological studies confirm the presence of human sacrifices at numerous ceremonial centers (Román 1990, 1991; Welsh 1988a, 1988b; Ruz 1968). Not surprisingly, prominent human sacrificial themes are also becoming well known in Teotihuacan, as recent archaeological findings and iconographic studies demonstrate. Sacrificial ceremonies are usually depicted relating to deities or sacred animals in Teotihuacan. In particular, the mythical Feathered Serpent is often represented in association with blood rituals in the city and abroad (see Chapters 4 and 6).

Since Mesoamerican ceremonies normally occurred according to calendar systems, the sacrificial rituals in question may have taken place at a specific time that held astronomical and sociopolitical significance. The studies of Drucker (1974) and Carlson (1991) propose that ritual activities in the Ciudadela were regulated by calendrical astrological significance, particularly of the Venus calendar. The TMU study suggests that Teotihuacan's major monumental works explicitly expressed a cosmogonical worldview and reckoning system of time and space. In particular, the FSP seems to have been the central place of Venus symbolism. The Venus almanac, in conjunction with other kinds of astronomical cycles, may have played a leading role in the determination of dates of warfare-related ceremonies and subsequent sacrificial rituals in the Ciudadela (see Maya cases in Nahm 1994; Aveni and Hotaling 1994). According to certain Postclassic mythologies, the Feathered Serpent symbolized Venus and was believed to have given time (the calendar) and delineated space (the present world) to mankind (López 1990). Quetzalcoatl, a Mexican deity symbolizing Venus, was often depicted as a divine being who traveled to the Underworld, fought against deities of obscurity, and returned with subsistence to feed the present world (*Codex Chimalpopoca* 1992: 145–47; Seler 1963: pls. 29–46). The FSP in Teotihuacan is the oldest known monumental structure in Mesoamerica with an exterior which commemorates the mythological Feathered Serpent in the watery Underworld that may convey such martial and Venus symbolism.

The rendering of the Feathered Serpent at the FSP depicts a being carrying on his body a headdress of another mythical entity. As we have seen in Chapter 4, this entity had a strong association with the calendar system. It may represent a Primordial Crocodile, a predecessor of the Postclassic Cipactli, a successor of the Preclassic Olmec Dragon, or a contemporaneous Oaxacan reptile deity and the Mayan celestial crocodilian monster, Yax Ain, wearing his own headdress of calendric significance. As a whole, the study supports the view that the FSP celebrated "the beginning of time" (Coe 1981: 167–68; Millon 1981: 230–33). The city layout, the FSP architecture and its iconography, and its sacrificial burial complex bearing symbolic offerings, together reflect and project a cohesive worldview that shaped the FSP and other monumental buildings in Teotihuacan. In the native point of view, the FSP would have been a fundamental reason for the entire site to be the center of the universe. Through this structure, only divine individuals could communicate with supernatural powers to govern the present world.

Sociopolitical implications

I here summarize results of my studies along with the questions that arose at the beginning of this volume: what can we learn about Teotihuacan urban life, society, and politics from reconstructing ideational aspects expressed at the major monuments? How can we evaluate sociopolitical functions of the ancient state's symbolic behaviors? And what can we generalize about the nature of ancient states with archaeological data from Teotihuacan society, which was evidently captivated by the conceptualization of time and space?

This synchronic view, which focused on coherent ritual meanings, does not imply that all monumental constructions discussed simultaneously took place within a short period. We simply do not know exactly how many years elapsed between the construction of the Sun Pyramid, the Moon Pyramid, and the Ciudadela, or whether the chronological span of the Ciudadela corresponded exactly with that of the FSP.[1] Indications are that the process of monumental construction was complex; significant differences in ceramic sherds included in the major monuments suggest that they were not built at the same time, and that occupations existed previously at the major monuments. At the Moon Pyramid we revealed that the monument was modified or enlarged at least six times until it got the form of the Moon Pyramid as we see it today. However, because Teotihuacan ceramic chronology for the early periods has not yet been correlated precisely with absolute dates (Rattray 1991), the chronological relationships of major monuments are still a matter for argument (see Chapter 3). At any rate, the events discussed in this book occurred about AD 200, as the constructions of the original city plan with major monuments were concluding in the city. The FSP and its burial complex seemingly marked the completion of the entire site's construction, as if the Feathered Serpent consecrated a new sacred center.

After this event, construction of new major monuments seems to have ceased. Modification, enlargement, additional building, or desecration continued to be carried out at the major monuments; in spite of such changes, the ideological principles laid out in the original city plan seem to have persisted for centuries, apparently until the city collapsed. The city seems to have entered a prosperous period, as data after the third century in the city and abroad suggest. At the FSP, a symbolic and/or political shift may have occurred, with the partial destruction of the temple, extensive looting activities, and the construction of the Adosada platform that partially covered the pyramid, as also happened at the Sun Pyramid and at the Moon Pyramid (Sugiyama 1998c, 1998d; Sugiyama and Cabrera 2000, 2003). However, no further monumental construction was undertaken, replacing the FSP or the Adosada platform; no similar dedicatory mass-sacrificial burials took place later in Teotihuacan's history, at least not on the scale observed at the FSP. Again, this supports the idea that the FSP burial complex was unique in terms of historical significance in Teotihuacan.

In the following discussion, I comment on underlying sociopolitical implications of the FSP's monumental program. It focuses on three main themes, which I believe the FSP symbolized most strongly: human sacrifice, militarism, and rulership. Although all three features were expressed in overwhelmingly religious terms, they evidently functioned together as political institutions that structured Teotihuacan society. It is my underlying proposition that the symbols at the FSP functioned as a social operation system for the state. After examining native views of symbols which carried specific ritual meanings, I offer an interpretation of this native social operation system and symbolic action that may give us a better understanding of the past society and the politics responsible for the event.

Human sacrifice

Archaeological data indicate that various types of sacrificial burials were carried out in Teotihuacan human sacrifice (see Chapter 7). Dismemberment burials, skull burials, and infant burials have been documented mainly from locations occupied after the pyramid's erection. Since major monuments were constructed in the early period of the city's history, dedicatory sacrifices to the monuments likewise belong to that period. The FSP burials form a strong contrast to later sacrificial burials uncovered in residential zones. Although skeletal materials do not seem to show any evidence of cut marks or other indications of sacrifice, the excavation contexts indicate that more than 200 individuals were sacrificed and interred in a complicated way in dedication to the FSP.

No simple classification of the individuals buried is possible, because descriptive variables vary widely in their distribution. I present in the following discussions only four basic categories of persons interred (Fig. 108), based on the types of offerings associated with them. Burial patterns by different variables support this classification, especially three related factors: number of individuals, sex, and location.

The first category includes those persons wearing greenstone nose pendants, earplugs, and beads. This category consists of sixteen persons in Grave 14, one individual in Grave 13 (the rest are unknown), and the individuals in Graves 1 and 203. If the human bones and offerings found at the top of the pyramid constituted a primary burial (see Chapters 5 and 7), this also belongs to the first category. All persons of the first category were male and were most likely from the group with the highest social status or at least disguised as such, according to associated artifacts.

The second category is composed of individuals wearing necklaces of small shell beads of certain types (types 110 or 112) from Graves 153, 172, and four individuals in the northern part of Grave 14 (individuals 14-A, B, C, and D). Individuals in

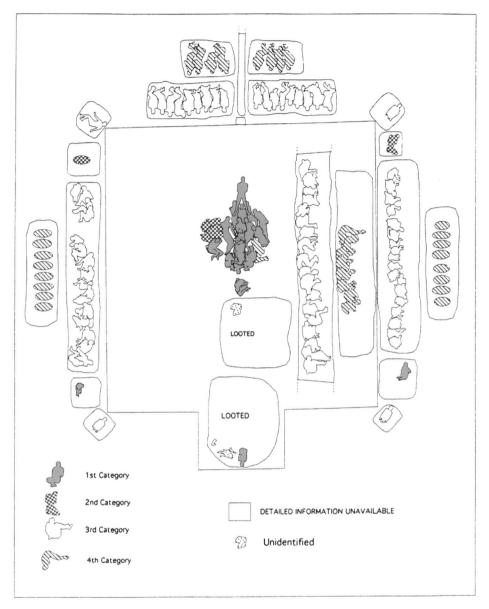

1st Category

2nd Category

3rd Category

4th Category

DETAILED INFORMATION UNAVAILABLE

Unidentified

Fig. 108 Possible affiliation of individuals buried at the FSP, suggested by burial patterns and associated offerings found at the FSP. Four basic categories are suggested. GIS map: author.

Grave 14 possibly had other offerings (see Chapter 6), while individuals in the other graves had no offerings beside beads. All were identified as male. The same type of shell bead also was worn by individuals 1, 14-E, H, L, M, and N, classified as the first category. This, and their spatial relations, indicate that second-category persons may have had closer relationships with the first category than with individuals of other categories.

The third category consists of persons from Graves 190, 4, 204, 5, 6, and the individuals found at the four corners of the pyramid, who wore collars with maxilla pendants. Most carried back disks and abundant projectile points, and all were identified as male except those found at the corners, whose sex is unknown. They evidently comprised the most clearly military group of the burial complex.

The fourth and last category consists of all female individuals wearing (as a diagnostic element of this category) shell earplugs and a few cylindrical shell beads; projectile points were also found with them. Individuals from Graves 2, 10, 11, 16, and 17 comprised this category. Although one person in Grave 14 (14-M) was identified as male, he may have been more closely associated with the female category than any other male.

These four categories appear to have been basic units reflected in burial patterns despite the fact that some variations in offerings make further, more complex subdivision possible. Social differentiation appears to have been involved in this classification. Persons of high social status may have been involved in the FSP burial complex, as suggested by richly adorned individuals of the first category; however, almost all graves, including the central grave, apparently contained sacrificial victims. In addition, intracategory differentiation was minimally manifested, as if burial forms were ritually determined as a dedication program, in which individuals were treated anonymously (see Chapter 5).

Elite burials may possibly have been integrated into this monumental construction. In particular, the grave pit in front of the staircase may have contained the body of an elite person. Even this possible elite (or royal) tomb, if it existed, seems to have had a form in which an elite (or royal) was also dedicated to the monument, since it was located at the bottom of the stairway that rose to the temple atop the FSP. This dedicatory feature seems to be emphasized by the fact that the central grave contained twenty individuals arranged in a highly symbolic mode, with no individual who stood out from the others.

Osteological analyses used to identify the individuals buried at the FSP have not been completed; however, excavation contexts and associated offerings give some suggestions about the victims. The arm positions on the backs of individuals suggest that many were unwilling captives – foreigners, rivals, or antagonistic groups within Teotihuacan society. In Mesoamerica, sacrifice of war captives was widely described in ethnohistorical records and depicted in various works of art in a form similar to those of the reconstructed bodies at the FSP (Fig. 51). The individuals depicted were not necessarily always humiliated or dressed poorly. Sacrifices of high-ranking persons had religious and political significance and were often displayed in public areas, as later discussed (Marcus 1983: 138; Nagao 1989; Schele 1984: 29–30).

All individuals at the FSP were adorned with ornaments or offerings, indicating that they were not simply stripped and that what they wore conveyed ritual meaning or functioned as identification. This was particularly so in persons of the first category, who were buried in an orderly fashion with strong cohesion among graves, as indicated by burial patterns and the associated offerings. Importantly, I suggest that the significance of ornaments and offerings was tightly associated with the symbolism of the FSP, and that they were most likely not symbols of the sacrificed persons. The dedicated individuals were clearly prepared to be integrated into the symbolism of the FSP.

Individuality was minimally expressed in terms of locations, positions, and offerings in the FSP dedicatory burial complex. Analyses indicate that differential mortuary treatments were more conspicuous between graves than between individuals within a grave. Intergrave differentiation is especially true for the burials of the first category (Graves 14, 12, and 13), which were distinguished from those of other categories by their locations, grave forms, positions of the interred bodies, as well as variety, quality, and quantity of offerings. The individuals seem to have been ritually prepared elite victims who were in some sense antagonists to the sacrificers.

If these persons were foreigners, they might have been from the Oaxaca region, as suggested by the maxilla pendants worn by 54 percent of all individuals found at the FSP. As we have seen, maxilla pendants were most unusual in Mesoamerica. The few examples of clearly human maxilla pendants we know of came from the Oaxaca region, date vaguely to the Classic and Early Postclassic periods, and are found on ceramic statues that carry elements indicating human sacrifice. These similarities indicate that maxilla pendants as symbols of sacrifice were shared at least in Teotihuacan and Oaxaca.

Dental modification was another unusual feature of the FSP burial complex. Half of the males buried at the pyramid evidenced some type of dental modification. The exceptionally high percentage discovered at Teotihuacan (where the custom was rare) may suggest that the individuals were foreigners. In a comparison of modification types found at the FSP, the most similar cases are found in Monte Albán, as suggested by Serrano et al. (1993); however, the high concentration and wide variety of dental modification types at the FSP would be exceptional even in Oaxaca.

Although the above two features suggest that the origin of the victims was Oaxaca, interpretation of the victims as war captives should be approached cautiously. Previous references to maxilla pendants in later periods suggest diffusion over time rather than contact between the two regions at the time of the FSP erection. Our data simply suggest that maxilla pendants and dental modifications appeared in Oaxaca following the construction of the FSP, implying that individuals wearing maxilla pendants were not necessarily from Oaxaca, and that both features might instead have been diffused from Teotihuacan to Monte Albán and perhaps elsewhere in Mesoamerica. In addition, a few Teotihuacan representations of human figures with possible maxilla pendants have been found, suggesting that the pendants were not entirely uncommon at Teotihuacan. There is no evidence to indicate that the origin of sacrificed persons must have been one region; the individuals could have been of different social status from various places. Those sacrificed could also have been Teotihuacan-affiliated soldiers or displayed as such with the maxilla pendants as a Teotihuacan military emblem.

Recently concluded isotope analysis of the victims' bones by White et al. (2002) in fact suggests that some lived in Teotihuacan while others were brought from different regions. Oxygen-isotope ratios in skeletal phosphate from forty-one victims of the sacrifical complex at the FSP were analyzed on the assumption that they are markers of geographic identity. A comparison of teeth enamel and bone values, which apparently reflect environments experienced during growth and adulthood respectively, suggest that individuals identified as soldiers (third category) had either lived locally since childhood or moved to Teotihuacan from several foreign locations including distant areas. Most, however, had lived in Teotihuacan for a prolonged period before their death. The analysis also indicates that the women (fourth category) had either lived all their lives in Teotihuacan or moved from there to a foreign location, and that most of the individuals in the center of the pyramid (first and second categories) had neither come from Teotihuacan, nor lived in the city long before their deaths. Although the sample size and variety for comparison are still insufficient to identify the origins precisely, the study clearly indicates that the sacrificial complex were composed of diversified ethnic groups; a majority were brought from various regions in Mesoamerica at different stages of life. This preliminary interpretation is, however, subject to further studies of various kinds, including ongoing DNA analysis for the biological identification of the victims.

Whether or not the victims were foreigners or affiliates, it can be argued that differentially presented burials and offerings were prepared by Teotihuacan sacrificers in dedication to Teotihuacan deities. Burial patterns and offerings made exclusively at the FSP indicate the intention of Teotihuacan sacrificers to express their own ritual meanings, suggesting that individual offerings may not necessarily represent the ethnic origin or social status of the dead. Some offerings, such as shell maxilla pendants, obsidian projectile points of high quality, eccentrics, greenstone ornaments, and figurines were found in great numbers at the FSP despite their very low frequency among Teotihuacan materials. Some rare objects have been found only in monuments. In pictorial works of later periods, several types of ornaments and the offerings found at the FSP were repeatedly shown as associated with soldiers or elites, perhaps affiliated with the Feathered Serpent. Therefore, the victims could even have been impersonators of sacred soldiers from other social categories who were prepared to play ritual roles in Teotihuacan fashion (see Aztec analogies in Sahagún 1981: bk. 2).

It is also possible that the buried individuals included actual Teotihuacan soldiers or Teotihuacanos from some other social level. They may have been dedicated to their own temple, although they apparently were not dedicated voluntarily, as suggested by the tied position of the bodies.

If a king was buried in Grave 13, as suggested by Millon (1992: 362) and Cowgill (1992a: 107), they could have been retainers of Teotihuacan or foreign origin who accompanied the king. This interpretation is supported by the fact that the victims' ornaments and other offerings were iconographically linked to Teotihuacan images of soldiers or elites. An exact number of people might have been chosen for the dedication to the dead ruler and his associated pyramid and buried with their own ornaments made in Teotihuacan. However, the burial contexts I discussed earlier suggest that this interpretation remains dependent on the question of whether a king was buried during the original pyramid construction period. I discuss this in the final section on rulership.

Whether or not the ruler's body was involved, I suggest that the main purpose of the burial complex was a dramatization of the mass sacrifice of sacred soldiers, manifested not only by the persons sacrificed and interred, but also by the tools of sacrifice buried with them and their patterned spatial distributions (see Chapter 6). In particular, the central grave seems to have symbolized cosmogonic meanings of human sacrifice, and perhaps the materials discovered there were remains of a sacrificial ritual accompanying a scattering ceremony similar to scenes repeatedly depicted in murals. A large number of obsidian bifacial knives, blades with sharp points, and "piercers," all of which could have been tools for sacrifice or auto-sacrifice, were intricately integrated with objects of highest quality scattered into the symbolic mortuary presentation. This symbolic behavior of dramatizing sacrifice should be understood as a ruling group's political action, proclaiming through this blood ritual the significance of militarism and rulership.

Militarism

Militarism was another sociopolitical feature symbolically manifested at the FSP, again expressed by ritual offerings associated with interred individuals: projectile points, slate disks found at the back of waists, and pendants of human and canine maxillae that can be interpreted as war trophies. These are most likely elements indicative of soldiers. Burial contexts provide further references to militarism.

Although projectile points are often found in graves at Teotihuacan, their unusual concentration in the burial complex (more than 1,267 points) clearly manifests their primary martial role in the offering set. It is worth repeating that women also had projectile points, an indication that they were an integral part of military symbolism.

Ninety-five percent of male individuals found in Graves 190, 204, 4, 5, and 6 carried slate disks. According to later iconographic representations in the Mexican Highlands, these were a diagnostic element for soldiers. Mirrors may also have involved specific mythological meanings associated with the Feathered Serpent. Taube (1992b) has proposed that disks or mirrors in Teotihuacan seem to have symbolized eyes, faces, flowers, fire, water, webs, woven shields, the sun, and caves. The Feathered Serpents on the FSP's facades are attached to disks fringed with feathers (Fig. 17a). As Taube (1992b: 197) has pointed out, the mirrors (disks) may represent vital passageways by which the Feathered Serpents emerged from the watery Underworld. Disks worn by soldiers at the FSP might also have a similar meaning of mythical connection with the Underworld, from which they were believed to have emerged as sacred soldiers.

Maxilla pendants also seem to have been trophies for soldiers and may have carried other religious meanings or an identification code. The inclusion of real human maxillae as pendants also might imply human sacrifice, since maxillae for pendants may have been extracted from victims through sacrifice. Canine maxillae strengthen the idea that persons with maxilla pendants represented both ritual warfare and human sacrifice, since coyote representations in Teotihuacan and later Classic and

Postclassic societies explicitly indicate attributes of soldiers and sacrificers (Fig. 88) (C. Millon 1988b: 207–9).

These individuals, adorned with martial objects, were differentiated from and probably subordinate to those of the first category (Graves 12, 13, 14, 1, and 203), who wore objects of greenstone and other materials. Nose pendants in the form of serpent rattles (as identified by Oralia Cabrera) indicate that persons of this category possibly represented an elite class associated with the Feathered Serpent. Individuals of the first category also carried projectile points but were without maxilla pendants, suggesting their military association.

Eccentrics, recovered around the FSP but found in greater concentration in the central area, have often been discovered in association with monuments. Type C eccentrics, representing a combination of projectile points and Feathered Serpents, seem to have been found only at the FSP in Teotihuacan, primarily in the central grave, except for six type C eccentrics discovered in graves of the third and fourth categories in peripheral zones (20 percent). The eccentrics seem to have linked the central grave to those of the other categories. Their morphology evidently represents the martial nature of the Feathered Serpent with which soldiers were associated.

In conclusion, all four categories of burials within the complex seem to have represented a mythical and/or real social hierarchy of sacred soldiers dedicated to the Feathered Serpent. As we have seen, associated offerings indicate that the soldiers were not enemies buried with their own ornaments of foreign affiliation but were sacrificed individuals consecrated to the Feathered Serpent. They may have come from various regions in Mesoamerica at different stages of life as suggested by the isotope analysis. Whether or not they were foreigners or Teotihuacanos, they most likely represented divine soldiers dedicated to the FSP, in that they had been set with the trappings of success in war and sacrifice. This is strongly suggested by false shell maxilla pendants used as war trophies but seemingly produced exclusively for this burial complex. The individuals' positions, seated with the temple to their backs or facing upward with their heads toward the pyramid, support the idea that the soldiers were prepared for the temple dedication as if they were guarding the pyramid of the Feathered Serpents, and were linked mythologically with warfare. According to archaeological and ethnohistorical information of the Late Classic and Postclassic centers like Cacaxtla, Tula, Chichén Itzá, or Tenochtitlán, the Feathered Serpent played a role as a supernatural patron of warrior activities (Nicholson 2000: 158–59). Perhaps the FSP at Teotihuacan that entombed sacred mass soldier sacrifices was the earliest instance of the association of the deity with warfare celebrated on a grand scale in Mesoamerica; this mortuary program apparently reflected a commemorative ritual performance rather than a victory celebration related to a real war.

Military figures in Teotihuacan iconography often appeared in murals in residential compounds a few centuries after the FSP was constructed. Teotihuacan-related armed figures identified in the Maya lowlands also date from after the first half of the fourth century AD (Schele and Miller 1986; Schele and Grube 1994).

These data suggest that the interment of the soldiers at the FSP was exceptional in that it took place before other records of Teotihuacan-related militarism became visible.

R. Millon (1988b: 109) has argued that the military arm of the Teotihuacan polity must have developed into a powerful force early in its history, before its impact was felt in most of Mesoamerica. Although the sacrificial victims at the FSP might have been related to a celebration of a specific war victory, the data suggest that they were more likely integrated into a commemoration of mythological warfare as honored soldiers in an early phase of the city. Whether they were real or surrogate soldiers is still to be determined; however, they most likely served the state to justify this military hierarchy institutionalized on an extraordinary scale. The proposition that the sacrificial burials were an integral element of the city planning may strengthen the idea that militarism was a crucial factor of state formation, as discussed later.

Rulership

Discussions on rulership are now more grounded in archaeological data than before the 1980s because of the recent discoveries at the FSP. Although we have not yet found the bodies of rulers, it is difficult to interpret the burial complex, offerings of exceptional quality, and associated monumental architecture without linking them with a decision-making entity at the highest level in the Teotihuacan state. In this section, I summarize my views on the Teotihuacan polity, focusing on the nature of symbolic materials manipulated by the ruling group who erected the FSP.

It has been pointed out that the socioeconomic structure of Tenochtitlán was closely tied to its religion (Berdan et al. 1996; Carrasco and Broda 1978), and that Aztec rulers tried to locate their hegemony symbolically, within the order of the cosmos (Broda et al. 1988). This materialization of the creation myth in the center of the "universe" can be better understood as an essentially political strategy. In particular, political proclamation by rulers was embedded in religious metaphor at the Templo Mayor, the principal Aztec pyramid. The main temple-pyramid represented the sacred mountain, where Aztec rulers declared themselves to be the legitimate descendants of the Toltecs and claimed the governance of the present world with divine solar authority. The pyramid and its monumental sculptures also functioned theatrically as a metaphorical commemoration of historical events, particularly of war victories (Carrasco 1991; Umberger 1987b).

Teotihuacan seems to have become a sacred religious center relatively swiftly. According to Millon's reconstruction, the city's early stage is characterized by major construction works which were begun by the third century AD. If major construction works were carried out under a master plan, as suggested by my study of the city layout, it would imply that a strong state administration existed for the creation of the sacred city from its beginning; the FSP construction would have been one of the last integral monuments of that program. Exceptionally high energy expenditure for the FSP's sculptural works indicates that the erection must have been carried out by the state administration, which enabled planners to organize large amounts of labor and subsistence. The burial complex was one of the state's most expensive investments, as indicated by a large number of foreign materials and the high quality and quantity of objects. Some artifacts, especially those of rare greenstone, seem to have been restricted to elite groups, as they were in other Mesoamerican societies (Grove and Gillespie 1992: 30). The following summary of information previously discussed may make the nature of this powerful polity clearer and more specific.

In Mesoamerica, militarism and human sacrifice were characteristically major institutions controlled by ruling groups. In the cases of the Aztecs and Maya, whose historical events were recorded in documents and inscriptions, individual rulers of fundamentally religious character headed the ruling groups. This pervasive cultural tradition may lead one to suspect that the same was true in Teotihuacan, since rich ritual displays of militarism and mass human sacrifice were among the principal factors in the erection of the FSP. In fact, some symbol sets we identified at the pyramid were used in later Mesoamerican societies as symbols of their individualistic religious rulership (Pendergast 1990; Schele and Grube 1994).

One of the most characteristic objects in the burial complex is tools for sacrifices. Large obsidian knives, such as those used by Aztecs for heart sacrifice, may have been symbols of authority for sacrificers to execute bloody rituals. In particular, obsidian biface miniatures and "piercers' indicate the performance of auto-sacrifice. Among the Lowland Maya, royal bloodletting was a dominant subject of monumental art and the hieroglyphic inscriptions associated with kingship (Stuart 1988). In Teotihuacan iconography, only one instance of auto-sacrifice has been identified recently, in relation to images of high-ranked priests (C. Millon 1988c). Archaeologically, the tools found at the FSP are the most plausible evidence for auto-sacrificial rituals at Teotihuacan. The fragile nature and morphology of the tools, and the burial contexts in which they were found, suggest that auto-sacrifice was involved in mortuary rituals carried out at the FSP's central graves; this may imply that individuals of the first category were qualified as members of royalty.

Represented mythical entities further define attributes of the pyramid. Feathered Serpent images were not only represented on the building's facades but also displayed in certain offerings. Numerous zoomorphic obsidian figures evidently represent Feathered Serpents; they would have served to enhance meanings of the divine commission of Graves 13 and 14. The wooden baton with a Feathered Serpent representation seems to have had special significance and function (Fig. 93); it seems to have been a tool of proclamation of individual authority. As discussed in Chapter 4, representations of the Feathered Serpent in later Teotihuacan periods also indicate its strong association with individual authority. For example, mat representations, used widely as a locative icon for authority in Mesoamerica, are depicted exclusively with the Feathered Serpent among mythical entities in Teotihuacan (Figs. 20c–e and 22g). Therefore, the baton seems to have been a personal insignia of rulership. Feathered Serpent images were also used as an identification code of important personages in post-Teotihuacan political centers such as Xochicalco, Cacaxtla, Chichén Itzá, Tula, etc. As suggested by Carrasco (1982) and others, the Feathered Serpent could have been the symbol of rulership as early as the time of the FSP in Teotihuacan.

At the FSP, the Feathered Serpent may have been related to the Storm God. In some cases, Feathered Serpents were depicted metaphorically, as the lightning that Tlaloc grasps (Fig. 94). Bolts of lightning were often considered as spears that the Storm God holds with a spear-thrower. Therefore, it is possible that Feathered Serpents carried the meaning of spears, or that the spear was seen as a metaphor for the Feathered Serpent. In fact, obsidian eccentrics of type C found in the FSP symbolized this transformation of the Feathered Serpent into projectile points (Fig. 60). Therefore, the baton with the serpent head could have been, in a sense, the Storm God's lightning, which may metaphorically have been conceived as a spear (projectile point). The baton could have been an item of the regalia of ruling individuals associated with the Storm God as well as the Feathered Serpent itself.

In addition to these symbolic objects, greenstone ornaments of unusual quality and quantity were deposited in a complicated way at the FSP. In particular, first-category burials (Graves 1, 203, 14, and 13) included greenstone nose pendants of unusual types. Type A, in the form of rattles representing affiliation to the Feathered Serpent, were worn by persons who were most adorned with other kinds of ornaments and offerings in the central grave (Grave 14) and two individual graves outside the FSP (Graves 1 and 203). The data suggest that these individuals belonged to, or were surrogates for, special classes affiliated with the Feathered Serpent cult. However, these persons labeled with a Feathered Serpent icon were not necessarily from the highest class (since some were found with hands crossed behind the back) but instead may have been set as dedicatory to the Feathered Serpent by persons in charge of the event.

Type B nose pendants, in the form of a rectangle with two fang-like hangings below, were found only in a looted grave (Grave 13). Although the ritual meanings of the form are unknown, they are similar to those worn by richly ornamented anthropomorphic figures in Teotihuacan iconography and abroad (Fig. 67). Some have been interpreted as the Storm God (Caso 1967a: 252), the Great Goddess (Pasztory 1992; Berlo 1992), or rulers (Cowgill 1992b; Schele 1994, personal communication). This would have been a most significant identification code for the social status of particular individuals. Probably more than two persons in Grave 13 wore them.

The difference between the two types of nose pendants, clearly divided into two graves, is unquestionable. Other grave variables – location, depth of the pits, and some offerings exclusive to specific graves – support this difference. As mentioned in the following section, these two graves probably contained two different elite groups who were likely sacrificed. Both types A and B nose pendants, contrasting one to another, seem to have been identification codes of victims who ritually, and perhaps in reality, belonged to two different affiliations. Excavation contexts indicate that the individuals interred in Graves 14 and 13 were not rulers, since they were numerous, twenty and perhaps about eighteen individuals respectively. Nose pendants of the two contrasting types seem to have been strategic values applied in these two anonymous and collective graves incorporated into a theatrical ritual.

The construction work involving sacrificial burials with these symbolic objects was completed with the masonry facades. The mortuary program, which was once displayed with chanting priests for the public (or at least for some audience), was completely concealed and remained invisible to later visitors. In contrast, the facade itself was evidently programmed more consciously for permanent public display. The iconographic study of the facade presented here indicates that the foundation of the FSP was carried out as a dedication program for the Feathered Serpent and, perhaps, the Storm God, two principal deities in Teotihuacan. The Feathered Serpent was the principal motif in the four facades of the pyramid. The temple atop the pyramid may have had large images of the Storm God, who was also manifested by at least six Storm God jars included in the pyramid. The symbols of the two interrelated deities, as suggested by iconographic representations of later periods, seem to have played a major role for the foundation of the FSP. In extension, the symbolism at the FSP seems to have functioned for the state as a religious metaphor, which arbitrarily and conventionally links ritual meanings with their sociopolitical functions.

Besides the discovery of symbolic objects related to individual rulership, the FSP excavations disclosed the possibility that a ruler's body was involved in the burial complex. However, the proposition is still to be confirmed archaeologically. Unfortunately, the most probable candidates for royal tombs have been heavily looted or completely destroyed since Teotihuacan times, and the existence of a royal tomb at the FSP may never be proved definitively. In addition, the meanings of the FSP burial complex, in which the symbols of rulership are potentially involved, are not precisely understood. I however believe the data support the following interpretation of three possible elite graves better than other current alternatives.

As we have seen, Grave 13 may have contained a ruler's body. Nonetheless, I incline to the idea that Grave 13 contained a multiple burial of anonymous sacrificial victims, analogous to that of Grave 14. The similarity of the bodies' spatial distribution between Graves 13 and 14 supports this interpretation (see Chapter 5). Although there were significant differences between the two graves with regard to burial contexts and associated materials, the differences may be insufficient to separate one from the other as sacrificial burial versus royal tomb (or royal tomb including sacrificed retainers). In addition, the offerings in the graves may not necessarily reflect the people buried. The presentations of both Graves 13 and 14 seem to have been arranged by others in order to contrast one with the other.

Grave 14, which contained twenty individuals with exceptionally rich offerings, seems to have been a collective anonymous presentation of sacrifice. The offering clusters found there were part of scattering rituals associated with sacrifice, possibly like those depicted in several murals. If the interpretation of these murals as a depiction of a scattering ritual associated with sacrifice is correct, the priests (the main motif of the murals) may have been the sacrificers (or rulers) who executed the rituals. They (the sacrificers) are scattering apparently valuable materials like trumpet shells, bivalves, miniature headdresses, greenstone figureheads, earplugs, beads, nose pendants, flowers, and seeds, all probably included in the FSP's burial cache. A Tetitla figure (Figs. 67a and 104a) is scattering, among other things, type B greenstone nose pendants identical to those he/she wears on his/her face. Other figures depicted in the Maguey Priest Mural (Fig. 18c) are chanting over precious objects, including miniature representations of headdresses. They were scattering or chanting over the most important objects, including their own emblems, to identify their high social status. A similar ritual may have taken place at the center of the FSP, although archaeological evidence shows only sacrificed victims and what the sacrificers may have thrown on their bodies, without any physical evidence of the sacrificers themselves. Some general offerings were placed on the bodies in Grave 14 and perhaps Grave 13. Possibly, the most important things for sacrificers were also scattered as general offerings in this symbolic act, as the mural representations demonstrate. Thus, analogous ritual contexts support the idea that Graves 14, and perhaps 13, were sacrificial burials rather than royal tombs.

The burial pit in front of the FSP stairway is, to me, a stronger candidate for a royal tomb. This proposition is supported by data from elite tombs found at Mounds A and B of Kaminaljuyú, Guatemala (see Chapter 7). As suggested by Teotihuacan-influenced architectural style, modification program, and offerings, mortuary practices for elites seem to have followed the patterns of the mother culture. Elite tombs were prepared under or in front of the staircase and on occasion under the footpath, or under the Adosada platforms, at Kaminaljuyú. Since analogous architectural features can be seen in the large pit in front of the FSP and in the modification program of the Adosada platform at Teotihuacan, this grave pit was the most probable place for an important individual who died a natural death. But burial contents were almost completely removed by looting, and it is still to be confirmed whether the pit contained the body of a ruler and, if so, whether he or she was a ruler or an elite, with or without accompanying sacrificed individuals. The topic should also be discussed in the larger context of the city's elite burials, especially those associated with major monuments; the case of the Sun Pyramid provides supporting information and a hypothetical interpretation that royal graves were probably associated with the main staircase of the corresponding Adosada platform (see Chapter 7).

The recently discovered burial complex at a middle level of the Moon Pyramid opened another possibility for a royal grave. The burial complex found at the top of Building 5 with jade ornaments symbolizing rulership suggests that the FSP might also have had an elite burial at the top level of the pyramid. However, fragmented bones and offerings recovered were insufficient to further develop interpretations and need to be complemented by other similar instances to indicate a royal grave pattern associated with monuments.

Whether or not the body of a ruler was included, the symbolic materials studied suggest the presence of strong rulership in the erection of the FSP. For me, the most conspicuous symbols for individual rulership are the representations of headdress complexes (including nose pendants) sculptured on the facade of the FSP. As with many Teotihuacan murals and vessel paintings, which included headdress representations at important focal points of the scenes, the FSP shows a type of headdress in high relief as if it were juxtaposed with the Feathered Serpent. I identify the headdress form as a Primordial Crocodile, which bears cosmogonical calendrical significance. It is worth emphasizing *why* the mythical entity carries a headdress on his body, the nature of which is for human use; I believe this symbolic mythical scene was structured to demonstrate publicly the political hegemony and divine authorization of the person who wore the headdress to rule the "universe" brought into being by the Feathered Serpent. The headdress, symbolizing the beginning of time, was to be given to the individual who was believed to be designated to control a new "universe" by using that headdress. The planner of the FSP, the executor of mass human sacrifice, presumably would have been the person who used the headdress. In summary, the FSP may have been a monument commemorating the accession of a ruler who, through the realization of mass human sacrifice and the cosmogonic scene of a new era, was designated to be privileged to administer the present world on behalf of the gods.

If these symbolic programs were operating in the public arena, this particular way of expressing political authority seems to relate the Teotihuacan polity to individual rulership based on a sacred/religious charter in an early period of Teotihuacan history. In particular, the enactment of mass human sacrifice at the FSP was evidently part of a most effective program for political proclamation. At many levels, the data indicate that the events at the FSP were prepared within a larger state program of consecrating the politico-religious center, in both physical and ideational senses. The state was responsible for the coordination of all aspects of this dedicatory event: preparation of offerings, execution of sacrificial burial, monument construction, and decoration.

It has long been believed that Teotihuacan was one of the most sacred places that did not reflect personalized authority. For example, Grove (1994) states that "from 1000 BC onward the ideological systems of Central Mexican societies were characterized by anonymous rulership; place rather than personalized rulership received the emphasis in public art." In my view of Teotihuacan through the FSP, this is misleading. I believe, on the basis of the archaeological evidence brought to bear here in these pages, that Teotihuacan was among Mesoamerican societies in which individual rulership of a religious character played a leading role in an early stage of state formation, and that public art explicitly but symbolically manifested that rulership. Warfare and subsequent human sacrifice (or human sacrifice and the prescribed warfare necessary for it, in native minds) seem to have been important institutions that structured society and characterized Teotihuacan politics and cultural contents. The Feathered Serpent represented, in mythical metaphor, the rulership that manipulated them.

Materialization of power in ancient states

In this final section, I briefly summarize what this study may suggest in the historical context of Mesoamerica and beyond, in order to elucidate patterns shared among certain states and characteristics of ancient urbanism. The previous discussion mainly stressed planned city layout with coherent cosmological meanings, the symbols of militarism and charismatic rulership, and the religious nature of the Teotihuacan polity. As a next step, these features, interpreted through a major monument and associated material symbols, need to be evaluated contextually in wider comparative studies with the data from other monuments and relevant sites in the city, particularly with those from the Moon Pyramid, which has recently been intensively explored. The discussion below is meant to suggest an interpretative framework for such comparative studies.

In certain aspects, the Teotihuacan state may stand in contrast to the earliest cities of ancient Egypt, Mesopotamia, or the Indus Valley, which were associated with a major river flowing through desert, rooted in the local cultures of their own region, and developed to a certain degree without substantial interaction with other cultural centers. The ecological and social spheres of the Teotihuacan state may be more comparable to the cities of the second urbanization phases developed on the Ganges–Yamuna river system of the Indian subcontinent, Chinese capitals of the Chou dynasty, or the Andean states of Chimu or Tihuanaco, where certain conditions preexisted, including high agricultural potential with fertile soil, advanced technologies, intensive intra- and interregional trade systems, and cultural traditions shared with distant societies. Their political relationship with other relevant centers would have been critical in the formation of new centers.

The Mesoamerican cultural sphere is characterized by diversified ethnic groups living in different geographic areas and by intensive interaction among them for millennia in the form of war conquest, political alliance, migration, colonization, and trade. The Valley of Mexico at the dawn of Teotihuacan does not seem exceptional; contemporaneous regional centers in ecologically rich basins with high agricultural potential are characterized by their hierarchical settlements, craft specialization, exchange networks, and certain kinds of pan-Mesoamerican belief systems. Although archaeological evidence is still too scarce to discuss specific social interaction of the emerging Teotihuacan state with hilltop sites or lakeshore centers with monumental architecture, like Cuicuilco and Tlapacoya (Fig. 1), the interaction must have been significant. Decision-making processes by successful ruling entities would have been influenced substantially by regional interactions, either competitively or cooperatively, since the very beginnings of Teotihuacan, as suggested by extensive settlement pattern surveys (Blanton et al. 1993; Sanders 1981).

The role of warfare suggested by this study would have been one of the most radical strategies in societal formation and transformation, as it would have been for other complex ancient societies (Haas 1981; Tainter 1988; Wilcox and Haas 1994; Yoffee and Cowgill 1988). Lamberg-Karlovsky (1982: 66) argues that confrontational regional interactions may be a structural common factor of ancient urban process worldwide. He cites conflict and warfare within the primary urbanization of Sumer, Elam, Turan, and the Indus; texts from Egypt (ca. 3000 BC) and Sumer-Elam (ca. 2800 BC) indicating enmity and warfare; and the first fortification systems constructed around Early Harappan sites. The role of warfare among the southwestern prehistoric sites in the United States has recently been stressed in terms of the formation of tribal organization and group boundaries, with data of site clusters, defensive features, burning, massacres, scalps, trophy heads, etc. (Hegmon 2000). In many ancient states, from which historical accounts are available, we see that war conquests were centrally involved in their foundation and expansion processes.

It has often been argued that warfare in Mesoamerica was at the root of the collapse or political fragmentation of states, including Maya centers (Webster 1977) and Teotihuacan (R. Millon 1988a). Militarism is also cited as an important institution from the very beginning of state formation (Marcus and Flannery 1996). It is well documented that the Aztec empire in the Central Mexican Highlands grew rapidly by incorporating new territories through conquest or alliance. A military campaign was an efficient strategy to integrate preexisting local organizations into the empire (Berdan et al. 1996; Hassig 1988). However, a systematic review of material remains in provinces subjugated by the Aztecs indicates that conquest may not always be inferred with only archaeological information, since the materialization of Aztec hegemony depended on varied strategies in the empire that would have left local authorities and cultural traits unchanged (Umberger 1996). It is noteworthy that Aztec conquests were displayed more conspicuously through symbolic proclamation by the conquerors in their own monumental sculptures and construction programs of sacred public space than in local archaeological contexts (López 1994; Umberger 1987b).

Formation of the Teotihuacan state was not discussed specifically in terms of military expansionism until new data recently began to address the issue (Sugiyama 2002) because relevant data were insufficient (see exceptions in Millon 1981). Excavation contexts at the FSP have substantially demonstrated that Teotihuacan's early rulership was publicly declared in relation with military forces. The significance of warfare in the city's foreign policy was ritually imbued in a worldview materialized through a mortuary program of anonymous deified soldiers. The event would have been an early and unique official proclamation of militarism by the state. Whether it actually implies a takeover of certain conflicting centers is not certain, since evidence of specific conquests has not been identified. However, a territorial and/or hegemonic integration by military force over a large area by that time should be discussed, since the erection of the FSP corresponded to the final stage of the realization of the grand city plan that required a large amount of labor and resources far exceeding the capacity of the city alone.

Teotihuacan's warlike policy is also suggested by material symbolism from the later periods of the state, although this does not necessarily mean that actual wars took place frequently throughout its history. New discoveries cited previously, and recent iconographic studies of various kinds of materials, evidently indicate that warfare and its consequent human sacrificial rituals were among the central concerns of the state throughout its history, just as they were in other Mesoamerican societies (Langley 1986; Berrin 1988; Berrin and Pasztory 1993; Millon 1992; Sugiyama 1992). At the Ciudadela, the discovery in 1982 of a ceramic workshop revealed that military symbolism, which originated at the FSP, was later shifted to butterfly-soldier symbolism mainly manifested by censer and tripod production controlled by state officials living in the Ciudadela (Langley 1992; Múnera 1985; Sugiyama 1998a). New archaeological discoveries have also sparked reinterpretations of representations, figurines, architecture, and city layout that appear to emphasize militaristic aspects and its symbolism in urban life (Garcia-Des Lauriers 2000; Headrick 1996;

Sugiyama 1998b, 2000). Warren Barbour (1995, personal communication), citing Florencia Müller's interpretation, argues convincingly that portrait figurines, one of the most numerous figurine types at Teotihuacan, may actually represent a vast army of male soldiers (Berrin and Pasztory 1993: 228).

Outside the city, Teotihuacan influence was ubiquitous (R. Millon 1988a: 114–42). Representations of so-called Teotihuacan "missionaries" were found in major contemporaneous centers, where local ruling groups often depicted Teotihuacan elites with their own historical persons in realistic styles and with texts; the scenes suggest that Teotihuacan officials actually visited distant major centers (Marcus 1983; C. Millon 1988a). Maya rulers used Teotihuacan costumes, arms, and symbols, some of which have been identified at the FSP, in order to legitimize their divine authority with military character. These data imply that the Teotihuacan state engaged, over an extensive area, in militaristic campaigns, political alliances, and trade, which resulted in ideological influence permeated with military symbolism at high diplomatic levels by the time of their appearance abroad (late fourth century AD and after). This foreign relationship seems to have continued until at least the sixth century AD or later, the time when the metropolis collapsed, evidently from collusion among internal or external sectors (R. Millon 1988a). In post-Teotihuacan periods, warfare became much more conspicuous at Late Classic and Postclassic regional centers in the Mexican Highlands (Diehl and Berlo 1989). Deciphered inscriptions and iconography tell us that for the Maya elites, warfare and sacrificial rituals were major concerns of rulers during the Late Classic and Postclassic periods (Martin and Grube 2000; Wren 1994).

Teotihuacan would not have been an exception to this conflict-laden political atmosphere in Mesoamerica from the emerging phase of the state. The argument may be specifically supported by a parallel feature observed at the FSP and certain other early urban centers: the themes of militarism and conquest were conspicuously manifested in early public monuments. Monte Albán fully developed pictorial programs with a writing system and demonstrated its militaristic power and conquest history through them at least by Period II (200 BC–AD 100), by which time statehood had unmistakably developed (Flannery and Marcus 1983: 79–143). In Period IIIa (AD 100–400), formerly called Transition II–IIIa and approximately contemporaneous with the FSP soldiers' burial complex in Teotihuacan, the depiction of rulers, their captives, and conquests were major themes integrated into foundation programs of monuments (Fig. 51a–b; Marcus 1983: 137–43). Slabs with sculptured images of captives were incorporated mainly on the facades of the southern monuments, which may have represented the Underworld (Masson and Orr 1998), as if they were sacrificial offerings dedicated as a part of the foundation program of the conquerors' main pyramids. These analogous features between two major centers, which correlate well with one another, seem to strengthen the idea that the burials at the FSP were a peculiar but shared feature among major Mesoamerican centers for the public proclamation of militaristic expansionism.

Captive sacrifice, manifested as a dedicatory act to a monument in the form of either actual graves or representations, also became a characteristic of later programs

Fig. 109 Mural of Structure B, Cacaxtla, showing sacrificed and sacrificers with martial objects. Drawing: Kumiko Sugiyama, from drawing by Debra Nagao in Diehl and Berlo 1989: fig. 1).

of foundation and/or expansionism in the Mexican Highlands. The sacrificial scene of war captives at Cacaxtla (Fig. 109) seems to have represented the celebration of warfare expressed with Venus–Tlaloc symbolism that Carlson (1991) suspects might have originated specifically at the FSP. Both the war captives being sacrificed and the sacrificers were depicted in a band on a long wall facing a main plaza of the site with the highest platform complex behind them, as if the sacrificed were dedicated to a major monumental compound of the site. The central position and richer attire of the sacrificed, as opposed to those of the sacrificers, suggest that the victims constituted the main message of the scene. At this Epiclassic hilltop center with strong defenses, the founders may have proclaimed militarism in religious metaphors portrayed in interregional styles, perhaps to imply extensive political authority whether it existed or not (Nagao 1989). It is also well documented in ethnohistorical records that Aztec temple dedication ceremonies were often integrated with rituals sacrificing war captives at monuments (Durán 1967: 333–49), which has been supported by excavations at the Templo Mayor (López 1994).

Thus, explicit manifestation of sacred militarism during the stage of state foundation or expansion seems to have constituted a Mesoamerican pattern of political strategy, shared by certain other ancient warlike states worldwide. One of the most grand-scale manifestations may have been the royal tomb of the ruler Qin Shi Huang; thousands of lifesized terracotta statues of warriors and horses were buried in association with the royal grave as if they were the afterlife army of the emperor, who created an empire through militaristic campaigns. Although the specific form of the martial symbolism at the FSP is uniquely characterized by the religious metaphor involved, the political proclamation makes sense in social histories of ancient militaristic expansionist states.

This symbolic proclamation seems to have been distinguished by features of early Mesoamerican monuments. Trigger (1990) interprets monuments as conspicuous consumption involving wasteful spending to enhance social prestige and power. Early Egyptian pyramids, prominently those of the Fourth Dynasty of the Old Kingdom (which were exceptional in size, masonry work, and quality of adornment), testify to the central administration and the political power to control resources, labor, and a body of knowledge (Trigger et al. 1983: 87). In contrast to Egyptian pyramids (each symbolizing rulership associated with a king buried in it), major Teotihuacan monuments seem to have been constructed to materialize jointly a specific world-view on a citywide level during a relatively short period, implying that early powerful rulership, perhaps lasting a few generations, centralized political power to an exceptional degree allowing such a grand citywide construction program. The rapid completion of the city plan with major monuments seems to indicate that the planner already had divine sanction, social prestige, and economic resources in hand before the project began. The monuments apparently functioned continuously, simultaneously, and coherently during the following centuries, and rulers after the completion of the original city plan apparently did not construct vast new monuments on the same scale but concentrated conspicuous consumption in modification programs of extant pyramids and in the elaboration of their royal graves on the principal facades or inside.

Early charismatic rulership and its ideology were not only demonstrated by the monumental constructions and mortuary programs we have discussed, but also seem to have been centrally displayed to the public through ceremonies including scattering rituals; these have been lost forever but are suggested by several kinds of material symbols used and buried, particularly by later murals of similar rituals. The symbolic artifacts discussed here would have produced essentially social transactions when they were arranged in a ritual context. In particular, ceremonies involving human sacrifices might have served as political sanctions in which the victims themselves became social symbols, as documented in other preindustrialized complex societies. Sacrificial burials at Cahokia, Illinois, demonstrate the importance and ceremonial nature of the structure and varied social status involved in mortuary rituals (Fowler 1975; Fowler and Hall 1978). Graves of more than 260 individuals in Mound 72 were found with certain patterns and specific orientations into 25 distinct burial units, including elite graves, decapitated burials, and a mass-dedication pit grave for 52 persons. Rulers seem to have carried out social transactions through ceremonies of astronomical significance at the mound, in which sacrificial burials would have been symbols of dedication for the community at different construction stages (see also cases of temple sacrifice in Hawaiian chiefdoms; Valeri 1985).

At the FSP, the distinctive political proclamation rituals by a Teotihuacan ruler took place by means of the most valued belief complexes, such as a time-reckoning system, a distinctive worldview, and a deity complex. In fact, the strategy was long used by Mesoamerican elites to legitimize their divine authority on earth; visual arts and early writing systems with a unique calendar complex developed as strategic tools for rulers to commemorate their political events (rituals) in cosmological terms (Freidel and Schele 1988b; Justeson and Kaufman 1993; Marcus 1992a; Reilly 1996). The feature also reminds us that rulers of other civilizations enhanced social power by materializing worldview, scaling time and space, and connecting themselves with supernatural powers living in under or upper worlds (Chang 1980; Zuidema 1990).

The long-term project of the FSP erection, consecrated by rituals and burials, was finally concluded with a sculptural program that most explicitly displayed the belief system of the Teotihuacan state. Although the particular forms of representations appear unique, an architectural feature integrating sculptures on facades to express underlying Mesoamerican cosmology seems to have been shared with other contemporaneous societies for a certain period. Late Formative Maya rulers appear to have been concerned with representing avian, reptilian, or jaguar-like deities in sculptures embedded in the facades of major monuments at El Mirador, Uaxactun, Tikal, and Cerros, among others. These supernatural entities, essentially involving cosmogonical and astronomical significance, seem to have represented a common religious ideology pervasive in early Mayan societies. Although the way to express this unique ideology was often anonymous or collective, the erection of such a monument would in fact have been a symbolic proclamation of an emerging ruler (Freidel and Schele 1988a; Hansen 1992; Reese 1996). The period characterized by the monuments with early supernatural entities was followed by dynastic histories of Early Classic Maya rulers who began to erect temples, stelae, sculptures, murals, and other commemorative objects to celebrate their rulership with texts; thus, individual rulers became more conspicuous. Rulership before the invention of a writing system still remains anonymous in the archaeological assemblage despite the rulers' strongly implied presence in monuments via visual metaphors and material symbols. The sculptural facades of the FSP, and the Adosada platform of the Sun Pyramid, which was also decorated with sculptures, seem to have been a version of this horizon style in Late Formative Mesoamerica.

In conclusion, various programs at the FSP can be better understood in Mesoamerican historical contexts as repeated features of a legitimatization process based on divine authority and militarism. These characteristics would have further implications in constructing repetitive patterns of growth and decline of states in Mesoamerica and beyond (Carrasco et al. 2000; Marcus 1992b). The mortuary program, with its large investment of lives and material wealth, constituted a legacy in the minds of the city's inhabitants; the ritual act served to glorify the role of soldiers sacrificed for the benefit of the state in the foundation period of the sacred city. Through these monumental constructions, associated rituals, and works of art, commoners acknowledged the glorification of the divine power of rulers along with their own subordinate status. Thus, strategic dominance of ideational realms through the materialization of a belief system seems to have operated centrally as a means of social negotiation and generating power for the state, as is repeated in other complex ancient societies widely separated in time and space (DeMarrais et al. 1996; Joyce and Winter 1996; Patterson 1986).

The Teotihuacan polity has often been explained in terms of anonymous (or masked) rulership with collective or corporate organization and distinct ideology or timeless sacred landscape including the "mythical cave" under the Sun Pyramid (Pasztory 1997). In this book, I have dealt with a religious state polity explicitly in terms of strategic action (or manipulation) orchestrated by leading entities, instead of assuming that ideological conventions anonymously structured the actors' behavior (Conrad and Demarest 1984). I argue that, by itself, anonymous or corporate leadership attached to the holy space does not seem to have been conspicuous before the emergence of Teotihuacan urbanism. The sacredness was created by particular individuals who consequently gained political authority through the consecration process. As happened in many ancient states in the world, powerful charismatic rulers at Teotihuacan, crucially identified with sacred military orders and a new belief system, instigated the change of a rich, natural landscape surrounded by interacting religious centers into an exceptional holy metropolis. Like post-Teotihuacan centers in the Mexican Highlands, Monte Albán, Mayan cities, and the Aztec capital, Teotihuacan was another warlike center, where rulers were involved in conspicuous energy consumption by conducting bloody rituals as a main duty of the state in order to embody and mystify their differentiated divine status, especially during the foundation stage of the state. Whether or not the state actually engaged in frequent warfare, it explicitly displayed military and sacrificial symbols to maintain the equilibrium of social powers. For the same reason, even the very secular role of the military sector had to be highly consecrated to the divine authority. Although esoteric religion has veiled their personal faces in Teotihuacan imagery, charismatic individuals are indicated in the uneven accumulation of resources and most prominently in the symbolic cognitive systems that characterized Teotihuacan society and urban life. The city was in full operation until a new political entity emerged in different contexts of social interaction, taking advantage of the well-founded ideology of human sacrifice, militarism, and rulership that the Feathered Serpent once symbolized in mythical metaphor.

Chapter 1 Introduction: cognition of state symbols and polity

1 The absolute dates of each phase indicated in this text were taken from Millon: 1973; I have recently suggested an alternate chronological framework modified with new C14 dates from the Moon Pyramid (see Table 1).

2 The present manuscript was originally written before new excavations at the Moon Pyramid by Rubén Cabrera and the author began in 1998, and therefore only includes new data and recent interpretations without substantially changing the structure (see Acknowledgments in this volume).

3 Preliminary reports on the excavations have been published in different forms. A brief report of the 1982 excavation was published by Cabrera and Sugiyama (1982) and a technical report by the same was submitted to the Archive of the INAH (Cabrera and Sugiyama 1983). For discoveries of burials in 1983–84, see Sugiyama 1988b, 1989a, and 1991a. Concerning the discoveries of burials by PTQ88–89, see the report by Cabrera et al. (1990); Spanish version by Cabrera et al. (1989), or English version by Cabrera, Sugiyama, and Cowgill (1991). Specific topics about the excavations and materials have also been published in preliminary form (e.g., Cowgill and Cabrera 1991; Sugiyama 1991b, 1992, 1993; Serrano et al. 1991, 1993). Detailed technical reports of the excavation by Cabrera, Cowgill, and myself will be published in Spanish and English. I have also published extensive electronic files of the excavation data as World Wide Web pages (http://archaeology.la.asu.edu/teo/). Concerning the looting activities at the FSP see Sugiyama 1998c.

4 Before the 1970s, Teotihuacan imageries were dealt with in terms of ahistorical deities or mythological entities. Hermann Beyer (1922a, 1922b), Alfonso Caso (1967a), and Pedro Armillas (1945, 1947) discussed religious aspects of Teotihuacan imagery as part of the overall cultural tradition of Mesoamerica. Hasso von Winning (1987) identified deities and mythical animals and their attributes in ritual terms. Esther Pasztory (1974, 1976, 1977) analyzed images contextually as sacred mythical entities. George Kubler (1967) suggested a probable discontinuity of meanings with those of sixteenth-century societies and applied linguistic models in an iconographic interpretation of Teotihuacan, although his interpretations remain within the context of mythological narratives. Laurette Séjourné (1970) was the first iconographer to stress the importance of martial and sacrificial aspects of Teotihuacan imageries. Presuming cultural continuity from Teotihuacan to Aztec times, perhaps more strongly than any other, she believed that bloody scenes are explicitly represented in Teotihuacan iconography, an argument which recent iconographic and archaeological studies support.

Chapter 2 Background: data, and ideation

1 During the mapping of the FSP, I had been impressed with its highly regular and symmetrical architectural plan, and I was looking for the measurement unit used at Teotihuacan (Sugiyama 1983, 1993). In fact, the Teotihuacan measurement unit (TMU) I propose in

Chapter 3 – 83 cm – originally derived from the measurements of this pyramid, which was precisely planned on principles of symmetry.

2 I was charged with mapping architecture and topography for excavation, conservation, and further research designs (Sugiyama 1982), and I intended to map all structures unearthed to date, to the scale of 1:100. When about 70 percent of the mapping was complete, the project was suddenly suspended and the PAT80–82 closed. However, the maps with their architectural features, stored in the INAH's archive, were major sources for my study of the Teotihuacan city layout and architecture described in this book.

3 Anna M. Jarquín and Enrique Martínez of PAT80–82 later found an individual grave (Fig. 5, Grave 172), again with small shell beads, north of the pyramid, corresponding to Grave 153 with respect to the building's east–west centerline. Thus, it was considered highly probable that Grave 153 had another counterpart with respect to the north–south centerline and that another grave might be found on the north–south centerline.

4 The Adosada ceramics and those from the FSP's interior seem to be significantly different; preliminary analysis suggests that the difference represents a transition from Miccaotli-Early Tlamimilolpa to Late Tlamimilolpa. According to Cowgill's review, cylindrical tripod vases, a single-chambered candelero, molded censer ornaments, and San Martín Orange were included in the Adosada but not in the FSP (Cabrera, Sugiyama, and Cowgill 1991: 89).

5 Excessive looting and temple destruction belong to another historical event revealed extensively since the 1982 excavation; I have discussed these activities elsewhere (Sugiyama 1988b, 1998c, 1998d).

6 Although the Mesoamerican worldview of fusion of temporal and spatial dimensions is different from modern Westerners' conceptualization of time and space, it was not unique in human history. Cases similar to it (which could be described as a prototype of an underlying cognitive system that developed in various preindustrial societies) have also been observed in China and neighboring cultural areas. To some, similarities suggest a common origin (Coe 1981: 161–62).

Chapter 3 The Ciudadela and the city layout

1 INAH's recent excavations of the Sun Pyramid complex may modify this chronological sequence as ceramic analyses progress; preliminary reviews by Evelyn Rattray (1995, personal communication) suggest that outermost layers of the original Sun Pyramid (before modification) and the innermost stage of its great surrounding platform complex could have been as late as a transition period from Miccaotli to Early Tlamimilolpa. Cowgill's preliminary review of the materials from a new tunnel in the Sun Pyramid resulted in the same conclusion. The confirmation of this ceramic chronology would support my proposition that the city's major monuments were built around AD 200 with a master plan.

2 Research by Drewitt and Drucker gave me confidence in 80–83 cm as a Teotihuacan measurement unit at the initial stage of this study. However, since the difference between 80.5 and 83 cm is significantly large for major structures, the 80.5 cm unit remained to be examined as another measurement unit. Séjourné's proposal of 60 m as a unit also might be appropriate. About 60 m seems to have been a large unit used to define residential compounds, at least in a district. Seventy-three TMU ($0.83 \times 73 = 60.59$ m), the number of Tonalpohualli in a fifty-two-year cycle, might have been applied in determining the size of some residential compounds. We are recently elaborating precise three-dimensional plans of the city's central zone as a program of the ongoing Project of the Moon Pyramid using aerial photos and architectural data surveyed with total station. Spatial analyses with these new data in the near future would provide much more precise interpretations than the propositions presented here.

3 The decimal system may not have been practiced in Teotihuacan, since the vigesimal system is known to have been used widely throughout Mesoamerica. If the vigesimal system is applied, the round numbers mentioned are 2.10.0 (2 × 20 × 20 + 10 × 20 + 0), 5.0.0 (5 × 20 × 20 + 0 × 20 + 0), and 10.0.0 (10 × 20 × 20 + 0 × 20 + 0) TMU, respectively; they are still well-punctuated numbers in the vigesimal system.

4 If the centers of the channelized rivers are considered the boundaries of the divisions, the north portion is 1,654 m, and the south portion is 1,678 m. From the current topography of the rivers, it is impossible to know exactly where the channelized rivers were almost twenty centuries ago and from which part of the river the Teotihuacanos measured. The Río San Juan and the Río San Lorenzo have been highly eroded and currently measure about 16 m and 40 m wide respectively; this may give readers an idea about the degree of accuracy with which the study of the TMU can be carried out on this scale. I believe, however, that the distance does not correspond accidentally to 2,000 TMU.

5 Distances should be considered to be approximate, since they were calculated with available data. Several factors make accurate computation difficult or impossible: the axis of the Sun Pyramid can be traced in different ways, depending on the architectural features on which the calculation is based; and the fact that Teotihuacan north–south and east–west orientations do not form an exact 90-degree angle. In particular, the minimum difference between the two distances (833 − 829 = 4 m) may also be due to the earlier inside construction of the Moon Pyramid, which would make the distance of the north portion approximate to the south portion, or exactly 1,000 TMU.

6 The same measurement may have been used in the Great Compound (Fig. 15): according to the TMP's reconstruction, the Great Compound's main plaza is 214–18 m in the north–south direction (Millon et al. 1973).

7 Expressions of horizontal dimension in terms indicating vertical differentiation with cosmological, political, or social implications can be recognized worldwide. The English "downtown/uptown" is a case in which different sociopolitical meanings are implied. *Shita-machi* (downtown)/*yama-no-te* (hand/direction of hill) in Tokyo also imply sociopolitical hierarchy: *shita-machi* demarcates a geographically lower area near the Sumida river where folk traditions still live; *yama-no-te* demarcates an elevated area where people of higher social status once lived, since Shogun families established their castle and state administrative offices there in the sixteenth century. The two terms are still in use to imply changing cultural and sociopolitical differentiation beyond geographical verticality

8 Freidel et al. (1993: 59–122) propose in their book *Maya Cosmos* that the significant ancient north–south cosmic axis was in fact the Milky Way for the Maya, often represented as the so-called World Tree in Mesoamerican cosmologies. Freidel (personal communication) kindly pointed out that the cosmogram arranged along with the Avenue of the Dead would have been celestial at the same time; as indicated by Reilly (1996), the underworld may rotate up at sunset from under the earthly realm to become the night sky. These intriguing ideas need to be explored in Teotihuacan contexts, as more specific meanings associated with the monuments are discerned.

Chapter 4 Architecture and sculpture

1 Tablero-talud architectural style, however, might have originated earlier in other regions (García 1981: 252; Plunket and Uruñuela 1998: 295).

2 Manta compounds are mold-made square plaques used as adornments of so-called Teotihuacan Theater-type censers. The surface on one side is filled with a set of symbols with some structural analogy. Although their specific meanings are not clear, Manta Compounds are assumed to have strong calendrical associations, particularly with Xiuhmolpilli, the Mesoamerican fifty-two-year ritual calendrical cycle, and the New Fire ceremony carried out for its commemoration (e.g., Langley 1986: 153–67).

3 Many sculptural blocks on the FSP's facades seem to have been removed from the spot to be reused in other building, possibly from later Teotihuacan periods to post-Teotihuacan times. Only four percent of the total number of blocks originally used on the facades were found in excavations.

4 Taube's interpretation differs from mine in that he interprets the headdress head as dualistic – a War Serpent juxtaposed with the Feathered Serpent. I do not see War Serpents as an entity distinct from Feathered Serpents: the Feathered Serpent at the FSP seems to have contained martial attributes as part of its nature. This is represented metaphorically in obsidian figurines of Feathered Serpents transforming into projectile points that were discovered at the pyramid (see Chapter 6).

5 The Feathered Serpent body and headdress in the Zacuala Palace mural seems to have been the central motif of that scene (Fig. 17c; Séjourné 1966a: fig. 9); however, as René Millon (1995 personal communication) recalled, this section seems to have formed a part of a column or a semicolumn projecting from a wall in the portico of the main temple in the residential compound. In the mural called "Mythological Animals," Feathered Serpents were painted in the central zone of a wall in a room (Fig. 18e), but in this case the Feathered Serpent was only one of several principal entities in the whole scene.

6 Quincross signs were associated with other motifs and appeared in other places. An entity with which it was associated was the Storm God (Fig. 19b), a combination often represented in abstract form, such as the quincross sign combined with the so-called mustache of Tlaloc with three dots (Batres 1906: 22). This association would make sense if the FSP were dedicated to the Storm God as later suggested.

7 According to archaeological data, the FSP was constructed about AD 200 and probably destroyed sometime in the fourth century (Sugiyama 1998c), after which the symbolism of the pyramid shifted, and the pyramid probably became a target of looting. Representations of War Serpents among the Maya cited by Taube are mainly from the Late Classic period, and many date to after the collapse of Teotihuacan. This spatial and temporal gap does not mean that the Maya did not copy war symbolism that originated several centuries earlier at the FSP; however, we should not easily suppose that the symbolism used by the Maya was the same as that used at the original place.

8 Taube thinks the bead-like texture indicates shell beads and showed me an example discovered in an archaeological context (Smith and Kidder 1951: figs. 42 and 69). It is clear that the shell beads found near the head of a burial discovered at Nebaj, Guatemala, were components of the headdress worn by that person.

Chapter 5 Burials

1 These features are analogous to those of the grave pits found in Kaminaljuyú (discussed in Chapter 7), and the double edge of the pit is similar to those of Tombs B-III and B-IV. Postholes such as the one mentioned here were also found in elite graves at Kaminaljuyú (Kidder et al. 1946: 47, 50, 51, 54, 68, 73).

2 The information of the burials from the top of the pyramid later motivated me to explore the top of a substructure found in the Moon Pyramid in 2000–2003. Under the well-preserved upper floor of the fifth substructure, a grave complex with abundant offerings and three individuals of special status was found. This discovery leads me to reconsider the possibility that the remains found at the top of the FSP could have been the rest of a elite grave (see also "Elite burials in Teotihuacan," in Chapter 7).

3 During fieldwork, physical anthropologists identified individuals of Burials 14-F, J, and M as female and those in Burials 14-A, G, and S as indeterminate. In the field, all individuals of Burial 2 had been identified as young males; in the laboratory, detailed analyses with retrieved bones indicated they were all female (Serrano et al. 1991). Although the analyses described here support the biocultural interpretation that clear distinction in mortuary

treatments between eighteen and eight buried persons may reflect sex distinction, the incomplete skeletons, especially of very young people, are best left unclassified.

There also have been discrepancies in sex determination of other burials. Burial 204-I once was identified as female by excavators and a physical anthropologist (Mercado 1987), and Burial 153 had been identified as female by Emma Flores and Serrano (Sugiyama 1989a: 88). All were later determined to be male by Serrano et al. (1991).

4 The extended body position is rare in Teotihuacan but not exclusive to the FSP burials. One adult lay on its back in an extended position, with rich offerings placed in the round structure complex just north of the Ciudadela (González and Fuentes 1982: 446). This position was also noted at the Barrio Oaxaqueño by the University of the Americas excavation of 1966 (Rattray 1992: 28). Paddock (1983) and Rattray (1992: 75) discovered a multiple burial of three individuals in extended positions, with standard Teotihuacan vessels of the Late Xolalpan phase and a Monte Albán Transition II–IIIA urn. Recent excavations by Michael Spence also unearthed Zapotec-style tombs containing individuals in extended positions with Zapotec funerary vessels. Spence (1992: 60) cites the extended position as a feature of Zapotec identity used by the inhabitants of the Oaxaca Barrio; however, it was also a tradition of the Mexican Highlands since at least the Middle Preclassic period (Romano 1972), and it is possible that those found at the FSP reflected the tradition of that region. Although the extended position was unusual in the burials found in Mounds A and B at Kaminaljuyú, the earliest burials (A-I and A-II) also had extended dorsal positions. All others in Mounds A and B had seated positions. A burial complex found recently at the Moon Pyramid also included three individuals in extended positions; the data support the idea that the position was not foreign to the Teotihuacan burial tradition.

Chapter 6 Offerings

1 Many of offerings found in the Moon Pyramid are similar to those uncovered at the FSP. The comparative analyses of them in near future would provide many insights into the state ideology and politics that this book deals with.

2 The Storm God vessel is a type of typical effigy ceramic representing the Storm God (once called Tlaloc), a popular deity in Teotihuacan. The vessels were produced from the Tzacualli period throughout the city's history and were probably used in rituals of pouring water, since the Storm Gods do this in many mural paintings.

3 Although the results of these analyses represent entire grave contents and distribution patterns of offerings, further analyses will be required to examine all possible combinations of patterning of the data set, because formal analyses of offerings by other researchers have not been concluded and some data are not available. In addition, new excavations at the FSP, now directed by Cabrera and his Mexican associates, have taken place. The results presented here therefore remain preliminary until all information is integrated into the analyses.

4 Quantitative data on the offerings used here were recorded by Alejandro Sarabia, who carried out formal analysis of the materials. Since his work has not been published, some interpretations based on his data are still preliminary. In the following sections, I discuss the morphology and symbolic nature of offerings from my own point of view independent of his classifications.

5 Previously, 175 projectile points were found at the foot of the FSP staircase by Pérez (1939; Rubín de la Borbolla 1947). Others, found farther west of the staircase under the Adosada construction, may have been part of offerings originally belonging to the looted grave in front of the staircase or the remains of caches. In 1922, Marquina found at least sixteen knives associated with sepulchers located atop the FSP. Detailed information about these objects is not available; therefore, I do not discuss them here.

6 A large number of blades was also found in Pérez's 1939 excavation in front of the FSP staircase. Whether they were offerings associated with a burial or caches is not clear because of the absence of sufficient excavation data. Information about more than 297 blade fragments, found in a small area, remains undisclosed.

7 However, in the cases of Burials 2 and 4, some blades might have been intentionally buried. This is suggested by a high percentage of blades found in the lowest layer of the grave fill.

8 This interpretation is shared by Taube (1992a: 63), who has independently identified the undulating obsidian serpent as an ancestral form, the itzcoatl, the obsidian lightning serpent of Postclassic Central Mexico.

9 Since 16 of 330 beads found in Grave 14 were not geocoded in the map, this argument remains preliminary. Some of the six individuals not listed here might also have had a single bead in proximity to the thorax.

10 Among 123 earspools found in the grave, 117 pieces were geocoded. Four of six earspools, whose precise locations are unknown, were found around individuals 14-G, P, and S, who are already known to have worn one or two earspools. Others (two pieces) were found at a higher level in the fill of the grave. Therefore, one more person could have had earspools.

11 The data on shell offerings used here were analyzed by Clara Paz and myself, and we will publish a detailed analysis separately.

12 One piece of canine imitation (type 36) was found in the fill of Grave 2, along with another piece (type 14). These are interpreted as possible intrusion; all other shell beads found in female graves are of type 1 (93 percent) or 29 (7 percent), both of cylindrical forms.

Chapter 7 Overview: sacrificial and elite burials

1 Manzanilla's excavation of a tunnel at the east side of the Sun Pyramid complex in 1992 supports this argument. Based on magnetometric analyses, she proposed that the tunnel under the Sun Pyramid continues to the east and west, and her team excavated a vertical and then horizontal tunnel to find the proposed extension. Although she did not discover such a continuation, she recognized the similarity between her tunnel and that under the Sun Pyramid in that both have an irregular, undulating, natural cave-like form. Nineteen centuries ago the ancient Teotihuacanos would have faced the same difficulties in digging straight tunnels due to the solid basaltic flows. Subsequent geological examination supports this argument, as described in the reports (Manzanilla et al. 1994).

2 Analysis of the samples obtained in the Adosada provides absolute dates indicative for the construction. Three carbon samples taken from the construction fill of the Adosada indicate calibrated dates of AD 134 (65–250), AD 385 (265–414), and AD 343 (238–421). The first one seems to indicate the date of the construction of the FSP, as the construction fill of the Adosada included materials used for the temple of the FSP, while the others indicate the construction period of the Adosada platform itself (Sugiyama 1998c).

Chapter 8 Conclusion: the Feathered Serpent Pyramid as symbol

1 Recently available chronological data seem to support this cohesive interrelation among major monuments. Ceramic chronology and one C14 dating (AD 80 ± 75) for a charcoal sample included in the Sun Pyramid, and substantial data from the Moon Pyramid recently explored, suggest that the realization of the original city plan may have begun sometime before AD 150 and appears to have been concluded around AD 200 although modification and enlargement programs at the major monuments took place during the following two centuries (Millon et al. 1965; Cowgill 1996, personal communication; Rattray 1995, personal communication; Smith 1987; Sugiyama and Cabrera 2003). The Feathered Serpent

Pyramid, the last major monument to be built in the city, is known more precisely (with eleven C14 samples, all calibrated) to have been built around AD 210 (Sugiyama 1998c). The data do not necessarily indicate that one monument corresponded to one ruler, one dynasty, or one calendrical period, then was followed by another monument symbolizing the next time span. A decision-making entity would have carried out the citywide construction plan during a relatively short period.

Acosta, J. R. 1964. *El Palacio de Quetzalpapalotl.* Memorias del Instituto Nacional de Antropología e Historia, No. 10. Mexico, D.F., Instituto Nacional de Antropología e Historia.

Almaráz, R. 1865. Apuntes sobre las pirámides de San Juan. In *Memoria de los trabajos ejecutados por la comision científica de Pachuca en el año de 1864,* pp. 349–58. Mexico, D.F., Ministerio de Fomento.

Alva Ixtlilxóchitl, F. de. 1975–77. *Obras históricas de Fernando de Alva Ixtlilxóchitl: Historia de la nación chichimeca,* 2 vols. Mexico, D.F., Universidad Nacional Autónoma de México.

Alva, W., and C. B. Donnan. 1993. *Royal Tombs of Sipán.* Los Angeles, Fowler Museum of Cultural History, UCLA.

Armillas, P. 1945. Los dioses de Teotihuacan. *Anales del Instituto de Etnografía Americana* 6: 3–32.

1947. La serpiente emplumada, Quetzalcoatl y Tlaloc. *Cuadernos americanos* 1: 161–78.

1950. Teotihuacan Tula y los Toltecas: las culturas post-arcaicas y pre-aztecas del centro de México: excavaciones y estudios, 1922–1950. *Runa*, 3: 37–70.

Arroyo de Anda, L. A. 1963. *La estela teotihuacana de la Ventilla.* Mexico, D.F., Instituto Nacional de Antropología e Historia.

Ashmore, W. 1989. Construction and Cosmology: Politics and Ideology in Lowland Maya Settlement Patterns. In *Word and Image in Maya Culture: Exploration in Language, Writing, and Representation,* ed. W. F. Hanks and Don S. Rice, pp. 272–86. Salt Lake City, University of Utah Press.

1991. Site-Planning Principles and Concepts of Directionality among the Ancient Maya. *Latin American Antiquity* 2 (3): 199–226.

Aveni, A. F. 1980. *Skywatchers of Ancient Mexico.* Austin, University of Texas Press.

Aveni, A. F., and L. D. Hotaling. 1994. Monumental Inscriptions and the Observational Basis of Maya Planetary Astronomy. *Archaeoastronomy* 19: 21–54.

Bandelier, A. F. 1880. On the Art of War and Mode of Warfare of the Ancient Mexicans. *Reports of the Peabody Museum of American Archaeology and Ethnology* 2: 95–161.

Barbour, W. 1976. The Figurines and Figurine Chronology of Ancient Teotihuacán. Ph.D. dissertation, Dept. of Anthropology, University of Rochester, N.Y.

Bastien, R. 1946. *Informe sobre las exploraciones hechas en "El Pozo de las Calaveras," Teotihuacan.* Estado de México, San Juan Teotihuacan, 1690–1891, 1918–46. Mexico, D.F., Archivo Técnico de la Dirección de Arqueología, Instituto Nacional de Antropología e Historia.

Batres, L. 1906. *Teotihuacán ó la ciudad sagrada de los Tolteca.* Mexico, D.F., Imprenta de Hull.

Becker, M. J. 1988. Caches as Burials, Burials as Caches: The Meaning of Ritual Deposits among the Classic Period Lowland Maya. In *Recent Studies in Pre-Columbian Archaeology,* ed. N. J. Saunders and O. de Montmollin. BAR International Series, No. 421 (I). Oxford, BAR.

Bender B. 1993. *Landscape Politics and Perspectives.* Providence, R.I., Berg Publishers.

Berdan, F. F., and P. R. Anawalt, eds. 1992. *The Codex Mendoza.* 4 vols. Berkeley, University of California Press.

Berdan, F. F., R. E. Blanton, E. H. Boone, M. G. Hodge, M. E. Smith, and E. Umberger, eds. 1996. *Aztec Imperial Strategies*. Washington, D.C., Dumbarton Oaks.

Berlo, J. C. 1983. The Warrior and the Butterfly: Central Mexican Ideologies of Sacred Warfare and Teotihuacan Iconography. In *Text and Image in Pre-Columbian Art: Essays on the Interrelationship of the Verbal and Visual Arts*, ed. J. C. Berlo, pp. 79–117. BAR International Series, No. 180. Oxford, BAR.

——— 1984. *Teotihuacan Art Abroad: A Study of Metropolitan Style and Provincial Transformation in Incensario Workshops*. 2 vols. BAR International Series, No. 199, Parts I and II. Oxford, BAR.

——— 1992. Icons and Ideologies at Teotihuacan: The Great Goddess Reconsidered. In *Art, Ideology and the City of Teotihuacan*, ed. J. C. Berlo, pp. 129–68. Washington, D.C., Dumbarton Oaks.

Bernal, I., ed. 1963. *Teotihuacán: descubrimientos, reconstrucciones*. Mexico, D.F., Instituto Nacional de Antropología e Historia.

Berrin, K., ed. 1988. *Feathered Serpents and Flowering Trees: Reconstructing the Murals of Teotihuacan*. Seattle, The Fine Arts Museums of San Francisco and the University of Washington Press.

Berrin, K., and E. Pasztory, eds. 1993. *Teotihuacan: Art from the City of the Gods*. New York, Thames and Hudson and The Fine Arts Museums of San Francisco.

Beyer, H. 1922a. Estudio interpretativo de algunas grandes esculturas. In *La población del Valle de Teotihuacán*, ed. Manuel Gamio, 3 vols., vol.1, pp. 168–74. Mexico, D.F., Secretaria de Agricultura y Fomento. Repr. 1979, 5 vols. Mexico, D.F., Instituto Nacional Indigenista.

——— 1922b. Relaciones entre la civilizacion Teotihuacana y la Azteca. In *La población del Valle de Teotihuacán*, ed. Manuel Gamio, 3 vols., vol. 1, pp. 273–93. Mexico, D.F., Secretaria de Agricultura y Fomento. Repr. 1979, 5 vols. Mexico, D.F., Instituto Nacional Indigenista.

——— 1969. Nota bibliográfica y crítica sobre el quinto tomo de las memorias científicas de Seler. *El México antiguo* 11: 81–86. Reprinted from *El México antiguo* 1, 1921.

Binford, L. R. 1971. Mortuary Practices: Their Study and Their Potential. In *Approaches to the Social Dimensions of Mortuary Practices*, ed. J. A. Brown. Society for American Archaeology, Memoirs 25: 6–29.

Blanton, R. E., G. M. Feinman, S. A. Kowalewski, and P. N. Peregrine. 1996. A Dual-Processual Theory for the Evolution of Mesoamerican Civilization. *Current Anthropology* 37 (1): 1–14.

Blanton, R. E., S. A. Kowalewski, G. M. Feinman, and L. M. Finsten. 1993. *Ancient Mesoamerica: A Comparison of Change in Three Regions*, 2nd edn. Cambridge, Cambridge University Press.

Boone, E. H., ed. 1984. *Ritual Human Sacrifice in Mesoamerica*. Washington, D.C., Dumbarton Oaks.

Bourdieu, P. 1978. *Outline of a Theory of Practice*, trans. R. Nice. Cambridge, Cambridge University Press.

Bracamontes Q., S. 2002. Las vasijas Tlaloc de Teotihuacan. B.S. thesis, Dept. of Anthropology, Universidad de las Américas-Puebla, Cholula.

Braun, D. P. 1981. A Critique of Some Recent North American Mortuary Studies. *American Antiquity* 46 (2): 398–416.

Broda, J. 1978. Relaciones políticas ritualizadas: el ritual como expresión de una ideología. In *Economía política e ideología en el México prehispánico*, ed. P. Carrasco and J. Broda, pp. 221–55. Mexico, D.F., Centro de Investigaciones Superiores del Instituto Nacional de Antropología e Historia and Editorial Nueva Imagen.

Broda, J., D. Carrasco, and E. Matos M., eds. 1988. *The Great Temple of Tenochtitlan: Center and Periphery in the Aztec World*. Berkeley, University of California Press.

Brotherston, G. 1975. Time and Script in Ancient Mesoamerica. *Indiana* 3: 8–30.

Brown, K. L. 1977. Toward a Systematic Explanation of Culture Change within the Middle Classic Period of the Valley of Guatemala. In *Teotihuacan and Kaminaljuyú: A Study in Prehistoric Culture Contact*, ed. W. T. Sanders and J. W. Michels, pp. 411–40. University Park, Pa., Penn State University Press.

Cabrera, M. O. 1995. La lapidaria del Proyecto Templo de Quetzalcoatl 1988–1989. B.S. thesis, Escuela Nacional de Antropología e Historia, Mexico, D.F.

Cabrera C., R. 1992. A Survey of Recently Excavated Murals at Teotihuacan. In *Art, Ideology, and the City of Teotihuacan*, ed. J. C. Berlo, pp. 113–28. Washington, D.C., Dumbarton Oaks.

Cabrera C., R., G. L. Cowgill, and S. Sugiyama. 1990. El Proyecto Templo de Quetzalcóatl y la práctica a gran escala del sacrificio humano. In *La época clásica: nuevos hallazgos, nuevas ideas*, ed. A. Cardos de Mendez, pp. 123–46. Mexico, D.F., Museo Nacional de Antropología, Instituto Nacional de Antropología e Historia.

Cabrera C., R., G. L. Cowgill, S. Sugiyama, and C. Serrano. 1989. El Proyecto Templo de Quetzalcóatl. *Arqueología* 5: 51–79.

Cabrera C., R., I. Rodriguez G., and N. Morelos G., eds. 1982a *Teotihuacan 80–82: primeros resultados*. Mexico, D.F., Instituto Nacional de Antropología e Historia.

1982b. *Memoria del Proyecto Arqueológico Teotihuacán 80–82*, vol. 1. Mexico, D.F., Instituto Nacional de Antropología e Historia.

1991. *Teotihuacan 1980–1982: Nuevas interpretaciones*. Mexico, D.F., Instituto Nacional de Antropología e Historia.

Cabrera C., R., and S. Sugiyama. 1982. La reexploración y restauración del Temple Viejo de Quetzalcóatl. In *Memoria del Proyecto Arqueológico Teotihuacán 80–82*, vol. 1, ed. R. Cabrera C, I. Rodríguez G., and N. Morelos G., pp. 163–83. Mexico, D.F., Instituto Nacional de Antropología e Historia.

1983. Informe de la reexploración y restauración del Temple Viejo de Quetzalcóatl. MS., Archivo Técnico de la Dirección de Arqueología, Instituto Nacional de Antropología e Historia, Mexico, D.F.

Cabrera C., R., S. Sugiyama, and G. Cowgill. 1991. The Temple of Quetzalcoatl Project at Teotihuacan: A Preliminary Report. *Ancient Mesoamerica* 2 (1): 77–92.

Carlson, J. B. 1991. *Venus-Regulated Warfare and Ritual Sacrifice in Mesoamerica: Teotihuacan and Cacaxtla "Star Wars" Connection*. Center for Archaeoastronomy Technical Publication, No. 7. College Park, University of Maryland.

Carr, C. 1995. Mortuary Practices: Their Social, Philosophical-Religious, Circumstantial, and Physical Determinants. *Journal of Archaeological Method and Theory* 2 (2): 105–99.

Carrasco, D. 1982. *Quetzalcoatl and the Irony of Empire: Myths and Prophecies in the Aztec Tradition*. Chicago, University of Chicago Press.

Carrasco, D., ed. 1991. *To Change Place: Aztec Ceremonial Landscapes*. Niwot, University Press of Colorado.

Carrasco, D., L. Jones, and S. Sessions, eds. 2000. *Mesoamerica's Classic Heritage: From Teotihuacan to the Aztecs*. Boulder, University Press of Colorado.

Carrasco, P. 1978. La economía del México prehispánico. In *Economía política e ideología en el México prehispánico*, ed. P. Carrasco and J. Broda, pp. 13–76. Mexico, D.F., Centro de Investigaciones Superiores del Instituto Nacional de Antropología e Historia and Editorial Nueva Imagen.

Carrasco, P., and J. Broda, eds. 1978. *Economía política e ideología en el México prehispánico*. Mexico, D.F., Centro de Investigaciones Superiores del Instituto Nacional de Antropología eltistoria and Editorial Nueva Imagen.

Caso, A. 1928. *Las estelas zapotecas*. Mexico, D.F., Museo Nacional de Arqueología, Historia e Etnografía.

1937. ¿Tenían los teotihuacanos conocimiento del tonalpohualli? *El México antiguo* 4: 131–43.

1962. Calendario y escritura en Xochicalco. *Revista mexicana de estudios antropológicos* 18 (1): 49–80.

1967a. Dioses y signos teotihuacanos. In *Teotihuacan: XI mesa redonda*, vol. 1, pp. 249–79. Mexico, D.F., Sociedad Mexicana de Antropología.

1967b. *Los calendarios prehispánicos*. Serie de cultura Nahuatl, Monograph No. 6. Mexico, D.F., Universidad Nacional Autónoma de México.

1971. Calendrical Systems of Central Mexico. In *Handbook of Middle American Indians*, ed. G. F. Ekholm and I. Bernal, vol. 10, pp. 333–48. Austin, University of Texas Press.

1977. *Reyes y reinos de la Mixteca*. Mexico, D.F., Fondo de Cultura Económica.

Caso, A., and I. Bernal. 1952. *Urnas de Oaxaca*. Memorias 2. Mexico, D.F., Instituto Nacional de Antropología e Historia.

Castillo F., V. M. 1972. Unidades nahuas de medida. *Estudios de cultura Náhuatl* 10: 195–223.

Chang, K. C. 1980. *Shang Civilization*. New Haven, Yale University Press.

Chapman, R., I. Kinnes, and K. Randsborg. 1981. *The Archaeology of Death*. Cambridge, Cambridge University Press.

Charlton, T. H. 1978. Teotihuacan, Tepeapulco, and Obsidian Exploitation. *Science* 200: 1227–36.

Cheek, C. D. 1971. Excavations at the Palangana, Kaminaljuyú, Guatemala. Ph.D. dissertation, Dept. of Anthropology, University of Arizona, Tucson.

Codex Chimalpopoca. 1992. Trans. J. Bierhorst, *History and Mythology of the Aztec: Codex Chimalpopoca*. Tucson, University of Arizona Press.

Codex Cospi: Calendario messicano 4093. 1968. Graz, Biblioteca Universitaria Bologna, Akademische Druck- u. Verlagsanstalt.

Codex Fejérváry Mayer: M 12014. City of Liverpool Museums. 1971. Graz, Akademische Druck- u. Verlagsanstalt.

Códice Borbónico. 1979. Mexico, D.F., Siglo XXI.

Códice Borgia. 1963. Mexico, D.F., Fondo de Cultura Económica.

Códice Vindobonensis. 1992. Codices méxicanos no. 1. Vienna and Mexico, D.F., Adademische Druck- u. Verlagsanstalt and Fondo de Cultura Económica.

Coe, M. D. 1978. *Lords of the Underworld: Masterpieces of Classic Maya Ceramics*. Princeton, Princeton University Art Museum.

1981. Religion and the Rise of Mesoamerican States. In *The Transition to Statehood in the New World*, ed. G. D. Jones and R. R. Kautz, pp. 157–71. Cambridge, Cambridge University Press.

1994. *Mexico: From the Olmecs to the Aztecs*. 4th edn. London, Thames and Hudson.

Coe, W. R. 1959. *Piedras Negras Archaeology: Artifacts, Caches and Burials*. Philadelphia, University of Pennsylvania Museum.

Coggins, C. 1975. Painting and Drawing Style at Tikal: A Historical and Iconographic Reconstruction. 2 vols. Ph.D. dissertation, Harvard University. Ann Arbor, Mich., University Microfilms.

1980. The Shape of Time: Some Political Implications of a Four-Part Figure. *American Antiquity* 45: 727–39.

1986. Reflections on Teotihuacan. Paper presented at the 51st Annual Meeting of the Society for American Archaeology, New Orleans.

1993. The Age of Teotihuacan and Its Mission Abroad. In *Teotihuacan: Art from the City of the Gods*, ed. K. Berrin, and E. Pasztory, pp. 140–55. New York, Thames and Hudson and The Fine Arts Museums of San Francisco.

Coggins, C., ed. 1992. *Artifacts from the Cenote of Sacrifice, Chichén Itzá, Yucatan*. Cambridge, Mass., Peabody Museum of Archaeology and Ethnology, Harvard University.

Conides, C. 1998. New Interpretations of Pictorial Themes on Teotihuacan Stuccoed and Painted Ceramics. *Teotihuacan Notes: Internet Journal for Teotihucan Archaeology and Iconography* (http://archaeology.la.asu.edu/teo/notes/ CC/noteI_6.htm). Tempe, Archaeological Research Institute, Arizona State University (in preparation).

Conrad, G. W., and A. A. Demarest. 1984. *Religion and Empire: The Dynamics of Aztec and Inca Expansionism.* Cambridge, Cambridge University Press.

Cook de Leonard, C. 1957a. Proyecto del CIAM en Teotihuacan. *Boletín del Centro de Investigaciones Antropológicas de México* 4: 1–2.

1957b. Excavaciones en La Plaza #1, "Tres Palos," Teotihuacan. *Boletín del Centro de Investigaciones Antropológicas de México* 4: 3–5.

1971. Ceramics of the Classic Period in Central Mexico. In *Handbook of Middle American Indians*, ed. G. F. Ekholm and I. Bernal, vol. 10, pp. 179–205. Austin, University of Texas Press.

Cowgill, G. L. 1974. Quantitative Studies of Urbanization at Teotihuacán. In *Mesoamerican Archaeology: New Approaches*, ed. N. Hammond, pp. 363–96. Austin, University of Texas Press.

1983. Rulership and the Ciudadela: Political Inferences from Teotihuacan Architecture. In *Civilization in the Ancient Americas: Essays in Honor of Gordon R. Willey*, ed. R. M. Leventhal and A. L. Kolata, pp. 313–43. Albuquerque, University of New Mexico Press and Peabody Museum of Harvard University.

1987. Métodos para el estudio de relaciones espaciales en los datos de la superficie de Teotihuacan. In *Teotihuacan: nuevos datos, nuevas síntesis, nuevos problemas*, ed. E. McClung de T., and E. C. Rattray, pp. 389–98. Mexico, D.F., Universidad Nacional Autónoma de México.

1992a. Toward a Political History of Teotihuacan. In *Ideology and Pre-Columbian Civilizations*, ed. A. A. Demarest and G. W. Conrad, pp. 87–114. Santa Fe, N.M., School of American Research Press.

1992b. Social Differentiation at Teotihuacan. In *Mesoamerican Elites: An Archaeological Assessment*, ed. Diane Chase and Arlen Chase, pp. 206–20. Santa Fe, N.M., School of American Research Press.

1996. Discussion. *Ancient Mesoamerica* 7 (2): 325–31.

Cowgill, G. L., J. H. Altschul, and R. S. Sload. 1984. Spatial Analysis of Teotihuacan: A Mesoamerican Metropolis. In *Intrasite Spatial Analysis in Archaeology,* ed. H. J. Hietala, pp. 154–95. Cambridge, Cambridge University Press.

Cowgill, G. L., and O. Cabrera C. 1991. Excavaciones realizadas en 1988 por el Frente B del Proyecto Templo de Quetzalcoatl y algunos resultados del análisis de la cerámica. *Arqueología* 6: 41–52.

Darling, J. A. 1995. Mass Inhumation and the Execution of Witches in the American Southwest. Paper presented at the 60th Annual Meeting of the Society for American Archaeology, Minneapolis.

Davies, N. 1984. Human Sacrifice in the Old World and the New: Some Similarities and Differences. In *Ritual Human Sacrifice in Mesoamerica,* ed. E. H. Boone, pp. 211–26. Washington, D.C., Dumbarton Oaks.

Demarest, A. A. 1984. Overview: Mesoamerican Human Sacrifice in Evolutionary Perspective. In *Ritual Human Sacrifice in Mesoamerica,* ed. E. H. Boone, pp. 227–43. Washington, D.C., Dumbarton Oaks.

Demarest, A. A. and G. W. Conrad, eds. 1992. *Ideology and Pre-Columbian Civilizations.* Santa Fe, N.M., School of American Research Press.

DeMarrais, E., L. J. Castillo, and T. Earle. 1996. Ideology, Materialization, and Power Strategies. *Current Anthropology* 37 (1): 15–31.

Diehl, R. A., and J. C. Berlo, eds. 1989. *Mesoamerica After the Decline of Teotihuacan A.D. 700–900.* Washington, D.C., Dumbarton Oaks.

Dosal, P. 1925a. Descubrimientos arqueológicos en el Templo de Quetzalcóatl, Teotihuacan. *Anales del Museo Nacional de Antropología e Historia y Etnografía* 1925(July/Aug.): 216–19.

1925b. Descubrimientos arqueológicos en el Templo de Quetzalcoatl, Teotihuacan. Unpublished MS.

Dow, J. W. 1967. Astronomical Orientations at Teotihuacan: A Case Study in Astro-Archaeology. *American Antiquity* 32: 326–34.

Drewitt, R. B. 1967. Planeación en la antigua ciudad de Teotihuacan. In *Teotihuacan: XI mesa redonda*, vol. 1, pp. 79–94. Mexico, D.F., Sociedad Mexicana de Antropología.

1969. Data Bearing on Urban Planning at Teotihuacan. Paper presented at the 68th Annual Meeting of the American Anthropological Association, New Orleans.

1987. Measurement Units and Building Axes at Teotihuacan. In *Teotihuacan: nuevos datos, nuevas síntesis, nuevos problemas*, ed. E. McClung de Tapia and E. C. Rattray, pp. 389–98. Mexico, D.F., Universidad Nacional Autónoma de México.

Drucker, R. D. 1971. A Measurement System for Teotihuacán. Unpublished MS.

1974. Renovating a Reconstruction. The Ciudadela at Teotihuacan, Mexico: Construction Sequence, Layout, and Possible Uses of the Structure. Ph.D. dissertation, Dept. of Anthropology, University of Rochester, N.Y. Ann Arbor, Mich., University Microfilms.

1977a. Precolumbian Mesoamerican Measurement Systems: Unit Standards for Length. Paper presented at the 76th Annual Meeting of the American Anthropological Association, Houston.

1977b. A Solar Orientation Framework for Teotihuacan. Paper presented at the 15th Mesa Redonda of the Sociedad Mexicana de Antropología, Guanajuato.

Durán, D. 1967. *Historia de las indias de Nueva España e islas de la tierra firme*, ed. A. M. Garibay K., vol. 2. Mexico, D.F., Editorial Porrua, S.A.

Eliade, M. 1959. Methodological Remarks on the Study of Religious Symbolism. In *The History of Religions: Essays in Methodology*, ed. M. Eliade and J. M. Kitagawa, pp. 86–107. Chicago, University of Chicago Press.

Flannery, K. V., and J. Marcus, eds. 1983. *The Cloud People: Divergent Evolution of the Zapotec and Mixtec Civilizations*. New York, Academic Press.

Fowler, M. L. 1975. A Pre-Columbian Urban Center on the Mississippi. *Scientific American* 23 (2): 92–101.

Fowler, M. L., and R. L. Hall. 1978. Late Prehistory of the Illinois Area. In *Handbook of North American Indians*, ed. B. G. Triggers, vol. 15, pp. 560–68. Washington, D.C., Smithsonian Institution.

Freeman, P. R. 1976. A Bayesian Analysis of the Megalithic Yard. *Journal of the Royal Statistical Society* 139 (1): 20–43.

Freidel, D. 1985. Polychrome Facades of the Lowland Maya Preclassic. In *Painted Architecture and Polychrome Monumental Sculpture in Mesoamerica*, ed. E. H. Boone, pp. 5–30. Washington, D.C., Dumbarton Oaks.

Freidel, D., and L. Schele. 1988a. Kingship in the Late Preclassic Maya Lowlands: The Instruments and Places of Ritual Power. *American Anthropologist* 90 (3): 547–67.

1988b. Symbol and Power: A History of the Lowland Maya Cosmogram. In *Maya Iconography,* ed. E. P. Benson and G. G. Griffin, pp. 44–93. Princeton, Princeton University Press.

Freidel, D., L. Schele, and J. Parker. 1993. *Maya Cosmos: Three Thousand Years on the Shaman's Path*. New York, William Morrow and Co. Inc.

Freidel, D., and C. Suhler. 1999. The Path of Life: Toward a Functional Analysis of Ancient Maya Architecture. In *Mesoamerican Architecture as a Cultural Symbol*, ed. J. K. Kowalski, pp. 250–73. New York, Oxford University Press.

Fuente, B. de la, ed. 1995. *La pintura mural prehispánica en México*, 2 vols., vol. 1, *Teotihuacan*. Mexico, D.F., Universidad Nacional Autónoma de México.

Galván V., L. J. 1991. *Las tumbas de tiro del Valle de Atemajac, Jalisco.* Mexico, D.F., Instituto Nacional de Antropología e Historia.

Gamio, M. 1922. *La población del Valle de Teotihuacán*, 3 vols. Mexico, D.F., Secretaría de Agricultura y Fomento. Repr. 1979, 5 vols. Mexico, D.F., Instituto Nacional Indigenista.

1926–27. Cultural Evolution in Guatemala and Its Geographical and Historic Handicaps. *Art and Archaeology* 22 and 23.

García C., A. 1981. The Historical Importance of Tlaxcala in the Cultural Development of the Central Highlands. In *Supplement to the Handbook of Middle American Indians,* vol. 1, *Archaeology,* ed. V. Bricker and J. Sabloff, pp. 244–76. Austin, University of Texas Press.

Garcia-Des Lauriers, C. 2000. Trappings of Sacred War: The Warrior Costume of Teotihuacan. M.S. thesis, Dept. of the History of Art, University of California, Riverside.

Garibay K., A. M. 1965. *Teogonia e historia de los mexicanos: Tres opusculos del siglo XVI.* Mexico, D.F., Editorial Porrua, S.A.

Geertz, C. 1973. *The Interpretation of Cultures.* New York, Basic Books.

1984. "From the Native's Point of View": On the Nature of Anthropological Understanding. In *Culture Theory,* ed. R. Shweder and R. LeVine, pp. 123–36. Cambridge, Cambridge University Press.

Gómez, S. 2000. La Ventilla: Un barrio de la antigua ciudad de Teotihuacán. B.S. thesis, Escuela Nacional de Antropología e Historia, Mexico, D.F.

González M., L. A. 1993. Analisis de restos oseos humanos de Teotihuacan con presencia de huellas rituales. Paper presented at the 13th International Congress of Anthropological and Ethnological Sciences, Mexico, D.F.

González M., L. A., and D. Fuentes G. 1982. Informe prelliminar acerca de los enterramientos prehispánicos en la zona arqueológica de Teotihuacan, México. In *Teotihuacan 80–82: primeros resultados,* ed. R. Cabrera C., I. Rodriguez G., and N. Morelos G., pp. 421–49. Mexico, D.F., Instituto Nacional de Antropología e Historia.

Grove, D. C. 1994. Review of *Art, Ideology, and the City of Teotihuacan: A Symposium at Dumbarton, 8th and 9th October 1988. Archaeology* 96: 215–16.

Grove, D. C., and S. D. Gillespie. 1992. Ideology and Evolution at the Pre-State Level: Formative Period Mesoamerica. In *Ideology and Pre-Columbian Civilizations,* ed. A. Demarest and G. Conrad, pp. 15–36. Santa Fe, N.M., School of American Research Press.

Haas, J. 1981. Class Conflict and the State in the New World. In *The Transition to Statehood in the New World,* ed. G. D. Jones and R. R. Kautz, pp. 80–102. Cambridge, Cambridge University Press.

Hansen, R. D. 1992. The Archaeology of Ideology: A Study of Maya Preclassic Architectural Sculpture at Nakbe, Peten, Guatemala. Ph.D. dissertation, Dept. of Anthropology, University of California, Los Angeles.

Harvey, H. R. 1988. The Oztoticpac Lands Map: A Re-examination. In *XLV Congreso Internacional de Americanistas: Arqueología de las Americas,* ed. E. Reichel D., pp. 339–53. Bogotá, Banco Poular, Fondo de Promoción de la Cultura.

Hassig, R. 1988. *Aztec Warfare: Imperial Expansion and Political Control.* University of Oklahoma Press, Norman.

Headrick, A. 1996. The Teotihuacan Trinity: UnMASKing the Political Structure. Ph.D dissertation, Dept. of Art and Art History, University of Texas, Austin.

Hegmon, M., ed. 2000. *The Archaeology of Regional Interaction: Religion, Warfare, and Exchange Across the American Southwest and Beyond.* Boulder, University Press of Colorado.

Hellmuth, N. M. 1975. *The Escuintla Hoards: Teotihuacan Art in Guatemala.* Guatemala City, Foundation for Latin American Anthropological Research.

Herrera, M. 1922. Esculturas Zoomorfas. In *La población del Valle de Teotihuacán,* ed. Manuel Gamio, 3 vols., vol. 1, pp. 187–95. Mexico, D.F., Secretaría de Agricultura y Fomento. Repr. 1979, 5 vols. Mexico, D.F., Instituto Nacional Indigenista.

Heyden, D. 1975. An Interpretation of the Cave Underneath the Pyramid of the Sun in Teotihuacán, Mexico. *American Antiquity* 40: 131–47.

1979. El "signo de año" en Teotihuacán, su supervivencia, y el sentido sociopolítico del símbolo. In *Mesoamérica: homenaje al Dr. Paul Kirchhoff*, ed. B. Dalhgren, pp. 61–86. Mexico, D.F., Instituto Nacional de Antropología e Historia.

1981. Caves, Gods, and Myths: World-View and Planning in Teotihuacan. In *Mesoamerican Sites and World-Views*, ed. E. Benson, pp. 1–39. Washington, D.C., Dumbarton Oaks.

Hodder, I. 1986. *Reading the Past: Current Approaches to Interpretation in Archaeology.* Cambridge, Cambridge University Press.

Hopkins, Nicholas A. 1996. Metonym and Metaphor in Chol (Mayan) Ritual Language. Paper presented at the 95th Annual Meeting of the American Anthropological Association, San Francisco.

Hubert, H., and M. Mauss. 1964. *Sacrifice: Its Nature and Function*. Chicago, University of Chicago Press.

Jarquín P., A. M., and E. Martínez V. 1982. Las excavaciones en el Conjunto 1D. In *Memoria el Proyecto Arqueológico de Teotihuacan 80–82*, ed. R. Cabrera C., I. Rodriguez G., and N. Morelos G., pp. 89–126. Mexico, D.F., Instituto Nacional de Antropología e Historia.

1991. Sacrificio de niños: Una ofrenda a la deidad de la lluvia en Teotihuacan. *Arqueología* 6: 69–84.

Jones, C., and L. Satterthwaite. 1982. *Tikal Report No. 33, Part A. The Monuments and Inscriptions of Tikal: The Carved Monuments*. Philadelphia, University of Pennsylvania Museum.

Joyce, A. A., and M. Winter. 1996. Ideology, Power, and Urban Society in Pre-Hispanic Oaxaca. *Current Anthropology* 37 (1): 33–47.

Justeson, J. S., and T. Kaufman. 1993. A Decipherment of Epi-Olmec Hieroglyphic Writing. *Science* 259: 1703–11.

Kidder, A. V., J. D. Jennings, and E. M. Shook. 1946. *Excavations at Kaminaljuyu, Guatemala.* Publication 561. Washington, D.C., Carnegie Institution.

Kishi, T. 1976. Japanese Palace-Cities and Chinese City-Castles. In *Research of Japanese Ancient Culture: City-Castles*, ed. M. Ueda, pp. 99–139. Tokyo, Shakai-Shisou-Sha.

Klein, C. F. 1987. The Ideology of Autosacrifice at the Templo Mayor. In *The Aztec Templo Mayor*, ed. E. H. Boone, pp. 293–370. Washington, D.C., Dumbarton Oaks.

Kolata, A., and C. P. Sangines. 1992. Tiwanaku: The City at the Center. In *The Ancient Americas: Art from Sacred Landscapes*, ed. R. F. Townsend, pp. 317–33. Chicago, Art Institute of Chicago.

Kolb, C. C. 1987. *Marine Shell Trade and Classic Teotihuacan, Mexico.* BAR International Series, No. 364. Oxford, BAR.

Kroeber, A. L. 1927. Disposal of the Dead. *American Anthropologist* 29: 308–15.

Krotser, G. R. 1968. Field Notes, TE 16B. Teotihuacan Mapping Project. MS., Teotihuacan Archaeological Research Facility, San Juan Teotihuacan, Mexico.

Kubler, G. 1962. *The Shape of Time.* New Haven, Yale University Press.

1967. *The Iconography of the Art of Teotihuacan.* Washington, D.C., Dumbarton Oaks.

1972. Jaguars in the Valley of Mexico. In *The Cult of the Feline*, ed. E. P. Benson, pp. 19–50. Washington, D.C., Dumbarton Oaks.

Kubler, G., ed. 1986. *Pre-Columbian Art of Mexico and Central America.* New Haven, Yale University Art Gallery.

Lamberg-Karlovsky, C. C. 1982. Sumer, Elam and the Indus: Three Urban Processes Equal One Structure? In *Harappan Civilization: A Contemporary Perspective*, ed. G. L. Possehl, pp. 61–68. New Delhi, Oxford, University Press and IBH Publishing Co.

Langley, J. C. 1986. *Symbolic Notation of Teotihuacan: Elements of Writing in a Mesoamerican Culture of the Classic Period.* BAR International Series, No. 313. Oxford, BAR.

1991. The Forms and Usage of Notation at Teotihuacan. *Ancient Mesoamerica* 2 (2): 285–98.

1992. Teotihuacan Sign Clusters: Emblem or Articulation? In *Art, Ideology and the City of Teotihuacan*, ed. J. C. Berlo, pp. 339–429. Washington, D.C., Dumbarton Oaks.

Laporte, J. P., and V. Fialko C. 1990. New Perspectives on Old Problems: Dynastic References for the Early Classic at Tikal. In *Vision and Revision in Maya Studies*, ed. F. S. Clancy and P. D. Harrison, pp. 33–66. Albuquerque, University of New Mexico Press.

León-Portilla, M. 1963. *Aztec Thought and Culture: A Study of the Ancient Nahuatl Mind.* Norman, University of Oklahoma Press.

Leone, M. P. 1982. Some Opinions about Recovering Mind. *American Antiquity* 47 (4): 742–60.

Linné, S. 1934. *Archaeological Researches at Teotihuacan, Mexico.* Stockholm, Ethnographical Museum of Sweden.

López A., A. 1973. *Hombre-dios: religión y política en el mundo náhuatl.* Mexico, D.F., Universidad Nacional Autónoma de México.

1990. *Los mitos del tlacuache: caminos de la mitología mesoamericana.* Mexico, D.F., Alianza Editorial.

López A., A., L. López L., and S. Sugiyama. 1991. The Feathered Serpent Pyramid at Teotihuacan: Its Possible Ideological Significance. *Ancient Mesoamerica* 2 (1): 93–106.

1992. El Templo de Quetzalcóatl en Teotihuacán: su posible significado ideológico. *Anales del Instituto de Investigaciones Estéticas* 16 (62): 35–52.

López L., L. 1994. *The Offerings of the Templo Mayor of Tenochtitlan*, trans. B. R. Ortiz de Montellano and T. Ortiz de Montellano. Niwot, University Press of Colorado.

Macleod, B. 1989. The 819-Day-Count: Soulful Mechanism. In *Word and Image in Maya Culture: Explorations in Language, Writing, and Representation*, ed. W. F. Hanks and D. S. Rice, pp. 112–26. Salt Lake City, University of Utah Press.

Malmstrom, V. H. 1978. A Reconstruction of the Chronology of Mesoamerican Calendrical Systems. *Journal of the History of Astronomy* 9 (2), no. 25: 105–16.

Manzanilla, L. 1992. The Economic Organization of the Teotihuacan Priesthood: Hypotheses and Considerations. In *Art, Ideology and the City of Teotihuacan*, ed. J. C. Berlo, pp. 33–429. Washington, D.C., Dumbarton Oaks.

1994. Geografía sagrada e inframundo en Teotihuacan. *Antropológicas* 11: 53–65.

Manzanilla, L. ed. 1993. *Anatomía de un conjunto residencial teotihuacano en Oztoyahualco*, 2 vols. Mexico, D.F., Universidad Nacional Autónoma de México.

Manzanilla, L., L. Barba., R. Chávez, J. Arzate, and L. Flores. 1989. El inframundo de Teotihuacan: Geofísica y arqueología. *Ciencia y desarrollo* 85: 21–35.

Manzanilla, L., L. Barba, R. Chávez, A. Tejero, G. Cifuentes, and N. Peralta. 1994. Caves and Geophysics: an Approximation to the Underworld of Teotihuacan, Mexico. *Archaeometry* 36 (1): 141–57.

Manzanilla, L., A. Ortiz B., and M. A. Jiménez. 1993. VI: La cerámica del conjunto residencial excavado. In *Anatomía de un conjunto residencial teotihuacano en Oztoyahualco*, vol. 1, *Las excavaciones*, ed. L. Manzanilla, pp. 195–387. Mexico, D.F., Universidad Nacional Autónoma de México.

MapInfo Corporation. 1992–94. *MapInfo: Macintosh Reference.* Troy, N.Y., MapInfo Corporation.

Marcus, J. 1983. Stone Monuments and Tomb Murals of Monte Albán IIIa. In *The Cloud People: Divergent Evolution of the Zapotec and Mixtec Civilizations*, ed. K. Flannery and J. Marcus, pp. 137–43. New York, Academic Press.

1992a. *Mesoamerican Writing Systems: Propaganda, Myth, and History in Four Ancient Civilizations.* Princeton, Princeton University Press.

1992b. Political Fluctuations in Mesoamerica. *National Geographic Research and Exploration* 8 (4): 392–411.

Marcus, J., and D. V. Flannery. 1996. *Zapotec Civilization: How Urban Society Evolved in Mexico's Oaxaca Valley*. London, Thames and Hudson.

Marquina, I. 1922. Arquitectura y escultura, Part 1, Arquitectura. In *La población del Valle de Teotihuacán*, ed. Manuel Gamio, 3 vols., vol. 1, pp. 99–164. Mexico, D.F., Secretaria de Agricultura y Fomento. Repr. 1979, 5 vols. Mexico, D.F., Instituto Nacional Indigenista.

1951. *Arquitectura prehispanica*, 2 vols. Mexico, D.F., Instituto Nacional de Antropología e Historia.

Martin, S., and N. Grube. 2000. *Chronicle of the Maya Kings and Queens: Deciphering the Dynasties of the Ancient Maya*. New York, Thames and Hudson.

Martínez V., E., and L. A. González M. 1991. Una estructura funeraria teotihuacana. In *Teotihuacan 1980–1982: nuevas interpretaciones*, ed. R. Cabrera C., I, Rodríguez G., and N. Morelos G., pp. 327–33. Mexico, D.F., Instituto Nacional de Antropología e Historia.

Masson, M. A., and H. Orr. 1998. The Writing on the Wall: Political Representation and Sacred Geography at Monte Alban. In *The Sowing and the Dawning: Termination, Dedication, and Transformation in the Archaeological and Ethnographic Record of Mesoamerica*, ed. S. Mock, pp. 165–75. Albuquerque, University of New Mexico Press.

Mastache, A. G., and R. H. Cobean. 1989. The Coyotlatelco Culture and the Origins of the Toltec State. In *Mesoamerica After the Decline of Teotihuacan A.D. 700–900*, ed. R. A. Diehl and J. C. Berlo, pp. 49–67. Washington, D.C., Dumbarton Oaks.

Matos M., E. 1984. The Templo Mayor of Tenochtitlan: Economics and Ideology. In *Ritual Human Sacrifice in Mesoamerica*, ed. E. H. Boone, pp. 133–64. Washington, D.C., Dumbarton Oaks.

1987. Symbolism of the Templo Mayor. In *The Aztec Templo Mayor*, ed. E. Boone, pp. 185–210. Washington, D.C., Dumbarton Oaks.

1995. *La Pirámide del Sol, Teotihuacan*. Artes de México. Mexico, D.F., Instituto Cultural Domecq, A.C.

McClung de Tapia, E. 1987. Patrones de subsistencia urbana en Teotihuacan. In *Teotihuacan: nuevos datos, nuevas síntesis, nuevos problemas*, ed. E. McClung de Tapia and E. C. Rattray, pp. 389–98. Mexico, D.F., Universidad Nacional Autónoma de México.

Medellín Z., A. 1983. *Obras maestras del Museo de Xalapa*. Mexico, D.F., Studio Beatrice Trueblood, S.A.

Mercado R., A. 1987. Una sacerdotisa en Teotihuacan? *México Desconocido* 121: 6–9.

Milbrath, S. 1997. Decapitated Lunar Goddesses in Aztec Art, Myth, and Ritual. *Ancient Mesoamerica* 8: 185–206.

Miller, A. G. 1973. *The Mural Painting of Teotihuacán*. Washington, D.C., Dumbarton Oaks.

Miller, V. E. 1991. *The Frieze of the Palace of the Stuccoes, Acanceh, Yucatan, Mexico*. Washington, D.C., Dumbarton Oaks.

Millon, C. 1972. The History of Mural Art at Teotihuacan. In *Teotihuacan: XI mesa redonda*, vol. 2, pp. 1–16. Mexico, D.F., Sociedad Mexicana de Antropología.

1973. Painting, Writing, and Polity in Teotihuacan, Mexico. *American Antiquity* 38: 294–313.

1988a. A Reexamination of the Teotihuacan Tassel Headdress Insignia. In *Feathered Serpents and Flowering Trees: Reconstructing the Murals of Teotihuacan*, ed. K. Berrin, pp. 114–34. Seattle, The Fine Arts Museums of San Francisco and the University of Washington Press.

1988b. Coyote with Sacrificial Knife. In *Feathered Serpents and Flowering Trees: Reconstructing the Murals of Teotihuacan*, ed. K. Berrin, pp. 207–17. Seattle, The Fine Arts Museums of San Francisco and the University of Washington Press.

1988c. Maguey Bloodletting Ritual. In *Feathered Serpents and Flowering Trees: Reconstructing the Murals of Teotihuacan*, ed. K. Berrin, pp. 195–205. Seattle, The Fine Arts Museums of San Francisco and the University of Washington Press.

Millon, R. 1957. New Data on Teotihuacan I in Teotihuacan. *Boletín del Centro de Investigaciones Antropológicas de México* 4: 12–18.

1967. Extensión y población de la ciudad de Teotihuacán en sus diferentes períodos: Un cálculo provisional. In *Teotihuacán: XI mesa redonda*, vol. 2, pp. 57–78. Mexico, D.F., Sociedad Mexicana de Antropología.

1973. *Urbanization at Teotihuacan, Mexico*, vol. 1, *The Teotihuacan Map*. Part I: *Text*. Austin, University of Texas Press.

1974. The Study of Urbanism at Teotihuacan, Mexico. In *Mesoamerican Archaeology: New Approaches*, ed. N. Hammond, pp. 335–62. Austin, University of Texas Press.

1976. Social Relations in Ancient Teotihuacán. In *The Valley of Mexico: Studies in Pre-Hispanic Ecology and Society*, ed. E. R. Wolf, pp. 205–48. Albuquerque, University of New Mexico Press.

1981. Teotihuacan: City, State, and Civilization. In *Supplement to the Handbook of Middle American Indians*, vol. 1, *Archaeology*, ed. V. Bricker and J. Sabloff, pp. 198–243. Austin, University of Texas Press.

1988a. The Last Years of Teotihuacan Dominance. In *The Collapse of Ancient States and Civilizations*, ed. N. Yoffee and G. Cowgill, pp. 102–64. Tucson, University of Arizona Press.

1988b. Where Do They All Come From? The Provenance of the Wagner Murals from Teotihuacan. In *Feathered Serpents and Flowering Trees: Reconstructing the Murals of Teotihuacan*, ed. K. Berrin, pp. 78–113. Seattle, The Fine Arts Museums of San Francisco and the University of Washington Press.

1992. Teotihuacan Studies: From 1950 to 1990 and Beyond. In *Art, Ideology and the City of Teotihuacan*, ed. J. C. Berlo, pp. 339–429. Washington, D.C., Dumbarton Oaks.

1993. The Place Where Time Began. In *Teotihuacan: Art from the City of the Gods*, ed. K. Berrin and E. Pasztory, pp. 17–43. San Francisco, Thames and Hudson and The Fine Arts Museums of San Francisco.

Millon, R., B. Drewitt, and A. A. Bennyhoff. 1965. The Pyramid of the Sun at Teotihuacán: 1959 Investigations. In *Transactions of the American Philosophical Society*, New Series, vol. 55, Part 6. Philadelphia, The American Philosophical Society.

Millon, R., B. Drewitt, and G. L. Cowgill. 1973. *Urbanization at Teotihuacan, Mexico*, vol. 1, *The Teotihuacan Map*. Part II: *Maps*. University of Texas Press, Austin.

Mogor, J. 1966. Pit Report: Cut N17E1 in Oaxaca Barrio Excavations. MS., University of the Americas, Puebla.

Morelos, N. 1993. *Proceso de producción de espacios y estructuras en Teotihuacán: conjunto Plaza Oeste y complejo Calle de los Muertos*. Mexico, D.F., Instituto Nacional de Antropología e Historia.

Mountjoy, J. B., and J. P. Smith. 1985. An Archaeological Patolli from Tomatlan, Jalisco, Mexico. In *Contributions to the Archaeology and Ethnohistory of Greater Mesoamerica*, ed. W. J. Follan. Carbondale and Edwardsville, Southern Illinois University Press.

Muller, Florencia. 1965. Proyecto Teotihuacan: el material lítico de Teotihuacan. MS., Instituto Nacional de Antropología e Historia, Mexico, D.F.

Múnera B., L. C. 1985. Un taller de cerámica ritual en la Ciudadela, Teotihuacan. B.S. thesis, Escuela Nacional de Antropología e Historia, México, D.F.

1991. Una representación de bulto mortuorio. In *Teotihuacan 1980–1982: nuevas interpretaciones*, ed. R. Cabrera C., I. Rodríguez G., and N. Morelos G., pp. 335–41. Mexico, D.F., Instituto Nacional de Antropología e Historia.

Múnera B., L. C., and S. Sugiyama. 1993. Cerámica ritual del taller de la Ciudadela, Teotihuacan: Catálogo. MS.
Nagao, D. 1985. *Mexican Buried Offerings: A Historical and Contextual Analysis.* BAR Inter-
  national Series, No. 235. Oxford, BAR.
  1989. Public Proclamation in the Art of Cacaxtla and Xochicalco. In *Mesoamerica After
  the Decline of Teotihuacan A.D. 700–900,* ed. R. A. Diehl and J. C. Berlo, pp. 83–104.
  Washington, D.C., Dumbarton Oaks.
Nahm, W. 1994. Maya Warfare and the Venus Year. *Mexicon* 16 (1): 6–10.
Nichols, D. L. 1987. Prehispanic Irrigation at Teotihuacan, New Evidence: The Tlajinga
  Canals. In *Teotihuacan: nuevos datos, nuevas síntesis, nuevos problemas,* ed. E. McClung de
  Tapia and E. C. Rattray, pp. 133–60. Mexico, D.F., Universidad Nacional Autónoma de
  México.
Nicholson, H. B. 1971. Religion in Pre-Hispanic Central Mexico. In *Handbook of Middle
  American Indians,* vol. 10, *Archaeology of Northern Mesoamerica,* ed. G. F. Ekholm and I.
  Bernal, pp. 395–446. Austin, University of Texas Press.
  2000. The Iconography of the Feathered Serpent in Late Postclassic Central Mexico. In
  Mesoamerica's Classic Heritage: From Teotihuacan to the Aztecs, ed. D. Carrasco, L. Jones,
  and S. Sessions, pp. 145–64. Boulder, University Press of Colorado.
Noguera, E., and J. Leonard. 1957. Descubrimiento de la Casa de las Aguilas en Teotihuacan.
  Boletín del Centro de Investigaciones Antropológicas de México 4: 6–9.
O'Brien, P. J., and H. D. Christiansen. 1986. An Ancient Maya Measurement System. *Amer-
  ican Antiquity* 51 (1): 136–51.
Ortíz de Montellano, B. R. 1978. Aztec Cannibalism: An Ecological Necessity? *Science* 200:
  611–17.
Ortner, S. B. 1984. Theory in Anthropology since the Sixties. *Comparative Studies in Society
  and History* 26: 126–66.
Paddock, J. 1983. The Oaxaca Barrio at Teotihuacan. In *The Cloud People: Divergent Evolution
  of the Zapotec and Mixtec Civilizations,* ed. K. V. Flannery and J. Marcus, pp. 170–75.
  New York, Academic Press.
Parker Pearson, M. 1982. Mortuary Practices, Society and Ideology: An Ethnoarchaeological
  Study. In *Symbolic and Structural Archaeology,* ed. I. Hodder, pp. 99–113. Cambridge,
  Cambridge University Press.
Parsons, M. L. 1988. The Iconography of Blood and Sacrifice in the Murals of the White
  Patio, Atetelco, Teotihuacan. M.A. thesis, Dept. of Art and Art History, University of
  Texas, Austin.
Pasztory, E. 1974. *The Iconography of the Teotihuacan Tlaloc.* Washington, D.C., Dumbarton
  Oaks.
  1976. *The Murals of Tepantitla, Teotihuacan.* New York, Garland Publishing Inc.
  1977. The Gods of Teotihuacan: A Synthetic Approach in Teotihuacan Iconography. In
  Studies in Precolumbian Art and Archaeology, No. 15. Washington, D.C., Dumbarton
  Oaks.
  1978. Artistic Traditions of the Middle Classic Period. In *Middle Classic Mesoamerica:
  A.D. 400–700,* ed. E. Pasztory, pp. 108–42. New York, Columbia University Press.
  1983. *Aztec Art.* New York, Harry N. Abrams, Inc.
  1988. A Reinterpretation of Teotihuacan and its Mural Painting Tradition. In *Feathered
  Serpents and Flowering Trees: Reconstructing the Murals of Teotihuacan,* ed. K. Berrin, pp. 45–
  77. Seattle, The Fine Arts Museums of San Francisco and the University of Washington
  Press.
  1992. Abstraction and the Rise of a Utopian State at Teotihuacan. In *Art, Ideology, and the
  City of Teotihuacan,* ed. J. C. Berlo, pp. 281–320. Washington, D.C., Dumbarton Oaks.
  1997. *Teotihuacan: An Experiment in Living.* Norman, University of Oklahoma Press.

Patterson, T. C. 1986. Ideology, Class Formation, and Resistance in the Inca State. In *Critique of Anthroplogy* 6 (1): 75–85.

Pendergast, D. M. 1971. Evidence of Early Teotihuacán–Lowland Maya Contact at Altun Ha. *American Antiquity* 36: 455–60.

    1990. *Excavations at Altun Ha, Belize, 1964–1970*, vol. 3. Toronto, Royal Ontario Museum.

Pérez, J. 1939. Informe general del proceso de excavaciones practicadas en sistema de pozos y tuneles en diversos sitios de mayor interés del interior de monumentos de la Ciudadela en la zona arqueológica de San Juan Teotihuacán, Estado de México. MS. Dirección de Monumentos Prehispánicos, Instituto Nacional de Antropología e Historia, Mexico, D.F.

Pijoan A., C. M. 1981. Evidencias rituales en restos oseos. In *Cuadernos de trabajo del Museo Nacional de Antropologia, Mexico*, pp. 5–13. Mexico, D.F., Instituto Nacional de Antropología e Historia.

Plunket, P., and G. Uruñuela. 1998. Preclassic Household Patterns Preserved under Volcanic Ash at Tetimpa, Puebla, Mexico. *Latin American Antiquity* 9 (4): 287–309.

Pohl, J. M. D. 1994. *The Politics of Symbolism in the Mixtec Codices.* Vanderbilt University Publications in Anthropology. Nashville, Tenn., Vanderbilt University.

Popol Vuh: The Definitive Edition of the Mayan Book of the Dawn of Life and the Glories of Gods and Kings. 1985. Trans. D. Tedlock. New York, Simon and Schuster.

Quintanilla M., P. 1982. Pozo de agua. In *Memoria del Proyecto Arqueológico Teotihuacan 80–82*, ed. R. Cabrera C., I. Rodríguez G., and N. Morelos G, pp. 185–87. Mexico, D.F., Instituto Nacional de Antropología e Historia.

Rattray, E. C. 1990. The Identification of Ethnic Affiliation at the Merchant's Barrio, Teotihuacan. *Etnoarqueología: coloquio Bosch-Gimpera*, ed. Y. Sugiura and M. Serra P., pp. 113–38. Mexico, D.F., Universidad Nacional Autónoma de México.

    1991. Fechamientos por radiocarbono en Teotihuacan. *Arqueología* 6: 3–18.

    1992. *The Teotihuacan Burials and Offerings: A Commentary and Inventory.* Vanderbilt University Publications in Anthropology, No. 42. Nashville, Tenn., Vanderbilt University.

    2001. *Teotihuacan: Ceramics, Chronology and Cultural Trends.* Mexico, D.F., University of Pittsburgh, and Instituto Nacional de Antropología e Historia.

Rattray, E. C., and Ruiz, M. E. 1980. Interpretaciones culturales de La Ventilla, Teotihuacán. *Anales de antropología* 17 (1): 105–14.

Reese, K. V. 1996. Narratives of Power: Late Formative Public Architecture and Civic Center Design at Cerros, Belize. Ph.D. dissertation, Dept. of Anthropology, University of Texas at Austin.

Reiba, M. 1976. Chinese City-Castles. In *Research of Japanese Ancient Culture: City-Castles*, ed. M. Ueda, pp. 303–33. Tokyo, Shakai-Shisou-Sha.

Reilly, F. K. 1996. Art, Ritual, and Rulership in the Olmec World. In *The Olmec World: Ritual and Rulership*, ed. J. Guthrie, pp. 27–45. Princeton, N.J., Princeton University Art Museum.

Renfrew, C., and E. B. W. Zubrow, eds. 1994. *The Ancient Mind: Elements of Cognitive Archaeology.* Cambridge, Cambridge University Press.

Reygadas V., J. 1930. Las últimas excavaciones en la zona arqueológica de Teotihucán. *Anales del XX Congreso Internacional de Americanistas, Río de Janeiro* 2 (1): 161–67.

Robicsek, F., and D. Hales. 1984. Maya Heart Sacrifice: Cultural Perspective and Surgical Technique. In *Ritual Human Sacrifice in Mesoamerica*, ed. E. H. Boone, pp. 49–90. Washington, D.C., Dumbarton Oaks.

Rodríguez G., I. 1982. Frente 2. In *Memoria del Proyecto Arqueológico Teotihuacan 80–82*, ed. R. Cabrera C., I. Rodríguez G., and N. Morelos. G., pp. 55–73. Mexico, D.F., Instituto Nacional de Antropología e Historia.

Rodríguez M., V. 1992. Patrón de enterramiento en Teotihuacán durante el período clásico: estudio de 814 entierros. B.S. thesis, Escuela Nacional de Anthropología e Historia, Mexico, D.F.

Román B., J. A. 1990. *Sacrificio de niños en el Templo Mayor*. Mexico, D.F., Asociación de Amigos del Templo Mayor, Instituto Nacional de Antropología e Historia, and García y Valadés Editores.

1991. A Study of Skeletal Materials from Tlatelolco. In *To Change Place: Aztec Ceremonial Landscapes*, ed. D. Carrasco, pp. 9–19. Niwot, University Press of Colorado.

Romano, A. 1972. Sistema de enterramiento en Tlatilco. In *Sociedad Mexicana de Antropología, XII mesa redonda: religión en Mesoamerica*, ed. J. L. King and N. Castillo Tejero, pp. 365–68. Mexico, D.F., Sociedad Mexicana de Antropología.

Romero M., J. 1958. *Mutilaciones dentarias prehispanicas de Mexico y America en general*. Mexico, D.F., Instituto Nacional de Antropología e Historia.

1986. *Catálogo de la colección de dientes mutilados prehispánicos*, Part IV. Mexico, D.F, Instituto Nacional de Antropología e Historia.

Romero N., M. 1982. Frente 1B Talud Sur. In *Memoria del Proyecto Arqueológico Teotihuacán 80–82*, ed. R. Cabrera C., I. Rodríguez G., and N. Morelos G., vol. 1, pp. 49–54. Mexico, D.F., Instituto Nacional de Antropología e Historia.

Roys, R. L. 1933. *The Book of Chilam Balam of Chumayel*. Washington, D.C., Carnegie Institution.

1943. *The Indian Background of Colonial Yucatan*. Washington, D.C., Carnegie Institution.

Rubín de la Borbolla, D. F. 1947. Teotihuacan: ofrendas de los Templos de Quetzalcoatl. *Anales del Instituto Nacional de Antropología e Historia* 6 (2): 61–72.

Ruz L., A. 1965. Tombs and Funerary Practices of the Maya Lowlands. In *Handbook of Middle American Indians*, vol. 2, *Archaeology of Southern Mesoamerica*, Part I, ed. G. R. Willey, pp. 441–61. Austin, University of Texas Press.

1968. *Costumbres funerarias de los antiguos mayas*. Mexico, D.F., Universidad Nacional Autónoma de México.

1973. *El Templo de las Inscripciones Palenque*. Coleccion cientifica 7, Arqueología. Mexico, D.F., Instituto Nacional de Antropología e Historia.

Sahagún, F. B. 1950–82. *Florentine Codex: General History of the Things of New Spain*, trans. A. J. O. Anderson and C. E. Dibble. Santa Fe, N.M., School of American Research and the University of Utah.

Sanders, W. T. 1978. Ethnographic Analogy and the Teotihuacan Horizon Style. In *Middle Classic Mesoamerica: A.D. 400–500*, ed. E. Pasztory, pp. 34–44. New York, Columbia University Press.

1981. Ecological Adaptation in the Basin of Mexico: 23,000 B.C. to the Present. In *Supplement to the Handbook of Middle American Indians*, vol. 1, *Archaeology*, ed. V. Bricker and J. Sabloff, pp. 147–97. Austin, University of Texas Press.

Sanders, W. T., and J. W. Michels, eds. 1969. *The Pennsylvania State University Kaminaljuyu Project: 1968 Seasons*, Part I, *The Excavations*. Occasional Papers in Anthropology, No. 2. University Park, Pa., Pennsylvania State University.

1977. *Teotihuacan and Kaminaljuyu: A Study in Prehistoric Culture Contact*. University Park, Pa., Penn State University Press.

Sanders, W. T., J. R. Parsons, and R. S. Santley. 1979. *The Basin of Mexico: Ecological Processes in the Evolution of a Civilization*. New York, Academic Press.

Schele, L. 1984. Human Sacrifice among the Classic Maya. In *Ritual Human Sacrifice in Mesoamerica*, ed. E. H. Boone, pp. 7–48. Washington, D.C., Dumbarton Oaks.

Schele, L., and D. Freidel. 1990. *A Forest of Kings: The Untold Story of the Ancient Maya*. New York, William Morrow and Co., Inc.

Schele, L., and N. Grube. 1994. *Notebook for the 18th Maya Hieroglyphic Workshop at Texas.* Austin, University of Texas at Austin.

Schele, L., and M. E. Miller. 1986 *The Blood of Kings: Dynasty and Ritual in Maya Art.* New York, G. Braziller.

Schneider, D. M. 1976. Notes Toward a Theory of Culture. In *Meaning in Anthropology*, ed. K. Basso and H. Selby, pp. 197–220. Albuquerque, University of New Mexico Press.

Scott, S. 1993. *Teotihuacan Mazapan Figurines and the Xipe Totec Statue: A Link Between the Basin of Mexico and the Valley of Oaxaca.* Vanderbilt University Publications in Anthropology, No. 44. Nashville, Tenn., Vanderbilt University.

Séjourné, L. 1956 *Burning Water: Thought and Religion in Ancient Mexico.* London, Thames and Hudson.

   1959. *Un palacio en la ciudad de los dioses.* Mexico, D.F., INAH.

   1961. El culto de Xochipilli y los braseros teotihuacanos. *El México antiguo* 9: 111–24.

   1964. La simbología del fuego. *Cuadernos americanos* 135 (4): 149–78.

   1966a. *Arquitectura y pintura en Teotihuacan.* México, D.F, Siglo XXI.

   1966b. *Arqueología de Teotihuacan: la cerámica.* México, D.F., Fondo de Cultura Económica.

   1966c. *El lenguaje de las formas.* México, D.F., Gabriel Mancera.

   1970. *Pensamiento y religión en el México antiguo.* México, D.F., Fondo de Cultura Económica.

Seler, E. 1963. *Comentarios al Códice Borgia*, 2 vols. México, D.F., Fondo de Cultura Económica.

Sempowski, M. 1983. Mortuary Practices at Teotihuacán, Mexico: Their Implications for Social Status. Ph.D. dissertation, Dept. of Anthropology, University of Rochester, N.Y. Ann Arbor, Mich., University Microfilms.

   1994. Mortuary Practices at Teotihuacan. In *Mortuary Practices and Skeletal Remains at Teotihuacan*, ed. M. Sempowski and M. Spence, pp. 1–314. Salt Lake City, University of Utah Press.

Sempowski L., M., and M. W. Spence. 1994. *Mortuary Practices and Skeletal Remains at Teotihuacan.* Salt Lake City, University of Utah Press.

Serrano, C. 1993. Funerary Practices and Human Sacrifice in Teotihuacan Burials. In *Teotihuacan: Art from the City of the Gods*, ed. K. Berrin and E. Pasztory, pp. 108–15. New York, Thames and Hudson and The Fine Arts Museums of San Francisco.

Serrano S., C., and Z. Lagunas. 1975. Sistema de enterramiento y notas sobre el material osteológico de La Ventilla, Teotihuacan, México. *Anales del Instituto Nacional de Antropología e Historia* 7a (4): 105–44.

Serrano S., C., M. Pimienta, and A. Gallardo. 1991. Los entierros del Templo de Quetzalcoatl: patrón de distribución por edad y sexo. *Arqueología* 6: 53–67.

   1993. Mutilación dentaria y filiación étnica en los entierros del Templo de Quetzalcoatl, Teotihuacan. In *II Coloquio Pedro Bosh-Gimpera*, ed. M. T. Cabrero G., pp. 263–76. Mexico, D.F., Universidad Nacional Autónoma de México.

Sharer, R. J. 1994. *The Ancient Maya.* 5th edn. Stanford, Stanford University Press.

Shook, E. M. 1951. The Present Status of Reseach on the Preclassic Horizon in Guatemala. In *The Civilizations of Ancient America*, ed. S. Tax, pp. 93–100. Selected papers of the 24th International Congress of Americanists. Chicago, University of Chicago Press.

Shook, E. M. and A. V. Kidder. 1952. Mound E-III-Kaminaljuyu, Guatemala. Carnegie Institution of Washington Publication 596, vol. 9, pp. 33–128. Washington, D.C., Carnegie Institution.

Siliceo P., P. 1925. Representaciones prehispánicas de dientes humanos hechas en concha. *Anales del Museo Nacional de Arqueología, Historia y Etnografía* 4 (3): 220–22.

Smith, A. L., and A. V. Kidder. 1951. *Excavations at Nebaj, Guatemala.* Washington, D.C., Carnegie Institution.

Smith, R. E. 1987. *A Ceramic Sequence from the Pyramid of the Sun, Teotihuacan, Mexico.* Cambridge, Mass., Peabody Museum of Archaeology and Ethnology, Harvard University.

Smith, V. G. 1984. *Izapa Relief Carving: Form, Content, Rules for Design, and Role in Mesoamerican Art History and Archaeology.* Washington, D.C., Dumbarton Oaks.

Spence, M. W. 1977. Teotihuacan y el intercambio de obsidiana en Mesoamerica. In *Los procesos de cambio: XV mesa redonda*, pp. 293–300. Mexico, D.F., Sociedad Mexicana de Antropología.

1981. Obsidian Production and the State in Teotihuacan. *American Antiquity* 46: 769–88.

1987. The Scale and Structure of Obsidian Production in Teotihuacan. *Teotihuacan: nuevos datos, nuevas síntesis, nuevos problemas*, ed. E. McClung de Tapia and E. C. Rattray, pp. 429–50. Mexico, D.F., Universidad Nacional Autónoma de México.

1992. Tlailotlacan: A Zapotec Enclave in Teotihuacan. In *Art, Ideology, and the City of Teotihuacan*, ed. J. C. Berlo, pp. 59–88. Washington, D.C., Dumbarton Oaks.

1994. Human Skeletal Material from Teotihuacan. In *Mortuary Practices and Skeletal Remains at Teotihuacan*, ed. M. Sempowski and M. Spence, pp. 315–427. Salt Lake City, University of Utah Press.

Storey, R. 1992. *Life and Death in the Ancient City of Teotihuacan: A Modern Paleodemographic Synthesis.* Tuscaloosa, University of Alabama Press.

Stuart, D. 1988. Blood Symbolism in Maya Iconography. In *Maya Iconography*, ed. E. Benson and G. Griffin, pp. 175–221. Princeton, Princeton University Press.

2000. "The Arrival of Strangers": Teotihuacan and Tollan in Classic Maya History. In *Mesoamerica's Classic Heritage: From Teotihuacan to the Aztecs*, ed. D. Carrasco, L. Jones, and S. Sessions, pp. 465–513. Boulder, University Press of Colorado.

Sugiyama, S. 1982. Los trabajos efectuados por la Sección de Topografía. In *Memoria del Proyecto Arqueológico Teotihuacán 80–82*, ed. R. Cabrera C., I. Rodríguez G., and N. Morelos G., vol. 1, pp. 467–75. Mexico, D.F., Instituto Nacional de Antropología e Historia.

1983. Estudio preliminar sobre el sistema de medida teotihuacana. Paper presented at the Round Table of the Sociedad Mexicana de Antropología, Taxco.

1986. Recent Discoveries of Burials at the Temple of Quetzalcoatl and their Significance. Paper presented at the 51st Annual Meeting of the Society for American Archaeology, New Orleans.

1988a. Los animales en la iconografía teotihuacana. *Revista mexicana de estudios antropológicos* 34 (1): 13–52.

1988b. Nuevos datos arqueológicos sobre el Templo de Quetzalcóatl en la Ciudadela de Teotihuacán y algunas consideraciones hipotéticas. In *XLV Congreso Internacional de Americanistas: Arqueología de las Américas*, ed. E. Reichel D., pp. 405–29. Bogotá, Banco Popular, Fondo de Promoción de la Cultura.

1989a. Burials Dedicated to the Old Temple of Quetzalcoatl at Teotihuacan, Mexico. *American Antiquity* 54 (1): 85–106.

1989b. Iconographic Interpretation of the Temple of Quetzalcoatl at Teotihuacan. *Mexicon* 11 (4): 68–74.

1991a. Descubrimientos de entierros y ofrendas dedicadas al Templo Viejo de Quetzalcóatl. In *Teotihuacan 1980–1982: nuevas interpretaciones*, ed. R. Cabrera C., I. Rodríguez G., and N. Morelos G., pp. 275–326. Mexìco, D.F., Instituto Nacional de Antropología e Historia.

1991b. El entierro central al interior de la Pirámide de la Serpiente Emplumada en Teotihuacán: implicaciones generales. *Arqueología* 6: 33–40.

1992. Rulership, Warfare, and Human Sacrifice at the Ciudadela, Teotihuacan: An Iconographic Study of Feathered Serpent Representations. In *Art, Ideology, and the City of Teotihuacan*, ed. J. C. Berlo, pp. 205–30. Washington, D.C., Dumbarton Oaks.

1993. Worldview Materialized in Teotihuacan, Mexico. *Latin American Antiquity* 4 (2): 103–29.

1996. Polity Reflected in the Urbanization Process of the Teotihuacan State. Paper presented at the 61st Annual Meeting of the Society for American Archaeology, San Francisco.

1998a. Archaeology and Iconography of Teotihuacan Censers: Official Military Emblems Originated from the Ciudadela? *Teotihuacan Notes: Internet Journal for Teotihucan Archaeology and Iconography* (http://archaeology.la.asu.edu/teo/notes/SS/noteI_2SS.htm). Tempe, Archaeological Research Institute, Arizona State University.

1998b. Teotihuacan Militarism and Its Implications in Maya Social Histories. Paper presented at the 63rd Annual Meeting of the Society for American Archaeology, Seattle.

1998c. Termination Programs and Prehispanic Looting at the Feathered Serpent Pyramid in Teotihuacan, Mexico. In *The Sowing and the Dawning: Termination, Dedication, and Transformation in the Archaeological and Ethnographic Record of Mesoamerica*, ed. S. Mock. Albuquerque, University of New Mexico Press.

1998d. Cronología de sucesos ocurridos en el Templo de Quetzalcoatl, Teotihuacán. In *Los ritmos de cambio en Teotihuacán: reflexiones y discusiones de su cronología*, ed. R. Brambila P. and R. Cabrera C. Mexico, D.F., Instituto Nacional de Antropología e Historia.

2000. Teotihuacan as an Origin for Postclassic Feathered Serpent Symbolism. In *Mesoamerica's Classic Heritage: From Teotihuacan to the Aztecs*, ed. D. Carrasco, L. Jones, and S. Sessions, pp. 117–43, Boulder, University Press of Colorado.

2002. Militarismo plasmado en Teotihuacan. *Ideología y política a través de materiales, imágenes y símbolos: memoria de la primera mesa redonda de Teotihuacan*, ed. M. E. Ruiz G., pp. 185–209. Mexico, D.F., Universidad Nacional Autónoma de México and Instituto Nacional de Antropología e Historia.

Forthcoming. Excavacion y resultados del Frente C. In *Proyecto Templo de Quetzalcoatl 1988–1989*, vol. 1, *Excavaciones y resultados*, ed. R. Cabrera, G. L. Cowgill, and S. Sugiyama, ch. 4. Pittsburgh, Pa., University of Pittsburgh and Mexico, D.F., Instituto Nacional de Antropología e Historia.

Sugiyama, S., and R. Cabrera C. 2000. Proyecto Pirámide de la Luna: algunos resultados de la segunda temporada 1999. In *Arqueologia 23* 2: 161–72.

2003. Hallazgos recientes en la Pirámide de la Luna. *Arqueología mexicana* 11 (64): 42–49.

Sullivan, Thelma D. 1986. A Scattering of Jades: The Words of Aztec Elders. In *Symbol and Meaning Beyond the Closed Community: Essays in Mesoamerican Ideas*, ed. G. H. Gossen, pp. 9–17. Albany, Institute for Mesoamerican Studies, State University of New York, Albany.

Tainter, J. A. 1978. Mortuary Practices and the Study of Prehistoric Social Systems. *Advances in Archaeological Method and Theory* 1: 105–41.

1988. *The Collapse of Complex Societies*. Cambridge, Cambridge University Press.

Taube, K. 1986. The Teotihuacan Cave of Origin. *RES: Anthropology and Aesthetics* 12: 51–82.

1988. The Iconography of Lightning at Chichén Itzá. Paper presented at the 53rd Annual Meeting of the Society for American Archaeology, Phoenix.

1992a. The Temple of Quetzalcoatl and the Cult of Sacred War at Teotihuacan. *RES: Anthropology and Aesthetics* 21: 53–87.

1992b. The Iconography of Mirrors at Teotihuacan. In *Art, Ideology, and the City of Teotihuacan*, ed. J. C. Berlo, pp. 169–204. Washington, D.C., Dumbarton Oaks.

2000. The Turquoise Hearth: Fire, Self Sacrifice, and the Central Mexican Cult of War. In *Mesoamerica's Classic Heritage: From Teotihuacan to the Aztecs*, ed. D. Carrasco, L. Jones, and S. Sessions, pp. 269–340. Boulder, University Press of Colorado.

Thompson, J. E. S. 1934. Sky Bearers, Colors and Directions in Maya and Mexican Religion. In *Contributions to American Archaeology*, Publication 436, Contribution 10. Washington, D.C., Carnegie Institution.

1960. *Maya Hieroglyphic Writing: An Introduction*. Norman, University of Oklahoma Press.

1962. *A Catalog of Maya Hieroglyphs*. Norman, University of Oklahoma Press.

1972. *A Commentary on the Dresden Codex*. Philadelphia, American Philosophical Society.

Tobriner, S. 1972. The Fertile Mountain: An Investigation of Cerro Gordo's Importance to the Town Plan and Iconography of Teotihuacan. In *Teotihuacan: XI mesa redonda*, pp. 103–16. Mexico, D.F., Sociedad Mexicana de Antropología.

Townsend, R. F. 1979. *State and Cosmos in the Art of Tenochtitlan*. Washington, D.C., Dumbarton Oaks.

Tozzer, A. M. 1941. *Landa's Relación de las cosas de Yucatán: A Translation*. Papers of the Peabody Museum of American Archaeology and Ethnology, vol. 18. Cambridge, Mass.: Peabody Museum, Harvard University.

Trigger, B. 1990. Monumental Architecture: A Thermodynamic Explanation of Symbolic Behaviour. *World Archaeology* 22 (2): 119–32.

Trigger, B. G., B. J. Kemp, D. O'Connor, and A. B. Lloyd. 1983. *Ancient Egypt: A Social History*. Cambridge, Cambridge University Press.

Turner, C. G. II, and J. A. Turner. 1995. Cannibalism in the Prehistoric American Southwest: Occurrence, Taphonomy, Explanation, and Suggestions for Standardized World Definition. *Anthropological Sciences* 103 (1): 1–22.

Turner, M. H. 1992. Style in Lapidary Technology: Identifying the Teotihuacan Lapidary Industry. In *Art, Ideology, and the City of Teotihuacan*, ed. J. C. Berlo, pp. 89–112. Dumbarton Oaks, Washington, D.C.

Turner, V. 1977. Sacrifice as Quintessential Process: Prophylaxis or Abandonment? *History of Religions* 16: 189–215.

Umberger, E. 1987a. Antiques, Revivals, and References to the Past in Aztec Art. *RES: Anthropology and Aesthetics* 13: 63–105.

1987b. Events Commemorated by Date Plaques at the Templo Mayor: Further Thoughts on the Solar Metaphor. In *The Aztec Templo Mayor*, ed. E. H. Boone, pp. 411–49. Washington, D.C., Dumbarton Oaks.

1996. Aztec Presence and Material Remains in the Outer Provinces. In *Aztec Imperial Strategies*, ed. F. Berdan, R. E. Blanton, E. H. Boone, M. G. Hodge, M. E. Smith, and E. Umberger, pp. 151–79. Washington, D.C., Dumbarton Oaks.

Urcid S., J. 2001. *Zapotec Hieroglyphic Writing*. Washington, D.C., Dumbarton Oaks.

Valeri, V. 1985. *Kingship and Sacrifice*. Chicago, University of Chicago Press.

Villacorta C., J. A., and C. A. Villacorta R. 1930. *Arqueologia guatemalteca*. Colección Villacorta de historia antigua de Guatemala, vol. 2. Guatemala City, Tipografía Nacional.

von Winning, H. 1948. The Teotihuacan Owl and Weapon Symbol and its Association with "Sepent Head X" at Kaminaljuyú. *American Antiquity* 14 (2): 129–32.

1961. Teotihuacan Symbols: The Reptile's Eye Glyph. *Ethnos* 26: 121–66.

1979. The "Binding of the Year" and the "New Fire" in Teotihuacan. *Indiana* 5: 15–32.

1987. *La iconografía de Teotihuacan: los dioses y los signos*. 2 vols. Mexico, D.F., Universidad Nacional Autónoma de México.

Weaver, M. P. 1994. *The Aztecs, Maya, and Their Predecessors: Archaeology of Mesoamerica*. 3rd edn. New York, Academic Press.

Webster, D. 1977. Warfare and the Evolution of Maya Society. In *The Origins of Maya Civilization*, ed. R. E. W. Adams, pp. 335–72. Albuquerque, University of New Mexico.

Welsh, W. B. M. 1988a. *An Analysis of Classic Lowland Maya Burials*. BAR International Series, No. 409. Oxford, BAR.

1988b. A Case for the Practice of Human Sacrifice Among the Classic Lowland Maya. In *Recent Studies in Pre-Columbian Archaeology*, ed. N. J. Saunders and O. de Montmollin, Part I, pp. 143–65. BAR International Series, No. 421 (I). Oxford, BAR.

Wheatley, P. 1971. *The Pivot of the Four Quarters: A Preliminary Inquiry into the Origin and Character of the Ancient Chinese City*. Chicago, Aldine Publishing Co.

White, C. D., M. W. Spence, F. J. Longstaffe, H. Stuart-Williams, and K. R. Law. 2002. Geographic Identities of the Sacrificial Victims from the Feathered Serpent Pyramid, Teotihuacan: Implications for the Nature of State Power. *Latin American Antiquity* 13 (2): 217–36.

Widmer, R. J. 1987. The Evolution of Form and Function in a Teotihuacan Apartment Compound. In *Teotihuacan: nuevos datos, nuevas síntesis, nuevos problemas*, ed. E. McClung de Tapia and E. C. Rattray, pp. 317–68. Mexico, D.F., Universidad Nacional Autónoma de México.

Wilcox, D. R., and J. Haas. 1994. The Scream of the Butterfly: Competition and Conflict in the Prehistoric Southwest. In *Themes in Southwest Prehistory*, ed. G. J. Gumerman, pp. 211–38. Santa Fe, N.M., School of American Research Press.

Wilkerson, S. J. K. 1984. In Search of the Mountain of Foam: Human Sacrifice in Eastern Mesoamerica. In *Ritual Human Sacrifice in Mesoamerica*, ed. H. Boone, pp. 101–32. Washington, D.C., Dumbarton Oaks.

Woolley, L. 1954. *Excavations at Ur*. New York, Crowell.

Wren, L. 1994. Ceremonialism in the Reliefs of the North Temple, Chichen Itza. In *Seventh Palenque Round Table, 1989*, ed. M. G. Robertson and V. M. Fields, pp. 25–31. San Francisco, The Pre-Columbian Art Research Institute.

Yoffee, N., and G. L. Cowgill, eds. 1988. *The Collapse of Ancient States and Civilizations*. Tucson, University of Arizona Press.

Zuidema, R. T. 1983. Hierarchy and Space in Incaic Social Organization. *Ethnohistory* 30 (2): 49–75.

1990. At the King's Table: Inca Concepts of Sacred Kingship in Cuzco. In *King and the Kings*, ed. J. Galey, pp. 253–70. New York, Harwood Aademic Publishers.

Other books published in the series:

Ian Hodder and Clive Orton: *Spatial analysis in archaeology*

Keith Muckelroy: *Maritime archaeology*

R. Gould: *Living archaeology*

Stephen Plog: *Stylistic variation in prehistoric ceramics*

Patrick Vinton Kirch: *Evolution of the Polynesian chiefdoms*

Dean Arnold: *Ceramic Theory and Cultural Process*

Geoffry W. Conrad and Arthur A. Demarest: *Religion and empire: the dynamics of Aztec and Inca expansion*

Graham Barker: *Prehistoric farming in Europe*

Daniel Miller: *Artefacts as categories*

Rosalind Hunter-Anderson: *Prehistoric adaptation in the American Southwest*

Robin Torrence: *Production and exchange of stone tools*

Bo Gräslund: *The birth of prehistoric chronology*

Ian Morris: *Burial and ancient society: the rise of the early Greek state*

Joseph Tainter: *The collapse of complex societies*

John Fox: *Maya postclassic state formation*

Alasdair Whittle: *Problems in Neolithic archaeology*

Peter Bogucki: *Forest Farmers and Stockherders*

Olivier de Montmollin: *The Archaeology of Political Structure: settlement analysis in a classic Maya polity*

Robert Chapman: *Emerging complexity: the later prehistory of south-east Spain, Iberia and the west Mediterranean*

Steven Mithen: *Thoughtful foragers: a study of prehistoric decision making*

Roger Cribb: *Nomads in archaeology*

James Whitley: *Style and society in Dark Age Greece: the changing face of a pre-literate society 1100–700 BC*

Philip Arnold: *Domestic ceramic production and spatial organization*

Julian Thomas: *Rethinking the Neolithic*

E. N. Chernykh: *Ancient metallurgy in the USSR: the early Metal Age*, translated by Sarah Wright

Lynne Sebastian: *The Chaco Anasazi: sociopolitical evolution in the prehistoric Southwest*

Anna Maria Bietti Sestieri: *The Iron Age community of Osteria del'Osa: a study of sociopolitical development in central Tyrrhenian Italy*

Christine A. Hastorf: *Agriculture and the onset of political inequality before the Inca*